Pauli Murray

A PERSONAL AND POLITICAL LIFE

Troy R. Saxby

THE UNIVERSITY OF NORTH CAROLINA PRESS

CHAPEL HILL

Jacket photograph: Pauli Murray in 1977; courtesy of the Schlesinger Library,
Radcliffe Institute, Harvard University.

Cataloging-in-Publication data for this title is available at the
Library of Congress, https://lccn.loc.gov/2019049765.
ISBN 978-1-4696-5492-8 (cloth: alk. paper)
ISBN 978-1-4696-5493-5 (ebook)

Pauli Murray

. . . . .

for Luke & James

Contents

Figures

PREFACE

June 1923

The train that services Croom in southern Maryland has only two carriages, the first for white passengers and the second for baggage and colored passengers. Pauli Murray, twelve years old and slightly built, sits alone in the second carriage. As the train rattles north along the single-track line toward Baltimore, there is little in the scenery—swamplands and undergrowth, mostly—and no company to distract her from thinking about the tragedy that has prompted this hastily arranged trip. The plan had been to spend an entire happy summer in Croom with her Aunt Sallie's family, as she has done the past two years. Pauli loves the freedom and open spaces of Croom, the abundance of good food, playing with her two baby cousins, and taking country drives in her uncle's Model T Ford, which can reach exhilarating speeds of over thirty miles an hour. But early in the summer a telegram's arrival brought this vacation to a sudden halt. As she sits in the second carriage, all she knows is the telegram's message: her father is dead, and she is expected at the funeral in Baltimore.

She journeys alone in part because she is now orphaned—her mother died when Pauli was three, and her father was committed to a psychiatric facility shortly thereafter. Following her mother's death, Pauli went to live with maternal relatives in North Carolina and had almost no contact with the Murray family she now travels to be with. Because she knows only what the telegram announced, her father's death does not yet seem real. It's difficult enough to picture him alive; she really only has two images to conjure. One is a revered impression she created from photographs and the reminiscences of her mother's sisters. In this vision he is a handsome, dapper young man: a sportsman, musician, poet, and well-respected school principal. The other impression, in stark contrast, she formed four years earlier when she visited him at Crownsville State Hospital for the Negro Insane. In this version, he is disheveled and neglected, dressed in patched, discolored overalls and cracked shoes. He looks much older than his forty-seven years: he shuffles; his eyes are dull, his face unshaven, his hair unkempt; and, worst of all, he fails to recognize her. Pauli doesn't know it yet, but soon after her train journey ends she will acquire a third, even more distressing image of her father.

Everything about arriving in Baltimore seems to possess an unsettling, bewildering quality. In rural Croom, the nearest neighbor's house can barely be seen across a field, but here the city streets are paved, and on block after block sit endless rows of identical attached brick houses without porches or front yards. The house Pauli enters is distinguished only by a mourning wreath on the door. Inside, Aunt Rose and Uncle Bubber's home is larger and grander than she is used to; the three stories plus basement, indoor plumbing, and modern furnishings all impress her, as does the neat, fashionable attire of her Baltimore relations. By contrast, Pauli is a "tomboy" in secondhand clothes who speaks with a southern accent. She is also darker-skinned than many of her relatives; some of them can, and sometimes do, pass as white. Most bewildering of all, Pauli's five siblings live in this house. She has only seen them once since their mother died and she alone left Baltimore. Her siblings have led very different lives since then, not least because in North Carolina Pauli learned all about her parents, whereas her siblings are forbidden from mentioning their mother and father. As mourners arrive at the house, Pauli's alienation takes a disturbing turn. Aunt Rose keeps introducing all the children, Pauli included, as her own. Pauli learns still worse news: her father had been murdered at Crownsville, and the asylum will soon ship his body to this house.

Had Pauli's adult relations known what to expect, Pauli later maintained, they would surely have requested that the casket be sealed. After looking at the remains, Aunt Rose places a handkerchief over her dead brother's face, and the coffin is placed in the parlor until the funeral can take place the following day. Mourners, almost all of them unknown to Pauli, gather in other rooms of the house. That night Pauli hears the grownups discussing a rumor that her father had argued with a white Crownsville hospital attendant, after which the attendant asserted, "I'll get that nigger later." Several hours later the attendant cornered her father in a basement and beat him to death with a bat. The force of the blows fractured his skull from ear to ear. The *Baltimore Afro-American* front-page headline on the morning of the funeral screams, "Killing Insane Principal, Most Brutal in State's History."[1]

In the hours between the coffin's arrival and the funeral the following day, the urge to see her father proves overpowering. Over and over again, when nobody is watching, Pauli creeps into the parlor and up to the gray casket. She opens the lid and looks inside. She sees her father's body dressed in a shabby, oversized suit and the handkerchief covering his face. She reaches a hand into the coffin and removes the handkerchief. She stares at the disfigurement: his face purplish with bruising, grotesquely swollen in places, mangled in others, and his head, roughly shaven, exposes a skull held loosely together with large, jagged stitching performed after a crude postmortem examination. Nothing about her father looks human except his hands. Over and over again, to convince herself it's really him, she reaches into the coffin to touch and hold his hand. This is the only time Pauli remembers touching either of her parents.[2]

TWELVE YEARS OLD AND ATTENDING her father's funeral is not the way Pauli Murray is typically recalled and certainly not the reason I became interested in writing her biography. Murray has become increasingly well known in the last decade for innovating many famous nonviolent direct-action civil rights protests, helping found the National Organization for Women (NOW), having distinguished legal and scholarly careers, authoring several books, befriending influential figures such as Eleanor Roosevelt, and becoming the first Black woman Episcopal priest.[3] I first learned of Murray from an essay on women's participation in the civil rights movement that described her keynote speech to the National Council of Negro Women in late 1963. When she delivers this speech, Murray is already a veteran civil rights activist, has just finished serving on a presidential commission into the status of women in America, and is completing a Yale law doctorate. In the months after the iconic March on Washington, popularly remembered as a day of unity and the high point of a noble movement embodying inclusivity, Murray rose to the podium to lambast the exclusion of Black women from leading roles in the march. She described the whole movement as in danger of becoming a vehicle to "prestige and power" for civil rights spokesmen and likened some of their actions to relegating women to the "back of the bus." Women in the audience took the message to heart, and the subsequent reporting of Murray's speech in the Black press further galvanized women in the struggle.[4]

This Pauli Murray presents a seemingly marked contrast to the Pauli Murray from forty years earlier when she attended her father's funeral. In one image she is a twelve-year-old orphan standing before a coffin and trying to convince herself that the mutilated corpse is her father, and in the other she is a fifty-two-year-old legal scholar standing before a microphone speaking out for race and gender equality. On the surface, the biographer's goal appears a simple one: describe how the grieving child became the inspiring advocate. Of course, realizing that goal is less straightforward. There is an almost instinctive urge among biographers to demonstrate how a subject achieved, if not greatness, then at least some notable deeds, which perhaps stems from a belief that the more important the subject's deeds, the more important the biography. In writing about Murray, there is an added compulsion to celebrate her achievements because she suffered so much personal loss and endured so many forms of discrimination. In other words, to interpret her life as anything other than an outstanding success seems at best mean-spirited and at worst a further form of discrimination. The urge, therefore, is to acknowledge that she suffered and then to focus on what she achieved. This would mean passing lightly over the disempowering image of a helpless youth standing before her disfigured father's corpse and focusing on the empowering vision of a mature scholar on the public stage.

I set out wanting to tell the story of an unsung hero who rose from extreme disadvantage to achieve notable "firsts" and made remarkable contributions to race and gender equality. While researching Murray's life, however, I became just as interested in the complicated personality behind the achievements. Murray often acted heroically, but she rarely felt it. She was not some kind of butterfly-like creature who magically transformed from a potentially traumatized child to an apparently empowered advocate. Rather, throughout her life Murray bore the psychological wounds of her early experiences in addition to the accumulated hurts and humiliations of a society that went to great lengths to make many of its members feel inferior. In addition to racism and sexism, at various times in her life Murray also endured homophobia, transphobia, and political persecution — all of which had implications for her mental and physical health, employment, relationships, and intellectual pursuits. Although things like finding love, job satisfaction, and creative outlets, as well as enduring indebtedness, ill-health, and relationship turmoil, may not commonly feature in the biographies of individuals who participate in public life, examining such things is essential to understanding Murray and the world she inhabited.

This biography's purpose, then, is not just to celebrate Murray's many accomplishments but also to describe as fully as possible her lived experience. Of course, not every life experience can be covered in a single volume; the "definitive" biography I imagined writing at the outset, I am now convinced, is an impossible task. This book offers a detailed description of Murray's life, yet it is still *an* account of Murray's life rather than *the* story of Murray's life. The sheer breadth of Murray's activities and the abundant evidence about her life required selectivity at every turn. In choosing material, I have included as many of Murray's diverse life experiences as practical and avoided weighting her achievements more heavily than her heartaches. Or, to put it another way, I have given as much attention to what Murray felt as to what she did. I also remained attentive to the fact that turning a life into a story can impose a coherence, meaning, and direction that do not always reflect lived experience. A life journey as it unfolds can often seem more like a maze; only when it is looked back on does the path seem clear. With this in mind, I have included as many of the misadventures and messy complications that formed Murray's life—indeed, that form any life—as possible.

I hope this approach helps readers appreciate Murray's incredibly varied life. Knowing more about the private struggles she endured deepens admiration for the many things Murray achieved in public life while simultaneously highlighting the difficulties confronting oppressed people. If it's not already asking too much, I also hope readers gain a greater appreciation for historical biographies that do not focus on the deeds of "great" individuals, which often means biographies of the privileged that potentially perpetuate societal obsessions with power and prestige. Had Murray never accomplished any conventionally recognizable notable deeds, she would still be a fascinating figure. Her relationship difficulties, desire and ability to pass as a man at times, extreme financial hardship, innumerable physical and mental health issues, ongoing family problems, and constant encounters with race and sex discrimination all make an ordinary day in the life of Pauli Murray extraordinary to witness.

THE SOURCES OF EVIDENCE FOR THIS book include the work of scholars from various fields of study who have used their expertise to illuminate aspects of Murray's life. Black history scholars have established Murray's place as a previously unsung hero of the long civil rights movement, women's history scholars have noted her significant contributions to second-wave feminism, and scholars of legal history and theology have also documented her contributions to those fields, as have scholars working in gender, sexuality, and literature.[5] Three books focusing on Murray have been indispensable to this one. Sarah Azaransky's *The Dream Is Freedom* succinctly analyzes Murray's contributions to democracy and theology. Patricia Bell-Scott's *The Firebrand and the First Lady* provides a fascinating portrait of the friendship between Eleanor Roosevelt and Pauli Murray.[6] And Rosalind Rosenberg's *Jane Crow*, the only other cradle-to-grave biography, contextualizes Murray's life and record of achievement, particularly her role in the struggle for women's legal equality, and documents Murray's struggles around her sexuality and gender identity.

My primary aim—to provide readers with a sense of what life was like for this remarkable individual—is an approach that complements the existing Pauli Murray literature. For example, *Jane Crow* covers Murray's childhood succinctly, whereas I devote considerable attention to it because I see Murray's formative years as significant in shaping her personality and aspirations. Conversely, *Jane Crow* provides, for example, a lengthy discussion of *Mendez v. Westminster* (1947), a legal case for which Murray helped write a brief later studied by NAACP lawyers preparing for the *Brown v. Board of Education* (1954) case.[7] I cover this in a few sentences because my focus is more tilted to how Murray felt, thought, and acted rather than how the world later interpreted, and benefited from, her work. The two book titles neatly capture the different emphases: Rosenberg's *Jane Crow* references Murray's label for the gender discrimination she fought to overcome, and mine, *Pauli Murray*, homes in on the person behind the accomplishments.

This approach would not have been possible had Murray not gone to great lengths to create and preserve so much evidence about so many aspects of her life. Murray worked sporadically on an autobiography over the last two decades of her life—published posthumously as *Song in a Weary Throat*—during which time she became well acquainted with the challenges of biography.[8] The autobiography took so long, in part, because she agonized over what to include. At one point she asked confidants, "How far am I ready to reveal myself?"[9] Her mentor, academic historian Caroline Ware, suggested to Murray that she was stuck not on an issue of self-revelation, but on an issue of emphasis: "If the focus of the book is to be mainly psychological—how a Negro woman with your background, generation and circumstances puts and keeps the pieces of herself together . . . you would handle it one way. . . . If it is to be mainly socio-political, a reflection of the changing scene in the life of a Negro woman activist and pioneer . . . the line would be different." Murray replied uncertainly, suggesting she could either leave unpublished "Notes for My Biographer," or publish a "socio-political" autobiography. In the end she accomplished both, writing a socio-political autobiography and leaving a voluminous archive "to supply insights to future biographers."[10]

Although her collection of personal papers is rarely counted as one of the many achievements she is lauded for, I consider it Murray's crowning success. The collection she donated to Schlesinger Library includes over 135 boxes of correspondence (sent and received), diaries, short stories, photographs, medical records, school reports, legal cases, newspaper clippings, interviews, and all other manner of material. Painstakingly, Murray collected and preserved the documents of her existence, lugging the ever-accumulating boxes with her through a rarely settled life. The information contained within provides numerous insights into not only what she accomplished but also, as importantly, what she thought and felt. Murray felt constrained about discussing many things in her own lifetime—particularly relating to her sexuality, her "experimentation on the male side," and the mental health problems she and her siblings endured—but she still recognized their potential historical significance. Thanks to Murray's bravery and foresight in preserving so many intimate life details, this biography is able to connect Murray's inner life with her incredibly active public life and highlight the interplay between the two.

This is one reason that, above all other experiences from Pauli Murray's remarkable life, her father's death comes to my mind most frequently. It seems to me as if the air around that private Baltimore home in 1923 is thick with the consequences of centuries of systematic oppression. In the parlor lies the most appalling evidence of just how dangerous it is to be Black in America—Pauli's brilliant and beautiful father crushed psychically and then physically, no longer recognizably human except for his poet's hands. While twelve-year-old Pauli strokes his hand and tries to convince herself that this battered body is her father, in another room an aunt Pauli barely knows introduces her as daughter along with five siblings equally unfamiliar to her. Even in this most intimate setting, Pauli Murray stands apart, somehow "other." The weight of family tragedies will pull on her as she moves through life, trying desperately to overcome the forces that destroyed her parents while forging her own sense of identity and belonging. It's a life journey that, like the journey to her father's funeral, is often lonely and filled with uncertainty and heartbreak, but it takes her to the forefront of struggles to make the world a more equitable place.

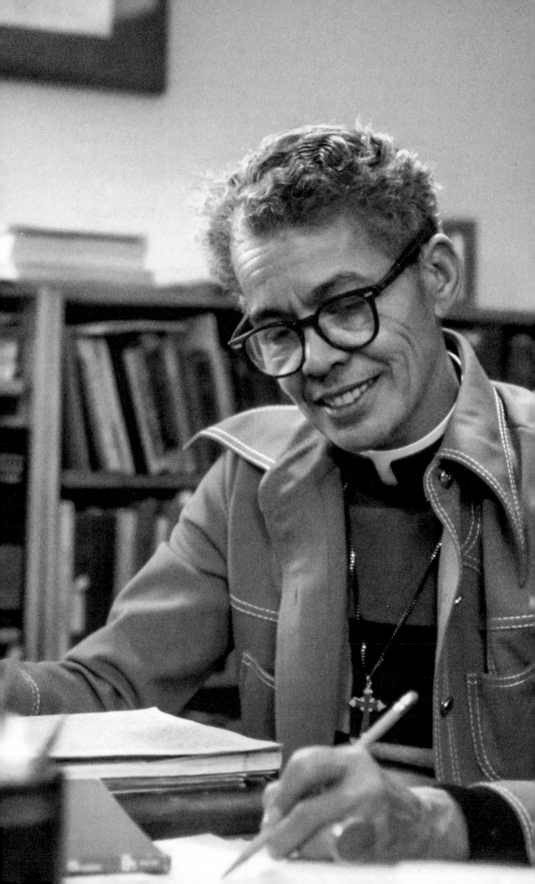

Pauli Murray

Murray's parents, Agnes Fitzgerald Murray and William H. Murray, ca. 1908.

(Schlesinger Library, Radcliffe Institute, Harvard University)

one

A CHILD OF DESTINY OR

A NOBODY WITHOUT IDENTITY,

1910–1926

. . . . .

I

Pauli Murray long believed that she was born on November 20, 1910, and named Anna Pauline Murray. It came as a shock to discover, then, when she began research for an autobiography, that her birth certificate said her birth occurred a day later and her baptism certificate listed her name as Annie, not Anna.[1] The sudden confusion around the basic elements of her personal identity illustrate a more general uncertainty that appeared at different points in Murray's life: uncertainty as to whether what she believed of herself was true, or whether what society said about her was true. Had her parents remained in her life for longer, Pauli might have asked them for confirmation, but instead their early absence created further uncertainty. As a child Pauli "fed voraciously" on other people's memories of her parents— these reminiscences had a profound influence on her development. In the opening paragraphs of her autobiography she explained, "Their striving to achieve filled me with pride and incentive, while their misfortunes left a legacy of mournfulness hovering like a gray mist over my early childhood."[2] Through the gray mist of tragic events and unreliable evidence, Pauli looked back to fashion a coherent, encouraging story of her own beginning. The story shifted over time, but her final autobiographical account went along the following lines.

Pauli Murray believed that she inherited an energetic nature from her father. William Murray liked to hunt and fish, play baseball and basketball, compose poetry and music, and play the piano and flute. Despite severely limited education and employment opportunities for African Americans—William's mother washed clothes, while his father waited tables—"Will" showed tremendous grit to graduate in 1899, at age twenty-seven, from Howard University's college preparatory department. He gained employment as a teacher in Baltimore's segregated school system and married another teacher, but the marriage soon ended in tragedy when he lost both his wife and their first child during labor. Grief didn't slow William down for long. Soon after his first wife's death, Will attended a summer school in Hampton, Virginia, where he met Agnes Fitzgerald.

Pauli Murray believed that she inherited a fiery temperament from her mother. Those who knew "Aggie" well described her as quick-tempered, though her rage subsided equally quickly and she didn't hold grudges. Six years younger than William Murray, Agnes was born on Christmas night 1878 and grew up participating in all the manual work required to keep the family's North Carolina farm going, yet when she decided that she wanted to be a nurse, her parents said no. Like many at the time, her parents believed a nursing career would be too physically demanding and too likely to expose their daughter to indignities. Her three older sisters chose more acceptable careers—two went into teaching, and the other became a dressmaker—but Agnes wanted to be a nurse and would not be deterred. Through a combination of persuasion and stubbornness Agnes gained her parents' permission, if not their blessing, to attend Hampton Training School for Nurses, where she met William Murray in 1901.

He noticed her at a dance. Agnes was hard not to notice—her expressive eyes and mass of curly hair were especially striking. On this night she wore her hair pulled back and tied with a pink ribbon that matched the pink dotted dress she had made for the occasion; Agnes only realized when she got home that evening that she had worn the dress inside out. If William noticed, he didn't care. His eyes followed her all evening, but he dared not approach her. Will had escorted Aggie's cousin Sadie to the dance and, as the campus YMCA president, he did not want to appear frivolous. Nevertheless, he made sure he left the dance at the same time as Agnes, then maneuvered Cousin Sadie through a crowded streetcar to gain an introduction. Agnes and William began courting immediately. People who saw the handsome pair together thought they could be siblings—both were lean, with expressive eyes, dark wavy hair, and coppery-colored skin. The courtship continued through correspondence after the summer ended and William returned to Baltimore.

Two years after they met, on July 1, 1903, William Murray, supported by a retinue of young men, went to Durham to marry Agnes Fitzgerald. The

A Child of Destiny or a Nobody without Identity

dashing men from Baltimore, combined with the fact that Agnes was a Fitzgerald — her Uncle Richard became one of the wealthiest African Americans in the nation — made this marriage an occasion in Black Durham. Many of Durham's Black elite plus extended family and the groom's party all packed into the Emmanuel Church at the appointed time for the ceremony — the only thing missing was the bride. The minutes ticked by with no sign of Agnes. A stifling hot day added to the discomfort as everyone sweated on her arrival. Minutes past the appointed time became hours and the hot weather became stormy, adding an element of chaos to the occasion. Agnes, it turned out, had been having final adjustments made to her dress by her heavily pregnant sister, Maria, when Maria went into labor. Agnes switched from bride-to-be to graduate nurse to help deliver a healthy nephew. The wedding eventually took place late that afternoon, and a hastily reconvened reception occurred at Uncle Richard's lavish home.[3]

THE STORY OF HER PARENTS' ROMANCE, which Pauli pieced together using her maternal relations' memories, has all the qualities of a fairy tale, complete with a dramatic last-minute disruption that could have derailed the occasion completely. Yet Pauli did not see it this way entirely. She knew that this fairy-tale romance lacked a happily ever after. Rather than interpret the wedding day events as a case of love conquering all, Pauli wondered if the long delay and then the storm — she always saw greater significance in weather events — were actually omens of the "bad times" to come.

Although quite near, further signs of the bad times ahead were scarce as Will and Aggie settled in to married life in Baltimore. Will certainly seemed on the rise — his dogged pursuit of further qualifications led to his appointment as a school principal. Money remained tight — a Black teacher could only earn about half a white teacher's wage — yet the Murrays were more prosperous than most African Americans. They had a nice brick row house with marble steps in a segregated but up-and-coming neighborhood of young professional families, similar to themselves. Agnes grew roses in the small backyard while in the upstairs study Will completed schoolwork and wrote poetry with the aid of copious amounts of coffee and cigarettes. They also held a mortgage on a second property that they rented out, and they employed a domestic worker. Aggie's eighteen-year-old younger sister, Bertie, came to stay with the couple in search of excitement and confirmed in letters to her sisters back in Durham that money was tight but also that the Murrays had status. Bertie promised her sisters that if they visited she would introduce them "to some of the swell 400 of the elite and you will have a no. 1 time."[4]

Two years after the Murrays wed and still five years before Pauli's birth, the bad times arrived with seeming suddenness. In August 1905 typhoid fever struck Will down. Agnes nursed him as best she could, including continually packing ice around his neck and head, where the pain was worst. She told her parents, "I have been up both day and night since he has taken [to] his bed two weeks ago. I am so tired and weary I must close."[5] Will survived, but typhoid killed Bertie Fitzgerald. In the same sad year that Agnes lost her younger sister and very nearly her husband, she gave birth to her first child, Grace Murray.[6] The demands on Agnes grew because William also developed "brain fever," a label applied to a wide range of symptoms at the time. Pauli thought it may have been encephalitis, but she also thought that a contributing factor may have been overwork in an effort to disprove racial stereotypes about Black inferiority. Whatever the actual trigger, according to family legend, something caused a significant, permanent change in William Murray.

After the illness Will suffered depressive episodes and developed an unpredictable, violent temper. Amid this disturbing development, the family grew rapidly—after Grace in 1905 came Mildred in 1906 and William in 1909.[7] The violence continued throughout. In later life Pauli learned more about the violence's extent and nature, but she would not disclose what she learned, publicly or privately; she only told a niece that the details were so horrific that "the miracle is that any one of the Murrays has been able to carry on without serious psychopathic symptoms."[8] At the time, Agnes steadfastly refused her family's urging to have Will committed to a psychiatric facility. She nevertheless feared for her safety and her children's. Agnes regularly took their children and fled to her family home in Durham, only to return to her husband after short periods. On two occasions while Agnes was in Durham, William's relations committed him. But on each occasion Agnes hurried back to Baltimore to have her husband released into her care.

During one separation, around Christmas 1909, Aggie's family convinced her to divorce Will. She returned to Baltimore with that intention, but instead became pregnant with Pauli, the couple's fourth child. Pauli described her conception as part of a "passionate reunion," and that she was "a child of reconciliation conceived in love," but other evidence made it difficult not to interpret her creation as compounding the family's problems.[9] Further periods of marital separation followed. During one separation when Pauli was fifteen months old, Agnes decided to return to her husband after discovering she was pregnant again.

She gathered her parcels and herded her four small children onto the train at Durham station with the help of her eldest sister, Pauline Dame—

A Child of Destiny or a Nobody without Identity

she had lived with the Murrays in Baltimore for a brief time and was god-mother and namesake to the youngest Murray child. Moments before the train's departure, Pauline made a snap decision and grabbed her goddaugh-ter from the train. Over the din of the station noise, Pauline told Agnes that she would look after little Pauline for a time, since Agnes had too many children to care for with another one on the way. There was no time for de-bate, or even to retrieve the child's clothing from the train. Pauli Murray re-mained in Durham for at least the next nine months.

Things in Baltimore did not improve. Will must have worked intermit-tently, at best. Agnes wrote to Pauline explaining that she had to let the housekeeper go. Although she badly needed the help, she needed the money more. Before the bad times began in 1905, Agnes had no children, a hus-band earning more than most African Americans, a housekeeper, and sisters who regularly stayed with her; when she wrote to her sister in 1912 she had a newborn child plus three other young children and a dangerous, unstable husband to care for, and none of the earlier support. Her desperation comes through in the letter to her sister: "If I can only stay on my feet, and keep my family on theirs, I will be so thankful. My little baby [Rosetta] is so frail and tiny. . . . I am working hard to keep her well, for I was so sick myself be-fore she was born, she has not a strong foundation to build on. . . . Is little Pauline still using her diapers? I do hope you will train her to use the cham-ber[pot], for all these children require so much to be done for them, and I am not so strong."[10] Around the time she wrote this letter, Agnes fell preg-nant again. She gave birth to her sixth baby when the fifth child, the sickly Rosetta, wasn't yet fourteen months old; because of his frailty, the newborn Robert had to remain in the hospital for the first six months of his life. Two months after Robert's birth, Agnes became pregnant again—her seventh pregnancy in nine years.

On Thursday March 26, 1914, all of the Murray children except Robert were living in the Baltimore home. Although only three at the time, Pauli remembered being alone in a room—isolated from her siblings because of chicken pox—sitting on a trunk banging her heels on its side. This arresting image is the only memory she retained from the time of her mother's death. Pauli suspected that her inability to recall more details owed to more than just her young age. She reflected, "It is as if a protective shield of forgetful-ness was drawn over the shock and confusion that enveloped our house-hold, a burden too great for my memory to bear."[11] Not only could Pauli remember nothing further of this day, she also retained no memory of her mother's face, voice, or touch; she could only remember her mother's fra-grance and movements, and becoming entangled in her skirts.

Agnes was thirty-five years old and four months pregnant when she died. She died in the home where Pauli sat on a trunk banging her heels. The cause of death remained something of a mystery, and in Pauli Murray's life of uncertainties this one loomed large throughout. Pauli eventually acquired a copy of the death certificate that cited "apoplexy" as the cause, which she interpreted as a massive cerebral hemorrhage brought on from "the strain of too frequent pregnancies and my father's mental condition."[12] It's a depressing enough conclusion, since it implicates her father and her own creation as causes, but a massive stroke is at least a natural cause of death. This conclusion did not, however, prevent Pauli from contemplating down the years how else a thirty-five-year-old woman might suddenly and unexpectedly die at home.[13]

Pauli's "protective shield of forgetfulness" meant she had no memory regarding the decision that she should leave Baltimore following her mother's death. Her three elder siblings remained with their father, while a nearby paternal aunt took her two younger siblings. Pauli alone went to live with her maternal relatives in North Carolina. Aunt Pauline later told Pauli that this is what her mother had wanted if anything should happen to her, but Aunt Pauline also told Pauli that she let her decide whether to go to Durham or stay in Baltimore.[14] It is doubtful that a three-year-old made such an important decision, although conceivable if her father was not fit to decide and a custodial contest occurred between paternal and maternal aunts. In any case, the literal truth of whether Pauli decided to go to North Carolina is less important than the fact that she grew up believing she made the momentous decision to leave her father and siblings—a belief that led Pauli to experience a persistent feeling of being pulled between wanting to identify with her immediate family and clinging to the aunt who seemed to offer security. "In a sense," she recalled, "this is a history of my life, being pulled between my family and other things."[15]

Decades later, when aspiring to a writing career, Murray reimagined the critical events surrounding her permanent departure from Baltimore in an unpublished short story called "Problem Child." Pauli's fictional self, three-year-old Bennie (her childhood nickname was Lenie), also has chicken pox and is isolated from her siblings, seated on a trunk in the kitchen. Her mother has placed her there "hard," telling her not to move. Her mother then goes upstairs and Bennie hears a thump—the sound of her mother falling down dead. Although Bennie does not understand what has happened, she instinctively grabs her mother's apron from a kitchen chair. Bennie eventually falls asleep holding her mother's apron and later awakens on her father's bed. Her father could not be more caring—he picks her up, holds

A Child of Destiny or a Nobody without Identity

her tight, kisses her, and explains with a tear in his eye that Mommy has gone away. Bennie falls asleep again, and when she wakes the next morning, Aunt Bernadine (Aunt Pauline) is by her bed. Bernadine also takes Bennie in her arms.

The story concludes with a discussion between Bernadine and Bennie's father. Bernadine suggests she should take Bennie, and the father responds, "Bernadine, I hate to part with her. She's like her mother — she's got spirit. She's like me too — she's a strange child, hard to handle. I'm afraid she'll be ruined if she stays here with the rest of the children. She's not like the rest." He agrees to let Bernadine take Bennie, but then the choice is ultimately Bennie's. The father is curiously absent from the final scene, in which a paternal aunt tries to coax Bennie into coming along with her and Bennie's two younger siblings. Bennie detects harshness in her voice, however, and chooses to go with Aunt Bernadine, who did not try to influence her decision.[16]

Even in fiction, Pauli's mother remains absent from the story. The only mention is of her mother "placing her down hard," which could be a euphemism for abandonment — her mother left her to face life's hard realities alone, without protection and emotionally bereft. It could more simply be Pauli's perception that in her mother's final moments, sick, noisy Pauli became one burden too many. Concerning her father, "Problem Child" presumably elaborates Pauli's wish that his willingness to let her alone leave Baltimore was not an act of abandonment, but a painful decision by a loving father who recognized her exceptional qualities.

Having a scarcity of (mostly unpleasant) information about her earliest years did not help Murray devise a consistent "storied self," which psychologists describe as vital to providing a "sense of inner sameness and continuity."[17] As a rebellious young adult, Pauli sketched a blunt assessment of her origins in a notebook: "Agnes wed a young widower from Baltimore, highly intelligent, musical, but given to periods of insanity. Six children were born within nine years and the poor worn-out mother died suddenly during the pregnancy of the seventh."[18] Late in life, when writing her autobiography, Pauli described her parents' marriage as a Shakespearean tragedy: "Their passionate devotion to one another throughout the perplexities of their nearly eleven years of married life invested them with an aura of legendary, star-crossed lovers."[19] Over the years, stories of her parents' marriage engendered as much uncertainty and insecurity as identity cohesion and personal stability; nevertheless, she tried to weave them into an inspiring story and in doing so gained an implicit understanding that identities are not necessarily fixed, but can be created anew.

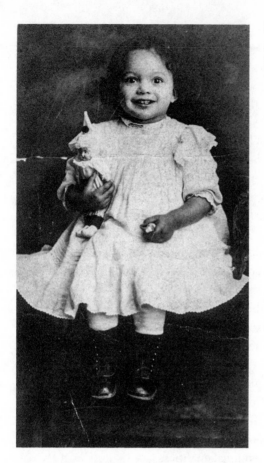

Murray as a child, 1913.
(Schlesinger Library, Radcliffe Institute, Harvard University)

. . . . .

II

Dire circumstance plucked three-year-old Pauli Murray from her family home in big city Baltimore and placed her in the semirural Durham home of her maternal grandparents. She had already spent considerable time in Durham, but the magnitude of the adjustment required was still enormous, not least because her siblings or father would never come to visit her. The very active child, still recovering from chicken pox, shared her new home environment with four mature adults: her grandparents, Robert and Cornelia Fitzgerald, in their seventies, and two of their daughters, Pauline Dame and Sallie Fitzgerald, forty-three and thirty-six years old, respectively. Pauli found things to admire in all four guardians, but she also found fault with them all. Her assessments of these four figures illuminate not only the key personalities that shaped her childhood but also the world that shaped those personalities.

A Child of Destiny or a Nobody without Identity

Aunt Pauline certainly wanted Pauli to come to Durham. Rather than express that strong desire, however, she later emphasized that it was Pauli's mother's wishes, and indeed Pauli's own wish, that Pauli come to Durham. This explanation made sense in terms of helping Pauli accept the decision that separated her from her father and siblings, but it also reflects an aspect of Aunt Pauline's personality—she cared deeply, but often struggled to express affection. Instead, Aunt Pauline adopted a dutiful air about the things she undertook. Indeed, her very appearance projected dutifulness. Her rimless spectacles, prim clothing and hairstyle, and severe expression, which looked like a weapon designed for quelling unruly schoolchildren, all made Aunt Pauline seem like an archetypal early twentieth-century primary school teacher. Her appearance may have evolved to reflect the vocation she first took up as a fourteen-year-old, but life had also dealt Aunt Pauline so many cruel blows that she had little reason for cheer. At the time Pauli came to Durham, the deaths of Aunt Pauline's younger sisters, Agnes and Bertie, were only the most recent in a series of dreadful losses.

Aunt Pauline had married Morton Dame, a "near white" graduate from Howard University Law School, three years after the infamous *Plessy v. Ferguson* (1896) Supreme Court decision, which provided legal cover for racial segregation. The redheaded, blue-eyed Morton Dame and his similarly fair-skinned bride rendered the notion of racial separation absurd.[20] However artificial the attempt to segregate African Americans, Morton's struggle to make a living as a Negro lawyer revealed its very real consequences. Adding to the financial woe, in 1900 Pauline gave birth to a girl, Venus, who died within a week. The couple fell pregnant again in 1902, but the marriage ended around the same time. Morton Dame decided to abandon his current life and relationships to create a new life as a white man in a new location. After returning to her parents' home Aunt Pauline gave birth to a boy in March 1903. Nine months later the child died from meningitis.[21]

The stories Murray recounted concerning Aunt Pauline's marriage provide insight into race issues at the turn of the twentieth century, as well as Pauli's continual efforts to craft her life story in ways that balanced honest exploration of the consequences of oppression with the need to respect the memories of her loved ones. Her autobiography stated that Aunt Pauline's marriage "floundered on an issue of principle," because Aunt Pauline refused to join Morton Dame in starting a new life as a white couple. Yet in the forthright unpublished account she wrote as a young adult, Murray described Morton Dame as possessing only "a diploma and a blond mustache" and said that Aunt Pauline "followed her ne'er-do-well husband all over Virginia and West Virginia and finally came back to her mother, a deserted and disillusioned woman."[22] Rumors that Morton Dame became a very success-ful white lawyer in a neighboring state made Aunt Pauline's abandonment more galling.[23]

Following the separation, Pauline Dame remained a "spinster" primary school teacher who, aside from a brief stint with the Murrays in Baltimore, lived with her parents. Aunt Pauline became the dutiful eldest daughter, caring for her aging parents and working to support them. Or, as Pauli de-scribed it, Aunt Pauline slipped into an "accustomed harness, and it was taken for granted that she would have no further life of her own."[24] Aunt Pauline's role as a teacher granted her respectability status in Durham's Black community—unlike most working women at the time, women teach-ers retained middle-class status provided they remained unmarried and childless, though they were also simultaneously pitiable for this childless-ness.[25] This became another reason that friends, and even Fitzgerald family members, cautioned Aunt Pauline against taking on the additional respon-sibility of raising a three-year-old child.[26] In most matters Aunt Pauline de-ferred to the wishes of others; in this matter, however, she would not yield. Aunt Pauline's unhappy life experiences no doubt added to her determina-tion to take care of her goddaughter, but those same experiences, combined with her community leadership role and perhaps an implicit awareness that independence and resilience were essential characteristics enabling a Black girl to survive in the Jim Crow South, inhibited her ability to show Pauli care in a demonstrative, affectionate manner.

Pauli's resistance to anyone taking the place of her mother also combined with Aunt Pauline's personality to limit the physical affection in the relation-ship. Pauli described Aunt Pauline as a master artisan and a compassionate spirit with a strong affinity for children that made her a fine teacher. But she also characterized Aunt Pauline as issuing orders like a general on a battle-field, being inflexible, intolerant of weaknesses or excuses, and gloomy and sparing with praise, which led Murray to nickname Aunt Pauline "General Sourpuss."[27] These descriptions reveal Pauli's complex relationship with the woman who cared for her following the death of her mother—she appreci-ated Aunt Pauline's efforts but remained critical. Aunt Pauline helped Pauli cope with the loss of her parents, though she could not replace them, some-thing Pauli made explicit by eventually calling Aunt Pauline "Mother" rather than "Mama" or any other intimate derivation.[28]

Aunt Pauline's younger sister, Sallie Fitzgerald, provided Pauli's next-strongest maternal influence. Although Aunt Sallie was also a schoolteacher and was fiercely loyal to her sister, she possessed a very different person-ality. Whereas Pauli depicted Aunt Pauline as a "doer of few words, who

A Child of Destiny or a Nobody without Identity

was intensely practical and who seldom smiled," she described Aunt Sallie as "imaginative and entertaining. She had a contagious laugh, a sense of humor, and an endless repertoire of engaging stories, but she tended to be disorganized and followed a pattern of stops and starts." Privately, Murray put it more bluntly, describing Aunt Sallie as "someone who fails at every task."[29] Therefore, Pauli could "talk out my troubles with Aunt Sallie, but in any emergency requiring action I automatically turned to Aunt Pauline."[30] Aunt Sallie competed with her sister for Pauli's affections by telling Pauli that she had been the "pal sister" to Pauli's mother. Sallie also took pleasure from what she saw as Pauli's closer resemblance to her—as a youth Pauli shared Aunt Sallie's rounder face and big smile, though the main similarity was their brown skin tone, which set them apart from the other, lighter-complexioned household members. Aunt Pauline came to exert the greater influence on Pauli, however, when Sallie married and moved away two years after Pauli's arrival in the Fitzgerald home.

Aunt Pauline inherited some of her unsmiling demeanor from her father, Robert Fitzgerald. Born in 1840, Grandfather Robert grew up a free man in the North. He wore a thick dropping moustache that stayed black in old age, as did his bushy brows, and much of his hair, which all contrasted with his dull ivory skin color. Never a tall man, by the time Pauli came into the house Robert barely measured five and half feet, but he seemed bigger—he stood erect, with his chin thrust aggressively out at the world. He always dressed immaculately, usually in a suit, even though most days he never went farther than the front porch.[31] Robert had fought for the Union during the Civil War, during which he survived a gunshot wound that left a bullet embedded behind his left eyeball.[32] Following the war he migrated to North Carolina, where despite his impaired vision he taught freedmen, then farmed and started a brickmaking business. Robert maintained a martial attitude throughout his life, which he tried to instill in his descendants, not least by making them march in military formation and resorting to corporal punishment without hesitation. Aunt Pauline said of her father, "He was very strict and would switch me for the smallest thing I'd do. I was four years old and could read and write—I had to do it."[33]

By the time Pauli came to live in the Fitzgerald house, full blindness left Grandfather Robert unable to carry out the traditional duties of a male head of the household. Despite his advanced age and diminishing capacity to contribute to the house, Robert remained intimidating in demeanor and appearance, especially his eyes—they had lost the power to see but had increased in intimidatory strength through a fixed, far-away look. Pauli recalled he had a reputation for "whaling the daylights out of grandchildren who did not move fast enough when he called; he'd lash out at them with whatever he happened to be holding at the time — his saber, a saw, a broom handle or his cane."[34] Pauli could never be sure when Grandfather might blindly lash out and therefore remained nervous and vigilant in his presence.

Not surprisingly, Pauli had mixed feelings about Grandfather. She reflected, "He was kind of an enigma to me. That is, I was very ambivalent about him. I resented him and admired him. Here was the impact of this person."[35] His lack of affection and harsh disciplinarian attitude are factors in her resentment, but she also resented the patriarchal privilege he enjoyed: for example, he received the larger share of the family's meager food supplies even though he was less able to contribute to the cultivation of food.[36] Her reasons for admiring him stem from his dedication to the cause of African American uplift, particularly through his Civil War service and career teaching freedmen. Murray's admiration was such that she eventually wrote a Fitzgerald family history, *Proud Shoes*, primarily about his life.

Pauli's grandmother, Cornelia Fitzgerald, provided respite from the inflexible discipline of Aunt Pauline and Grandfather Robert. She recalled, "I loved my grandmother more than anyone else in the world, I think. She was the one person I remember who rocked me in her arms when I was little, who called me 'Baby' and petted me."[37] In another unpublished short story about "Bennie," Pauli's fictionalized self, she elaborated:

> Everyone else was too occupied with grown-up troubles to notice that Bennie sometimes got very lonely. Grandmother was different; she was the only person who would take Bennie on her lap, holding her tight and rocking her. Bennie loved the sweet, soft, delicious feeling of being held and rocked; away from the world and all its hurts, the mysterious, new things she could not understand, the strange inexplicable, lost feeling which steals over a little girl who lives among serious older people, the sternness, the harshness, the endless arguments, the inflexible discipline — all these dissolved and withered away when Bennie buried her head in Gran'ma's flabby bosom and swung her legs back and forth in complete abandonment and well being.[38]

Grandmother Cornelia had a long thin nose, high cheekbones, and dark, almost melancholy eyes, set against grayish skin and long straight white hair. She possessed a bundle of nervous energy that meant she rarely sat still, and her short, plump stature hid a large and volatile personality.[39] The opening chapter of *Proud Shoes* describes Grandmother working herself into a rage about people trespassing on their property. Goaded by the neighbors for their amusement, Cornelia exploded with a tirade of invective, holler-

A Child of Destiny or a Nobody without Identity

ing, "I ain't going to let these dirty niggers walk all over me"[40] and calling a neighbor a "no-mannered slut!" and a "spraddle-legged whore."[41] The scene climaxes with five-year-old Pauli physically preventing Grandmother from climbing a fence to attack a fourteen-year-old girl with a mattock.[42]

Born into slavery in 1844, Cornelia described her biological mother, a slave named Harriet, as three-quarters white and one-quarter Cherokee. The slave owner's two sons, Frank and Sidney Smith, both lusted after Harriet. Sidney Smith drove off Harriet's husband, a local free Black man, then raped her, which resulted in Cornelia's conception. Sidney's sexual abuse of Harriet ended when his brother Frank physically assaulted him before taking Harriet for himself. Sidney Smith turned to drink and let his legal practice disintegrate. The drunkard Sidney acknowledged Cornelia was his child and showed her affection on occasion and openly acknowledged her as his daughter, even in front of company, in part to embarrass his family. Cornelia grew up thinking of herself more as a Smith than as a slave, but the space she occupied in the Smith house was ambiguous.

The actions of the Smith brothers' sister, Mary Ruffin Smith, who acquired legal ownership of Cornelia, created further ambiguity. "Miss Mary" had no children of her own and took a close interest in Cornelia's life. She told Cornelia that she was free, but never actually freed her from slavery. She took Cornelia along to the Episcopal Church, but Cornelia had to sit in the balcony, not downstairs in the Smith family pew. Miss Mary also spared Cornelia much of the work carried out by other house slaves, but also never taught Cornelia to read and write. Even after emancipation, Mary Ruffin Smith retained a strong influence over Cornelia: for example, she granted Grandfather Robert permission to marry her.[43]

Even as Cornelia endured the legacy of her slave ancestry, she rejected that heritage and chose to identify as the daughter of a white lawyer, raised by the lawyer's wealthy sister. When neighbors insulted Grandmother as a bastard child, Cornelia responded, "I'll tell anybody I'm a white man's child. A fine white man at that. A southern aristocrat. . . . My father was one of the best criminal lawyers in the South. He was in the North Carolina legislature. Before the Civil War he saved fourteen poor Negroes from the gallows free of charge."[44] Grandmother also asserted pride in her white heritage by hanging a painting bequeathed to her by Mary Ruffin Smith over the Fitzgerald mantlepiece.[45] Cornelia viewed it as a prized possession, though she might have just as easily viewed it as an insult—the childless Miss Mary willed much of the sizable Smith estate to the University of North Carolina and bequeathed to her biological niece only a small parcel of low-value land and a few trinkets.[46]

Grandmother's actions rendered the social categories of white and Black, around which much of southern social life was organized, complex and conditional. Cornelia's parentage reveals the illusionary foundations of race-based power structures in the South, but the illusionary foundations still supported a very real edifice that had a pervasive impact on its survivors and their descendants, not least through the additional arbitrary divisions that were created in the scramble for dignity. Murray explained, "Colored people grasped at any distinction to put distance between themselves and slavery. If one couldn't fall back on the amount of white blood he had in him, as Grandmother did, he'd rely on a free parent or free grandparent. And I could talk of free great-grandparents, something truly to be proud of in those times."[47]

Pauli's free ancestors were Grandfather Robert's parents, whom she described as a free northern "mulatto" and a white woman.[48] In her archival writing, Murray recorded a family legend that Robert's ancestors were "petty lords" from Ireland who only became identified with the "colored race" through "some mix-up." Half of the children disappeared from the family record after marrying whites, and the other half, including Robert Fitzgerald, married as "near white" as they could, "choosing for their mates mulattos, octaroons, or 'passing fair.'"[49] Similar to Cornelia, who described her mother as three-quarters white and one-quarter Native American, Robert's ancestors had at times sought to disassociate themselves from any Black ancestry.

Murray's personal papers include a sketch of her Fitzgerald forebears, written in the 1930s when she was least committed to middle-class values and ideology, which is devoid of the racial uplift content found in Murray's later published memoirs.[50] She described her grandfather thus:

> Captivated by a high-spirited Southern belle, and possible heir to much property, he married her before consulting his family. They never forgave him. In their opinion, Robert had married out of his station— a slave girl without education for all her white ancestry and fine culture. Her supposed millions had turned out to be a few paltry acres of untilled land and no money with which to stock it. The struggle against poverty had changed her from a strong, youthful woman to a haggard toothless matron, given to fits of temper and constant nagging. She was never accepted by her husband's people and his children were snubbed accordingly.[51]

Cornelia's pride in her white ancestry, then, can be seen not only as evidence of the shame felt by former slaves but also as a defiant assertion of personal pride in response to her in-laws' rejection.

A Child of Destiny or a Nobody without Identity

Murray's archival notes described her grandparents as suffering from an acute "color complex." Their children could only have friends and suitors whom they deemed sufficiently fair-skinned.[52] The Fitzgeralds had approved of William Murray's light brown skin. They no doubt also approved of Aunt Pauline's husband, Morton Dame, who could easily pass for white, though this apparent virtue according to the family color complex ultimately facilitated the marriage breakup. In a manner befitting Aunt Sallie's contrasting personality, she ignored her parents' prejudice when it came to marriage.

Aunt Sallie eventually accepted the marriage proposal of a West Indian Episcopalian minister who had long pursued her. Despite his very respectable profession, when Sallie's suitor first visited the Fitzgerald home one evening, a young Pauli called him a "big black bear" to his face, and blind Grandfather Robert ordered him out of the house. That night Aunt Pauline had a dream in which her future brother-in-law appeared as a giant black snake devouring her. When Pauline reported her dream the following morning, the Fitzgeralds decided that Reverend Small would most definitely not be welcome back in the home.[53] Although a fascinating insight into the ways in which extreme racism permeated American society, this incident never made it into Murray's published memoirs. Not surprisingly, in print she expressed a greater level of respect for her kin than in private, though it is often her unpublished reflections that better illuminate the period and its influence on family dynamics.

Incorporating the family history of racial "passing" proved a chief difficulty in writing her autobiography.[54] In addition to three surviving Fitzgerald aunts, Pauli had an uncle, Tommie, whom she didn't mention in her autobiography. He ran away at nineteen and was never heard from again; some thought he started a new life as a white man.[55] As an example of passing's humorous side that also highlighted the absurdity of dividing people by race categories, she described in her autobiography how a cousin's passing was exposed when the wig he wore to hide his kinky hair blew off at work.[56] The most personal incident Pauli recalled involved an unnamed lighter-skinned relative asking her to wait outside a store so the relative could pass as white inside the establishment to receive better service. Pauli did not describe how this made her feel. Rather, the incident served to illustrate Aunt Pauline's race pride — Aunt Pauline was furious when she learned what happened, and she never allowed Pauli to go anywhere with that relative again.[57]

Among the extended Fitzgerald family in Durham — Pauli's main source of playmates — Pauli's yellow-brown complexion placed her at the dark end of the family's skin tone spectrum, which she described as ranging from "fair" to "Indian copper."[58] In both her published and unpublished writing, Murray provided few details about how her relatively dark complexion influenced her treatment within the family. The closest she came is in a passage in *Proud Shoes* when she described, using examples of distressing dialogue, how the world she inhabited revolved on color and variations of color: "Brush your hair, child, don't let it get kinky! Cold-cream your face, child, don't let it get sunburned! Don't suck your lips, child, you'll make them too niggerish! Black is evil, don't mix with mean niggers!"[59] It sounds like Grandmother, yet Murray did not attribute this dialogue to anyone in particular—she did not even explicitly state that it was directed at her, let alone how such comments made her feel about herself or her family. In the most personal of matters, she reverted from the personal to the societal, narrating the types of views expressed at the time rather than recalling specific incidents from her home life.

Although revealing the damage done to the Fitzgeralds by racial oppression never became easy, Murray's writings about the most influential people in her childhood provide numerous insights into their personalities and the world that shaped them. Pauli's mere physical descriptions of her four Fitzgerald guardians expose the absurdity of a Black and white color line: "Grandma looked like the grey marble. . . . Mother [Aunt Pauline] was strawberry pink, Grandpa was ivory white, Aunt Sallie was taffy-colored like molasses candy when it has been pulled a little while."[60] However artificial the division, the consequences were real—Murray's writing documented how each of the Fitzgeralds' lives were shaped by racism and how it was reflected in their experiences and personalities. Murray is least revealing about how the Fitzgerald color complex directly impacted her, but she suggests clearly enough that it did. The plain though difficult-to-express reality of how it affected her childhood is perhaps best summed up in the response she gave to an interviewer who asked late in Murray's life if her "mixed" heritage had caused her problems growing up. Murray responded, "Oh, yes," then burst into laughter.[61]

. . . . .

III

At the time Pauli arrived, Durham was fast becoming one of the nation's most prominent centers of Black life. In 1912, the year before Murray's permanent arrival, W. E. B. DuBois praised the progress of African Americans in Durham, which he believed characterized "the progress of the American Negro." Some of the nation's wealthiest Black citizens resided in Durham—

Murray's grandparents, Robert and Cornelia Fitzgerald, ca. 1910.
(Schlesinger Library, Radcliffe Institute, Harvard University)

African Americans owned and operated numerous large industrial businesses as well as numerous retail shops and cultural and educational institutions such as schools and a library.[62] The success of some African Americans in the thriving industrial city bred white resentment and the vigorous enforcement of segregation. The financial prosperity of a minority of African Americans also served to highlight differences within Durham's Black community. Few families could have experienced these divisions more acutely than the Fitzgeralds.[63]

Grandmother Cornelia never received a substantial inheritance from her wealthy white ancestors, and Grandfather Robert's farm and brickmaking business failed along with his eyesight.[64] Murray wrote, "Their life was one of endless struggle and disappointment. What with a blind father, a nervous high-strung, unsystematic mother and six mouths to feed—the wolf was forever beating his tail against the door."[65] Grandmother developed pellagra, an illness caused by dietary deficiencies and an overreliance on corn products. In its advanced stages, pellagra can cause insanity (possibly accounting for some of Cornelia's volatility). In the early twentieth century, pellagra was stigmatized as a disease of the very poor—African Americans in Murray's neighborhood considered it nearly as shameful as venereal disease.[66]

The Fitzgerald's impoverishment contrasted greatly with Grandfather Robert's successful brother, the red-headed, blue-eyed Richard Fitzgerald. The two brothers had started brickmaking businesses, but only Richard's became a spectacular success.[67] He made so much money from brickmaking that he could afford to establish several other prominent Black businesses, including the Mechanics and Farmers Bank, which opened in 1907 with him as the first president. Richard also became a partner in the Durham Drug Company, president of the Coleman Cotton Mill, and president of the Real Estate, Mercantile, and Manufacturing Company.[68] Both Booker T. Washington and W. E. B. DuBois acknowledged Richard as a model businessman.[69] The contrasting fortunes of the Fitzgerald brothers led to their families' delineation as "the rich Fitzgeralds" and "the poor Fitzgeralds."[70] The success of the "rich Fitzgeralds" led Murray to sometimes view her family's hardships as resulting from ill fate and personal failings rather than a consequence of class and racial oppression.

The poor Fitzgeralds still clung to middle-class status, however. Race oppression meant that material wealth alone did not determine class status in Black communities—things such as education, deportment, and skin tone also counted.[71] In combating the overwhelming hostility of the white world, Black middle-class understandings of how uplift occurred often reinforced ruling-class values. E. Franklin Frazier described the Black middle-class as status obsessed; "moreover, they have unconditionally accepted the values of the white bourgeois world: its morals and its canons of respectability, its standards of beauty and consumption. In fact they have tended to over-emphasize their conformity to white ideals."[72] In trying to assert a positive identity that refuted claims about Black inferiority, proponents of uplift ideology often created and exacerbated differences with Black communities.[73]

Despite the wolf forever beating his tail at the family door, Pauli was taught to believe that "a Fitzgerald was *somebody*" and that the family were not simply poor but, rather, "the respectable poor."[74] Murray recalled a number of incidents that indicate that "respectable" behavior was a more important signifier of class than material resources in her autobiography, though she seemed oblivious to the class dimensions of these incidents. In one instance, Pauli asked for more meat during dinner at the home of a local Black doctor (Murray's appetite sometimes got her in trouble); the hosts were willing, but Aunt Pauline said no. When Pauli persisted, Aunt Pauline took her into another room to give her "one of the few whippings" of her life.[75] In many small ways, the family continued to emphasize dignified behavior as a marker of respectable middle-class status.[76]

IN THE 1890S ROBERT SUPERVISED construction of a sturdy home a mile from Durham's center. The two-story wooden structure at 906 Carroll Street (now a restored heritage site) consisted of two bedrooms upstairs and one more downstairs, plus a kitchen, dining room, and parlor.[77] Pauli slept in a little white iron crib in the hallway until Aunt Sallie married and moved away, and then at age five Pauli moved into Aunt Pauline's upstairs bedroom. As she grew older, the parlor became her favorite room. The rarely used room provided a quiet sanctuary to read and to study the family photographs on display, which included one of the Murrays taken when Pauli was about two. Her favorite photograph, however, featured her mother as a young woman, just before her marriage, dressed in her nursing uniform.[78]

Durham had grown rapidly in the years since the house's construction. By the time Pauli arrived, the land downhill from and fronting the property had become a Black neighborhood known as "the Bottoms," which comprised small communities living in shacks at the bottom of hills near streams and gullies.[79] Murray recalled, "It was as if the town had swallowed more than it could hold and had regurgitated, for the Bottoms was an odorous conglomeration of trash piles, garbage dumps, cow stalls, pigpens and crowded humanity. You could tell it at night by the straggling lights from oil lamps glimmering along the hollows and the smell of putrefaction, pig swill, cow dung and frying foods. Even if you lived on a hill just above the Bottoms, it seemed lower and danker than the meanest hut on a graded street."[80]

The Fitzgeralds were as materially poor as many of their neighbors, if not poorer—they were the last in the neighborhood to install inside plumbing and electricity—but their home ownership and their values still divided them from many of their neighbors. Murray acknowledged both these things when she recalled, "Money was hard to come by, we didn't have a car, we didn't have a cow, we didn't have a horse or buggy, we were really the respectable poor. But our values were middle class and therefore, to that extent, I think that there was polite interchange, there was neighborly kindness, but there wasn't social visiting back and forth between the kids who lived in The Bottom and me."[81] The estrangement from the community in which Pauli lived compounded her loneliness and complicated her identity formation—she was both Black and poor and yet not Black and not poor.

Pauli's ambiguous race and class identities physically manifested themselves in the location of the poor Fitzgerald's home. While the taint of the Bottoms threatened the Fitzgerald home to the front, an expanding, whites-only graveyard posed a threat behind the home. A chicken-wire fence separated the Fitzgerald backyard from Maplewood Cemetery, the segregated burial place for many of Durham County's white elites.[82] The graveyard, which looked to Pauli like it was tumbling down the steep hill toward the back of the house, provided an unwelcome reminder of both segregation and death. Murray remembered, "The oppressive nearness of this silent white world of stony angels, doves, lambs, tree trunks and columns gave me the feeling that death was always waiting just outside our back door to grasp me."[83] Had the cemetery's location been planned with symbolism in mind, it could not have been positioned more fittingly—at the top of the hill sat a Confederate cannon that pointed downhill directly at the Fitzgeralds' back door.

It very much seemed as if the Fitzgeralds were at war with Maplewood Cemetery. After losing his eyesight, Grandfather lost his brickmaking business and then the option on the land behind the house, which the graveyard began to take over. Over the years the expanding cemetery seemed to Murray like "a powerful enemy advancing relentlessly upon us, pushing us slowly downward into the Bottoms." The Fitzgeralds fought the incursion—Robert sued the city, while Cornelia harangued workmen expanding Maplewood in much the same way as she did her neighbors—but to no avail. The graveyard's march downhill toward the Fitzgerald home also posed physical health risks: as burial plots were dug closer to the Fitzgerald house, fluids from decomposed corpses seeped into the family's yard, forcing their well to be condemned. The family had to slosh around in boots much of the time, and Pauli recalled, "We were seldom free from the sickening odor of standing water and rotting weeds."[84]

Although the literal stench of segregation threatened the home from the rear, the Fitzgeralds still preferred to describe the home's location as "behind Maplewood Cemetery" rather than "in the Bottoms."[85] It was an unenviable choice, but the urge for class differentiation proved so strong that the poor Fitzgeralds believed the white graveyard conferred more status than the Black community facing their home. For their part, the neighbors similarly disdained the Fitzgeralds. Murray explained, "The dead behind us were closer and seemed more friendly at times than the living neighbors in front of us." If this bothered Grandmother Cornelia, she hid it well. "Dead neighbors made good neighbors," she would pronounce; "they kept their mouths shut and weren't always meddling into other folks' business." During summer days, Pauli spent more time playing in the cemetery than her own large front yard, which she likened to a moat separating her from other people—no neighborhood children came into the Fitzgerald front yard, and Aunt Pauline never let Pauli go to their yards to play.[86] Having already lost her mother and been separated from her father and five siblings, Pauli's experienced ongoing loneliness living in a house of serious mature adults— a loneliness that only intensified as she could only watch the children of the Bottoms play from her front porch during the day and fear the nocturnal sounds from the encroaching graveyard at night.

THE FITZGERALDS' CLAIM TO middle-class status extended beyond shunning their neighbors and demonstrating skin tone bias; they also asserted their status by taking pride in the achievements of African Americans, particularly in education. The Fitzgeralds' attitudes reflected broader patterns in which Black middle-class families often simultaneously perpetuated skin tone bias while countering external racism by fostering race pride.[87] Pauli's guardians gloried in the achievements of African Americans—they interpreted the success of Black individuals as progress for the race and celebrated accordingly.[88]

In her book *Proud Shoes* Murray used Grandfather's youthful experience to explore notions of "proving the race," notions to which she was still subject when writing the book in the 1950s. She explained, "A Negro was forever on trial, carrying always a heavy burden of proof that he was not by nature degraded or inferior. . . . Each learned that since he could never escape the burden of race, he must dedicate himself to it—to the cause of 'my people' . . . Robert Fitzgerald and his classmates would agonize over each unseemly act of the black man with the shame of personal guilt and exult over each triumph with the pride of personal achievement. And their descendants would do the same for many generations."[89] The feeling of being "forever on trial" and carrying a "heavy burden of proof" stayed with Murray throughout her life and made her unwilling to publicly acknowledge some aspects of her lived experience, lest they be construed as evidence that she was "by nature degraded or inferior."

Grandfather Robert's belief in education as the key to individual social mobility, instilled in Murray from a young age, aligned with collective racial uplift ideology.[90] Robert Fitzgerald and his family had long valued education—he established a school to teach freedmen following the Civil War, and his family strongly objected to his marriage to Cornelia partly because of her illiteracy.[91] Robert ensured that his children and grandchildren were literate. During Pauli's childhood, he made her read aloud from newspapers—to teach her, but also to keep himself informed. He especially liked hearing news from the battlefields of World War I—Grandfather's stern manner and propensity to lash out made her terrified of mispronouncing French battlefield names.[92] Grandfather's strict instruction meant Pauli learned quickly. Sitting in Aunt Pauline's primary school classroom before she reached school age also accelerated Pauli's education.[93] Aunt Pauline didn't take Pauli to classes with this in mind—she simply had no other childcare options—and it came as a shock to her when Pauli showed the desire and ability to complete the classwork assigned to the older children.[94]

Coming from a family of teachers gave Murray an educational advantage over many African Americans, but segregated education still didn't make it easy to develop and prove one's capabilities. In 1920 Durham had just three schools to serve thousands of Black children.[95] Set in the dirt with no play equipment, Pauli's school didn't look out of place positioned on the dirt road, which had a lumberyard at one end and a dump at the other. To get to the old wooden warehouse-like West End School building each morning, Murray had to walk past a new brick school where white children, who ignored her, played on new equipment.[96] Even as a child, the lie of "separate but equal" facilities was obvious and damaging. Southern white politicians defended the gross disparity on the basis that African Americans were intellectually inferior, though some white supremacists occasionally admitted that they feared formal education for African Americans for the same reasons that African Americans desired education—it could undermine the racial hierarchy. One Louisiana school official stated, "A little learning with the negro is a dangerous thing. Why should the white race be forced to aid and abet *a dangerous thing?*"[97]

Color prejudice in the playground provided Pauli with an additional challenge. She was one of only three light-skinned children in her primary school, which pushed her to the bottom of the schoolyard hierarchy.[98] She recalled, "In a world of black-white opposites, I had no place. Being neither very dark nor very fair, I was a nobody without identity. I was too dark at home and too light at school. The pride I learned at home was almost cancelled out by the cloak of shame I wore at school, especially when my schoolmates got angry and yelled at me, 'You half-white bastard! You dirty-faced Jew baby! Black is honest! Yaller is dishonest'" (because it indicated illegitimacy and transgressive sexual relations).[99]

Murray's position in the racial no-man's-land and the educational disadvantage of segregated schools led her to hate George Washington, mumble allegiance to the flag, resist standing for "The Star-Spangled Banner," and identify as Native American (from grandmother Cornelia's assertion that her biological mother was one-quarter Cherokee), which was not an uncommon assertion among the Black middle class.[100] Pauli also felt different from her classmates because she did not have visible parents. Less dramatically, but still an affecting influence for a child, Murray's lefthandedness at a time when it was forbidden posed a further challenge to her education — even Aunt Pauline's generally sympathetic attitude toward children did not extend to a toleration of lefthanded writing. Pauli's rebellious streak, a hallmark of her adult life, emerged at school — such was her ability to turn a classroom to chaos that one of her primary school teachers would take Pauli with her whenever she was called away from the classroom.[101]

AT AGE SEVEN, ON A RARE outing to a neighboring property in the Bottoms to get water from the neighbors' limestone well — it was believed that the lime would help cure Grandmother Cornelia's pellagra — Pauli heard excited talk of a shooting and followed the crowd to see what had gone on. The crowd gathered around a briar patch and quietly observed the dead body of an African American child. Some in the crowd whispered that a white man had shot the youth in the chest, either for stealing watermelons or "outta of pure down meanness."[102] Pauli knew the victim, John Henry Corniggins, a resident of the Bottoms a few years older than herself. The killer was never apprehended. Like most of her neighbors, Pauli believed the white man did it — a probability that left a terrible impression about the potential for racist violence, which could be inflicted, even on children, with impunity and for trivial reasons.

Like Corniggins's murderer, white people in general loomed as a dangerous yet elusive presence in Pauli's childhood. Living on the outskirts of town, she could avoid many of the daily humiliations segregation inflicted. When asked later about when she became aware of segregation, she explained, "I suppose this awareness to a child of my generation grows with you just like almost a part of your body and your being. It is hard to say when you become aware because you take it in all of the time . . . wherever you went in town, you saw the 'White' signs, the 'Colored' signs, drinking fountains, anytime that one would go down into the public center of town, one would be very, very conscious of it. Obviously, one would be conscious of separate schools and separate churches and the older people talking. It's something that you simply grow up with. It's not something that you suddenly experience."[103] Whenever Murray visited town, she boycotted segregated facilities—instead of taking public transport, she rode her bike, and instead of going to segregated movie theaters, she simply didn't go to movie theaters. In this regard she modeled typical Fitzgerald behavior—they avoided any contact with white people if it meant losing dignity, and since segregation routinely robbed African Americans of dignity, the Fitzgeralds severely restricted their movements. Pauli called it a "straightjacket existence."[104] It is little wonder, then, that she would seek to break free of it at the earliest opportunity.

· · · · ·

IV

Less than two weeks after the Great War ended, Pauli Murray celebrated her eighth birthday. Nearly five years had elapsed since her mother's death and, although she had not remained in contact with her father and siblings, she still thought of them often. Pauli later recalled the difference she felt in the Fitzgerald house: "I had a different name, I had my own family, of which I was very conscious, and in some ways, I was alien. I felt very much a part of the house, I was made to feel a part of the family, I knew that I was a Fitzgerald descendent and yet, there was always this longing for my family, my brothers and sisters, and a kind of . . . I guess 'sadness' about not having parents."[105] She had long cajoled Aunt Pauline about visiting the Murrays, but only early in the New Year did Aunt Pauline promise to take her once she had saved the money.

In the summer of 1919, Pauli and her reluctant aunt boarded an overnight Pullman train bound for Baltimore. The excitement that had been building in Pauli for months reached a fever pitch—she didn't touch the fried chicken Grandmother had packed, and she tossed and turned all night in the train car's upper berth, eagerly anticipating a joyous reunion with the family she knew only from old pictures and her aunt's descriptions.[106] But much had changed in Baltimore since either Pauli or Aunt Pauline had last been there. Most importantly, her father had been committed to Crownsville State Hospital for the Negro Insane. Pauli's five siblings now all lived with her paternal aunt and uncle, Rose and "Bubber" Murray (brother and sister). Her two younger siblings had lived with Rose and Bubber since their mother's death, and her three elder siblings joined them following their father's confinement two years before Pauli's visit.

Aunt Pauline and Pauli stayed with the Murrays during their visit to Baltimore, but this did little to foster a connection. The three older Murray siblings showed little interest in Pauli—they had their own friends and chores to do—while her two younger siblings were curious but shy. Pauli recalled, "I never lost the feeling of being an outsider in the Murray home and carried about with me an unsatisfied longing for the family I loved but could not wholly embrace."[107] Color divisions also affected relationships between the siblings, which Pauli later identified as a personal issue propelling her toward an activist life. She told an interviewer, "I told you there were six of us, six little Murrays. On the one visit that I made back to Baltimore, when I was about nine, it was very clear that at least four of us could go downtown to the movies on Saturdays, the white movie houses . . . and two of us couldn't. I happened to be one of the two and that says something to you about why I would become a crusader for civil rights. I don't think that I thought that in those days, but I'm sure that these experiences coming to me out from the intimacy of the family made an even greater impact than they would had they been from the society *per se*."[108] Pauli linked such experiences to her activism in her adult reflections, but during her childhood the issue of color only compounded her sense of difference.

Pauli's paternal aunt and uncle also unsettled her. Uncle Lewis "Bubber" Hampton Murray, another schoolteacher, was a tall, thin, redhead with a hawk-shaped nose and glasses that combined to give him a piercing look. Pauli described him as fastidious in appearance and exacting in everything he did—she felt uncomfortable in his presence, believing he kept her under constant, critical scrutiny.[109] He had, in her words, an "unerring faculty for finding a weak spot and impaling one on his rapier-like criticism," making Pauli feel insecure, particularly about her personal appearance as a "rough and tumble tomboy." She felt like an easy target for his criticisms. "Under his probing eyes," she became "even more self-conscious" about the dresses she wore, which Aunt Sallie usually acquired by selecting from the church mission box items that were more durable than fashionable.[110]

Pauli felt even greater antipathy toward Aunt Rose—the aunt who wanted to take Pauli and her two younger siblings following their mother's death.[111]

A woman of enormous bulk, Aunt Rose had red hair, eyes that didn't always align, and a freckled, babyish face and voice, at least until she yelled: then her voice grew shrill and unsettling.[112] "Because of her great weight," Pauli recalled, "Aunt Rose moved about as little as possible and would yell her orders to the older children from whatever room she happened to be sitting in."[113] Aunt Rose suffered teasing as a child, prompting her to leave school and marry at the earliest opportunity. The marriage failed and she returned to her family, according to Pauli, "to live in the shadow of her menfolk, haunted by a deep sense of inferiority over her lack of formal education."[114]

Aunt Rose forbade mention of Pauli's parents in her household and raised Pauli's two younger siblings to believe that she was their biological mother. The discovery of these facts shocked Pauli and fueled much of her hostility toward Aunt Rose. Erasing her parents' existence seemed inconceivable to Pauli, who often studied the photographs of her parents displayed in the Fitzgerald home and continually pestered Aunt Pauline for details of her parents' lives and made a game of asking Aunt Pauline which parent she resembled at different times. In complete contrast to Aunt Pauline's indulging Pauli's fascination with her parents, Aunt Rose essentially denied their existence. She always introduced the Murray children, including Pauli during the visit, as her own. Even in Aunt Pauline's presence, Aunt Rose introduced Pauli to a friend as one of her children who had been living down south. Pauli felt this as a threat to her very sense of self.[115]

Pauli's concerns about Aunt Rose's actions, in combination with the failure to connect with her siblings, boiled over in an incident she came to regret later. Her two younger siblings, gradually overcoming their shyness, questioned Pauli on their family connection while they played together in the backyard—specifically, they wanted to know why, if Pauli was their sister, she called Aunt Pauline "Mother" and called their mother "Aunt Rose." Pauli did not hesitate to explain what had been carefully concealed from them for the past five years. Pauli's younger siblings ran crying inside to Aunt Rose. Aunt Rose and Pauli then faced off. Pauli steadfastly refused to apologize. She believed Aunt Rose would have struck her had Aunt Pauline not intervened. Banished to a bedroom, Pauli remained there sobbing, refusing to come down for dinner. "Aunt Rose had to drag her heavy body up three flights of stairs and smash the door open to get me out," Pauli recalled.[116]

Pauli's dispute with Aunt Rose became entangled with long-standing acrimony between the Murrays and the Fitzgeralds. Aunt Pauline had been reluctant to make even this one trip to Baltimore because of the historical animosity. Pauli explained, "The roots of the hostility between the two families lay in things which had happened before I was born or was too young to know about, but the animosity left a residue of ill feeling which would force me to take sides in a subtle war of attrition more damaging to its victims than those who began it would ever know."[117] Although uncertain as to the conflict's origins, she believed it centered on Aunt Rose, though this could have been a reflection of her own deep dislike for her aunt. According to Pauli, Aunt Rose did not conform to her "proud in-laws'" notions of respectability: they considered her a "sporty" woman, meaning she drank whiskey, played cards, and bet on horses and the numbers.[118] To the pious Fitzgeralds such behavior seemed indecent and especially repulsive for a woman.[119]

Rose and Bubber, no doubt, interpreted the Murrays' status as superior to the Fitzgeralds'—after all, the Murrays were city folk who dressed fashionably and lived in a nicely furnished home with full indoor plumbing, in contrast to the general poverty and the condemned well of the southern, rural Fitzgeralds. Uncle Bubber and Aunt Rose never let any of Pauli's siblings visit their maternal relations' home in Durham, which deeply wounded the Fitzgeralds, who had come to know the older Murray children well during Agnes's frequent separations from William. In perhaps the greatest show of antipathy, Rose and Bubber even renamed Pauli's youngest sibling, who had not yet been released from the hospital when his mother died. He had been named Robert after Grandfather Robert Fitzgerald, but Rose and Bubber renamed him Raymond—another fact Pauli revealed during her frank discussion with her two younger siblings.[120]

In addition to family conflict, the trip to Baltimore raised disturbing concerns about the mental health of Pauli's relations. Pauli's personal papers reveal that Rose and Bubber were subject to neighborhood "cracks," though the papers don't explain why. The fact that they were a brother and sister living together while raising their institutionalized brother's children may have been enough. Rose's size and "sporty" behavior may have also contributed, as might have Bubber's passion for writing, directing, and acting in musical theater productions.[121] Regardless of why they were stigmatized, the fact that they were must have added to Pauli's emerging concerns about traits she feared might be hereditary.[122]

Pauli also heard a far more devastating rumor in Baltimore, this one concerning her mother's death. According to what she later described as the "careless gossip of adults," Pauli learned that her mother might have committed suicide. Neighborhood children had long been taunting her siblings, "Your daddy went crazy and your mother killed herself!" Pauli didn't disclose whether she discussed the rumor with her siblings at this time; she only described confronting Aunt Pauline with it.[123] The usually monotone

Aunt Pauline hotly denied it, telling Pauli that the doctor had showed her Agnes's temple bruising, which Aunt Pauline accepted as evidence of a hemorrhaged blood vessel. Murray's autobiography then states that "nothing" could make the Fitzgeralds believe their Aggie took her own life—which may suggest that she presented them with further evidence. In any case, Aunt Pauline's denials didn't reassure Pauli—she remained haunted ever after by the possibility that her mother had committed suicide.[124]

AUNT PAULINE HAD PROMISED PAULI that they would visit her father at Crownsville State Hospital for the Negro Insane before the trip ended. The state government established Crownsville in 1910 following a report by the Maryland State Lunacy Commission that described "shame and humiliation among the Negro insane."[125] It was only the nation's third "insane asylum" for African Americans, and here, unlike at the other two facilities, all of the employees were white. Conditions were appalling. The death rate among patients was nearly two times the discharge rate.[126] There were four untrained attendants to care for 275 patients, and the attendants carried clubs and broomsticks with which they regularly beat patients.[127] Crownsville housed African Americans deemed criminally insane, mentally ill, or "retarded," yet many others also ended up there. Alcoholics, sex offenders, and people with syphilis, epilepsy, and tuberculosis were all included in Crownsville's "Negro insane" population. Adults and children, male and female were all housed together.[128] There were not enough beds: some people slept on basement floors, and even those with beds had to share. Riots occurred, patients fashioned weapons for self-protection, and doctors conducted scientific experiments on patients without gaining their consent.[129]

Many years later, Pauli pieced together some of the incidents leading to her father's commitment to Crownsville. In the years after his wife died, William increasingly withdrew from society, even refusing visits from his siblings. His physician noted that William's "personal appearance had changed markedly from a fastidious attire to one of marked slovenliness, that he had been living a hermit life, keeping his children in close confinement, and that he had attacked officers with a razor."[130] Pauli's older sister later recalled that their great-uncle had said that "children shouldn't be without a woman" and arranged William's commitment in 1917.[131] Crownsville physicians diagnosed William as suffering from "anxiety neurosis" and later as a "manic depressive." William acknowledged having "feelings that people were against him, having been irrational, having lost control of himself and having done things contrary to the best interests of the children."[132] This could simply be an acknowledgment that he had kept them "in close

A Child of Destiny or a Nobody without Identity

confinement" and failed in his patriarchal duty to provide for them, or a veiled admission of something more.

Pauli didn't know all this yet. In 1919, she couldn't wait to see her father. She even harbored hopes that they could take him back to Durham, though Aunt Pauline—who had no idea what to expect—still warned Pauli that her father would need to stay in the hospital until doctors declared him well. Pauli's enthusiasm remained undampened. She recalled, "I knew exactly how he would look and I knew he would remember me because people said I looked so much like him and had his quick mind. I was bursting to tell him all about school and that I was on the Honor Roll in my class."[133] Pauli's sister Mildred wanted to accompany them on the visit, but just as they were setting off Aunt Rose forbade Mildred to go, so Pauli and Aunt Pauline went alone on a visit to see her revered father.

Pauli had no memory of her father from the first three years of her life, but she remembered plenty about seeing him at Crownsville. It was a stifling hot Sunday in late July. They traveled from Baltimore to Annapolis by electric train, then walked from the station among crowds of other visitors. Two shabbily dressed women—clearly not part of the crowd—hobbled along, pausing occasionally to pick up and eat discarded orange peels. In response to Pauli's questioning, Aunt Pauline said the women must be Crownsville patients. Once at Crownsville the crowd gathered in the waiting room. Patients entered, greeted their visitors, then headed out into the grounds with them. The crowd thinned and thinned until Pauli and her aunt were alone in the waiting room. Aunt Pauline sat nervously pursing her lips, while every few seconds Pauli ran to the door to peer down the corridor to look for him.

Finally, an old man shuffled in. Aunt Pauline asked, "It's Will, isn't it?" and Pauli blurted out, "He doesn't look like my father." She remembered gaping incredulously at his unkempt appearance: he more closely resembled the "wandering creatures" she had seen eating orange peels outside the grounds than the photographs of William Murray that she had studied. In no way did this old man—he was only forty-seven—match the descriptions she had memorized of a brilliant teacher, sportsman, musician, and poet. William didn't recognize his daughter either. He only looked at her, then turned to Aunt Pauline and asked, "Which one is this?" William never directly addressed his daughter during the visit. Pauli sat listening while he told Aunt Pauline about the frequent scrapes he got into because of his quick temper. When Aunt Pauline asked about his treatment, he replied, "To tell you the truth, in a place like this you never know what's going to happen. I have to watch my every move. The guards are worse than the patients. I want to get out of here and they tell me I'm ready to go, but there is nobody to have me signed out."

Beyond this, Pauli could only really recall her father sitting silently, "his face working as if there was something important he wanted to say. Before he could get it out, a uniformed guard came in." She recalled so many details from the day, but she could not recall whether she hugged him. She remembered walking out of the building, "too heavy with the things I had come to say and had not said to my father" to give much attention to the faces pressed against the glass inside the building, screaming at them as they moved away.[134]

Accounts of events that occurred some sixty years earlier may not provide a perfectly reliable account of the meeting, but they can tell us a good deal about the psychological impact the encounter had on the autobiographer. Murray carried no positive memory of the meeting. She did not recall experiencing any substantive connection with her father—not through recognition, conversation, or physical embrace. She mostly retained an impression that her father was mentally sound, but neglected, endangered, and in need of rescue.

If the day had not already gone badly enough, in an almost fitting conclusion to the troubling excursion to Crownsville, lightning struck the train carriage in which Pauli and her aunt were riding back to Baltimore. No one was injured, but it delayed the train for an hour. In between bolts of lightning, sitting in the darkened carriage while the frightening storm raged overhead, Pauli had ample time to consider her father's plight and all that had befallen her during the much-anticipated vacation. In one summer visit to Baltimore, eight-year-old Pauli had to absorb the shocking condition of her revered father, estrangement from her siblings, Aunt Rose's erasure of her parents' existence, Uncle Bubber's criticisms, and the rumors about her mother's possible suicide.

When the pair finally arrived back at the Murray home, a telegram awaited Aunt Pauline asking her to return to Durham immediately— Grandfather Fitzgerald had fallen gravely ill. Pauli had time just for a hurried conversation with her sister Mildred, the only one of her elder siblings who seemed interested in their father, or at least the only one she had established enough of a rapport with to discuss their father. After Pauli explained what she witnessed at Crownsville, the sisters made a vow to get their father released when they came of age. Pauli and Aunt Pauline then gathered their bags and headed on foot for the train station—hardly in the best frame of mind to deal with the everyday humiliations and dangers confronting African Americans traveling to the Jim Crow South.[135]

A Child of Destiny or a Nobody without Identity

Pauli and her aunt arrived in Durham to find Grandfather lying in his big iron bed looking extremely pale and small. Grandfather could still talk, but it was clear to all that he didn't have long left. In the coming days he stopped talking and grew still, his sightless eyes fixed on the ceiling; his breath came in gasps. Despite the seeming constant presence of death in her not yet nine years of living, Pauli had not seen anyone dying before now. Nor had she seen behavior like Grandmother's during the final days of Grandfather's life. Cornelia lived in an almost permanently agitated state, but now she unearthed another level—Pauli likened her to a "wild animal" and a "raging volcano."[136] Grandfather's two surviving sisters were too scared to visit. They were careful to only come as far as the back fence to inquire about their brother, because even before Grandfather's illness, Grandmother Cornelia reserved a special rancor for "trespassers."[137]

Before dawn on August 4, 1919, Grandfather died. Murray used this scene to close her Fitzgerald family history, *Proud Shoes*. She described having to run through Maplewood Cemetery before light—the cemetery at night terrified her—to fetch Grandfather's sisters, which she likened to outrunning death.[138] In the following days, Robert lay on his bier in front of the fireplace. Pauli peeked under the drape covering his body and saw that the man who had represented "strength and authority" now looked "tiny and shrunken" and shoeless. Although little of the man remained, Murray still likened Grandfather's death to "the shock of a great landmark tree crashing in the forest," and the memory of his corpse entered Pauli's mind for years after whenever she entered the parlor, her former sanctuary.

Many Fitzgerald kinsfolk gathered in the house behind Maplewood Cemetery during three days of mourning. "A ban on exiles was temporarily lifted," though Pauli did not reveal who had been exiled or why—it might have been some rich Fitzgeralds, or maybe even Aunt Sallie and her dark-complexioned husband, but probably not Uncle Tommie, who ran away at age nineteen because he couldn't stand his father. Irrespective of who had been banned, the sudden influx of visitors to the home provided a unique social opportunity for Pauli. In a measure of the acute isolation she endured, it seemed to her that she "had more visitors and playmates during those three days than I had in my entire life at Grandfather's house."[139]

Grandmother's erratic behavior intensified following her husband's death. As a young woman in the post–Civil War era, Cornelia had been terrorized by mounted Klansmen thundering around her isolated cabin at night, and now she began reliving something like that terror on most nights. Cornelia's delusions became so distracting to Aunt Pauline's work preparations that she left the home to stay with Aunt Sallie, leaving Pauli alone with Grandmother. Pauli dreaded nightfall. Before bed each night, Cornelia made Pauli assist her in fortifying the home: after locking all the downstairs doors and windows and securing them with crossbars, they would then barricade themselves in Grandmother's bedroom, piling barrels, baskets of clothing, and furniture against the door and windows. Once sealed in, Grandmother would prepare supper over the fireplace, but by that time Pauli usually felt too scared to eat. Pauli would eventually go to sleep in Grandma's double bed, underneath which Cornelia kept her deceased husband's Civil War musket, bayonet, and saber, in addition to a pearl-handled revolver and an ax.

In a pattern repeated many times, Grandmother's night terrors would begin sometime after midnight. Pauli recalled, "I would be awakened by heavy thuds and scrapings on the bare floor under the bed. Grandmother, convinced that an intruder was breaking in downstairs, was dragging the ax back and forth and pounding on the floorboards."[140] Cornelia would shout things at the imaginary intruders, such as "You get away from my window, you devil," then listen for a few seconds before resuming dragging and thumping the ax on the floorboards. This would continue until Grandmother exhausted herself and collapsed into bed. Cornelia would quickly fall into a deep sleep while Pauli remained awake, trembling, listening to the creaking house, which was set well back from the street in darkened shadows downhill from the cemetery, jumping whenever she heard an owl hoot, or a tree branch scrape against the roof. At the first sign of light entering through the cracks in the barricaded window, Pauli would jump up, remove the fortifications from the doorway, and run to a nearby classmate's home to prepare for school.

Aunt Pauline's absence from the family home during this time seems a strange act of abandonment. Her feelings about her mother's behavior perhaps contributed to a desire for a quieter space to prepare for school. Both Pauline and Sallie found their mother's neighborhood reputation as a "crazy old witch" deeply embarrassing; Cornelia's recent escalation in behavior might have become too much.[141] Even if that were the reason, it was no comfort to Pauli. After returning from the upsetting trip to Baltimore, Pauli had asked her aunt to adopt her formally.[142] The adoption became official in September 1919, but the paperwork didn't change the nature of their relationship. For her part, Aunt Pauline remained as serious and unaffectionate as ever. Aunt Pauline only reversed the practical decision to leave the home when she discovered Pauli washing her clothes in the school basement one morning.[143]

MURRAY LATER ATTRIBUTED THE independence thrust upon her at such a young age with fostering an identity that rejected traditional gender roles. Pauli had little interest in play coded as feminine and did not conform to traditional gender norms, later portraying herself as a tomboy who liked beefsteak, wore a soldier's hat, chopped wood for the family fireplace, preferred working with a hammer and tools than pots and pans, and wore her hair short, "for convenience," from age eleven.[144] When looking through a toy catalogue, she "passed over the dolls and dresses with a grunt," preferring instead to ogle the camping and outdoor equipment.[145] One year at school she made a Peter Pan–inspired outfit so poorly that wearing it at a school ceremony caused public humiliation. The incident ended her interest in sewing, but not her interest in Peter Pan, the fictional boy who never grew up and never knew his parents.[146]

Murray witnessed few examples of harmonious relationships as a child. Her parents' marriage had been marred by mental illness, violence, periods of separation, and ultimately the death of her mother. Her grandparents had also quarreled constantly. Uncle Bubber remained a lifelong bachelor and Aunt Rose had been abandoned by her husband, as had Aunt Pauline. Aunt Sallie's marriage also appeared to foster unhappiness. Sallie had married Reverend John Ethophilus Grattin Small, the West Indian minister who had been ejected from the Fitzgerald home because of his dark skin tone. A stout balding man with a goatee, Murray described Reverend Small as learned, but haughty and clinging to his British citizenship because he believed it accorded him higher status than that of an American Negro. In unpublished notes she put it more bluntly, describing him as "impulsive, quick-tempered, outspoken and with a general dislike for anything American except 'light Negro women.'"[147] Murray's autobiography did not acknowledge any family concerns about his skin tone or womanizing. Instead she described the Fitzgeralds as treating him with reserve—family members always referred to him as "Reverend Small," except for Aunt Sallie, who called her husband "Father Small."

Murray believed that Sallie only gave up her independence and teaching career to marry at nearly forty because of Reverend Small's persistence and her desire to serve the church as a minister's wife. For several years after the marriage, Reverend Small, Aunt Sallie, and their two children lived in a small nearby rectory, where Aunt Pauline had taken refuge to escape Grandmother Cornelia's night terrors. In 1921, Reverend Small became vicar of

Pauline Dame and Reverend John Small (*standing*), ca. 1924–26. Joshua, Sallie, and James Small are seated. (*Schlesinger Library, Radcliffe Institute, Harvard University*)

three small rural mission churches in southern Maryland. Murray described this as an advancement for her uncle, "but for Aunt Sallie it meant being uprooted from her lifelong hometown . . . and being isolated in the country, where her days would be filled with drudgery."[148]

At the age of ten, Pauli went with the Smalls to help them move to Croom. She spent most of her remaining pre-adulthood summers and holidays staying with the Smalls in the tiny Maryland village. Pauli relished the freedom of Croom, particularly the absence of "white only" stores and restaurants, and the highpoint of one holiday was a trip into Washington, which was twenty-five miles from Croom but felt like a different world. Only years later did Pauli ponder how lonely it must have been for Aunt Sallie, isolated in Croom without school teaching or community engagement and with barely the noise of a distant animal to break up the silent monotony. Reverend Small was often away tending the churches, making Pauli's visits especially important for Sallie, who talked nonstop. Sallie had hoped that, because of her closer proximity to Baltimore, Aunt Rose might let Pauli's siblings visit too, but the ongoing Murray/Fitzgerald hostility meant this never happened. While spending her third summer in Croom, Pauli learned that her father had died.[149]

On June 18, a white temporary employee of Crownsville State Hospital killed William Murray. According to reports, Walter Swiskowski attacked William with a bat-like object after the pair had scuffled earlier in the day (Swiskowski was eventually convicted of manslaughter and sentenced to ten years in prison).[150] Rumors circulated in the Murray household that after the initial altercation Swiskowski had threatened, "I'll get that nigger later," although the hospital report and *Afro-American* news accounts do not repeat this claim.[151] Regardless, Pauli always believed that her father was the victim of race violence.

The traumatic event had other long-term psychological consequences for Pauli. It instilled in her a prejudice against Poles — for many years afterward, she froze whenever she encountered a name that ended in "-ski." Pauli also developed an "irrational fear" of being hemmed in or attacked from behind like her father had been; consequently, she always tried to get a seat in the back row nearest the exit in theaters, churches, and other public meeting places. Furthermore, William's killing — at the hands of someone employed to look after him — before he could recover left her to wonder about the illness that precipitated his confinement. "My father's death had left the question of hereditary insanity unanswered," Murray recalled, "and I was never entirely free from apprehension that I might go berserk and do harm

Murray and brother William Murray on the day of their father's funeral, 1923. *(Schlesinger Library, Radcliffe Institute, Harvard University)*

to people around me." Trying to transform "psychic violence" into "creative energy" became a never-ending psychological struggle.[152]

Further distress followed close after her father's murder. A few months later, while Pauli and Grandmother were working in the backyard on a bitterly cold winter afternoon, eighty-year-old Cornelia dropped to her knees and began vomiting blood. They managed to get Grandmother inside, where a doctor visited her and diagnosed the problem as stomach ulcers. He recommended that she remain in bed and ingest only liquids and soft food. Never one to stay still for long, the irrepressible but still-weak Grandmother was back on her feet by spring. In the summer, Pauli went off to Croom again. One night during dinner with Aunt Sallie, Pauli became overcome with sadness and went outside. Later that night a message arrived stating that Grandmother Cornelia had died earlier in the evening.[153]

Murray credited Grandmother with instilling in her a defiant pride. She recalled Grandmother telling her, "Hold your head high and don't take a back seat to nobody. You got good blood in you—folks that counted for something—doctors, lawyers, judges, legislators. Aristocrats, that's what they were, going back seven generations right in this state."[154] Although Grandmother was referring to her white ancestry, her words provided some encouragement that Pauli's biological inheritance might include more positive elements than the hereditary illness she came to dread. Grandmother was also a kindred spirit. "We were nervous and excitable, easily stampeded, as vulnerable to imaginary terrors as we were to real dangers," Pauli ex-

A Child of Destiny or a Nobody without Identity

plained. "We were the sensitive exposed ones who couldn't stand pressures, took everything to heart, were torn by conflicts and cried out in protest when we were wronged or hurt, whether anyone heeded or even heard us."[155] As noted earlier, Murray also described Grandmother as the person she thought she loved most because Grandmother was the one who provided her with physical affection. Grandmother Cornelia's death, then, felt to thirteen-year-old Pauli like the end of her childhood.[156]

MURRAY'S HIGH SCHOOL PROVED TO BE a vast improvement on her warehouse-like primary school. She was among the first students to enroll at the newly constructed Hillside High School. One of only two Black high schools in North Carolina, Hillside High was a tremendous source of pride among African Americans in Durham. The school's resources were still not equivalent to those in the better white schools; nevertheless, it was a new, purpose-built, large brick school, staffed with new teachers, and the potential to advance educational opportunities for African Americans, who had very little opportunity for high school education at this time, not only in North Carolina but across the South.[157]

Hillside High was in Durham's Hayti section, which E. Franklin Frazer described as the nation's "capital of the black middle class."[158] The Fitzgeralds lived three miles from Hayti. They didn't have a car or horse, and public transport didn't cover the whole journey—even if Pauli had been willing to use segregated public transport—so she often walked to and from school until she could afford a bicycle, purchased with money earned from a Saturday newspaper route. The journey made her acutely conscious of separation from the hub of Black cultural life. One of the few times she could recall Aunt Pauline losing her temper with her occurred when Pauli referred to the "rich children of Hayti." Aunt Pauline broke out of her quiet monotone to angrily insist that Pauli was as good as any child.[159] At primary school Pauli had been made to feel ashamed of her lighter skin tone; at the new high school she observed another kind of difference, class difference, despite her adoptive mother's reluctance to acknowledge it.

Notwithstanding financial hardships and the traumatic events of her childhood, or perhaps because of them, Murray demonstrated remarkable determination to achieve. She described high school as providing better outlets for the "nervous energy" that had gotten her into trouble at primary school. She played sports, edited the school newspaper, and debated for the school team.[160] Her behavioral record remained imperfect, but she finished school at the top of her class. Her yearbook caption stated, "The best I can do to help others is to be the best I can myself," a motto she would adhere to for most of her life.[161] Top school results earned her a scholarship to the nation's oldest Black university, Wilberforce, but she declined it because she didn't want to attend a segregated school, even though many of the teachers who had inspired her were Wilberforce graduates. Turning down the scholarship was made easier because it barely covered tuition for one semester.[162]

Pauli also turned it down because she wanted to go to New York to continue her education. Years earlier, without ever having been there, Pauli had begun dreaming of New York, even as her early life experiences and Aunt Pauline's protectiveness caused her to fear it. In one of her only surviving childhood letters, ten-year-old Pauli wrote to Aunt Pauline from Croom: "Mother as you say there are lots of little girls raped between Washington and N. Y. . . . I'd like the NY Education but Mother I am afraid of being raped or assaulted."[163] Five years later, the summer before Pauli's final school year, the fear lifted when Aunt Pauline took her to New York, where she had the most exciting time of her life.[164] She knew immediately that she wanted to live there. After all, it seemed the perfect place to escape her "straightjacket" Durham existence — in New York she wouldn't be a "poor Fitzgerald" or a "mad Murray," but someone of her own making.

By the time Murray graduated from high school in 1926, she had lost both her parents, her maternal grandparents, and, in effect, her siblings. She coped with the losses, in part, by imagining for herself a providential life. Early in her autobiography, she identified the significant world events that coincided with the year of her birth: Halley's Comet passed Earth; the Urban League was founded; the NAACP published the first issue of *The Crisis*; and Leo Tolstoy died within twenty-four hours of her birth.[165] Aunt Pauline nurtured Pauli's providential view of herself. She took Pauli to visit a dying Episcopal bishop, who blessed Pauli and told her, "You are a child of destiny." Murray later recalled, "Those words were to have a lasting impact on my life. As long as she lived, Aunt Pauline reminded me that I have been blessed by a bishop on his deathbed. The solemnity of this act and the prophetic quality of Bishop Delany's words would follow me through the years."[166] In the years to come, Murray's providential self-perception will help her to combat the conflicting feeling that she is "a nobody without identity" and help to steel her for the many remarkable campaigns she will launch to advance herself and her causes.[167]

two

FOR ALL MY BRAVADO, DEEPLY ENGRAINED NOTIONS OF RESPECTABILITY FILLED ME WITH DISTRESS, 1926–1940

......

I

In 1926, a spindly fifteen-year-old Pauli Murray packed her suitcase and joined the southern exodus. Some seven hundred thousand African Americans migrated to the North during the 1920s, continuing the mass migrations that had begun during World War I.[1] Murray wasn't alone in choosing New York City as her destination — by the time of her arrival, New York had the largest Black population of any city in the nation.[2] Everything about the city excited Pauli, particularly the enormity of the skyscrapers and the Statue of Liberty, the entertainments of Coney Island and Broadway, the strange double-decker buses and automats that dispensed hot food, and, above all else, the absence of segregated public transportation and movie theaters. Although far less enthusiastic, Aunt Pauline still traveled to New York to help her bright-eyed adopted daughter get settled.

Murray wanted to study at Columbia University for the sole reason that her favorite high school teacher had attended Columbia (she did not realize that her teacher had attended Columbia Teachers College).[3] The plan to attend Columbia fell apart quickly. The admissions office informed Aunt Pauline that women were not admitted and referred them to Barnard College across the street, where they discovered that Aunt Pauline didn't have the money and Pauli didn't have the prior education required for admission. Barnard staff suggested they try Hunter College, a city school that did not

Aunt Pauline Dame with Murray, 1926.
(*Schlesinger Library, Radcliffe Institute, Harvard University*)

require tuition for New York residents. Any hopes of an easy transition to college in New York were again dashed when Hunter denied her admission because her North Carolina high school education ended in year eleven, not year twelve as required.[4] Undeterred, Murray set about completing another year of high school in New York City.

Murray moved in with Aunt Pauline's cousin, Maude, who had been close to Agnes Fitzgerald growing up in Durham. Maude had a husband and three young sons, but her only daughter died in infancy. Her daughter would have been a similar age to Pauli, leading Murray to believe that Cousin Maude wanted her to be a surrogate daughter. If true, the wish went unfulfilled. Murray appreciated Maude's hospitality, which extended as far as formally adopting Pauli to help with school residency requirements, but Pauli refused to play the role of dutiful daughter and assist in domestic activities — she had long eschewed domesticity in favor of tomboy interests and sometimes resisted mothering if it represented a threat to the place reserved for her deceased mother.[5]

Other factors also complicated the relationship. Most of the residents in the new Richmond Hill neighborhood of Queens, where Maude's family lived, were first- and second-generation European immigrants, including many Poles—likely reminding Pauli of her father's killer. Even if this wasn't a worry, the absence of African Americans—there were only two other Black families in the neighborhood—posed a definite problem for Pauli, or, rather, a problem for Maude's family that became a problem for Pauli. Even half a century later, when writing her autobiography, Murray treaded carefully in describing Maude's family's race passing. Murray described it as an "ambiguous situation," because her fair-skinned cousins—she didn't use their family name—had moved in when there were few houses in the area. Maude's family had not moved into the home to start new lives as white people, Murray asserted, they had simply remained silent about their racial background in the developing immigrant neighborhood and lost touch with Black friends from their old neighborhood.[6]

When Pauli came into the house, with her "unmistakable yellow-brown skin, kinky-curly hair, and southern accent," the family's racial identity became suspect. Murray felt like an embarrassment. She recalled, "Although the neighbors were nice enough, Cousin Maude saw the questions in their eyes and hinted that my presence made the difference. In spite of everything she did for me, I could not help feeling that I was a stranger who had upset the delicate balance in neighborhood relationships. I kept to myself and made no friends my age on the block."[7] Moving from Durham had not freed Murray from race problems or cured her loneliness—her new home environment in New York City offered no better social opportunities, and she still felt conscious of being too dark-complexioned at home.

Such experiences must have caused untold psychological harm, especially at age sixteen, but they also provided extra incentive and opportunity to succeed in her studies. Murray ultimately concluded that racial passing was an unsatisfying way around the race problem: "Given the choice of passing, it was easy to drift into the anonymity of the white background and settle for self-imposed mediocrity, working at less than one's capacity. It was a life without bitter struggle, it is true, but it was also a life without extra challenge, the incentive to excel." She did not articulate these conclusions until much later, yet her desire to excel was already clear. The admissions staff at Hunter College had provided a lengthy list of required high school subjects, including another year of English, Latin, and French, as well as completing a host of subjects she had never studied before. It should have taken a year and a half or two years to complete, but Murray wanted to do it all in a year.[8]

Murray undertook the year of intensive study at Richmond Hill High, where she was the only Black student among a cohort of four thousand students. Just what a daunting experience this must have been is hard to fathom. She recalled no racism and described the students as friendly and the staff as helpful; but, having never competed against white children, and fearing that failure would confirm her racial inferiority rather than her previous educational disadvantage, Murray experienced extreme anxiousness during her first few months. Her fears of not being able to compete with white students initially seemed to be coming true, with reports placing her well behind the top students. Murray responded by undertaking an even more exhaustive study regime, breaking only to eat and sleep — further explaining her unwillingness to contribute to domestic chores in Maude's home. The stress likely contributed to physical changes — she gained fifteen pounds, and her menstrual cycle stopped for five months — but at the end of the school year, Murray graduated with honor, finishing among the top twenty-five students in her class.[9] This became a pattern through her life — Murray had a strong desire to prove that she could succeed in predominantly white educational institutions, though it often came at a cost to personal relationships and her health and well-being.

Despite her academic achievement, Murray didn't move on immediately to college, but returned to Durham. Having completed such an intense year of study to gain college admission, it must have been a bitter pill to have been dragged back to Durham. Murray's papers and memoirs reveal little about what specifically prompted her return, though it likely related to Aunt Pauline's inability or unwillingness to continue financially supporting her. Murray recalled working at the *Carolina Times* doing odd jobs before taking a position as a junior stenographer at the Bankers Fire Insurance Company, where she remained until the next summer.[10] In between these two jobs, however, Murray worked from October to December 1927 as a stenographer at North Carolina Mutual Life Insurance, which at one point was the largest Black business in the world.[11] Three jobs in twelve months foreshadowed another long-term pattern: employment instability. Murray's twelve months in Durham also confirmed that she wanted something different for her life than administrative work in southern Black businesses.

TWO MONTHS BEFORE HER EIGHTEENTH birthday, Murray returned to Cousin Maude's and commenced study at the world's largest women's college, Hunter College, or, as some referred to it, "the poor girl's Radcliffe." Murray later asserted that she would have preferred to attend a residential coeducational college, but Hunter's free tuition settled the matter.[12] Attending an increasingly rare all-women college — five out of six college women attended coeducational institutions by the 1930s—proved to be a fortuitous stepping stone on the road to Murray later becoming a feminist. She remembered Hunter as "a natural training ground for feminism," since it developed women's confidence and leadership skills and encouraged resistance to subordinate roles.[13] In this respect college continued Murray's exposure to independent women role models—her blind grandfather had been the only man regularly present in her childhood.

Murray relished her first year of college. Her political science teacher's insistence that students read the *New York Times* encouraged a lifelong attention to current affairs—and the *Times's* capitalization of "Negro" also pleased her, as she believed capitalization gave dignity to her racial identity. She struggled in English at first but received an A– for the last paper she wrote in her first semester, an essay on Grandfather Robert Fitzgerald. Murray formed strong friendships, including one with Lula Burton, the only other Black student at the Brooklyn Annex campus they both attended. The ease with which Burton kept up with the work and the confidence she exuded interacting with white students boosted Murray's morale. Pauli formed another important friendship with a Jewish student who informally tutored her in a German class—which Pauli found particularly challenging—during the long train journey from the Brooklyn campus to their respective homes in Queens. It wasn't all work, however; many Hunter students caught the same train, and it didn't take long for Pauli to join the packs of teenage girls shrieking and running through the carriages.[14]

The bonds students might form at women's colleges were not always viewed innocently. A study conducted during the late 1920s noted that sexual intimacy between women became prevalent "when a few campus leaders in several of the larger women's colleges made it something of a fad."[15] Male authority figures condemned these relationships in unequivocal terms. Many still considered women's education as suspicious in itself. In the year Murray commenced college, medical writer John Meagher claimed, "It has been observed that a woman who yearns only for higher education and neglects love, is usually of the frigid type. Many homosexuals are intellectual and cultured, though sexually infantile."[16]

Intimate relationships between women also received closer public scrutiny in the late 1920s following the controversial publication of a few "lesbian themed" novels. The most famous, *The Well of Loneliness*, quickly sold a hundred thousand copies before becoming the subject of a widely reported pornography trial in New York in 1928. The book included a preface by sexologist Havelock Ellis, who theorized about "sexual inversion," and the novel's main character, Stephen Gordon, is a biological woman who dresses in masculine attire and pursues relationships with women. Although Murray never mentioned the novel, as an English student and a *New York Times* reader living in the city where the trial occurred, she surely knew of it—many women recalled it as the only book about lesbianism that they knew about for several more decades.[17]

Murray further immersed herself in women-centered environments in the months preceding her nineteenth birthday. In May 1929, she left Cousin Maude's home—to both her relief and Cousin Maude's—to move into a room in an expansive, 260-room housing facility operated by the Harlem branch of the Young Women's Christian Association (YWCA)—the only branch that admitted Black women. Unlike Maude's home in Queens, where Murray felt ashamed of her different skin color, in Harlem she joined with ninety thousand Black migrants who had arrived in the neighborhood over the past decade.[18] The Harlem YWCA's all-women living arrangement and management also provided additional role models and support. The leadership included women who went on to fill prominent roles in society, most notably Dorothy Height, who became president of the National Council of Negro Women.[19] Like women's colleges, the YWCA provided opportunity for romantic attractions to develop between women.[20] Murray later told doctors that her "emotional crises" involving women began around this time, at age nineteen.[21]

Harlem also had an emerging gay scene, particularly based around jazz music.[22] The extent to which Murray participated in this scene is unclear. She recalled enjoying performances at the Apollo Theater, as well as listening to the choir and organ from the Abyssinian Baptist Church, which she could hear from her YWCA bedroom window.[23] Enjoying the two was emblematic of a tension that emerged in Murray's life between pursuing interests associated with creative personal freedom and conforming to roles that adhered closely to middle-class notions of respectability. Unsurprisingly, for a young person now fully independent of close family supervision for the first time in her life, Murray enjoyed more fun than responsibility at this time. Her sense of adventure is neatly captured in her fondness for exploring the city on a pushbike. In a period when motorcars proliferated and road usage rules were largely determined by the car horn, Murray was knocked off her bike five times, escaping serious injury each time to continue tearing around the city as though she were still doing a paper run on the dirt roads of Durham's West End.[24]

Harlem in the late 1920s provided a perfect setting for pursuing creative self-expression. The year before her arrival in New York, Alain Locke published *The New Negro*. Locke claimed that African Americans "shook off the psychology of the 'Old Negro,' of the implied inferiority of the post-reconstruction era, to become the 'New Negro,' self-assertive and racially conscious as though for the first time."[25] Murray drew a similar distinction between herself and her forebears when, on her arrival at the YWCA, she announced to the membership secretary, "I have been living with my aunt and she represents old age and I represent intolerant youth."[26] New forms of artistic expression also emerged in the 1920s to inspire Murray.[27] A college classmate introduced Pauli to Harlem Renaissance poets, though the white poet Stephen Vincent Benét impressed her most. She described reading his epic Civil War poem *John Brown's Body* as one of her great college experiences.[28] Murray had read poetry in her grandparents' home, and Aunt Pauline dabbled in it and told Pauli that her father had done the same, but more than anything, her New York education and independence encouraged her writing dreams and opened her up to new ideas and ways of being in the world that hadn't existed in Durham.

· · · · ·

II

Moving to the Harlem YWCA granted unprecedented personal freedom, especially over the 1929 summer when Murray had no classes and only had the responsibility of a few odd jobs at the Y to support herself. When classes resumed in September, however, the combined pressures of work and study became problematic, and they intensified further a month later, when the October 1929 Wall Street crash ushered in the Great Depression. Murray suffered malnutrition and developed anemia during a "horror" school year.[29] The summer offered no respite as she struggled with two low-paying jobs and summer school. Her autobiography described withdrawing from school in the fall of 1930 to look for work, but in a student newspaper article she described withdrawing because of a nervous breakdown.[30]

The financial ruin brought on by the Depression also brought on a backlash against the perceived hedonism of the 1920s. Abyssinian Baptist Church pastor Adam Clayton Powell, the period's most famous Black clergyman, regularly delivered homophobic sermons. Murray could hear the Abyssinian organ from her bedroom window, so she might also have caught his homophobic preaching or read reprints of them in the Black press, which supported Powell's campaign against "immorality." The *New York Age* ran a front-page story reporting Powell's assertion that sexual relationships between women "has grown into one of the most, horrible, debasing, alarming and damning vices of present day civilization, and is . . . prevalent to an unbelievable degree."[31] At a time when Pauli first experienced emotional crises over attractions to women, public attacks on homosexuality might well have contributed to her breakdown and withdrawal from college. Concerns about her sexuality might also have prompted her very sudden decision, shortly after her breakdown, to get married.

On November 30, 1930, ten days after her twentieth birthday, Murray married William "Billy" Wynn, in a secretive ceremony at the Episcopal Church in Richmond Hill, the church Pauli had attended while living with Cousin Maude.[32] The two-paragraph account of their marriage is the only intimate relationship openly acknowledged in Murray's autobiography. She said little of Billy other than that he too was trying to study and work— as a caretaker at a "women's residence," where he slept in the basement. She labeled the marriage a "dreadful mistake" made by two people drawn together by "mutual loneliness and rootlessness." Her "straitlaced upbringing" prohibited premarital sex, so when matters became serious between them, they married. The cheap West Side hotel where they spent their weekend honeymoon made for a "bleak atmosphere" that added to their "discomfiture." The newlyweds had nowhere to meet in privacy and "after several months of mounting frustration . . . gave up in despair."[33] In an earlier draft, Murray described Billy's naïveté as matching her own, adding, "His boyish charm and my frustration over being out of school and at a loose end combined to make me vulnerable." She also mentioned "unsuccessful attempts at marital intimacy."[34] Most likely, she had this experience in mind when she later told doctors that she resisted whenever a man tried to have sex with her.[35]

Around the same period, Murray questioned her religious beliefs. Since moving to the YWCA, she had attended St. Philip's Church, where she began teaching Sunday school before faltering: "I was required to teach small boys of 10–12 the Life of Christ, and I had no teaching materials which would enable me to make this life relevant to small boys of that age. I needed a record of Jesus' life from ages 12 to 30, and none was available. So I left the Church and wandered in the wilderness for several years with all kinds of doubts about the Virgin Birth, the Trinity, the miracles, etc."[36] Murray's attractions to women, withdrawals from college and church, and short-lived marriage may not have all been connected, but it seems likely that at least some of these events were related. Her problems at this time were profound, striking at her foundational beliefs and aspirations. Murray's emerging sexual preference was subject to increased scrutiny and condemnation, the financial catastrophe further diminished her grim employment options, and both undoubtedly hampered her studies. She attempted to resolve problems in seemingly contradictory ways, via escaping restrictive spaces such as her extended family's home and the church and, conversely, by trying to conform to social expectations by marrying, but no measure proved lasting.

DURING THE WINTER OF 1930 she found work as a switchboard operator and stenographer with Open Road Inc., a travel agency that organized tours to the Soviet Union. Murray later explained that her employment came about unexpectedly when the organization contacted the YWCA seeking to hire "an intelligent colored girl," but it is possible that she gained a position with the Communist Party–associated organization because she had begun mixing in radical left-wing circles.[37] Regardless, the job represented a great opportunity financially—downtown firms rarely hired African Americans, and the pay was 25 percent more than she had previously earned. Despite these advantages, she lasted only a few months in the job. Her autobiography attributed her departure to Open Road's merger with another agency, but her private letters reveal that she became bored in the role, her work slackened, and after discussing it with her supervisor, they mutually agreed she should leave.[38]

After leaving the Open Road job, Murray briefly returned to college in February 1931, only to withdraw again the following month because of an unknown illness. The illness must not have been too physically debilitating, however, since in the same month she and her friend Dorothy "Toni" Hayden hitchhiked to Hayden's family home in Newport, Rhode Island, which also had a visible gay community at the time.[39] Again, Murray's autobiography barely mentions the trip, but her archives include photos of the pair styled in the masculine fashion of the period.[40] Their boyish appearance led to an incident in Bridgeport, Connecticut, that Murray never publicly acknowledged, though it made the local paper.

At the local train station, Pauli and Toni confronted a "bathroom dilemma" that is familiar to many transgender stories. Public bathrooms were—and remain—heavily "policed" sites of gender conformity; consequently, risks exist for transgender people whichever choice they make.[41] Toni chose to use the women's room, while Pauli entered the men's. Toni's choice raised concern: a woman observed Toni exiting the women's facilities, and a confrontation ensued. Toni convinced the person that she had entered the "correct" bathroom, but when Pauli emerged from the male bathroom the woman called the police. The problem wasn't Murray's appearance—rather, the witness became alarmed by the impropriety of a young boy and girl traveling together unaccompanied. When police arrived, Pauli told the officers she was female: "We weren't trying to fool you, but it was good fun while it lasted. It'll make great material for the book we are

The Dude – 1931

Murray during the period when she withdrew from college at age twenty, 1931. *(Schlesinger Library, Radcliffe Institute, Harvard University)*

going to write."[42] After the initial terrifying ordeal of the police detainment, nothing came of the incident to deter Murray from further experimentation. The police simply turned the pair over to the Bridgeport Protective Association, an agency for juvenile girls, in whose care they spent a night before returning to New York City. The police didn't charge Pauli with any offense, and the director of the Bridgeport Protective Association later wrote affectionately to Murray about her amusing adventures.[43]

Emboldened, Pauli undertook an even more daring adventure two months later when she crossed the continent with an unnamed friend of Toni who was driving home to Vallejo. Whether Murray planned to settle there or in nearby San Francisco, or somewhere else in California, isn't clear. She may

Deeply Engrained Notions of Respectability Filled Me with Distress

not have even decided; she may simply have left on an impulse when the opportunity arose. In her autobiography Murray explained that she undertook the move in the belief that a fresh start in California might improve her fortunes after a series of disappointments that culminated in losing the Open Road job.[44] She elaborated in an earlier draft, "My goal to save money and return to school seemed further away than ever, and I was fed up with myself, New York, and just about everything else. It was spring, I was restless, and there was little to restrain the reckless streak in my nature which revealed itself when too many pressures piled up."[45] Murray had escaped North Carolina for New York; now she sought to escape New York for California. Over the years to come, escape became a familiar response to the strain of too many pressures, though she could never escape her sense of responsibility for long.

When Pauli arrived at the unnamed friend's family home in Vallejo, a letter from Aunt Pauline awaited her. Pauli had not told her adoptive mother that she was moving to California, since Aunt Pauline would never approve, but the letter forwarded from New York arrived before her. The letter informed that Aunt Pauline was unwell and needed Pauli to return to Durham. Pauli immediately wired Durham to reveal her whereabouts and explain that she had no money to return. Aunt Pauline wired back to say she had no money to pay for the fare either. Pauli still felt immense pressure to answer her mother's plea. Her hosts in Vallejo suggested that, if she were willing, she could make the trip by hopping trains across the continent.[46]

Only two months earlier, nine Black youths and two white women dressed in overalls were discovered in a freight train carriage near Scottsboro, Alabama. Twenty minutes after they were stopped, one of the women accused the youths of rape, sparking one of America's most infamous and longest-running criminal cases.[47] Murray didn't know about this incident when contemplating the journey, but she did recall an incident from her childhood that gave her reason enough to hesitate. She and some other sixth graders had snuck into a Durham freight yard in search of tar to chew when they happened upon a burlap sack barely concealing the body of a man recently decapitated by a train. The little that remained of his head could be seen splattered along the tracks. Even this memory, however, wasn't enough to dissuade Pauli from answering Aunt Pauline's call.

Murray set off less than a week after arriving in California. She faced the dangers of not only jumping onto moving trains but also freezing when too exposed, burning when too close to engine embers, getting trapped or crushed by shifting freight, being attacked by other travelers, and being shot by trigger-happy railway guards. Murray completed the journey in ten days with no more serious damage than a few knocks against the sides of trains. The most worrying incident occurred when a railway employee caught hold of her toward the journey's end. Murray pleaded with him by telling him she was an only daughter rushing home to care for her sick mother. The man was suspicious—he didn't believe she was anyone's daughter—but he let her continue after Murray proved her biological sex to a female railway employee.[48]

This adventure is the only incident recounted in her autobiography where she acknowledged gender nonconformity. Murray explained, "It was well for me that . . . my sex was not immediately apparent to the hundreds of rough men and boys I encountered during the trip. I carried a small knapsack containing minimum camping equipment, and my attire — scout pants and shirt, knee-length socks, walking shoes, and a short leather jacket— together with my slight figure and bobbed hair made me appear to be a small teenage boy like thousands of others on the road. No one questioned me about my gender and I soon discovered that my boyish appearance was a protection."[49] Murray describes her gender passing as a fortuitous accident, inadvertently aiding safe passage. No doubt, passing as men helped protect "sisters of the road" from sexual violence and exploitation, but it also provided some protection to explore sexual relationships with women and other forms of gendered expression.[50]

Murray provided an alternative account of the journey in the short story "Three Thousand Miles on a Dime in Ten Days."[51] The story describes the daring adventure of a young man, "Pete," and an unnamed, ungendered narrator riding the rails home to New York from San Francisco. Murray may have omitted a travel companion from her autobiography, possibly the unnamed friend with whom she traveled to California. In private correspondence, she acknowledged changing "we" to "I" for some of the adventures recounted in her memoirs to protect the privacy of former lovers.[52] Furthermore, correspondence with the publication editor reveals that the short story was in fact an extract from a diary.[53] The story itself hints at a sexual relationship between the characters. Scholar Doreen Drury identified several erotic allusions in the story: for example, "I jumped from one flat on to another, took a leap and found myself lying on top of Pete underneath a carload of hot new machines. When it got so dark we couldn't see the countryside we all rolled up together, arms, legs, and hands entangled, and slept."[54]

The story's publication history also reveals that Murray's masculine gender presentation was intentional. "Three Thousand Miles" appeared in the 1934 tome *Negro: An Anthology*, a hefty volume (nearly 900 pages long) featuring 150 contributors from Africa, Europe, and the Americas. The story's inclusion in the collection was an impressive achievement for an aspiring writer, and the contribution was also somewhat unique in that it did not address race issues, unlike all the other stories included in *Negro*. Yet Murray rarely acknowledged this publication in later life. Undoubtedly, she overlooked it because in the accompanying picture Murray is dressed as "Pete." Before publication, Murray wrote to *Negro's* editor, Nancy Cunard, to seek assurances about how the publication would identify her. Cunard replied, "No, of course we won't tell the reader that you are a girl; it will just be the title and the lovely new photo you sent . . . and Pauli Murray, a name for a boy or girl." Cunard added, "Several friends have liked your photo as much as I do. It is wonderful, the BOY itself."[55]

AUNT PAULINE'S ILLNESS, WHICH HAD prompted Murray's daring journey across the continent, turned out to be not so dire that Murray needed to return permanently to Durham. Instead, she worked all summer as a waitress in a New Jersey hotel, sleeping in the laundry room to save money and pay down debts. She resumed her studies at Hunter College in September 1931, moving into a cheap room above a Harlem funeral parlor. For all her childhood experiences of death, Murray expressed no concern about the grim business taking place below the room she shared with an art student, Louise "Lou" Jefferson; in fact, she returned to college with renewed spirit. Over the next two years of living together Murray gained invaluable support from Lou, a small birdlike woman crippled by polio in childhood who still managed to become a local swimming champion. According to Murray's recollections, Lou's passion for order and precision work balanced her own "harum-scarum" impulsivity. Pauli also enjoyed the support of other friends, including Toni Hayden, Margaret "Pee Wee" Inness, and Maysie "Tom Thumb" Decosta.[56]

Murray also adopted various nicknames. She briefly used her mother's name, "Agnes," on her college record, but otherwise adopted masculine names, including "Pete," "Paul," "the dude," and "Petie."[57] Murray settled on the gender-neutral "Pauli"—the first part of her given name, Pauline, and the literal opposite of her childhood nickname, Lenie, taken from the latter part of her birth name, suggesting not only a desire for a gender-neutral name but also a strong desire to fashion an identity of her own while still acknowledging her family. Adopting different names is an obvious manifestation of conscious efforts to create new identities; Murray's assortment of nicknames befits her multiple identities. An artist friend of a friend, Maysie Stone, had to wrestle with this multiplicity when doing a clay sculpture of Murray: Stone titled the completed bust *The Girl of a Thousand Faces*.[58]

The Vagabond

Bridgeport, Conn. 1931

The photo of Murray as "Pete" used for "Three Thousand Miles on a Dime" in *Negro: An Anthology*, 1931. *(Schlesinger Library, Radcliffe Institute, Harvard University)*

One of the "thousand faces," the left-wing radical, became briefly visible when Murray contemplated joining a group of African Americans invited to the Soviet Union to participate in a film project about racial discrimination. Murray's autobiography described it as a tempting proposition, "since communism was beginning to attract Negro intellectuals, and a visit to Russia offered a chance to see the social experiment in action."[59] An earlier draft included a more defensive statement—that she had not wanted to go out of any "sympathy with Communism since my ideas about it were extremely vague."[60] According to the published version, she decided against going after an "inner struggle": she feared another disruption to her education would mean that she would never complete college. Murray added

Deeply Engrained Notions of Respectability Filled Me with Distress

that she later felt relieved she hadn't gone because the trip was a disaster.[61] In private correspondence, however, Murray doubted the decision right up until World War II, since the "glamour" surrounding those who went still lingered.[62]

Murray's college education suffered no further disruptions after she re-entered Hunter in September 1931. Her academic record remained "spotty" by her own admission: she barely made the grade point average for admission to the English Department in her junior year. This owed much to the fact that she had to work to survive throughout her studies, barely earning enough to cover her rent and often going hungry. A lack of interest in some subjects also contributed to her uneven record. She was particularly perturbed by the absence of African American content in her courses. A desire to correct this situation led to a long-term interest in Black history and a short-term plan to establish a Black student group to raise consciousness about Negro culture and achievements, though she graduated before she could see it come to fruition. Murray's graduation on January 17, 1933, a few weeks before President Franklin Roosevelt's inauguration, was a remarkable achievement — she was one of only four Black students in a class of 247, she was one of only a dozen or so entirely self-supporting students in the entire college, and she completed her studies during the worst years of the Depression.[63]

· · · · ·

III

In the six years between first coming to New York and graduating from Hunter, Murray had held at least nine different jobs.[64] The dire economic circumstances partly explain this record. In 1930, when Murray's education became so disrupted, the unemployment rate was approximately 25 percent, though the figure for African Americans was near 40 percent.[65] Domestic laboring jobs disappeared, and white workers now competed for other menial jobs that had been among the only occupations available to African Americans. Murray had a job as a housekeeper for one day: her duties included preparing dinner, but after tasting Pauli's first effort her employer paid her and told her not to come back the next day.[66] This was far from her most demeaning work experience.

On two separate occasions she waited tables at Alice Foote MacDougall restaurants, a restaurant chain with themed settings, such as "Mediterranean" and "Plantation," which typically employed light-skinned Black waiters to act as Italian peasants or plantation house servants. Murray didn't indicate in her memoirs whether she was thematically dressed or whether she knew the chain refused to employ dark-skinned African Americans in service roles, but she did recall that white staff were provided meals that they could eat in the dining area, while Negro staff had to eat leftovers in the basement. She also remembered walking off the job with her coworkers in spontaneous protest when the restaurant refused to serve a Black couple— as did many downtown restaurants—but the protest had no effect.[67]

The Depression combined with employment discrimination made it hard to find meaningful, decent-paying work, and this affected Murray's physical and mental health. Later she explained her patchy employment record thus: "During my student days, in part time jobs under sweatshop conditions, I was not noted for obsequiousness. Hence, on one or two occasions I was fired for refusal to obey what I thought were unreasonable orders."[68] At the time, however, she wondered if her difficulties stemmed from within. In a sketch titled "Contradictions," she described herself in the third person: "In her work life, her urge for lack of restraint made her express contempt for employers. She prided herself on her lack of fear to speak out forthrightly, hazarding discharge or the possibility of resignation. She was restive under discipline and rebellious when ordered to do this or that. Yet, just as earnestly she sought approval, masking herself in cooperative behavior and wearing a thin shell of compliance. Inwardly, however, she seethed with resentment, and while normally a highly capable worker at almost any task, she often made stupid errors and confounded her employer with obvious and thoughtless questions."[69] Murray found herself trapped in a cycle of having only unsatisfying, exploitative job opportunities that she lost through rebelliousness, resentment, and inattentiveness.

Hunter College had fueled Murray's interest in writing. She enrolled in a master's degree in English at Columbia University—the institution she had first come to New York to attend—but quickly dropped out after one discouraging philology lecture. After being encouraged by friends, Murray began to write about her family background, but she didn't get far with the project before abandoning it. She eventually gained a position as a field representative for *Opportunity*, the magazine of the National Urban League, which published some of her poetry. The job required traveling across states to sell magazine subscriptions at social work conferences and Urban League branches. Although she could ill afford it, Murray bought a used car to avoid using segregated public transport.[70]

After eleven months Murray quit the Urban League because of what she described in her autobiography as a bad attack of pleurisy that occurred around the time of her twenty-fourth birthday in November 1934. She did not reveal an underlying disorder, except to say that years of marginal living had caught up with her and that her doctor, famed Harlem physician May Chinn, told her she was in danger of developing tuberculosis and "insisted" she resign her job, "take a rest, and spend the winter in the sun." This was virtually impossible (presumably for financial reasons, though Murray does not elaborate), leaving her faced with "the prospect of long-term confinement in a sanatorium." Murray then stated that Dr. Chinn found her a place in a camp for unemployed women in the Bear Mountain area of upstate New York, which Dr. Chinn believed would be a reasonable substitute for a warm climate because it, in Murray's words, "provided outdoor life under regulated conditions."[71]

The inconsistencies in her doctor's treatment plan and the mention of possible long-term confinement in a sanatorium suggest that Murray's health problems were not simply a physical ailment. She admitted that she had sharp disagreements with her boss but denied they had any effect on her good relationship with him and gave no indication that this played a part in her resignation from the Urban League. Elsewhere, Murray described being "unemployed in part because of poor health due to malnutrition, and the effects of overstudy and overwork to complete my college education and in part because of difficulty in finding professional work in keeping with my educational training."[72] She had tried to get summer work at a camp in Bear Mountain Park during her college years, so it is likely that she pushed as hard as her doctor to get a place there.[73] She also told doctors a few years later that she suffered extreme periods of "ups and downs" and felt happier outdoors and alone during this period.[74] In another indication that her resignation and arrival at the camp was not simply on doctor's orders, Murray's camp roommate turned out to be her friend "Pee Wee."[75]

Camp TERA (Temporary Emergency Relief Assistance) spearheaded a small New Deal program of camps for unemployed women. At the insistence of influential New Deal women, including Eleanor Roosevelt, camps for unemployed women were established during that period, albeit on a greatly reduced scale to those established for unemployed men — eight thousand women attended the camps, compared to some 2.5 million men. The labor camps established for men incorporated work and training in tasks such as reforestation, but authorities considered this type of training inappropriate in women's camps and prohibited it.[76] Murray acknowledged that Camp TERA served no specific purpose beyond unemployment relief, explaining, "It was little more than a recreational camp for adult women at the time I was there, since it offered no work experience beyond our camp duties and was only one step removed from the dole."[77]

The lack of clear purpose for the women's camps fueled New Deal critics' concerns about what the camps might in fact be facilitating. The American Legion accused Camp TERA of using public funds to promote communism, and another point of condemnation centered on sexual deviance. Indeed, even camp supporters believed women living alone was problematic—Harry Gersh, a teacher at Camp TERA, described it as "a most unnatural environment for these young women. . . . No one had thought that sexual isolation would be a problem."[78] Both "problems" can be linked to Murray's departure from Camp TERA after just three months.

Murray had been relishing camp life. She enjoyed hiking with Pee Wee, a tiny Caribbean woman whose enthusiasm for pursuing grievances through letter writing Murray later adopted, describing the activity as "confrontation by typewriter." Pauli formed an even closer relationship with Peg Holmes, a slender blond camp counselor. Murray wrote in her autobiography, "Peg and I were about the same age and her intellectual curiosity matched my own. We also had a common interest in poetry, and after I overcame my shyness about my writing I showed her some of my work. Peg seemed utterly without racial or class prejudice although she was the daughter of a banker and came from conservative Putnam County, New York. When she read my poems she told me she was amazed that I could write with such compassion. 'I would be bitter if I were a Negro,' she said."[79]

Although Murray's autobiography revealed nothing further about the relationship, archival sources reveal that the pair shared an intimate relationship. Murray nicknamed Holmes "Pan," the name of the Greek god of sensual nature, among other things, though Murray might also have liked the pet name because her nickname was Pete, meaning together they formed Murray's favorite fictional character, Peter Pan.[80] Murray wrote a poem about Pan that ended:

Your face, beloved, half-shadowed—
Half-bathed in moonlight. . . .
Pulse of the heart in the pulse
of night . . . Pipes of Pan.[81]

The poem's appearance in the Camp TERA Christmas newsletter indicates a degree of openness about her strong feelings for Holmes within the camp community.

As with other incidents in her life involving her sexual preference, Murray's autobiography is elusive about the issues involved in her expulsion from Camp TERA. In the paragraph after discussing her affinity for Holmes, she asserts that she left because of a "personality clash" with the camp director, Miss Mills, who did not like her "cockiness." For her part, Murray resented Mills's patronizing attitude. The last sentence of the paragraph stated, "Miss Mills also discouraged any social contact between campers and counselors outside of scheduled activities, despite the fact that we were all adult women and in some instances had intellectual interests in common."[82] Murray says no more about how her social contact with a counselor might have contributed to her expulsion from the camp, though it seems likely to have played a part, since Peg Holmes left too.

Murray was more forthcoming in recalling the camp director's charges concerning her political radicalism. Miss Mills, a "raw-boned" former World War I ambulance driver who ran the camp along semi-military lines, criticized Murray for failing to show due respect during a camp visit by Eleanor Roosevelt. Murray had not stood to attention when Roosevelt entered the dining hall, which Pauli attributed not to a lack of respect but to a combination of nervous excitement and a belief that the First Lady would not appreciate such obsequiousness.

Following Roosevelt's visit, Murray asserted that Mills placed her under "surveillance." This led to Pauli being hauled back into Mills's office a few weeks later and verbally abused for a second time, this time for being a communist who had come to the camp solely to organize a communist cell. Murray didn't know the source of the accusation but assumed that Mills had spotted her copy of *Das Kapital* during a room inspection. Murray's autobiography defensively asserted that she had never read Karl Marx's famous work and only possessed it because it was assigned reading from a past college course.[83] As historian Doreen Drury pointed out, even forty years after the event Murray felt compelled to repudiate the charge of communism, while she could still not even name the charge of homosexuality.[84]

A month after leaving Camp TERA, Pauli and Peg hitchhiked to Nebraska and back. They were not the only ones on the move. Nearly 2 million women wanting work could not find it during the Depression; tens of thousands, typically dressed in overalls and traveling in pairs, became "sisters of the road." Murray remembered the trip fondly, noting that the Depression "permitted us the freedom to travel about in ways that were not otherwise socially acceptable."[85] This included sleeping wherever they could find shelter, including local jails. The trip wasn't simply a fun experiment to alleviate the monotony of unemployment, however. Murray's 1935 diary reveals that something more problematic than boredom motivated the trip. "Decided to leave before day to avoid undue curiosity," she wrote. "Still scared about the trip. Wondering if we're doing the right thing. Have no way of knowing yet. At least we're trying to solve our problem in the best way possible."[86] The following day she recorded that the pair "sneaked out" of New York City at

5:30 A.M.[87] Later in the diary, she described having a "serious talk with Peg re P-P relationship."[88]

Whatever the exact problem Pauli and Peg were trying to solve, the trip provided temporary relief. They rode trains, hitchhiked in cars and trucks, and walked many miles. They slept in garages, jails, and hotels (when local authorities paid for it). They washed dishes, chopped and sawed wood, and cut lawns for money or food. It was often cold and raining. For most of the trip, Pauli and Peg received generous treatment. Strangers provided food, rides, accommodation, cigarettes, and money to help them along. On one occasion, they were caught out at night until a railway station manager let them sleep in a boxcar, prompting Murray to record in her diary, "God is good and kind. We are thankful." They were refused service in one small town, then held for questioning by a sheriff the following morning—the reason Murray recorded in her diary, "Race again." Murray's cropped hair and masculine attire reduced the risk of their being identified as a lesbian couple, while her indeterminate racial appearance and her seeming youth—at twenty-four Murray looked closer to fourteen—reduced the even greater risk of their being identified as a Black man sleeping with a white woman. On at least one occasion Murray "passed" as a Boy Scout, on another as a Native American.[89]

Four weeks into the five-week adventure, Murray's diary entries end abruptly. Either during or shortly after the trip, she suffered another breakdown. Details are scant, many pages have been torn from her 1935 diary, and her autobiography sheds no light. Murray appears to have made a regrettable return to Durham, which she referred to in a letter written to Aunt Pauline years later: "You know the south, the hot days, and my trouble of 1935. I don't want a repetition."[90] Whether she tried to relocate permanently or simply went home to recuperate is unclear. Murray returned to New York City where she was admitted to Bellevue Hospital from August until September.[91]

The "P-P relationship" problem seems a likely contributor to the breakdown. Social condemnation placed a great strain on Murray's love life, but it wasn't the only problem. A few years later Murray described—again in the third person—uncertainty regarding her romantic attachments: "Her greatest torment was in her love life. She could never decide whether her devotion was an affirmation of love or because her own need for affection was so great she was willing to purchase it at any cost."[92] Murray suspected that her attractions to women were complicated not only by societal condemnation but also by the lasting impact of childhood events. She also told psychiatrists that she had the emotions of a child and that women always eventually mothered her, but she also reported hating the feeling of being dominated by women she did not like, prompting her to ask, "Do you think I have a mother fixation?"[93]

Pauli's collapse occurred in the same year that her older brother, Bill, suffered a psychological breakdown, resulting in his institutionalization.[94] Bill's hospitalization was a distressing enough event in itself, but given their father's experience it must have felt like compelling and terrifying evidence that mental illness could be hereditary—at a time when homosexuality too was often considered a mental illness.[95] The popularity of eugenics and biological determinism in the early twentieth century also encouraged Murray to perceive herself, rather than the society that tried to oppress her, as a problem.[96]

Pauli must have been alarmed by other eerie parallels with Bill's situation. After his girlfriend jilted him, Bill—the sibling to whom Pauli was closest in age and appearance—quit law school and spent time in an unemployed camp before being hospitalized.[97] Pauli later described a family tendency to "nearly go off their rockers" during relationship breakdowns—a belief that must have added to the substantial challenges facing a same-sex, interracial relationship in 1935.[98] The family behavioral patterns suggested to Murray a genetic defect, the prospect of which alone would be enough to create mental health issues, but when combined with experiences of racism, homophobia, transphobia, childhood trauma, and extreme financial marginalization, Murray's prolonged hospitalization seems more complex, but hardly surprising.

· · · · ·

IV

Shortly after leaving the hospital, Murray was arrested for the first time in her life. The arrest stemmed from trying to help her friend Ted Poston—a quick-witted, lanky, and successful journalist she had known for about five years. Initially, a friendship between the pair seemed unlikely, because Murray "foolishly" asked him if his dark skin tone was a great handicap. The question left Poston unimpressed, but he didn't hold it against her and grew to become a mentor to the aspiring writer. Her admiration for his journalism led to a "lunch counter friendship" whereby Poston would stop to chat briefly whenever he saw her sitting at a local diner. Although he was only four years older, Murray still described his interest in her writing as "fatherly."[99]

Poston and fellow union members had been arrested for picketing their employer—the Black weekly, the *Amsterdam News*—because the newspaper refused to recognize their membership in the American Newspaper Guild. Murray read reports of the arrest and immediately called Poston to see if she could help. He asked her to join the picket and she readily agreed, though she had never participated in an organized protest before. She later recalled that once she joined the picket, anxiety took hold: "For all my bravado, deeply engrained notions of respectability filled me with distress. It was one thing to ride freights anonymously or sleep in jails in strange towns where I was unknown. It was quite another to carry a picket sign in the heart of Harlem, where many people knew me. I felt as if I had been asked to parade in public undressed, and was extremely self-conscious when I first joined the line and faced a crowd of onlookers."[100]

At first glance it seems strange that someone who refused to pledge allegiance as a six-year-old would, twenty-years later, be afraid to protest, but when Murray had time to think, she had time for self-doubt. Participating in public protests risked public humiliation, a terrifying prospect for a sensitive person steeped from a young age in middle-class codes that stressed respectability and dignified behavior. Murray must have become especially panicked when, once on the picket line, the police arrived to arrest the picketers. The protestors, including Murray, spent several hours in jail, but the following day a judge dismissed the charges, and Murray and the other protestors returned to the picket line. Participating in the picket signaled Murray's first step toward organized activism, though this arrest would also be used against her later in life.

Murray's self-consciousness also emerged when she applied for work through the newly established Works Progress Administration (WPA). The WPA's initial $1.4 billion annual budget made it the largest New Deal agency; it used those funds to engage millions of unemployed workers in projects ranging from building roads to operating drama theaters. Because the projects were designed to provide work only for heads of households, far more men than women gained employment.[101] Murray's independence made her eligible, and her lack of steady employment for nearly a year made her desperate. At night Murray slept in the art studio of her friend Maysie Stone; during the days she read in the New York Public Library and washed in a public restroom.

On the day of the WPA interview she also, unusually, donned a dress. Murray typically wore pants, though not without a "terrific mental conflict." When she was in pants strangers assumed she was a boy, and when she was in dresses her friends laughed.[102] She suspected her awkwardness in dresses was obvious even to strangers: as she stepped up for the WPA interview, she imagined the male interviewer thinking that "dresses did not enhance that particular form." She imagined him being uncertain whether her face belonged to a boy or girl and noting something amiss "in the walk when its owner approached the desk—neither fast nor slow, but deliberate and a bit defiant he thought."[103]

Despite the awkward interview, on October 9, 1935, the WPA "saved" Murray.[104] It took her from homelessness to her largest ever income, $23.86 a week, which enabled her to rent a room in a largely Italian immigrant section of Greenwich Village, where she witnessed occasional pro-Mussolini rallies inspired by the Italo-Ethiopian War. One demonstration that she made her way through on the way to work included an effigy of the Ethiopian king swinging from gallows set up on cart.[105] It reminded Murray of lynching photos and, no doubt, prompted memories of her father. Murray remembered the protest for life—fear of violence was never too far from Murray's thoughts and shouldn't be overlooked as a major source of tension amid the many that she had to balance.

Murray worked on the Remedial Reading Project assisting school students' develop English skills. During college, she had contemplated then rejected the possibility of a teaching career—the profession of her father, adoptive mother, and numerous other relatives—but now she had no choice. She taught word construction and recognition to no more than three children at a time, yet found no greater contentment in this role than she had in any previous position. Murray felt the "stigma" of WPA status and considered her role an "unhappy one" because few teachers assigned students to the project, and those who did used it to rid themselves of students with behavioral problems. She described a school year of "mixed results," during which she suffered from "almost total isolation" from regularly appointed teachers. She recalled, "My lower-caste professional standing was so demoralizing that at the end of the school year, in spite of highly satisfactory ratings, I transferred to the WPA Workers' Education Project."[106]

Murray's claim that she joined the Workers' Education Project (WEP) immediately is not entirely accurate—she quit the Remedial Reading Project on September 18, 1936, but only joined the WEP in May 1937.[107] Between stints on the WPA projects she took up a scholarship to attend Brookwood Labor College, which opened in 1921 as a residential workers' college designed "to educate workers to work in the workers' movements and frankly aims not to elevate workers out of their class."[108] Brookwood's aims were antithetical to the ideology instilled in Murray since childhood—that individual success would bring collective uplift—but very much in keeping with her immersion in left-wing ideology. Many Brookwood founders and supporters, including its first director, the famed pacifist A. J. Muste, were aligned with the Socialist Party, which is where Murray's political sympathies lay, having voted for their presidential candidate in 1932.[109] Murray's association with left-wing political groups and personalities must have facilitated her scholarship to Brookwood, though in her memoirs she doesn't reveal how it came about.

Murray admitted to having attended Brookwood, but stated that she did so during a short leave of absence from the WEP to "get more labor background," making it sound more like a part of her professional development than an engagement with left-wing ideologies.[110] She also noted the American Federation of Labor's (AFL) role in establishing Brookwood, but overlooked the AFL's long-standing directive to affiliated unions to withdraw support for the college because it had become too radical.[111] Although Murray later downplayed her political radicalism, she certainly never denied involvement in the labor movement. While at Brookwood, she participated in volunteer union organizing at the Tarrytown automobile plant during the Automobile Workers' strike, which formed part of widespread strikes affecting the automobile industry and beyond.

Beginning with the December 30, 1936, "sit-down" strike at the General Motors factory in Flint, Michigan, strikes quickly spread. By March 1937 there were 170 similar sit-down strikes underway, not just in automobile factories but also in other industries, at colleges, and even among the New York Rovers ice hockey team. An estimated 170,000 people were on strike, leading the *Detroit News* to declare, "Sitting-down has replaced baseball as a national pastime."[112] Murray would later go on to instigate sit-in protests against segregation that replicated the sit-down strategy. Indeed, she likened Brookwood experiences—such as listening to inspiring speeches from labor leaders, singing union songs, and participating in group discussions—to the later civil and women's rights movements because of the intense, almost "religious fervor" generated.

Murray recalled one Brookwood experience as particularly influential. She believed a fellow student, "Red," a white autoworker from Georgia who had never interacted on an equal basis with African Americans, withdrew from Brookwood in part because she had triggered "a deep conflict within him which he could not resolve." She suspected her superior education shattered his belief in his skin color's superiority, which in turn shattered his self-esteem. Murray considered him crippled by racism, just as she had been crippled by it in other ways, recalling, "My own self-esteem was elusive and difficult to sustain. I was not entirely free from the prevalent idea that I must prove myself worthy of the rights that white individuals took for granted. This psychological conditioning along with fear had reduced my capacity for resistance to racial injustice. It had not occurred to me that a system of oppression draws much of its strength from the acquiescence of its victims, who have accepted the dominant image of themselves and are paralyzed by a sense of helplessness."[113]

The connections Murray began making between labor and race struggles led her to apply, unsuccessfully, for a scholarship to study "Negro labor" at Columbia University.[114] Brookwood wasn't working out either. She took every opportunity to escape the residential school in Katonah to return to the city. The school itself was rapidly falling apart due to declining student numbers, decreasing revenue, and infighting between faculty members—there were only nineteen students still attending when Murray returned to the WPA.[115]

Around this time Murray also joined a Marxist group commonly known as the Lovestoneites. Jay Lovestone, a former Communist Party secretary general who had been ousted from the Party, formed his own political party that aimed to adapt communist ideas to the American context. The Lovestoneites still identified as a faction within the broader communist movement, but preferred to formulate their own policies rather than follow political positions issued by the Soviet Union.[116] Murray already opposed the Communist Party because of its USSR-formulated position that African Americans should fight to establish an independent Black nation in the southern states; she believed this plan was both unrealistic and segregation by another name. Again, Murray later framed her membership and attendance at the Lovestoneites' New Workers School as "a valuable learning experience, which equipped me to hold my own in future encounters with Communist Party members who joined various liberal organizations with which I associated."[117] She also claimed to have resigned from the group because she opposed the Lovestoneites' decision to support the Communist Party candidate in the 1936 presidential election, but she didn't break with the Lovestoneites until the fall of 1937 at the earliest and possibly remained affiliated until 1938.[118]

While presumably still involved with the Lovestoneites, Murray returned to the WPA, joining the Workers' Education Project in May 1937.[119] The WEP incorporated around 1,000 instructors in thirty-three states, enrolling 6,500 workers in classes covering labor law, economics, history, union administration, and current events.[120] Murray taught things such as basic arithmetic and literacy at the New York office, one of the largest in the country. She took pride in the teaching programs she and her colleagues established, despite their lack of formal teaching qualifications, yet persistent rumors that the program would be shut down by New Deal critics tempered her pride.

Murray carrying Peg Holmes, 1937. *(Schlesinger Library, Radcliffe Institute, Harvard University)*

Critics viewed the entire WPA as a waste of money and its employees as parasites; Murray's fluctuating self-confidence made it difficult for her to resist such criticisms no matter how hard she worked.[121]

SIMILAR VULNERABILITIES AFFECTED HER love life. In August 1937, Pauli and Peg Holmes visited Toni Hayden's family home in Newport, Rhode Island. In photos of the trip, the nearly twenty-seven-year-old Murray is dressed in a sailor suit, complete with sailor hat fitted over her closely cropped hair. The distinctly male attire is enhanced by Murray's poses and handwritten captions identifying her as "Pete," except for the photos with

Holmes, which are titled "Pauli and Peggie."[122] The joyous photos present such a striking contrast to the troubled thoughts she came to express about her sexual desires in written notes. These moments of joy are less well documented in Murray's archive, but no doubt existed amid the better-evidenced sources of strain on her intimate life.

One source of strain, rampant homophobia, placed many Americans under immense psychological pressure during this period. Novels and theater productions typically denigrated lesbians as tragic, dangerous, and sick freaks.[123] In the same year as Murray's trip with Peg, a spate of salacious newspaper reports about "sex offenses" led FBI director J. Edgar Hoover to declare "War on the Sex criminal" and New York mayor Fiorello La Guardia to appoint a Committee for the Study of Sex Crimes. Pedophiles received most of the ire, but little distinction was made between pedophilia and homosexuality since the latter was also a crime and often considered a consequence of arrested sexual development. The New York committee, which included psychiatrists, lawyers, and criminologists, recommended that "sex offenders" receive indeterminate sentences in secure medical facilities until psychiatrists deemed them rehabilitated.[124] Given what happened to Pauli's father, her brother, and her own 1935 hospitalization, threats of indefinite confinement to a psychiatric hospital must have been a terrifying prospect, adding an unfathomable amount of stress to Pauli's same-sex attractions.

Four months after the trip with Peg Holmes, on December 12, 1937, Murray entered the Long Island Rest Home, a psychiatric hospital in Amityville, New York. Her breakdown was so severe that two days after admission she still had no idea who had paid for her admission to the private facility or who had passed her off as a Cuban (African Americans were not permitted). Nor did she understand why she was there. She fought with the attendants because they treated her as a "mental case" suffering "psychosis" and gave her copious sedatives without providing any laxatives. She demanded the opportunity to take walks and confer with the doctor. "Why the hell can't I see that guy?" she asked, "Is he so damned important that he can't take off a few minutes to see me?" She thought the hospital staff were "stalling" but acknowledged that she might be unduly suspicious because of her "distaste for mental institutions."

Over the course of a week Murray scribbled sixty-three questions for doctors as well as a few answers she received.[125] The questions began with requests relating to her care before becoming increasingly focused on her "conflict," which manifested itself in restlessness, overactivity, and wanting to help others. Still without naming the conflict, Murray questioned why she had an "inverted sex instinct," by which she meant a preference for wearing pants and wanting to be one of the men; why falling in love with women felt natural; why she desired monogamous married life; why she felt attracted to very feminine, heterosexual-identifying women; and why "terrific breakdowns" followed each breakup. She also wondered why she remained deeply religious and a nondrinker and asked, "Why do many other Homosexuals irritate me instead of causing a bond of sympathy, particularly when I think it is acquired?"

Without ever directly labeling her sexual preference, Murray implied its centrality to her conflict because it didn't align with other aspects of her selfhood in ways she expected. Murray asked whether medical science knew the causes of homosexuality and was told no, but this did not deter her from trying to discover the sources of her behavior. In her questions she grappled with both psychology and physiology and with their interrelatedness. She wondered if several "unresolved subconscious" conflicts were at work and specifically asked about "an ego drive." Although Murray never seemed convinced by psychoanalytic theories, they still fascinated her. A week after her initial disagreeable interactions with staff and declaring her distaste for mental institutions, Murray reported receiving "splendid treatment" and seemed to benefit greatly from the care and attention. She even asked if she could stay on at the psychiatric facility while she gained weight and learned the "trade."

Murray still tended to believe that her perceived problems' source lay in her body and that the solution lay with experimental medical science. This feeling is evident in her question "Why do I prefer experimentation on the male side, instead of attempted adjustment as a normal woman?" Disinterest in heterosexual womanhood, even if psychiatry could help achieve it, encouraged Murray to seek clues to the conflict in her physical composition. In her wide-ranging questioning, which leaped from topic to topic, she asked about such things as the cause of her slight stature and boyish appearance and, more curiously, "Why during periods of nervous upset, a perspiration between my buttox [sic]?" The doctors did know the answer to this question, but she noted that the answer to some of her questions could be glandular. Murray requested examination of her "embryological development" and ovaries to determine whether she was a "pseudo-hermaphrodite" and wanted doctors to experiment on her with "male" hormones. Her concerns about bodily function culminated in the question "What are the possibilities that one of [my] 'genitalia' is male in composition," to which she received the answer "Impossibility."[126]

Murray's ideas evolved from reading at the New York Public Library.

Deeply Engrained Notions of Respectability Filled Me with Distress

Scholars have logically assumed that Murray read the works of early sexologists, such as Havelock Ellis, who theorized about sexual "inversion." Ellis believed that homosexuality was acquired and could be treated with psychology, but he also believed some people, "pseudo-hermaphrodites," identified as members of the opposite sex because of anatomical and hormonal influences.[127] Murray may also have heard of contemporary research, especially urologist Hugh Hampton Young's widely discussed work. In the same year as her hospitalization, Young published *Genital Abnormalities, Hermaphroditism and Related Adrenal Diseases*, which classified intersex people based on voluminous case studies.[128]

We can't know for sure what Murray read, let alone how well she understood it, but clearly some things she read triggered a suspicion that her body might contain hidden male attributes that medical science could uncover and bring to the fore. Murray's questions for doctors provide rare evidence of the lived experiences and challenges faced by innumerable people who didn't fit within narrow definitions of appropriate gender and sexual expression at this time. They are still very limited, however; definitive conclusions about a life cannot be drawn from questions, not all coherently expressed, written by someone who has clearly experienced a significant mental health breakdown. Unsurprisingly, there is no consensus among scholars who have examined the notes—some, plausibly, see homophobia propelling Murray into a desperate quest to legitimize her attractions to women by transitioning to male, while others, equally plausibly, believe Murray conceived of herself as intersex because she "felt more strongly her male self than her female self."[129] Some combination of the two is also plausible, but to add further to these discussions would require somehow discerning a first cause for feelings from a few remaining notes and risk applying current labels that Murray may or may not have welcomed.

Importantly, Murray didn't mention societal attitudes—beyond mentioning that she generally received kind treatment by most people—in her questions about her ill-defined conflict. She absorbed negative societal attitudes about homosexuality, but her questions mostly focused inward. One question encapsulated many of the others: "Where do you think is the seat of the conflict—in the brain, the body, the glands—[else]where?"[130] Doctors couldn't answer most of her questions, nor could they provide the treatments she wanted, but Murray remained undeterred. Shortly after her hospitalization, Murray underwent physical examinations at a "neurological clinic" in New York. The tests revealed that her basic metabolism was normal, her "female" hormone levels were also normal, but her "male" hormone levels were low, even for a woman.[131] Despite these discouraging results, Murray felt far from ready to give up the belief that something was wrong with her which medical science might be able to fix.

· · · · ·

V

Murray resumed WPA employment with renewed vigor following the hospitalization. Most weeknights she taught classes, primarily in Harlem to Black workers, on topics ranging from Social Security and labor issues to "Social Problems" and "Can We Avoid the Next War." Through working on WPA projects she became better acquainted with left-wing activists and current and future influential Black activists, including Ella Baker and A. Philip Randolph.[132] Murray also appeared to be moving away from Marxism. In a 1938 letter to Peg Holmes, she discussed her "Marxian training" and her evolving view that "class love should be substituted for class hate, and love of mankind and the future of mankind should motivate all our decisions."[133] In a letter to Socialist Party leader Norman Thomas the following January, she asked whether he thought Christian and Marxist worldviews could be synthesized; she wrote, "Class struggle seems as fatal as the concept, turn the other cheek, if turning the other cheek means giving in to the capitalists."[134]

In the same year, Murray read *War without Violence*, by Krishnalal Shridharani, who had protested Britain's occupation of India with Gandhi. His book explained *Satyagraha*, which required adherents to engage in disciplined "non-violent resistance or direct action." Murray enthusiastically embraced his argument that *Satyagraha* provided a superior strategy to bring about social change because "its compelling force is aimed at converting instead of destroying the opponent."[135] For someone who feared she might go berserk and do harm to others while also fearing social stigma from activism, nonviolent direct-action protest offered a dignified means of channeling frustrations toward a positive end.[136] Murray's activist focus shifted from the labor movement to the Black freedom struggle as she encountered more Black and white pacifist activists studying the Indian independence movement.

In late 1938, Murray made her first publicized contribution to the African American freedom struggle by applying to study sociology at the University of North Carolina (UNC). UNC's Sociology Department was considered the South's leading institution for studying America's race problem, even though African Americans weren't eligible to attend the institution.[137] Applying to UNC despite North Carolina segregation laws that prohibited her admission was a political act, but it stemmed from very personal motives. Murray recalled, "I wrestled with the problem of my obligation to Aunt Pauline and my guilt over an unwillingness to return South to live and work. Although I had been in New York for more than ten years, she had not become reconciled to my living away from home: I was in the position of an unmarried daughter who is expected to take care of older members of her family, whatever adjustments in her career plans this entails."[138] The expectations on Murray were exacerbated because she had no viable career plans—even if the WPA wasn't disbanded, as was often threatened, she could only remain for another six months before she would reach the maximum limit of eighteen months' continuous WPA employment.[139]

Murray also had reason to believe that UNC would soon accept Black graduate students. The Supreme Court was deliberating over whether Missouri had violated the right of graduate student Lloyd Gaines to a "separate but equal" education. The University of Missouri Law School had denied Gaines entry solely based on race. Since there were no separate Black law schools in Missouri, the NAACP led a legal challenge asserting that Missouri had violated Gaines's right to an "equal" education. Of the sixteen states that had segregation laws, none provided African American graduate schools; six provided funding for tuition out of state, and the other ten, including North Carolina, provided nothing.[140] On December 12, the Supreme Court ruled in Gaines's favor, a decision that appeared to compel southern states to either integrate graduate schools or provide new segregated graduate facilities at existing Black colleges.

Murray submitted her UNC application just days before the *Gaines* Supreme Court decision. She denied knowing about the *Gaines* case when she applied, but she probably only said this to lessen the likelihood that her application would seem politically motivated.[141] The strongest evidence that Murray was aware of the case comes from a letter she wrote, a week before the *Gaines* decision, to North Carolina College for Negroes president James Shepard, asking whether the college had plans to build graduate facilities. It was well known that Shepard wanted graduate facilities built at his college (now known as North Carolina Central University), but she still asked him for his views before going on to liken supporting anything short of full equality to collaborating with the aims of Nazi Germany. She didn't mention her UNC plans in the letter; however, she did ask what support a Negro applicant "could expect from Negro educators and liberal forces." She closed the letter by invoking "the traditional place of respect which you hold in my family," since he and Aunt Pauline were friends.[142]

Murray typed prolifically on the day she wrote to Shepard. She also wrote an impassioned letter to President Roosevelt, who had praised UNC as an institution of liberal thought while accepting an honorary doctorate a day earlier. She asked if his praise for UNC's liberalism meant it was going to allow Negro students to attend and if he would use his prestige and influence to make it happen. Murray sent a copy of the letter to Eleanor Roosevelt (ER) with a cover letter explaining why she did not stand when ER visited Camp TERA three years earlier and expressing her admiration for the First Lady. She also asked that ER try to understand the spirit of the letter sent to her husband if he were too busy to read it.[143]

Murray gained little satisfaction from her December 6 burst of "confrontation by typewriter." After four weeks, President Shepard had not replied. She wrote again, "May I expect an immediate answer from your office?" with a crossed-out note at the bottom saying her letter had been copied to the press. Shepard replied the following day, stating curtly that he had been away and would not debate the issues with her.[144] Her letter to President Roosevelt received a hollow reply from one of her seniors at the WPA. Eleanor Roosevelt replied after two weeks, stating, "The South is changing, but don't push too fast." It was an inauspicious beginning to the ongoing correspondence between the pair, described at length in Patricia Bell-Scott's *The Firebrand and the First Lady*.[145]

Two days after the *Gaines* Supreme Court decision, Murray received the most significant correspondence of all—a rejection letter from UNC. The letter stated unequivocally, "Members of your race are not permitted here."[146] Murray expected the rejection, but it still angered her. There were surely few people more worthy of permission to study the race problem at UNC: Grandmother Cornelia was conceived because Sidney Smith, a white UNC graduate, raped a woman owned by his father, Dr. James S. Smith, a UNC trustee; and the Smith heir who owned Cornelia, Mary Ruffin Smith, willed the bulk of the Smith estate to UNC rather than to her biological niece, Cornelia.[147] Now, the robbed inheritance seemed set to continue in Cornelia's granddaughter's generation.

Murray believed UNC needed to reconsider her application or risk violating the *Gaines* ruling. She wrote to UNC president Frank P. Graham, threatening legal action if UNC continued to refuse to admit her on the grounds of race. She invoked the specter of European fascism in her letter, asking, "How can Negroes, the economic backbone of the South for centuries, defend our institutions against the threats of Fascism and barbarism if we too are treated the same as the Jews in Germany?"[148] Graham had expressed similar sentiments during a keynote address to the newly formed Southern Conference on Human Welfare. "In this day when democracy and freedom are in retreat everywhere in the face of totalitarian powers," Graham expounded, "the black man is the primary test of American democracy and Christianity."[149] But Graham exercised far more caution in responding to Murray's letter. He told her that UNC was subject to state laws and therefore it was a matter for the state to decide. Perhaps Graham thought the application was destined for the courts. Murray certainly thought so.

On the day she received his reply, Murray wrote excitedly to a former high school friend in Durham asking her to approach local lawyers about the application. "Listen Lisha, I need your help," Murray began. "We gotta work fast before the Supreme Court and the Southern legislatures stop us." Murray asked Lisha to forward the enclosed correspondence with President Graham to local lawyers. She also asked Lisha to take a copy of her letter to Graham to Aunt Pauline before it appeared in the press, "so as not to shock her." Murray closed the letter, "O. K. pal, stick with me and this race of ours in North Carolina will go places."[150] Murray sent copies of her application and correspondence to the NAACP. When Thurgood Marshall responded asking her to order a copy of her Hunter College transcript at the NAACP's expense, Murray could barely contain her excitement. "When do we get going?" she responded. "I feel like a race-horse champing at the bit."[151]

Murray wasn't the only one getting excited by her application's potential. Stories appeared in both local and national newspapers. New York's *Daily News* carried an associated press account under the headline "Colored Tries to Enter Carolina U."[152] The UNC student paper, the *Daily Tar Heel*, cited vehement opposition: "Students hearing of the movement vowed that they would tar and feather any 'nigger' that tried to come into class with them."[153] Murray's name didn't appear in these early reports—the white press referred to her as "colored girl" and other racial epithets, for what mattered to opponents was her racial identity, not her personal identity or academic abilities. The *Durham Morning Herald* ran the story under the headline "NEGRESS APPLIES TO ENTER CAROLINA," which Murray found extremely hurtful. The article content was hardly less damaging: "Rational members of both races understand that the policy of segregation of races with respect to schools is a fixed one in this part of the country. No one in his right mind favors trying to abandon or materially amend that policy at this juncture."[154]

Despite the threats, the hurtful racial epithets, and the questioning of her mental health—or perhaps because of them—Murray did not retreat. Instead she fired back. She wrote a direct response to the *Daily Tar Heel*'s editorial, identifying herself only as "the Negro from New York." She challenged UNC students:

You sit on the same seat with your Negro nurse as a child, you come to her to pour out all your childish woes, you depend upon her for sympathy and advice when you are in trouble, you eat the food she prepares with her own hands, and yet if that same Negro nurse decides that she too is a human being and desires to study under the same group of professors and with the same equipment as you, you go into tantrums, organize "lynching parties" and raise the old cry of Ku Klux Klan. Why not be honest with yourselves? You share our songs, our contributions to the field of entertainment and music, you "go wild" over our dance orchestras, you "just love our good old spirituals," you quote our "quaint philosophies" in your poetry and literature, you think we're "just grand in our place" and yet you resent our intelligence and our determination to also better ourselves. Or do you?[155]

If Murray was simply interested in having her application test the *Gaines* Supreme Court decision, she didn't need to make public challenges to UNC students. But it was impossible for her to remain silent; Murray's outrage compelled her to challenge the depiction of her as an unhinged "Negress" deserving of tarring and feathering.

Important figures within North Carolina opposed Murray's application. The governor alluded to the bogeyman of interracial sex when he expressed opposition to the social mixing of the races.[156] Howard Odum, the white sociologist Murray hoped to study under, supported building graduate schools at existing Black colleges as the best means of not upsetting "powerful folkways."[157] Murray later described Odum's opposition to her application as unsurprising. She had done enough background research to conclude that he was "too close to the Old South" to support integrated education, which suggests she had given far greater thought to challenging segregation than to what it might be like to move back to North Carolina to study the race problem with UNC's leading sociologist.[158]

Murray wasn't without white supporters. Dr. Howard Beale of UNC's History Department wrote to the *Daily Tar Heel* criticizing the paper's hostile editorial stand: "Liberalism cannot be pursued in all categories and then denied whenever the Negro appears."[159] Of the UNC graduate students polled by the *Tar Heel*, eighty-two were in favor and only thirty-two opposed to admitting African Americans. An interracial forum attended by more than one hundred people also adopted a resolution supporting Murray's application.[160] Nor was Murray without Black critics. Aunt Pauline's good friend Dr. Shepard argued, "Negroes could do their best work in their own schools," no doubt with funding for the North Carolina College for Negroes in mind.[161]

Unbeknownst to Murray, division over whether to support her application also existed within the NAACP. Roy Wilkins, then editor of the association's magazine, *Crisis*, wrote to NAACP executive secretary Walter White urging that the organization distance itself from Murray's application. Wilkins only signed off on reimbursing Murray the one-dollar cost of obtaining a transcript from Hunter College "under protest." He emphatically stated that the NAACP should have no "record anywhere as having had anything to do with Miss Murray's application." Since she had not consulted them before applying and they had not yet agreed to take the case, Wilkins argued, "she should be allowed to proceed by herself." His objection to supporting Murray's application stemmed from her "extensive correspondence," particularly her correspondence with UNC president Graham, with whom Wilkins believed the NAACP could form a constructive relationship. Walter White lamented the "unfortunate tone" of Murray's letter but remained willing to leave the decision whether to support Murray to the legal team. It is possible, but not certain, that Thurgood Marshall warned Murray that the NAACP disapproved of her independent campaigning.[162]

The application also threatened to drive a wedge between Pauli and Aunt Pauline. Murray's attempt to prepare her adoptive mother for the impending controversy by asking a friend to visit her had not put Aunt Pauline at ease. Indeed, there was no preparing for the hostility expressed in some accounts from the white media. Pauli felt immense strain from it too, so much so that she informed Aunt Pauline that she would not be home for Christmas. Aunt Pauline responded, "You hurt me so much that Christmas has lost its joy." After that blunt opening, Aunt Pauline then continued, "I do hope you will get all o.k. so if we are apart till Easter you will come home. I have had two very bad falls within one week and both seemed to tear every muscle in my body from its place."[163] Pauli's own health concerns preventing her from going home for Christmas appear to have been related to her gender identity—in January she underwent more physiological testing, which noted her "boyish" physique, but hormone tests again detected nothing unusual and doctors again suggested she seek psychological help.[164] Whatever Murray's specific health concerns at the time, her mother's response can't have been revitalizing.

Aunt Pauline wasn't just hurt about Christmas or worried about her own health; she also feared Pauli's actions would have ramifications for her. In a letter written shortly after Christmas she warned Pauli, "Please be careful what you do about all this, for you can make it very uncomfortable for me. You are away and don't hear it. . . . I too am working and hoping for the teachers' retirement pension and return of the pre-war salaries. Don't do anything rash, please. You know it will take time to change the South."[165] On receiving the letter Pauli immediately telephoned home and listened to Aunt Pauline's concerns, which included a fear that enraged whites would burn down her home.[166] Murray had applied to UNC in part to try to appease her now sixty-eight-year-old adoptive mother, yet her UNC application was providing a clear illustration of why it was impossible for her to live in North Carolina and pursue her goals.

Rather than heed Aunt Pauline's request to be careful, Pauli did almost the exact opposite and launched a publicity campaign in defense of her application. Murray's autobiography stated that the Black press somehow "discovered" that she was the applicant, but in fact they published her name with her full blessing.[167] She wrote to *Carolina Times* editor Lewis E. Austin informing him that she had decided to let the "cat out of the bag" and providing him with all her correspondence on the issue—including the personal letter UNC president Graham had written her—to do with as he pleased. The *Carolina Times* and other Black news outlets ran with the story. Murray's name and picture were widely published, including in the *Baltimore Afro-American* and the New York *Amsterdam News*, making Murray an overnight champion of Black America.[168]

Roy Wilkins was not impressed, however. Throughout his involvement in the NAACP, Wilkins openly acknowledged his quest to disassociate the organization from working with any person or group with links to radical left politics.[169] Furthermore, the NAACP's limited resources and the powerful forces arrayed against it resulted in a cautious political and legal strategy that only selected airtight cases and clients who wouldn't appear to be political agitators.[170] Wilkins again wrote to NAACP leader Walter White to point out Murray's release of information to the press—though White could hardly have missed the media storm. Wilkins insisted that Murray's application wasn't simply a legal matter and claimed that NAACP special counsel Charles Hamilton Houston "agreed most emphatically . . . that the Association should not be connected in any way with Miss Murray's application."[171]

In March 1939, NAACP chief counsel Thurgood Marshall informed Murray that the NAACP would not pursue her case. She later described the news as her "worst disappointment." Murray's autobiography explained that the NAACP's decision stemmed from the fact she wasn't a North Carolina resident when she applied, which cast doubt on whether her application could test the state's segregation laws.[172] Yet Murray suspected that other, nonlegal reasons influenced the NAACP's withdrawal. In a 1976 interview she recalled getting "the shock of her life" when Marshall told her the NAACP wouldn't pursue her case. According to her recollection, Marshall indicated that she was not "Simon-pure enough" and "too maverick." In a follow-up question, the interviewer asked Murray directly if she thought her radical activities had influenced the NAACP withdrawal. Murray answered, "Might well have" and said that Marshall "might have implied this."[173]

Historians differ over the NAACP's motives for declining to pursue the case — some argue that the NAACP only withdrew because of Murray's New York residence; others emphasize her independent activism and even her family history of mental illness and Murray's sexual and gender identities as possible reasons.[174] It is unlikely that issues not arising directly from the application were deciding factors, since the NAACP became involved in another Murray case the following year. Her independent activism in support of her application was clearly a problem, though, which made it easier to decline the case when combined with the legal technicality. Regardless of what caused the NAACP to withdraw, for Murray's well-being and self-perception it was important that she suspected for much of her life that the NAACP had rejected her because of reasons unrelated to her case's merits. As with numerous other instances in her life, from everyday interactions with shopkeepers, bus drivers, and the like, to potentially life-changing decisions of organizations like the NAACP, Murray could rarely be certain about the sources of any mistreatment she perceived. The abrupt end to a potentially landmark challenge to segregated education ratcheted up the numerous tensions she constantly lived with, which included financial, social, and political disenfranchisement, gender and sexual identity conflicts, her responsibility to Aunt Pauline, and a fiery, up-and-down temperament that evoked her father's memory and the fear that a fatal flaw might lurk within her genes.

Murray vented her frustration by attacking almost everyone. In personal correspondence, she referred to Dr. Shepard as a "handkerchief head" and "tool for further betrayal."[175] She was scarcely less scathing in public criticisms. In an article for Black Dispatches, she accused North Carolina's Black community leaders of a willingness to "sacrifice ultimate principles for temporary palliatives." She also accused young African Americans of dissipating their creative energies developing the "most grotesque 'jitterbug techniques' to the exclusion of all else." She lamented that three hundred thousand African Americans could fill the streets when Joe Lewis won a boxing match against a white man, but not for Black legal equality. She continued, "It is our failure which must be judged; our group lethargy, our lack of idealism, our timidity, our disorganization, and our proneness to do little more than mouth our grievances beyond 'the big gate.'"[176]

. . . . .

VI

Murray finally visited Aunt Pauline during the 1939 Easter break. While there, she made a point of walking around the UNC campus—no small act of bravery given the hysteria her application caused a few months earlier—and spoke with staff and students who supported her application.[177] She did not stay in North Carolina long, however; her life was very much in New York.

Murray still dreamed of a writing career. She took a night course on poetry and developed a mentoring relationship with the poet she most admired, Stephen Vincent Benét. She spent so much time writing poetry, prose, letters, and WPA lectures, often through the night—like her father, Pauli experienced prolonged periods of ceaseless activity before crashing—that the clacking of her typewriter resulted in three evictions in one year alone. Murray bounced around Harlem's furnished rented rooms, cramming all her books and ever-growing cartons of personal papers, a hot plate and ironing board, typewriter and work table, and two beaten trunks into tiny spaces that left nowhere for entertaining.

She gained some reprieve from neighbors' complaints when she moved into a room in an eight-room Harlem apartment where several other WPA, relief, and marginally employed women resided. The housemates minimized expenses by sharing food and went on small adventures together. In good times the company provided a fun outlet; in less happy moments the place felt claustrophobic—at one point there were thirteen people sharing the small apartment. Murray described "the giggles and grins, the cackling at morning and the tittering at night," as well as "the arguments and debates, the petty squabbles over less than a toothpick."[178]

Pauli shared her room with Adelene "Mac" McBean—a slender, high-spirited Black woman with a loud voice and an infectious laugh.[179] Aunt Sallie's two sons, aged twenty and seventeen, also came to live with them following their father's death. Reverend Small's death meant Aunt Sallie had moved back in with Aunt Pauline and had no means to provide for her sons.[180] Murray assured her aunts, "I'm quite a self-confident fellow to take moral responsibility for two boys in New York City."[181] Pauli described the arrangement in ways resembling a stereotypical nuclear family—Mac fretted over the boys and cooked for them, while Pauli set the rules and provided advice on important life choices. In one letter home she wrote, "Thursday night, Mac (my girl-friend) and I threw a small surprise birthday party in honor of Jimmy's birthday and Joshua's being here. Mac baked a beautiful birth-day cake with white icing and twenty deep blue candles on top. . . . I've decided that if he wants to really study music, to encourage him at it, so long as he gets a daytime job and makes his expenses."[182] Murray felt better about playing the role of substitute father than dutiful daughter. Housing her cousins also became a way to fulfill the family obligation to Aunt Pauline that she felt guilty for neglecting. "Somehow," Pauli informed Mac, "it helps pay back for all the times I didn't write, or didn't help out, or was deaf to pleas that were never actually written in letters."[183] While she accommodated Aunt Sallie's boys, Aunt Sallie took care of Aunt Pauline, who had injured herself in another fall.

Although spared the responsibility of returning home, assuming a parental role created different pressures, particularly after she reached the maximum allowed eighteen months' continuous employment by the WPA on July 23, 1939.[184] A week later Murray accepted an administrative position with the Negro People's Committee to Aid Spanish Democracy (NPC), despite her concerns that the Communist Party might dominate the organization. She made it clear when reluctantly accepting the position that she would resign if her suspicions proved true.[185] With that condition in place, Murray began working exhausting hours, but she still could not meet the extra financial burden created by her cousins' arrival, nor did they enjoy an easy transition to New York. Twenty-year-old James struggled to find lasting work, while seventeen-year-old Joshua struggled with the leap from segregated southern schools to the New York school system.[186]

A month after accepting the NPC job, Murray took a week's rest break at Peg Holmes's Rhode Island home.[187] Holmes retained a special place in Pauli's heart, but there is little in the surviving evidence to indicate the nature and extent of Holmes's feeling toward Murray. Any rejuvenation Murray gained from the break didn't last. Nazi Germany and Soviet Russia invaded Poland that same month. Despite her strident antifascism (and increasing anticommunism), on hearing the news Murray immediately thought, "A Pole killed my father."[188] Another problem, and a further reminder of her father's demise, emerged shortly after when she received the sad news that her older brother Bill's mental health problems had again led to his hospitalization.[189]

On a Sunday in early October, she traveled down to St. Elizabeth's Hospital in Washington to visit Bill. The journey must have evoked memories of her trip to Crownsville to visit her father twenty years earlier. As with her father, Pauli found her brother's disheveled appearance deeply disturbing, but she also described Bill as "quite rational and quite anxious to work in the cafeteria providing he could be out on the grounds." Desperate to help in any way, Pauli wrote to doctors after the visit to ask if there was anything she or her family could do to assist her brother.[190] A hospital physician replied stating that Bill had shown some recent improvement, leading the hospital to again consider granting him privileges "such as walking about the hospital reservation unattended and permitting him to visit the city overnight in the custody of his relatives." But they couldn't offer a way for Pauli to hasten her brother's recovery—as with her father, she could only wait and hope.

Aside from a further reminder of her father's brutal murder, the invasion of Poland also compounded NPC work difficulties. Fundraising for Spanish Civil War refugees among African Americans in Harlem during a prolonged economic crisis was never an easy assignment; now the far larger conflict engulfing Europe made it impossible. Association with the Communist Party, which Murray strongly opposed, also tainted the organization. Murray's letters to her aunts during this period reveal extreme fatigue and reluctance to continue in the role.[191] Two months after starting the NPC job, Murray reported to Aunt Pauline that she was exhausted, the work too hard, and her financial situation too precarious. The combination of different pressures piling up—financial strain, physical exhaustion, political factionalism, and family illness—brought her to the point of collapse.

Murray quit the NPC on November 10, three months after starting. The following day she wrote to her aunts, "The problem is this: I have not been well lately, and my nerves have been so bad that I just don't relish the idea of looking for a job immediately. I have been doing some conferring at the Post Graduate Hospital with some of the physicians in the endocrine department, and they may do some experimentation with hormones to help balance my emotional self. This may take a little time—I don't know yet until I've had a series of examinations."[192] Murray's inquiries to Post Graduate Hospital's endocrine clinic arose from newspaper accounts of hormone experiments conducted at the hospital, which were designed to turn "weak, effeminate" male youths into "strong, virile men."[193]

Murray's personal papers include a letter to the Amsterdam News signed by A. McBean, praising the newspaper's front-page coverage of the hormone experiments. Mac's letter, which reflects Murray's sentiments throughout, calls for sympathy regarding problems arising from "sexual maladjustments," which the letter described as sex inversion, homosexuality, virility in women, and effeminacy in men. The author(s), who didn't identify as sexually maladjusted, explained: "The tragedy of the thing is that individuals beset with these problems are in conflict not only with themselves, but with society at large. They are the minority of minorities, misunderstood by their family and friends, condemned without trial by social custom, isolated, excluded and made to endure a 'living death.' Our own racial group, perhaps more than any other, is guilty of great ignorance on this subject. We have almost no psychiatrists or neurologists among Negro physicians, and the bars of racial prejudice coupled with economic difficulties have made further scientific experimentation almost impossible."[194] The letter identified class, race, gender, and sexuality as intersecting forms of social oppression, though it went no further than appealing for sympathy until medical cures emerged.

Reports on breakthroughs in hormone research—the period between the wars has been described as an "endocrinological gold rush"—excited Murray about the possibilities for her situation.[195] For the third time in three years Murray underwent physiological testing. Doctors suggested, also not for the first time, that she seek psychiatric help, but she again declined. Although the testing revealed nothing to support her theory about her body, she still wanted to try the pills that turned "effeminate youths into strong, virile men." She asked clinicians if they would experiment on her with the "male hormone" (synthetic testosterone), but when the doctor instead suggested using "female" hormones, Murray did not return for treatment. At this point, her "desire to be male" felt too strong; she wanted to "wait and think long and earnestly before experimenting with female hormone."[196]

EARLY IN THE NEW YEAR, Murray sent another unsigned letter to both a local newspaper and Eleanor Roosevelt, this one describing the humiliation of having to reapply for relief. The letter—partially reprinted in ER's popular "My Day" column—detailed all the ways that seeking relief felt degrading for "our family of three." She wrote, "It is the sense of isolation, of being literally driven into these places by the whip of necessity, it is the inevitable loss of dignity, of self-assurance and personal identity when one has mustered the moral courage necessary to cross the threshold of a district office." The interview process for relief "makes the applicant feel like a prisoner awaiting trial. The moral and economic responsibility for oneself and loved ones makes the imprisonment all the more real." Murray had just spent three fruitless months trying to raise funds for Spanish refugees, and now she wondered if her situation differed: "Looking at all these miserable, frustrated, unused people, we cannot help thinking that the difference between our plight and that of the European refugees is only one of degree." The letter concluded, "Until democratic society can find a dignified use for all the individuals who comprise it, there can be no peace."[197] There was little peace in the world, or in Murray's mind, at the beginning of 1940.

Murray found welfare relief humiliating, but still preferable to returning to Durham. Her guilt over this had worsened because she couldn't support her cousins, neither of whom had work and came to her for money. Murray told Aunt Pauline in no uncertain terms that either the boys should remain in Durham or Aunt Sallie should come to New York to look after them. Although Murray's letter is strident, it is also laden with guilt and stress over the situation. She had initially expressed confidence in her ability to look out for her cousins, but now she told Aunt Pauline, "Joshua and Jimmy need a strong man's hand for guidance."[198] Murray's inability to provide for her cousins contributed to her feeling disempowered. The lingering effects of the Great Depression and her lack of professional qualifications combined with her marginalized racial, gender, and sexual identities to curtail employment opportunities other than working for leftist political organizations. Murray therefore had little option other than to consider another activist position, this time as executive secretary of the Annual National Sharecroppers' Week.

The Workers Defense League (WDL) and the Southern Tenant Farmers' Union (STFU)—Socialist Party members were prominent in founding both organizations—were jointly organizing Sharecroppers' Week, which aimed to raise both awareness about sharecroppers' plight and funds for the STFU.[199] Murray told a friend from the WPA who had recommended her for the job,

> You're going to think me perfectly insane when you read the intent of this letter. . . . Look Agnes, I've been searching myself with relation to this S. T. F. U. job, wondering if I really had all the qualities necessary to make it successful. I can't think of anything I'd like to do better — but you probably more than most people are aware of an instability which makes me hesitate. . . . The person who does the job must be stable, and experienced. I am neither. . . . To wait until I got in the middle of this project and then crack up would be unpardonable. . . . There are more aspects than I'm mentioning in this letter. But trust my instincts, will you?[200]

In the end, Murray couldn't afford to trust her own instincts; she took on the job despite her lack of confidence in either her ability or her mental state.

Shortly after taking up the role, Murray wrote to Eleanor Roosevelt to enlist her support. ER's secretary responded to say that the materials would be forwarded to relevant government agencies.[201] Murray persisted, requesting that a three-person delegation meet with ER, which was duly arranged

Deeply Engrained Notions of Respectability Filled Me with Distress

for January 15, 1940. Somehow on the day of the meeting the three-person delegation became six. Murray recalled that all in the delegation were nervous: one of her colleagues stumbled in front of the First Lady, another curtseyed, and Murray bowed, but ER put them at such ease that Murray soon forgot the First Lady's status. Roosevelt not only agreed to speak at the National Sharecroppers' Week dinner, she also agreed to award the prize for an essay contest and made a personal $100 contribution to the campaign. Murray came away from the meeting feeling as though she had chatted with an "affectionate older relative."[202]

As with other older relatives, Murray soon found fault with Roosevelt. Two weeks after their meeting, Murray criticized ER's decision to cross a Negro picket to attend the *Abe Lincoln in Illinois* film premiere. Civil rights activists picketed the premiere in part because the Washington movie theater hosting it had abandoned a plan to award the winner of an Abraham Lincoln look-alike promotional competition—because an African American had won. Roosevelt described in her "My Day" column how it had pained her to cross the picket line, but still Murray found the decision indefensible. She told the First Lady, "The continual day-to-day embarrassment of a group is a greater hardship than the momentary embarrassment of the individuals who attended the Keith Theatre performance of *Abe Lincoln in Illinois*. . . . There can be no compromise on the principle of equality."[203] In what must have come as a further disappointment, ER did not respond to the letter, despite their recent meeting.

Aunt Pauline was also dealing with disappointment after Pauli again failed to return home for Christmas. Afterward, Pauli wrote to her explaining that she had been unable to afford the trip because she spent the last of her money paying for her two cousins to return home to be with Aunt Sallie—Pauli had to borrow money just for her own Christmas lunch. Pauli also expressed her hope that cousin Joshua at least would not return to New York, since he had no work and she could not provide for him. The letter then turned to Sharecroppers' Week:

> The campaign here is so strenuous, it is even harder than the other job. I'm so weary when I come home that I fall into a stupor, and no one can wake me, not even to eat. When I am awakened to eat my dinner, I do it mechanically without knowing what I'm eating. Sometimes I don't get home from work until after midnight, and my job goes on Saturday all day and sometimes most of Sunday. Night meetings almost every night, committee meetings, conferences and interviews with various people, trying to get through bank loans, trying to

get important people to do favors for our campaign—you have no idea how rushed, harassed and worried I am.[204]

Murray was showing clear signs of the overwork and exhaustion that preceded the almost annual breakdowns that she had suffered for a decade. She described it as a manic-like state in which she suffered mental upsets, irritability, fear, anxiety, overactivity, disorganization, and created "tension and confusion in the office or at home." She also admitted to "taking on greater responsibilities than I am able to carry through to successful conclusion." It seems likely that Murray and Mac were experiencing relationship problems or that she had developed strong but unrequited feelings for a woman coworker.[205] Murray didn't disclose these experiences in her autobiography—she recalled the Sharecroppers' Week planning stages when she met with ER, but said little about the week itself. The autobiography simply noted a few of the highlights—which involved activities in more than twenty cities—and left readers to assume her presence, when in fact she was elsewhere.[206]

ON FRIDAY, MARCH 1, 1940, days before National Sharecroppers' Week commenced, state police detained Murray after finding her in an inconsolable state wandering along a highway in Provincetown, Rhode Island. It's not certain what brought her to Provincetown—it seems most likely that she was looking for Peg Holmes, who married and moved to California around this time.[207] The police handed Murray over to a probation officer to escort her into New York police custody. The probation officer recalled, years later, that Murray was dressed in men's attire and stated that she was a "homosexual" who had been taking hormone treatments at Bellevue Hospital to change her sex. New York police took Murray straight to Bellevue, where physicians diagnosed her as schizophrenic.[208] A notice arrived at Pauli and Mac's apartment declaring, "An application will be made to one of the Justices of the Supreme Court . . . for an order committing Pauli Murray to one of the State Hospital[s] as an alleged mentally sick person."[209] Murray's fear that she would "crack up" in the middle of the job had come to fruition.[210]

Mac quickly raised funds among friends to have Pauli transferred to the Rogers Hospital, a private psychiatric hospital. While there, Murray described the symptoms associated with her "nervous collapse." She noted that her regular collapses usually involved a woman: either falling in love with a woman "or finding no opportunity to express such an attraction in normal ways—sex life, marriage, dating, identification with the person and her environment." Murray also believed other people's responses intensified her collapses: she thought males misunderstood and therefore resented her, while women were kind and attracted but unable to respond and thus usually suggested psychiatric care. She wrote, "The unsophisticated people in the environment accept me pretty much as one of nature's experiments; a girl who should have been a boy, and react to me as if I were a boy."

She listed seven questions for which she had no satisfactory answers. Some questions echoed those from her hospital notes from two years earlier—questions about her boyish appearance and male "emotional attitude" and her attractions to heterosexual women—while other questions were new. She asked why her upsets were greatest during menstruation, which she equated with the experiences of menopausal women, prompting her to ask if she might be experiencing a "change of life" at age twenty-nine. Another question was "Do I have tumors which are causing my emotional disturbances? Would the removal of these tumors return me to normal female reactions?" In the final question, despite having been told two years earlier that it was impossible, she again wondered if she might have hidden testicles, and, if menstruation excluded this possibility, "Could it be possible that I have one normally functioning ovary, and one male organ, producing a physical and therefore emotional conflict?"[211]

This "Summary of Symptoms of Upset" identifies sexual preference and gender identity issues as central to the hospitalization. But another missive to Dr. Rogers penned on the same day complicates matters. In "Patient's Analysis of Nervous Collapse," Murray identified ten possible causes—only one related directly to her sexuality and gender identity, point 8, which stated, "Frustration in social adjustment—conflict with regard to sex; inability to integrate homosexual tendencies into a 'socially acceptable' pattern of living."[212] The other nine points relate to concerns about family responsibility, lack of opportunities for creative endeavors, physical well-being, employment anxiety, and the immediate trigger of the shock and anxiety regarding a friend who had gone missing over the weekend of February 23–26. Another potential contributing factor, not identified by Murray, could have been Sharecroppers' Week, where the First Lady of the United States was scheduled to speak at the culminating dinner. Murray had initially doubted her ability and capacity to do the work, then worked exhaustively to make it successful. The event's imminent commencement must have been extremely anxiety-inducing, and her breakdown on the eve of the week's events does not seem entirely coincidental.

Whatever the breakdown's causes, hospitalization had a marked restorative effect on Murray. From her hospital bed, she read about Sharecroppers' Week's successful completion in the *New York Times* and experienced a "quiet joy" over the events, especially the newspaper quotes from Eleanor Roosevelt's closing banquet address. Two days after the banquet, Murray wrote to the First Lady, "I was in the Hospital on the night of the Annual Dinner-Forum for National Sharecroppers Week, and my punishment was that I was unable to hear you speak, or to participate in the activities of our campaign, even by listening over the radio. I am still in the Hospital, but hope to be out by the first of next week." Murray also apologized for criticizing ER's decision to cross the *Abe Lincoln in Illinois* picket line, explaining that the newspaper account she had read didn't include all of Roosevelt's comments on the subject. Several days later, Murray's spirits were further boosted when she received a flower bouquet from ER with a get-well card suggesting a future get-together. Elated by the gesture, Murray took great pleasure from sharing the flowers with patients, staff, and friends.[213]

By March 11, a week after narrowly avoiding a court-ordered commitment to a psychiatric facility, Murray asked if she could leave the Rogers Hospital as early as the following day. She wrote to Dr. Rogers, "Frankly, I have little faith in psychiatric work, but have benefited a great deal from the one or two intellectual conferences we have held." The rest had been enjoyable, she acknowledged, but she was turning thirty in a few months and felt eager to get on with life. Murray outlined her posthospitalization plans, which involved tying up some loose ends on Sharecroppers' Week, then "hibernating" for the spring and summer, possibly at a friend's Vermont family home. If required to stay in New York, she hoped to improve her swimming technique, dance more frequently, take up experimental theater, and pursue an interest in photography. She also hoped that relief, a part-time job, or a loan could cover her financial needs for six months while she focused on her writing.[214] But before pursuing any of these exciting possibilities, Murray and Mac made plans to visit Aunt Pauline for Easter.

. . . . .

VII

Although Murray had been making the trip from New York to Durham for over a decade, she never grew accustomed to segregated bus seating; in fact, the more she experienced it, the more intolerant of it she grew. To her mind, it was the most abhorrent form of segregation because the humiliation was so public. Furthermore, the indifference, and sometimes arrogant swagger, of uniformed white drivers implementing rules that compelled African Americans to fill the bus from the farthest available row back came to remind Murray of Nazi storm troopers. During one trip home, Murray watched, seething, as a woman was forced to stand for many miles balancing a baby in her arms even though the front half of the bus was only sparsely occupied.[215]

For the Easter 1940 trip to Durham, Pauli and Mac hoped to cut costs and avoid segregated public transport by taking public transport only as far as Washington, then borrowing a car from a Murray family member for the remainder of the journey. When they arrived in the capital, they soon realized help would not be forthcoming. Her sister Mildred's car was in the shop. Uncle Bubber, who had criticized Pauli's dresses when she visited Baltimore as a child, refused to loan Pauli a car, then insulted her for wearing pants. Pauli's younger sister Rosetta frankly expressed her disapproval of Pauli and Mac's "friendship," forcing Pauli to listen painfully on the phone while Rosetta "expressed most strongly the attitude of society." Pauli's eldest sister, Grace, wanted to accompany her farther south, but Pauli found her sister "under strain" and in need of a few weeks' rest.[216] Pauli knew about being under strain, having recently been detained by police and hospitalized. She wired Aunt Pauline to let her know that they wouldn't be coming to Durham after all because the pair had no transport or money. Aunt Pauline, eager to see her adopted daughter, wired the bus fare for both Pauli and Mac, leaving Pauli no choice other than to subject herself to further strain on a loathsome segregated bus journey to Durham.

Following her trip last Easter, Murray had written to Trailways criticizing the bus operator's enforcement of segregated seating. Murray also attacked segregated bus station facilities — not only were separate Black facilities not equal, but some stations had no Black facilities at all. As Murray had discovered years earlier when police detained her outside a train station bathroom, public bathrooms could be troublesome sites for biological women who looked like adolescent boys. Race and sex-segregated bathrooms were even more problematic. On one trip home, Murray had needed to use a rest stop bathroom urgently, but there was a line to use the "colored" bathroom. She approached the driver about using the unoccupied "white" bathroom, but he refused her request, telling her to go into the nearby wide-open field, perhaps, though not certainly, assuming she was a boy. In response to Murray's complaint letter, a Trailways representative made the startling claim that "this question of segregation of the races is more embarrassing to us than it is to either of the races. I mean that very seriously." Despite the company's embarrassment, the representative resorted to the familiar refrain: "It seems to be a matter that only the years can work out."[217] A year after her complaint, nothing had changed.

Murray's familiarity with segregated travel's frustrations and humiliations made her nervous about taking Mac to Durham for Easter. She described Mac as "a peppery, self-assertive young woman of West Indian parentage, who had never been confronted with segregation law and believed that southern Negroes were altogether too timid about their rights."[218] Aunt Pauline also consistently discouraged the relationship for reasons that aren't clear.[219] Mac's peppery personality may also have been on show at the Rogers Hospital, where she had organized Pauli's recent admission. Something prompted Murray to write Dr. Rogers a note defending Mac's character and expressing deep regret over "the negative impression" that the doctor had formed of Mac.[220] While Murray valued her girlfriend, she simultaneously worried that others found Mac abrasive.

Someway into the bus journey, Murray's fears about the trip began to materialize. Mac complained of stabbing pain in her side, a discomfort exacerbated by having to ride in a seat situated over a rear wheelbase. Mac wanted to move forward, but Pauli knew that would mean violating segregated seating customs. She approached the driver to ask his permission; he refused and shoved her back with his arm. Pauli and Mac remained in the same seats, with Mac staring at the empty seats in front in an obvious, boiling rage. When the bus stopped to collect more passengers in Petersburg, Virginia — where Grandfather Robert had fought with the Union army — Pauli and Mac took the opportunity to move forward one row, only to realize the seat was broken, so they moved forward another row.[221] They were still behind all the white passengers, but they were violating the segregation custom of African Americans filling the bus from the farthest row back. When the driver noticed, he yelled at the pair, ordering them to move back. When they refused, he left to call the police.

Mac was both less studied in *Satyagraha* and more assertive than Pauli. Fearing the confrontation to follow, Murray took the opportunity to give details to another Black passenger bound for Durham; this passenger promised to contact Aunt Pauline and give her a message to contact the NAACP if the pair got arrested. Murray's autobiography described fellow passengers as otherwise unsupportive: whites pretended it was none of their business and Black passengers murmured but didn't dare interfere. As Murray feared, Mac exploded when the police finally arrived. Mac opened by telling them that they didn't scare her with their "brass buttons and shiny bullets." She fearlessly told them she knew her rights and would not sit in a broken seat while she felt ill. Despite Mac's fiery opening salvo, the two police officers attempted to defuse the situation by asking the driver to repair the seat in the row behind the seats Pauli and Mac occupied. After the driver did so, Murray tested the seat, then Mac agreed to move back one row. Considering the matter settled, the police left.

Mac wasn't quite finished with the driver, though. She told him that he should apologize. According to Murray's autobiography, the driver mumbled something about believing all people deserved a fair go before returning to the front of the bus. Before setting off, the driver decided to distribute incident forms to the white passengers only. Murray described her role in the "ludicrous affair" up until this point as "relatively minor," but she could not tolerate his latest action, which seemed to her the "final damning implication that black people were *nobodies*."[222] When Murray demanded to know why Black passengers weren't issued incident forms too, the driver's fury reignited—he took off after the police, who returned to arrest Pauli and Mac.

The pair did not resist. Murray gathered her typewriter, books, and briefcase and headed toward the front of the bus. A commotion behind caused her to pause—Mac had fainted onto passengers opposite, then had to be half-carried and half-dragged from the bus. The police called for a stretcher, while Pauli looked around for support. There were only "picnic-bound Negroes huddled together in frightened silence" who then boarded the bus, leaving only a crowd of white men. Murray recalled, "As I stood there shivering in the chilly twilight air, worrying over what had happened to Mac, all the horrors of the South which had shaped my childhood and lurked just beneath the level of consciousness came back and left me almost rigid with fear. I had seldom felt so alone and helpless as I did now, surrounded by strange white men who looked on with bawdy amusement."[223]

The police escorted Pauli and Mac to a hospital and then to Petersburg City Prison. Inside they were led down a long corridor and into a fifteen-by-thirty-foot cell with a rank-smelling toilet and rusty sink near the door and four double bunk beds pushed against the whitewashed walls. Each bed had a straw mattress, and a foul-smelling, grease-stained blanket constituted the only bedding. The three other women already occupying the cell warned Pauli and Mac about the bedbugs and the large water bugs that came out at night. The women had no privacy either from each other or from male prisoners, who were separated from the women only by a cell door under which they slid a mirror to keep them under constant watch.

In a "prison notebook" Murray wrote, "To this situation the sensitive, intellectually aware Negro woman is brought—with a hodge-podge of training in various Negro and mixed public schools, a hatred for filth and uncleanness, a resentment against inequality, and an almost pathetic loyalty to her racial group. She is most astonished at the relation of the Negro prisoners among themselves."[224] At first, the prisoners' slang intrigued her, but as time dragged on she attributed the monotonous "obscene, indecencies" to the "limited knowledge of the English language" of the "rural-Southern

Negro." For their part, the other prisoners mocked Pauli as an "uppity nigger" for requesting clean linen and hygiene products.[225] Pauli and Mac were
practicing *Satyagraha*—asserting dignified resistance to unjust treatment—
and once they explained this, other prisoners became supportive and even
began asking the pair for legal advice.[226]

It's easy to see why other prisoners turned to Murray for help: few other
prisoners could match her array of influential contacts. From jail Murray
reiterated her request for NAACP assistance, wiring Aunt Pauline, "EASTER
GRETTINGS. ARRESSTED. PETERSBURG WARRANT GREYHOUND BUS.
DON'T WORRY. CONTACT WALTER WHITE."[227] At the NAACP's behest, a
local lawyer soon visited Pauli and Mac. The New York–based Workers Defense League, whom Murray had worked with on Sharecroppers' Week, also
asked a local lawyer to investigate. Murray's sister Mildred contacted the
First Lady, who in turn appealed to Virginia's governor (he refused to intervene).[228] Three days after their arrest, Pauli and Mac appeared in a packed
courthouse represented by two lawyers. Murray gave evidence stressing
their dignified opposition to segregation customs but, predictably, the judge
still found them guilty of disturbing the peace and disorderly conduct and
fined them five dollars each plus court costs.[229] The defense lawyers immediately lodged an appeal.

Friends urged Pauli and Mac to go to prison to continue practicing *Satya-
grahi* until the appeal could be heard, but instead the pair decided to visit
Aunt Pauline and Aunt Sallie. Murray had been worried about how her
aunts would cope with the news of her arrest. From prison she had written
to an NAACP official, "Both Mrs. Dame and Mrs. Small are in poor health
and the anxiety and concern over our delay may cause serious illness on
their part."[230] Mac was also under the care of a physician from the "shock
and strain of the whole nightmare."[231] Murray herself was barely two weeks
out of a psychiatric hospital. It can't have raised anyone's spirits when, following the court case, they boarded the bus to Durham and saw that the
driver was the very same one who had requested their arrest days earlier.
He acted with the utmost courtesy, however, and according to Murray, her
and Mac's resistance to mistreatment sparked a change of policy toward
Negro patrons on the part of Greyhound, evidenced by the presence of two
guards on the bus.[232]

Pauli and Mac's lawyers remained hopeful that the appeal could be used
to test the constitutionality of segregated public transport. NAACP leaders
Charles Hamilton Houston, Thurgood Marshall, and Walter White all corresponded with each other and local lawyers about the case. A Petersburg
lawyer wrote to Pauli and Mac describing it as a potentially "far reaching

case," a phrase Murray underlined.[233] Pauli traveled to Washington to prepare for the case and excitedly reported to Aunt Pauline on April 25, "On Sunday afternoon, we're meeting with Attorney's Hastie, Marshall, Hill and Valentine (crack legal team of the NAACP) to work out evidence, testimony, etc. They seem to think we have a fine legal case, and they want us to stick right with them until it is finished."[234] Pauli and Mac returned to Petersburg for their appeal in early May.

Murray's dreams of being the defendant in a landmark legal challenge to segregation suffered a blow when the appeals court judge upheld the original verdict. An NAACP lawyer succeeded in getting a rehearing to argue that the state was pursuing segregation charges indirectly via the disorderly conduct charges. The judge heard the matter again four days later, only to again uphold the original verdict. The NAACP then dropped all interest in the case. Although disappointed in the decision, Murray claimed in her autobiography that she understood the NAACP's legal reasoning and that she and Mac "preferred to go back to jail rather than pay the fine."[235]

Her private correspondence reveals a different story. The NAACP's sudden withdrawal from the case shocked and hurt Murray. William Hastie, chairman of the National Legal Committee, could not even be contacted following the unsuccessful appeal. The Petersburg lawyers representing Murray called Hastie's office and learned that he was out of town until Tuesday, at which time they learned the NAACP thought a further appeal would be inadvisable. A further appeal would cost $300, and the only issue at stake would be whether "hysteria" and "raised voices" in the assertion of one's rights constituted disorderly conduct.[236]

On the day she went to prison, Murray wrote hurriedly to the Workers Defense League to see if they would appeal the case, but two days later she received a reply stating that their lawyers also thought an appeal was inadvisable.[237] The NAACP also refused to pay the pair's fines, since they had no precedent for paying defendants' fines. The local Petersburg NAACP branch had not raised money for the fines either. Pauli and Mac certainly didn't have the money—Murray had debts to pay off relating to her recent hospitalization. The NAACP's withdrawal from the case and refusal to pay the fines meant Pauli and Mac went to prison not out of preference but because they had no other option. After the pair had spent two days in prison, the Workers Defense League, which had covered most of the legal costs associated with the case, paid the fines so that they could leave prison.[238]

At the time of the event, Murray described the NAACP's actions as "disgusting." Her life had been disrupted for two months, and she and Mac had incurred expenses traveling back to Petersburg for two appeal hearings.

Pauli confided to Aunt Pauline, "We feel particularly badly, because they led us to believe that the case had such far-reaching implications that they were going to see it through. Then a white organization had to raise money to get us out of prison, which is bad for the prestige for a Negro organization like the NAACP. . . . I feel disillusioned and disappointed about the whole thing. The time wasted and the money spent in the thing might have been avoided and we could have paid a lower fine in the first place if we weren't going to fight the case through."[239]

Murray's adoptive mother showed little sympathy—she advised Pauli to "keep out of these radical things." Aunt Pauline blamed Mac for the arrest, writing, "Had you come alone, I do not believe you would have had that trouble but you would not take my advice." On a roll, Aunt Pauline continued, "You have placed yourself in the limelight all over the country. It is passed for the present and cannot now be remedied, but you can be careful as you go on." As she was prone to do, Aunt Pauline then switched: "I'm very sorry you've had to suffer so much, but such is life. . . . I do hope you can find something to your liking soon and not work too hard."[240]

Murray's autobiography put a much more uplifting spin on events: "Having now faced the fear of Southern justice," she wrote, she never again regarded it with the same terror. Murray concluded the chapter on the incident by stating, "The episode convinced me that creative nonviolent resistance could be a powerful weapon in the struggle for human dignity."[241] Such a claim is plausible only in an autobiographical narrative about overcoming discrimination written decades later, when she could highlight her groundbreaking part in the later victories of the civil rights movement. She couldn't have felt empowered in 1940 while sitting in prison wondering why the NAACP had suddenly abandoned her for the second time in two years.

MURRAY'S AUTOBIOGRAPHY ALSO MADE no mention of an eyewitness account, since uncovered by historian Glenda Gilmore.[242] Two days after Pauli and Mac left prison, a story about the arrest appeared in the May issue of *Opportunity*, the Urban League's journal, for which Murray had sold subscriptions in 1933.[243] In a further coincidence, the eyewitness was a sociology graduate student at the University of North Carolina, just as Murray had applied to be the year before. The eyewitness report mirrored Murray's version in many ways, but there were also discrepancies. Mac is even more assertive in the eyewitness account. The eyewitness, Harold Garfinkel, claimed that the dispute flared again not because Murray objected to the driver's issuing incident forms to white passengers only but because of Mac's demand for an apology from the driver. Garfinkel's version seems more plausible—a white bus driver who insisted that Black passengers move to the back of the bus only to be defied and subsequently delayed by two hours while he had to call his employers and the police would surely have reacted more strongly to Mac demanding an apology.

The other, more significant discrepancy between the accounts is Garfinkel's revelation that Murray was deliberately passing as a man at the time of the arrest. Garfinkel described Mac as "slender, light colored, but not very good looking." The description of Pauli was even less complimentary: "The young man with her was lighter than she, of slight build, thin shoulders, flat chest, sensitive, self-conscious in voice and manner."[244] The description grew even more unflattering: "His voice was just a bit too loud and too clear, an arrogant adolescent repeating by rote. Clearly he was not the one to deal with. The whites were not attracted to him because he was neither white nor black, spoke like neither, and threatened to upset a good fight." Garfinkel believed the nearly thirty-year-old biological female was an adolescent boy, as did other passengers. A white passenger is quoted as saying, "Why doesn't that guy shut up and let her [Mac] do the talking?"[245] Given Murray's fluctuating self-esteem, reading this account must have been devastating, both as a humiliating public description of her personhood and because the revelation of her gender passing might have influenced the NAACP's decision to withdraw from the case.

The intentionality of Murray's masculine gender expression is clear in Garfinkel's account. He accurately recalled Mac's surname, which she gave to the police on the bus, suggesting that Garfinkel either took notes during the incident or had an impressive memory. According to his account, when the police officers then asked for Murray's name, she answered, "Oliver Fleming."[246] Oliver Fleming wasn't simply Garfinkel's invention or a fake name made up by Murray on the spot: like Peter Pan and "the dude," it was an alter ego. Murray constructed the pseudonym from combining the first and last names of two characters from *Oliver Twist*—the first name of the title character and the surname of Oliver's deceased mother, Agnes Fleming.[247] Evidently, Murray strongly identified with Oliver—both were orphans with a deceased mother named Agnes struggling to survive deep impoverishment.

"Oliver Fleming" is a minor and unappealing participant in Garfinkel's account. Garfinkel described McBean as "abrasive" and Oliver Fleming as "cringing" when the police arrived on the scene. After the driver fixed the broken seat, Garfinkel described Oliver Fleming as trying to defuse the situation: "The young man with her [Mac] revealed himself as the weaker of the two by the spirit of his acceptance. While speaking he glanced quickly from one face to the other. 'Alice, that's fair enough. Isn't it? I think that's fair enough. Don't you? He's willing to meet us half way and I think we ought to do the same.'"[248] Garfinkel couldn't know Murray's obvious reason for such apprehension: she had middle-class values of respectability instilled in her; she was violating both racial and gender codes; she was more familiar with the dangers of the South than Mac; arrest was a distinct possibility; and, worse still, lynching was a real threat, especially considering the levels of transgression involved.

The accurate recall of so many details by Garfinkel ensured that anyone aware of the incident who read the May issue of *Opportunity* would immediately recognize Murray as Oliver Fleming. No doubt, many people read Garfinkel's story—*Opportunity* enjoyed a wide circulation among African Americans. Aunt Pauline heard about it. She wrote to Pauli asking, "I'm told that there is an article written about the Greyhound incident. No one seems to know to what race the writer belongs, but I'm told he tells just what happened from Richmond Va. to Petersburg Va. You were called a boy 'Fleming,' I'm told the other name they got right. If you can get [the article] send it to me."[249] Publicly, Murray never mentioned the hurtful report; privately, she worried that the NAACP abandoned her case because of it. She wrote to her Petersburg lawyers describing Garfinkel's account as "inaccurate" and "fictionary," and probed, "We were wondering if this article had anything to do with a change of opinion on the part of Attorney Hastie."[250] If she received a reply, she didn't keep it. As with the NAACP's decision not to pursue her case against UNC, Murray was again left to wonder if they had withdrawn from her case for reasons that had nothing to do with its legal merits.

Since the publication of Garfinkel's story, many people have assumed that it was fiction, such was the unlikelihood of such a defiant protest. Without consulting Garfinkel, the editors of *The Best Short Stories of 1941* reprinted "Color Trouble" as a work of fiction, preceded by a William Faulkner short story, and it appeared again in *Primer for White Folks* in 1945.[251] It was more than a little ironic that Murray, who longed to be a successful writer, had her real-life experience, which she never fully acknowledged, turned into a highly successful story almost unwittingly by a white student from the graduate school that had rejected her the year before. Garfinkel also titled his story "Color Trouble," the same title Murray had used for a poem she wrote two years before the bus incident.[252] In yet another coincidence, after graduating from UNC Garfinkel went on to become a distinguished sociologist, establishing the field of ethnomethodology and writing about "transgender shaming."[253] "Color Trouble" featured again in a 1989 scholarly article tracing the development of Garfinkel's ethnomethodology through this earlier "literary work."[254] Garfinkel recalled the Greyhound bus incident late in life but remained unaware that Oliver Fleming was transgender until Glenda Gilmore interviewed him shortly before his death.[255] A May 2011 obituary of Garfinkel published in the *New York Times* also mentioned his short story.[256] Challenging segregation in such a bold manner in 1940 seems like a fictional story—that the adolescent boy Oliver Fleming was actually a twenty-nine-year-old biological woman was beyond even imagining and something Murray could never claim ownership of in her lifetime.

three

AN UNKNOWN NEGRO GIRL

WITHOUT TITLE OR PRESTIGE,

1940–1946

.....

I

Murray spent much of the 1940 summer and fall attending Workers Defense League (WDL) committee meetings in New York. The WDL had been established by the Socialist Party in 1936 to provide legal representation for labor causes.[1] She really didn't know what use she could be to the organization. She felt bored and useless and attended simply because she felt indebted to the WDL for paying the costs associated with her arrest in Virginia and because they soon began paying her to do administrative work. Murray's apathy about WDL meetings changed dramatically when the board began discussing a murder case involving a Black sharecropper from Gretna, Virginia—only 125 miles from where Pauli and Mac had been jailed a few months earlier.[2]

Twenty-three years old, short and stocky, Odell Waller had worked for the past two years, sometimes directly and sometimes indirectly, for his white landlord, Oscar Davis. Davis didn't own the property either: he rented it and invited Odell Waller to farm a portion of the land in exchange for a share of the crop. Davis got three-quarters of the wheat and corn, as well as half of the tobacco Waller produced. The arrangement had worked satisfactorily enough for a year, but in the second year a freezing winter and a government cutback in the tobacco crop added strain to the relationship. The widespread phenomenon of sharecropping relied on the goodwill of all involved rather than legal contracts. But in early 1940 Odell Waller's goodwill for his landlord ran out. He believed Davis demonstrated none toward him

Murray writing a poem on Riverside Drive, New York City, ca. 1938 or 1939. *(Schlesinger Library, Radcliffe Institute, Harvard University)*

and simply exploited his willingness to work. Waller went off to work for another man, and in Waller's absence Davis called the sheriff to evict Waller's wife and mother from the property. Waller returned to the property on July 15, 1940, to claim his share of the crop. A dispute occurred, and Waller shot his white landlord four times, fatally wounding him.[3]

A posse of white men with dogs pursued Waller as he ran for his life. The manhunt became national news. Waller remained at large for nine days until his capture in Ohio.[4] A small Trotskyist organization, the Revolutionary Workers League (RWL), became interested in the case. The RWL did not have its own legal organization—the group was too small for that. Instead they enlisted a local Virginia lawyer, Thomas H. Stone, to represent Waller. Murray's organization, the WDL, also became interested in the case, but Trotskyist involvement concerned them. The WDL secretary-treasurer told Tom Stone, "If we decide to handle the case and give it widespread publicity it will be necessary for RWL to withdraw from active sponsorship; this political angle should not be allowed to prejudice Waller's chances and we would not want to risk the 'Red issue' being introduced on either side."[5] The RWL declined to withdraw, so Stone was Waller's sole representation at the murder trial.

Stone didn't have a law degree—it wasn't a requirement in Virginia at the time—and had only three days to prepare for a murder trial. At the trial, which began on September 19, 1940, Stone argued self-defense, telling the all-white male jurors that Waller shot Davis because he believed Davis had reached for a weapon. The trial ended after two days: the jury, which included eleven farmers, six of whom employed sharecroppers, took less than an hour to find Waller guilty. Waller was sentenced to die in the electric chair on December 27, 1940.[6] Just two and half months had elapsed since Waller shot Oscar Davis.

Murray's interest became fully awakened when the WDL executive board decided to join the case for the appeal, despite reservations about Trotskyist involvement.[7] Her interest immediately turned to apprehension, however, when the board further proposed that she travel to Virginia to raise support and funds for Waller's appeal.[8] In notes she made shortly after, she wrote, "Everybody began looking at me with one of those 'it's-one-of-your-own-race-you-ought-to-do-something-about-it' expressions. I was flabbergasted. In the first place I had sworn to myself never to go South again and in the second place I'd never taken on so much responsibility in my whole life. I knew nothing about handling a murder case, had no experience in raising money and had never spoken publicly more than once or twice—both times I was rigid with fear when I faced the audience. I doubted my ability to confront Southern whites face-to-face. For them I held little beyond a robust contempt."[9] Murray rarely seemed confident at the outset of jobs, but her concern in this case is especially understandable given her arrest and imprisonment in Virginia earlier in the year.

Murray raised objections around the fact she had never done any work like it before, but she was told there was simply no one else available—if she didn't go, then no one would, and the WDL wouldn't be in a position to fight Waller's execution. She also expressed extreme reluctance if it meant going back to Virginia on a segregated bus. A WDL supporter agreed to loan Murray her car. Pauli's friend, Gene Phillips, also agreed to accompany her.[10]

Yet the support offered by Phillips created another potential problem because Philips was white. Murray had traveled with white women before, but never to the South. She noted in her journal, "However free our relations might be in New York, we were expected to be separate in all our dealings once below the Mason Dixon line. A Negro and a white traveling together in the absolute South was defying the Jim Crow gods too much. We would scare immediately all liberals of both races into the belief we were Communists. Where would we stay—how would we eat?"[11]

THE PAIR SET OFF ON Election Day, November 5, 1940. They avoided problems during the journey by eating their own packed food in the car and staying with Pauli's relatives.[12] They spent the first night with a Fitzgerald relative, Cousin Sadie. According to Pauli's diary, Sadie assumed Gene Philips was Black until Philips failed to offer "the usual personal experiences about 'passing' which any 'fair' Negro is expected to boast of among other Negroes." In the morning, Sadie asked Pauli about Gene's race. When Sadie learned Gene was white, she told Pauli that they were "taking an awful chance" traveling together in the South.

After arriving in Richmond, a local socialist offered them accommodation in his home in a poor white section of town. Murray recalled apprehensively slipping in and out of the place. She had hoped that she could canvass the Black community while Phillips approached white sympathizers, but given the lack of transport options, there was no alternative other than to canvass together. They first called on the home of a white union leader whose wife had agreed to meet with them. Murray wanted to remain in the car when they arrived, but Phillips insisted she come. "Contrary to the experience of many Negroes who come from the South," Murray revealed,

I had never had personal dealings with whites except in official relations or in some business establishment. My ideas were not at all clear as to the folkways which flow between the races. I didn't know whether a Negro who comes to the door of a white residence in some other capacity than a servant is expected to use the front or the back entrance. I have never known whether such a Negro is expected to transact his business standing on the front porch or whether he will be invited in to sit down. Rather than risk the embarrassment I preferred to stay outside. These thoughts, not the Waller case, were uppermost in my mind as I rang Mrs. Squires' bell.[13]

Despite her fears, Murray experienced no ill treatment from any of the white liberals she met, but nor did she enlist much support for Waller's cause.

White liberals were sympathetic but unwilling to become involved in a legal case handled by Tom Stone, whom many local liberals viewed as a "dangerous radical."[14] Stone's past as a local Communist Party leader alienated liberals, socialists, and unionists. Murray revealed her own growing anticommunist tendency when she described herself as "intolerant" of Trotskyists.[15] She also had personal reasons to be wary of Stone. Murray did not reveal it then or later, but she already knew him—he had worked on her appeal following her Greyhound bus arrest earlier in the year.[16] For all she knew, Stone could have read the *Opportunity* article describing her as Oliver Fleming. As with so many of her responses to situations, a personal, anxiety-inducing element potentially complicated her activism.

Murray fared little better when presenting Waller's cause to Black community leaders. They were reluctant to become involved in the Waller case due to financial hardship and a belief that there were campaigns worthier of support, such as securing additional funding for Black schools and teachers. Comparatively, the case of a Black sharecropper who had admitted shooting a white man seemed both a lost cause and a disreputable one. Black community leaders also expressed concern about the organization Murray represented, which was unknown to them and therefore no more reputable than the Trotskyist RWL.

One experience at Virginia Union University thoroughly dejected and humiliated Murray. The professor with whom she had arranged the speaking engagement expected—after hearing Murray's voice on the telephone—a white speaker, but when Murray arrived he took one look at her and told her his superiors would never allow her to speak. Murray already felt upset, because she had driven over three hours that morning following an overnight visit with Aunt Pauline and then had a minor collision parking the car at the college. The rejection made Murray feel worse. It made her feel physically sick and led her to wonder if Waller was to die because "an unknown Negro girl without title or prestige came to plead his cause."[17]

Murray had little time for further lamentation. She had another speaking engagement that afternoon at a Black ministers' meeting where local church leaders gathered to discuss community issues and hear appeals to support various causes. Before Murray addressed the ministers, Dr. Leon A. Ransom, a lawyer and educator from Howard University, spoke about raising money for the NAACP to defend four young Black men accused of raping a white woman. As she listened to Ransom's confident articulation of the case, an exhausted Murray became increasingly dejected. When Ransom's address ended, she watched the ministers rush forward with donations and lost all hope. Murray tried to slip out of the meeting, but the organizer noticed her and called on her to speak. As she stood before the crowd of men she became overwhelmed and burst into sobbing tears. Unable to go on, the meeting organizer read her prepared notes for her. Murray regained enough composure then to pour out her feelings about the past week of failing to find anyone to help "this unknown, friendless sharecropper." The ministers all donated money, so Murray left the meeting with twenty-five dollars, making it far and away her most successful fundraising effort.[18]

The whole trip only raised $37.50 in cash, which barely covered expenses. A thoroughly dejected Murray drove the borrowed car back to New York through thick fog and an icy rainstorm, having to hold her head half out the window so she could see the road because the old car's wiper didn't work. The miserable journey felt like a fitting end to a failed mission.[19] Murray's report to the WDL focused on the RWL and Waller's lawyer; she recommended that Stone be persuaded to accept another lawyer as associate counsel and restrain his radicalism to avoid alienating public opinion. She concluded, "Frankly, if a man's life were not at stake, we would recommend that the WDL withdraw from the case because of these complications."[20] Although it didn't make it into her report, the trip did have one fortuitous personal benefit—Dr. Ransom told her, after they had both addressed the ministers' meeting, that she should consider studying law at Howard University, to which she replied, her bravado restored, that she would if she received a scholarship.[21]

DESPITE MURRAY'S DOWNBEAT REPORT, the WDL executive board pursued the Waller case and asked her to work full time on the campaign, which she did with a typically exhaustive effort. She initiated a correspondence with Odell Waller on death row, writing: "We want you to feel encouraged and to know that you have thousands of friends all over the country. . . . Try to keep well and strong because you have a tough job ahead of you. Many people are praying for you." She also enclosed two dollars "for your needs." Waller replied, "[I] was more than glad to hear from you and I know I have some friends same time I think every one have gone against me."[22] Murray also wrote to high-profile citizens to enlist their support, including prolific public intellectual John Dewey, who in turn campaigned vigorously for Waller.[23] Murray wrote to Eleanor Roosevelt about the case, and the First Lady forwarded the letter to Virginia governor James H. Price, requesting that he "look into the case and see that the young man has a fair trial." Price responded that he would ensure Waller's defense team had adequate time to prepare for a Supreme Court hearing.[24]

Murray wrote to ER during another exhausting workday, which also happened to be her thirtieth birthday. The only celebration she had entailed "a soul-searching session with myself after everyone had left the office." Murray reflected on her sketchy work history since finishing college seven years prior and concluded that she had lived a "grubby existence" in rented rooms on the "fringes of society." The reflection ended with her writing to Howard University Law School requesting an application form. She recalled it as a "tentative gesture" rather than "an act of firm decision," such was her uncertainty and lack of confidence.[25] Although edging toward abandoning a life outside the mainstream to pursue a professional vocation, Murray wasn't quite ready yet.

In December 1940, shortly after sending off the application, Pauli parted ways with her cousins. Along with Mac, she moved into the "Harlem Ashram," which she described as a Gandhi-inspired experiment in interracial, interfaith, cooperative living.[26] Other innovators of the nonviolent civil rights movement also resided at, or visited, the Ashram at various times, including James Farmer and Bayard Rustin. Like others among the notable contacts she accumulated through her restless involvement in various groups and activities, Murray immersed herself in ideas that had been utilized with great success in the Indian independence movement. She remained committed to pacifism for the remainder of her life, but she couldn't remain committed to the Ashram for more than a few months.

The experiment in cooperative living soured during an Ashram dinner attended by celebrated pacifist activist A. J. Muste. After eating, everyone adjourned to the living room to talk with Muste. When Murray, a lifelong heavy smoker, reached for a cigarette another Ashram resident, Haridas, touched Murray's arm and whispered, "No smoking." Murray replied that she would go upstairs to her room for a few minutes. While smoking in her room, she began ruminating on the incident. She decided not to go back downstairs to rejoin the company, which included some friends she had invited to the Ashram for the occasion. At 5:30 A.M. the following morning, she recorded in her diary, "I agree with Haridas that we must have discipline, but it must be self-imposed, not dictated from without. . . . I did not feel that I could co-operate with Haridas last night. His action would have made me feel artificial and a very resentful person in the group. . . . If the ashram is to become a convent or a monastery, then I have no place here."[27] Murray had trouble finding a place anywhere—the Ashram was her fourteenth permanent residence in the past five years alone.[28]

Despite ongoing instability in her living arrangements and career plans, Murray continued working on the Waller campaign at a relentless pace. In addition to putting together literature, corresponding with Waller and others connected to the case, and traveling to Virginia twice, Murray also spoke at two or three church, labor, or other organizations each day with Waller's adoptive mother, who came to New York to help with fundraising during November and December 1940.[29] Annie Waller's speaking events in New York helped raise over $1,000 and brought Waller's appeal national media attention. John F. Finerty, a high-profile lawyer who had represented Sacco and Vanzetti, joined Waller's legal team to argue the constitutional issues on appeal.[30] The campaign gained further impetus and a significant victory when Waller received a reprieve from imminent execution—the execution date changed from December 27 to March 14, 1941, the first of several reprieves.[31]

The campaign still experienced ongoing challenges. In mid-December, the Trotskyist RWL tried to get Waller's birth mother, Dollie Harris, to go to Cleveland and Chicago to speak at meetings. The WDL had planned speaking events for Waller's adoptive mother, Annie Waller, at a similar time. Things were in danger of becoming seriously confused—two organizations with similar names, the Revolutionary Workers League (RWL) and the Workers Defense League (WDL), were organizing speaking events for two Waller mothers. Murray wrote to Waller's adoptive mother imploring her to get Waller's birth mother to decline the RWL: "If other organizations enter the field and confuse things by suggesting tours for Mrs. Harris, the public will become confused and will ignore the whole case."[32] It must have been a bewildering experience for the two women desperate to help save Odell's life, but Annie Waller acted on Murray's advice, persuading Mrs. Harris to decline the RWL invitation.

Although Murray averted the confusing possibility of rival speaking events, the RWL's continuing involvement infuriated her. On December 28, 1940, she tried to end it once and for all by writing a long letter to Odell Waller asking him to decide which group should be responsible for organizing the campaign to save his life. She wrote, "You must make the choice as whether you want to be represented by the Workers Defense League and its cooperating groups, or whether you want to be represented by the Richmond Waller Defense Committee [established by the RWL] or any other organization which may seek to aid you. I CANNOT MAKE THAT CHOICE

FOR YOU OR INFLUENCE YOUR DECISION." Murray did seek to influence his decision, however. In the same letter she noted that the RWL "is not a defense agency; it is a political group, very small and with but a few members in the country. . . . It has been our experience that such a group is more interested in making publicity out of the case than it is in saving the life of the person involved." After writing to Waller, Murray wrote to the WDL leadership to explain her unilateral action: "There was only one recourse—to shoot the works." If it didn't work, she continued, "I'm ready to recommend that the Workers Defense League withdraw from the case and make a public statement as to its reasons."[33] The suggestion reveals more about Murray's hot temper and impulsivity than a serious proposal. Given how much energy she and others had already devoted to the campaign, and the desperate stakes of a man's life, withdrawing completely from the case would have been a remarkable course of action.

Rather than withdraw, Murray became more deeply involved in the case. She somehow managed to wangle her way in to visit Odell Waller in his death row prison cell despite a rule limiting visitors to lawyers, spiritual advisers, and family. Murray only spoke with Waller for a few minutes, but it was long enough to convince her that Waller didn't kill premeditatedly and to make her a lifelong opponent of capital punishment.[34] She also emerged from the visit with a letter from Waller to the WDL-employed lawyer, John F. Finerty, stating, "I want you to take my case in your hands and doo what you can I want you to Represent me as my Attorney in all matters Regarding my case. I will except what ever decision you make until Further notice. I understand you Represent the Workers Defense League, the sole Organization I give power to handle my case."[35] It must have been a vexing development for a man on death row, desperate for any help he could get, but like his adoptive and biological mothers, Waller put his trust in Murray and the WDL.

It was all in vain, though. The RWL weren't inclined to end their involvement simply because Waller no longer desired it. RWL members were difficult to work with. The group's origins dated back to a small group of Trotskyists expelled from the Communist Party in 1928. They then joined the American Workers Party only to be expelled from that organization in 1935, after which they formed their own group. According to one former member, "It was all downhill from the start." The group failed to recruit new members and founding members departed following numerous splits.[36] That Murray found this group difficult to work with is hardly surprising. Yet despite convincing the Waller family of the RWL's potential to damage the campaign, there was no option other than to accept the group's presence, since they refused to go away. The lawyer that the RWL had retained to represent Waller during the initial trial, Tom Stone, was also still needed, since Virginia law required that defendants be represented by a lawyer registered in the state.

MURRAY ADDED HER KNOWLEDGE TO the efforts of freelance journalist and later Pulitzer Prize winner Murray Kempton, in a pamphlet titled *All for Mr. Davis: The Story of Sharecropper Odell Waller*. The authors noted that Virginia had a voluntary $1.50 poll tax that had to be paid for three consecutive years before a person could vote. The tax couldn't be afforded by most of Pittsylvania County's African American residents, who were sharecroppers receiving as little as thirty-eight dollars a year. Of the county's 61,000 residents, 25,000 were Black, yet only 200 African Americans were eligible to vote. Since juries were typically recruited through voter rolls, a person who didn't pay the tax was highly unlikely to serve on a jury. Murray and Kempton therefore explained that Waller had not been judged by a jury of his peers, since the jurors in his trial were white farmers, most of whom employed sharecroppers. The authors effectively linked the local tragedy of Waller's case to the national issue of poll taxes, which was becoming a major political issue in the early 1940s, placing Murray at the forefront of another social justice campaign.[37]

Her ceaseless efforts on the Waller campaign continued into the New Year when the WDL sent her on a speaking tour with Annie Waller. Beginning on January 7 the pair made twenty-two speaking appearances in twenty days, addressing nearly seven thousand people in Chicago, Minneapolis, and Detroit. Murray enjoyed the freedom of the westward train journey, contrasting it with the Jim Crow rail cars. "I felt like a free human being for the first time in my life," she recalled. When the pair returned to New York, Murray again introduced Annie Waller before a mass meeting at the Abyssinian Baptist Church in New York, where Reverend Adam Clayton Powell, who also addressed the meeting, had launched homophobic campaigns a decade earlier. Through Murray's determined efforts, the Waller case was now by far the biggest project undertaken by the WDL, in terms of money raised and spent as well as national profile.[38]

The successful midwestern tour led the WDL to arrange a six-week national tour for Murray and Annie Waller in late April 1941. The pair visited major cities from coast to coast raising defense funds and awareness about the plight of some 9 million sharecroppers — Mrs. Waller provided the personal story of Odell's life, while Murray spoke of the broader inequalities of sharecropping and the poll tax. The Black press gave the tours widespread publicity. One journalist described Murray as "a slim, lissome and almost exquisitely pretty colored girl," while another described her as "a bright young city woman, educated, aggressive and articulate," and another remarked, "Frankly I thought of Joan of Arc when she spoke, and wondered if at some fortuitous time she might not become something of a deliverer of her people from bondage, from long-suffering ghastly indignities."[39] Murray's confidence had grown immeasurably since the campaign's beginning, when she expressed dread at the thought of public speaking.

She also gained confidence from being partnered with Annie Waller. Murray described their presentation in her autobiography: "Mrs. Waller would tell her personal story, 'crudely, honestly, touchingly,' as one reporter put it, and I would follow with a factual presentation of conditions among sharecroppers and the evils of the poll tax system."[40] In her diary, Murray described feeling torn between embarrassment and amusement at Mrs. Waller's appearance. While on a train journey between speaking engagements, she speculated on how others might view Annie Waller: "She is the only kind of her species ever seen by some of these mountain natives, I'm sure. One would observe that her young companion treats her with far too much deference for a maid and yet with too much reserve for a relative. I am filled with glee to note the gaping curiosity of the other passengers who would give a silver dollar to know who this incongruous couple are, *where* they came from, and *why on earth* they are going to Seattle."[41] Murray had long been acutely self-conscious, but now delighted in the role of race spokesperson and her sense of mission—a rare and empowering experience for someone so typically made to feel like a "nobody." Yet just as Murray imagined her fellow passengers' confusion about her, she still remained uncertain about who she wanted to be.

During the midwestern tour in January, Murray received a heartfelt letter from a coworker at the WDL, possibly Mac, though the letter is unsigned. The author pleaded with Pauli to accept herself as part of a third sex and not seek to change herself: "Although few people are willing to accept this fact, there definitely are three classes of human beings; the true man, the true woman and the homosexual. If you have tendencies to swerve toward the third class, then that is where you belong. Why try to change yourself?" The writer urged Murray to consider the other person involved: "Since you have this desire, then, as far as I am concerned you may go and never again will I think of you. The life you wish to enter into does not appeal to me, and I would rather forget about you, now, than keep on yearning for someone who has departed this life."[42] If Murray responded to this letter, she did not keep a copy.

One month after receiving the unsigned letter, Murray reflected on her relationship with Mac in a diary entry. "It came to me in a flash tonight," she wrote, "what [is] the peculiar mutual constitution Mac and I have given to each other. We are realists—we see the worst side each of the other [and] do not hesitate to inform the other fellow. It's hard medicine, but perhaps it has a purging effect."[43] Murray's relationship conflicts were matched by inner conflicts that were not only about gender identity and sexual preference. Murray felt conflicted between wanting to pursue identities and roles she associated with personal fulfillment and those she associated with responsibility. She described herself as carrying "the shell of a young woman of causes, when the elfin Pete, the lover of simple things, the vagabond spirit is lost and alone. . . . The poet looks at his ghost and walks behind the shell with bowed head and mute sorrow. Someday perhaps!"[44]

Increasing unhappiness with her working life is also evident in Murray's personal correspondence. Murray told a friend that she had never been keen on the WDL position and continued the work mostly out of loyalty to Morris Milgram, a WDL executive board member. She also confessed turning down a permanent position: "Frankly, the WDL needed someone to go to work immediately, and I am worn out, organizationally, from the hectic life of the past eight months. Secondly, I don't want to continue with the conflict of desire still disrupting my work. As long as I fight back the impulse to write, I can't give my best to any job. I've got to be sure of the direction in which I'm going by the end of this summer. It's almost now or never."[45] Murray had once again exhausted herself. Despite bonding with Mrs. Waller during two tours and meeting with Odell on death row, after completing the national tour Murray left the Waller campaign and she only briefly returned to paid work for the WDL a year later.

. . . . .

III

Through WDL contacts, Murray spent most of the 1941 summer in the Catskills Mountains. She shared a secluded two-room cabin, positioned on a cliff edge toward the top of Mount Airy, with only a newly acquired puppy, Petie, until Mac's unplanned arrival. Mac had gotten a summer job at a nearby sanitarium but quit after one day because, in Mac's words, the employer needed "two mules—not a human being."[46] Mac's arrival created some initial tension, but otherwise Pauli relished the opportunity, describing it as "an idyllic setting free from pressures." Murray sat on the screened porch wearing only a pair of shorts, feeling the crisp mountain air on her skin and taking inspiration from the spectacular views—on clear days she could see as far as the Berkshires in Massachusetts—while she smoked and typed. When the words didn't come, she would take Petie for walks in the surrounding woods.[47]

Murray mostly wrote autobiographical short stories, which she had been urged to write by the poet Stephen Vincent Benét, whom she regularly sent her draft poetry, prose, and journalism. He often promptly replied with a host of criticisms and even more encouragement.[48] The year before he had told her, "You seem to be —, well, loosening up a little is the way I'd put it — writing with more fluency and freedom. . . . You have such rich material, once you have learned to smelt it out at the core. And I think you are learning."[49] Loosening up was easier said than done, however. Murray rarely enjoyed prolonged time periods to focus on her writing, and even when she did, she could not write openly about all her experiences without examining painful memories. Murray struggled with fashioning her many negative life experiences into a positive, coherent story of self, which identity scholars refer to as establishing a "narrative self."[50] She felt further constrained in what she could write about if she intended to publish the stories, because of the potential impact on her surviving family members.

The tension between wanting to publish stories about her life and feeling unable to reveal all her experiences is evident in her autobiographical account of her decision to enter law school at the end of the summer. Murray's "tentative gesture" of applying for Howard University Law School on her thirtieth birthday resulted in a surprise offer of a tuition scholarship. Her autobiography described two incidents that convinced her to halt her creative writing and accept the Howard offer. Both incidents involved racial discrimination in New York City, but one of the incidents was only partially recounted. Murray described a building superintendent racially abusing her when she was housesitting for WDL executive director Morris Milgram at his apartment in Queens: the superintendent saw her exiting the building in the morning and "pounced on me, shouting that I had no business in that building. He told me to 'go back to Harlem where you belong,' and warned me not to return. While I was out he changed the locks on the apartment door, and in order to reenter to get my clothes I was forced to call the police."[51]

Murray's autobiography didn't acknowledge that Mac stayed with her in the mountain cabin or in the Queens apartment, or that the superintendent verbally abused both of them. Archival evidence reveals the superintendent accosted them both in the morning as Murray was leaving for Durham to care for Aunt Pauline, who was sick again. After saying goodbye, Mac returned to the apartment to find that the lock had been removed from the door. She went into the apartment and started to telephone the WDL office when the superintendent appeared in the doorway and then entered the apartment uninvited. Terrified, Mac asked him to leave. When he refused, she asked the telephone operator for the police. The superintendent punched Mac to the ground, then fled the apartment.

Murray learned what had happened after arriving in Durham, prompting her to recall the night before the attack. She and Mac had been asleep in the apartment when she awoke with the feeling that someone was shining a torchlight on them and around the room. Under the bedcovers, she quietly nudged Mac with her foot, but Mac sleepily dismissed her sensation as a dream.[52] After learning of the assault, Murray became convinced that she had not dreamed the incident.

The whole episode starkly illustrated the dangers confronting oppressed people, even in the supposedly more liberal New York City. Murray's unwillingness to share the full terrifying story in her autobiography can only be explained by the fact that it required acknowledging her relationship with Mac. Consequently, Murray also omitted the facts that Mac pressed charges against the superintendent and that the WDL worked on the case in consultation with the NAACP. The NAACP asked Pauli to return from Durham to be a witness in the superintendent's trial.

The request created another problem for Pauli, which she also described in a letter to her friend: "To make things worse my Mother is furious at the thought of my returning to New York on the 18th [August 1941], is accusing me of putting someone else before her, is a mixture of jealousy, loneliness and fear about her health — and I'm torn between concern for her welfare and the combined principle and loyalty involved in Mac's situation."[53] Murray's identities as daughter, lover, and advocate for justice were in conflict. A short story written that same August reveals that Murray returned to New York despite Aunt Pauline's fury. The story, "Leaving Home," described the difficulty of leaving her adoptive mother. As she was preparing to return to New York, gloomy Aunt Pauline, who suffered frequently from undiagnosed ailments, told Pauli they might never see each other again. Murray wrote, "Half of you is weeping yonder on the porch with your mother sitting alone in the pale sunset and half of you is rushing forward to embrace her whom you will meet at the other end."[54]

The fear that Aunt Pauline's health problems would force her to return permanently to North Carolina still weighed on Pauli. She confided her concerns about it to her sister Mildred: "Then there's Aunt Pauline to consider, I've almost been persuaded to stay here and work this winter to be near her in case of illness or emergency, I don't know whether I have the emotional stamina to take it. I think of my own collapse in recent years and about Willie [older brother] and Grace [eldest sister] and don't want to do anything to get myself down. You know how I hate the South and how free I am—the adjustment might be asking too much of myself."[55] Given what had happened to Mac in New York, there was no telling what dangers she might face if she returned permanently to the South.

Even moving as far south as Washington, D.C., to take up the Howard University tuition scholarship caused far more concern than she revealed in her memoirs. Washington brought her into closer contact with her siblings, whose problems were distressing. While considering the Howard opportunity, Pauli made a shocking discovery. Several months earlier, on April 23, 1941, Grace had been diagnosed as "schizophrenic, paranoid type," and committed to Crownsville—the same Maryland psychiatric hospital where their father's brutal murder occurred.[56] "Aunt Pauline hesitated a long time before she told me about Grace," Pauli confided to Mildred, "but I dug it out of her, and was so shocked it set me off on a siege of nervous indigestion." Pauli then added, "If it is true that Lewis [Grace's husband] put her in Crownsville, then he is a most despicable person, no matter what apparent justification. The least he could have done was to respect our father's memory and not have sent her to that god-forsaken place."[57]

The experiences of her brother Bill would have already been weighing on her mind. Bill had been a Howard University Law School student—a brilliant one, according to former classmate and future Supreme Court justice Thurgood Marshall. But Bill withdrew then spent most of the subsequent six years in mental health facilities.[58] Pauli must have worried that enrolling in the very same law school could lead her to the same fate, though she could never publicly disclose this concern. Nor could she have welcomed the prospect of being in closer proximity to her younger, disapproving sister, Rosetta. "I had thought if Rose were a different kind of person," she explained to Mildred. "I could go to school and help her manage the store, but you know how she is and what she thinks of me. So I probably won't come to Washington."[59] Financial hardship, family conflict, and the fear of becoming a "mad Murray" created significant worries about attending Howard.

The feeling of being "forever on trial" made it difficult to acknowledge all the fears complicating her decision to attend law school, but the same feeling motivated her. In a letter to a WDL supporter who assisted Murray financially throughout her studies, Pauli described law as "one of the highest profession[s]—ranked with medicine and religion," revealing the extent to which status and prestige influenced her thinking.[60] She speculated years later that her desire to enter the legal profession might have been, in part, an unconscious desire to match the achievements of her white great-grandfather, and lawyer, Sidney Smith.[61] Recent experiences with the legal system also demystified the profession—in the past year alone, she had been a defendant following her arrest on the Greyhound bus, a witness in the case stemming from Mac's assault, and a central organizer in the campaign to save Odell Waller from the electric chair. All these experiences helped push her to overcome her misgivings and make the move to Washington to study law.

· · · · ·

IV

Thirty-one-year-old Pauli Murray entered Howard University on September 6, 1941. Although a segregated institution, Howard had some white faculty and graduate students and attracted the leading Black scholars, such as Alain Locke and E. Franklin Frazier, to teach some of the around four thousand students enrolled there. Howard's reputation as the nation's leading Black university made it more palatable to Murray, who had not attended a segregated school since leaving high school fifteen years earlier.[62] In the intervening years Murray had been a rare Black student at a women's college; now she became a rare woman at a Black university.

When Murray looked around the room on the first day of class, she saw only one other woman—who soon dropped out—in a class of thirty people. The professor in her first class also noticed the two women when he surveyed the room. Having done so, he told the entire class that he didn't understand why women came to law school, but since they did the men would have to put up with them. The men in the room burst into laughter. This exemplified many experiences to come—Murray experienced no hostility from Howard men, but much ridicule thinly disguised as banter. She also noticed that instructors often overlooked her when asking questions, and in open discussion male voices drowned her out.

If Murray remained in any doubt that gender divisions mattered, that doubt dissolved when, during the first semester, an invitation circulated for "all male students of the First Year Class" to attend a fraternity gathering. Murray went to Leon Ransom's office to complain about women's exclusion and Ransom—one of the university's most liberal professors—chuckled and told her that she could form a sorority for women law students, a suggestion that made no sense when there were only two women law students.[63] She put her opposition in writing, arguing, "As a minority group, I fear the results of our applying the same policies of exclusion within our ranks against minorities which are applied against us by the majority group."[64] Already well aware of Jim Crow race discrimination, Murray quickly labeled sex discrimination as its counterpart, "Jane Crow."[65]

Murray countered gender discrimination the same way she countered race discrimination: by trying to prove her abilities. She quickly rose to the top of the class. The enforcement of segregation in Washington further committed the already studious Murray to her studies: rather than cooperate with the system, Murray spent her free time studying at the Howard University library.[66] While avoiding segregation when possible, she still continued to fight it. In fact, she felt an extra responsibility to fight it when the United States entered World War II three months after the school year commenced and Howard men began leaving for war service. Murray cowrote an article for *Threshold*, a national student magazine, asking what African Americans were fighting for, given a recent lynching in Missouri and many other horrific racist acts occurring across America, which the article documented in unflinching detail. One reader wrote to the editor describing it as the year's most poignant article.[67]

Many Black activists advocated for change by highlighting the hypocrisy of fighting fascism abroad while supporting race discrimination at home. Before U.S. involvement in World War II, A. Philip Randolph began organizing African American discontent into the March on Washington Movement (MOWM), which proposed mass acts of civil disobedience that would culminate in a hundred thousand African Americans marching on Washington. To prevent such a demonstration, President Roosevelt signed an executive order banning race-based employment discrimination in defense industries and government agencies. In exchange, Randolph postponed the march on Washington, but MOWM groups continued to meet and agitate for racial equality. The MOWM peaked in the summer of 1942, after Murray had completed her first year at Howard. On June 16, some twenty thousand African Americans demonstrated in Madison Square Garden, demanding justice, democracy, and freedom.[68]

Two weeks after the Madison Square rally, Virginia's governor refused to commute Odell Waller's sentence, extinguishing his last hope of avoiding execution. Waller's plight had become so well known that Randolph, who worked with the WDL and knew Murray, asked her to organize a Washington delegation to try to convince Roosevelt's administration to intervene. Murray worked all night to bring together nearly twenty prominent spokespeople—including Mary McLeod Bethune, Leon Ransom, and Ted Poston—in a frantic effort to save the life of a sharecropper from rural Virginia who most likely would have been executed two years earlier but for the national campaign to save his life that Murray largely created. Depressingly, the delegation couldn't secure a meeting with anyone from the Roosevelt administration: Eleanor Roosevelt called Randolph that night, the evening before the scheduled execution, to say that she had interrupted the president several times concerning the matter only to be told that he was powerless to intervene. Murray later described it as a day of "unrelieved failure and humiliation."[69]

Waller died in the electric chair on July 2, 1942. Murray didn't attend the funeral in Virginia—she "couldn't bear to stand that sorrowful occasion," since she "felt his death too keenly." Instead, she traveled to New York where she spoke at a memorial service, which Randolph also addressed. Murray gave a brief account of Waller's life and the campaign to save him, then quoted his dying statement, which read, "As my time comes near each second means I am one nearer my grave. I have asked God to forgive me and I believe he has. . . . All you people take this under consideration. Have you ever thought about [how] some people are allowed a chance over and over again then there are others [who] are allowed little chance—some no chance at all."[70] After Waller's execution, Randolph asked Murray to write an open letter to President Roosevelt. In it she described African Americans' disillusionment and willingness to "die right here in America to attain democracy." Several Black newspapers printed the letter, which members of the Washington delegation signed.[71]

Randolph also asked Murray to organize a silent parade in New York City to protest Waller's execution and two recent lynchings. Murray relied on Maida Springer of the Dressmakers Union and a few other women activists for assistance in organizing the event. Springer, who eventually became a close friend, later recalled her first impression of Pauli at a planning meeting: "I walked into this meeting with Dollie [Lowther] and other trade union people, and we heard this little small person with cropped hair, wearing these white sailor pants and standing on the table. She was on *fire*, talking about social injustice and Jim Crow. Pauli was, I guess, maybe size eight then."[72] Murray stood 5 feet 2.5 inches tall and weighed only 105 pounds, but she could speak in a deep, assertive voice when she could overcome her extreme self-consciousness.[73]

Despite Murray's passionate appeals, the parade that Pauli and Maida Springer led attracted a much smaller crowd than the previous March on Washington Movement demonstration. The NAACP provided no support, and friction developed between the two organizations supporting the demonstration—the New York MOWM group and the WDL. Some Black MOWM activists were suspicious of the predominantly white Socialist

Party–affiliated WDL.[74] The WDL paid Murray, but "loaned" her to the New York MOWM division, leaving her caught in the middle of organizational disagreements and privately lamenting the many petty squabbles in committee meetings.[75]

Only a few hundred people turned out for the parade, curiously mostly Communist Party members who had not participated in Waller's defense because of Trotskyist and socialist involvement. The white press largely ignored the event, though the Black press provided prominent coverage.[76] An early historian of Black protest in the war years described the parade as a "very minor achievement."[77] Murray situated the silent parade more positively in her autobiography, describing it as the small beginning to the much larger March on Washington led by Dr. Martin Luther King Jr. that occurred twenty-one years later.[78] In her report to Randolph at the time, however, she could think of little more positive to say about the event other than that it started on time and ended ahead of schedule.[79]

Given time and later movement victories, she looked back on her efforts with pride, understanding her contributions as providing links in a chain of activism that began before her and continued after her.[80] This is a view many historians support, rejecting the popular notion that the civil rights struggle burst out of nowhere in the late 1950s and early 1960s, instead understanding the rapid acceleration of the struggle as built on a longer-term effort by numerous people, many of them forgotten by history.[81] Murray's extensive personal papers and memoirs, however, mean her contributions can be evaluated as part of an intergenerational liberation struggle.

In the immediate aftermath of Waller's execution and the tiny silent parade, Murray had little to show for her efforts other than heartache. Feelings among those who had campaigned to save Odell Waller were extremely raw. Thomas Stone, Waller's lawyer, upset by the blame apportioned to him, tried to explain his role in the case in a long letter sent to several newspapers and magazines. Stone had been criticized because errors he made in the initial trial were later given as reasons for the Supreme Court's refusals to hear an appeal. His letter pointed out that he only had a few days to prepare Waller's defense and that it had to be done without any help from "the social democratic or liberal organizations or persons who now attack [me]."

An incensed Murray wrote a strong rebuttal, published, in part, in the *Richmond Afro-American*. She outlined the WDL's involvement before furthering the attack on Stone: "Had Mr. Stone and the Revolutionary Workers League never handled the case Waller would have had a fighting chance at least, though the patterns of Virginia justice would have remained the same. I'm for militancy and uncompromising struggle against racial and economic injustice, but the sooner unscrupulous radical organizations with purely political motives take their finger out of the Negro's fight and let him lead his own struggle the better it will be for all of us."[82] In her anger at Stone, Murray adopted a position she didn't really adhere to herself— she maintained a lifelong commitment to interracial organizations, such as the Socialist Party–affiliated, overwhelmingly white WDL, which paid her wage and had been criticized by Black activists in the MOWM on the same grounds on which she now criticized Stone. In the aftermath of not only a lost campaign but also a lost life, the "patterns of Virginia justice" received less attention by bereaved campaigners.

Murray directed further ire at President Roosevelt. In a letter she later described as "ill-conceived," she effectively praised the wartime internment of Japanese Americans. She demanded to know why the president used his wartime powers to evacuate Japanese Americans to prevent the perpetration of violence on them, but not evacuate African Americans from the South. She received a blistering response from the First Lady, whom she had sent a copy. "Your letter seems to me one of the most thoughtless I have ever read," ER wrote. Murray backpedaled immediately, explaining that she had not intended to offer any fundamental solution—she only wanted to convey the depth of her disgust at the president's failure to use his position to address racial injustices. ER did not bother responding to Murray's follow-up letter; rather, she surprised Pauli with an invitation to visit her New York apartment. When the meeting occurred, the First Lady greeted her with a hug; Murray left the meeting feeling unreserved affection for ER.[83] But the meeting proved to be the highlight of an otherwise difficult summer.

MURRAY WANTED TO BE IN New York in the summer not only for Waller's memorial. While organizing the silent parade, Murray wrote to Dr. Eidelsberg, whose experiments with testosterone she had first read about in 1939, explaining, "I am very anxious to have some medical care during my temporary stay in New York. . . . My life is somewhat unbearable in its present phase, and though a person of ability, this aspect continually blocks my efforts to do the things of which I am capable."[84] She included a two-page memorandum outlining her physical, mental, moral, and emotional characteristics—noting her top school results and strong religious beliefs and her tendency to vacillate "between extreme self-consciousness and bold aggressiveness"—then described her present state: "No crucial emotional crisis; motivated to seek help on a long standing emotional and mental conflict, popularly known as homosexuality."

Although she described it as an emotional and mental conflict, Murray listed four possible underlying causes, three of which were physiological: a "mental conflict"—the least acceptable explanation; a "glandular disturbance"—explaining her boyish appearance and aggressiveness; a "fibroid tumor or growth"—no explanation is given about how this caused her attractions to women; and the presence of "male organs secreted in the abdominal cavity." Murray wanted hormone tests, X-rays, fluoroscope, or exploratory surgery to explore this last theory, because "this is the most radical theory, and the most acceptable to the subject under discussion. It must be thoroughly exhausted before the subject will be willing to accept other conclusions." On this occasion, at least, Murray stated a clear desire to be cured of same-sex attractions and believed her appearance and behavior could provide the key to a cure.[85]

Murray's previous conversations concerning her mental and emotional conflict had taken place while she was hospitalized. Now, in her letter to Dr. Eidelsberg, she wanted to equalize the relationship, trying to sound calm, detached, and scientific when explaining her theories, as evidenced by identifying herself as "the subject." The effort bore no fruit, however: Dr. Eidelsberg replied stating that medical science did not support her conclusions, but he still offered to make an exhaustive study to determine whether she had any glandular disorder when his clinic reopened in September.[86]

Unwilling to wait, Murray wrote to Dr. Ruth Fox, whom she had consulted several years earlier, only to learn that the doctor was on holiday. Murray then sent a letter to Dr. Fox's vacation address in Martha's Vineyard stating that she was "coincidentally" planning to visit there for two weeks and asked if the doctor would experiment on her with hormones. Her "problem," she explained, had not improved in the last five years and made a satisfactory relationship with anyone impossible. She then declared that the doctor's answer would in fact partially determine whether she went to Martha's Vineyard or made inquiries at the Mayo Clinic. She needed to make an "inner adjustment" quickly, Murray revealed, if she were to cope with increased work responsibilities and social activities.[87] Dr. Fox replied within a week, restating her belief that Murray's problem was a "psychological matter" but encouraging her to pursue any physiological tests she desired.[88] Murray still went to Martha's Vineyard for most of August, but there is no evidence to indicate whether she met with Dr. Fox, coincidentally or otherwise.[89]

Once again Murray's quest for medical treatment coincided with an emotionally difficult period, even though she told doctors she wasn't in crisis. Murray wrote to Dr. Eidelsberg just eleven days after Waller's death and wrote to Dr. Fox on the day of the miserable silent parade. Over the past year's study at Howard Law School—the environment where her brother's

An Unknown Negro Girl without Title or Prestige

mental health trouble emerged—she had endured marginalization because of her biological sex while she endured isolation from Washington society because of segregation. Murray then had to absorb the terrible event of Waller's execution and the failure of her exhaustive efforts to oppose it as well as the acrimony between campaigners. There is no way to know whether emotions from these experiences spilled into her urgent quest for medical treatment in some way, but the possibility cannot be discounted entirely.

Murray succeeded in having some physiological testing done before returning to Howard. She underwent a "hysterosalpingogram" (an X-ray that looks inside the uterus and fallopian tubes) at North Harlem X-Ray Laboratories. The testing revealed typical female reproductive organs and uncovered no evidence of male reproductive organs.[90] This exam, like the tests she underwent in previous years, failed to confirm her favored theories about her body, leaving open the possibility, suggested by Dr. Fox, that her problems were psychological, which in turn kept the door open to a further possibility, that her mental and emotional conflict was evidence of her deepest fear: hereditary insanity.

. . . . .

V

By the commencement of Murray's second year at Howard, in the fall of 1942, many men had left for war service and more women had enrolled.[91] Murray gained a role model in Caroline Ware, a history professor who joined the predominantly male faculty. Ware, a self-described tomboy and social activist, became a mentor and friend to Murray for the remainder of her life.[92] Another important contact, Susie Elliot, Howard's dean of women and Pauli's cousin, created a bedroom for Pauli out of a "powder room" off a seldom-used dance hall on the first floor of the undergraduate woman's dormitory building.[93] The room had barely enough space for a cot, a desk, and a bookshelf, but because of Murray's maturity, activist background, and ongoing legal training, it became an informal meeting place for undergraduate women interested in civil rights. Murray returned to college with activism in mind: she told her WDL patron just before the semester began that activists needed to perfect nonviolent forms of protest so that in the coming year they could "strike out boldly for . . . the protection of minority rights."[94]

Murray joined the Fellowship of Reconciliation (FOR), an interfaith pacifist justice organization that dated back to World War I. FOR experienced a renewal during the current war, and some of its staff, including Bayard Rustin and James Farmer, became influential figures in the later civil rights movement. Murray and another FOR member, Henry Babcock, published "An Alternative Weapon" in the 1942–43 winter edition of *South Today*. They argued that a religious-based nonviolent activism involving redemptive suffering could heal the nation. "It is a strange thing to believe that out of the Negro's struggle and suffering may come the answer to the very problem which troubles so many Americans today," the authors stated.[95] She also became a member of the Congress of Racial Equality (CORE), a FOR offshoot that initiated an unsuccessful restaurant sit-in protest in Chicago in the spring of 1942.

After spending her first year avoiding Washington's segregated businesses, Murray found an opportunity to confront them using Gandhi-inspired nonviolent protest, similar to the unsuccessful one in Chicago.[96] In January 1943, a Washington restaurant refused service to three Howard sophomore women, including Ruth Powell, with whom Murray grew close. When the students refused to leave the manager called the police, but segregation in the nation's capital was based on custom, not law, so the police ordered restaurant staff to serve the students. The restaurant charged the students an inflated price, however, and when they refused to pay, police arrested them. News of the arrests motivated the students gathered around Murray's room to take further action: one student had been suggesting a "stool-sitting technique" for months, and Ruth Powell had routinely carried out such actions, staging what she called "sittings" whenever a downtown restaurant refused her service.[97] Rather than spontaneous individual protests, the students now began planning a coordinated action, with Murray in the role of student "legal adviser."[98]

The students established a Civil Rights Committee to study segregation laws, educate students on civil rights legislation, and encourage students to lobby their home-state politicians to support such legislation. As part of the awareness campaign, the student activists designed and distributed a survey to Howard students. Of the 292 survey respondents, 284 said they did not believe African Americans should suspend the struggle for equal rights until the end of the war, 262 agreed students should play an active part in the struggle, and 218 said they would join a campaign against segregation in the District of Columbia. The Direct Action Subcommittee, headed up by Ruth Powell, began training participants for nonviolent protests—they studied disorderly conduct and picketing laws to make sure they would comply with the law and they made potential participants sign pledges committing them to look and behave their best, regardless of provocation.[99] After careful consideration, the students decided to target the Little Palace Cafeteria, because it operated in a predominantly Black section of town yet still refused to serve African Americans.

On a rainy Saturday in April 1943, three Howard students entered the cafeteria and took up seats while another student observed from outside.[100] After being denied service the students didn't leave, rather they remained in their seats and began studying their schoolbooks. After a short while, another three Howard students entered and repeated the process. At staggered intervals twelve students, including Murray, occupied the cafeteria. Outside, the seven remaining students formed an orderly picket line and carried signs such as "We Die Together—Why Can't We Eat Together?"[101] The police arrived—led by the city's only Black lieutenant—but could do nothing, since no crime was being committed. Rather than serve the students, the cafeteria closed eight hours early. Murray and the students occupying the cafeteria joined the picket line, which continued for most of the afternoon.[102] The students returned on Monday morning to repeat the protest. Within forty-eight hours the cafeteria owner capitulated and began serving African Americans. The students similarly desegregated one other small restaurant in the area, again without major incident.

The protests Murray helped organize in 1943 have been celebrated for anticipating the famed 1960s sit-ins.[103] Indeed, one of the protest organizers, Juanita Morrow, provided a direct link to the civil rights movement when she became a leading CORE activist in the 1960s. The successful protests were also further testament to the capability of Black women activists— most of the nineteen protestors were women. Having suffered so many setbacks in her efforts to end segregation, the success elated Murray. She recalled, "We had proved that intelligent, imaginative action could bring positive results and, fortunately, we had won our first victory without an embarrassing incident."[104] Unlike Murray's other previous attempts to desegregate education and interstate transport, the restaurant sit-ins were not only links in an ongoing activist chain, but enjoyed tangible immediate successes. Her relief at having won the victories without embarrassing incidents indicates her sensitivity to public perception, which was crucial not only for defeating racism but also for maintaining self-belief.

THE SURVEY USED TO ENGAGE STUDENTS in the lead-up to the protests asked: "Am I screwball or am I a pioneer?"[105] The evocative question was in fact one Murray grappled with repeatedly. Daring to stand up against the established order required exposing herself to further marginalization as an unhinged radical, but accepting the established order meant accepting status as an inferior person. Either option had the potential to drive a person to despair, especially a person who already feared inherited mental illness.

This inner struggle may have run beneath Murray's intense spring of 1943: she threw herself into the campaign to desegregate the two restaurants, but it again took a toll. Activism while trying to complete her second year of law school, especially as simply passing was rarely enough for the high achiever, proved to be another exhausting experience.

Less than a month after the successful protests, Murray entered the Howard University infirmary, where she remained until she requested discharge six days later. Her hospital chart states that she was admitted for "bed rest" and felt very depressed and cried frequently when admitted.[106] In a later letter to a friend, Murray described missing her exams because of a "nervous breakdown"; she told another friend that "the crack up was serious."[107]

In addition to activist and exam stresses, the breakdown involved a third crucial element. Murray revealed how a young sophomore "sort of walked into my life without my realizing what was happening to me." Fearing expulsion from Howard, Murray unsuccessfully applied for work as a journalist and applied to another law school, but Dean Ransom refused to release her, because, according to Murray, he thought she had "legal genius."[108] Rather than expulsion, the Law School allowed Murray to postpone her second-year final exams until September, just before the commencement of the new school year.[109]

Less than two weeks after leaving the infirmary, Murray visited the White House to have tea with Eleanor Roosevelt. She had planned to bring along Aunt Pauline, but her adoptive mother was too unwell to attend. After attending the tea at the White House, Murray excitedly reported to Aunt Pauline what she had missed: "You would have thought I was talking to either you or Aunt Sallie, the way she talked to me."[110] Meeting with the First Lady provided a moment of joyous reprieve from the emotional storm engulfing Murray at this time.

Following the White House meeting, Murray spent a week recuperating at Caroline Ware's farm—a seventy-acre property in rural Virginia that Ware shared with her husband, economist Gardiner Means. Ware offered "The Farm" as both an extension of her classroom and a rest place for weary students. It was the ideal place for Murray—a great lover of the outdoors in times of crisis—to recuperate. Guests could take walks, usually accompanied by up to five Shetland dogs, which Ware called her "staff of psychiatric dogs," or find a quiet corner of the farmhouse to read books from the large collection on display, or chat around the fireplace with the couple and other guests.[111]

Murray used her time at The Farm to reflect on her latest collapse. She put some of her thoughts in a letter to Aunt Pauline: "I do feel the need of getting myself straightened out sort of once and for all," she explained. "This little 'boy-girl' personality as you jokingly call it sometimes gets me into trouble, Mother, and I'm no further along to adjustment than I was the summer of 1935 when I was home."[112] Pauli had ended her on-and-off three-year relationship with Mac, and now a new love interest had created problems. She described having done nothing to be ashamed of, "or even outside the rules of society," but she and the unnamed woman sophomore student were still subject to "gossip." Her older brother Bill's catastrophic exit from Howard a decade earlier must have been especially prominent in her thoughts when she explained, somewhat cryptically, that she had become a victim of "certain medical rivalries," whereby one doctor threatened to send her to the "Psychopathic Ward" at Gallinger Municipal Hospital for observation, "and of course I might have been really put out of commission for a long time on the basis of family history alone if that had been carried out."[113]

Exams, innovative sit-in protests, a potentially scandalous relationship, and the specter of hereditary insanity form a familiar confluence of mutually reinforcing pressures that resulted in breakdown and a renewed focus on her body. Murray's letter identified her sexual preference as creating past employment difficulties and ongoing uncertainty about the seat of her problems. She wrote,

> Mother, you've always been so understanding—both you and Aunt Sallie, but where you and a few people understand, the world does not understand nor accept my pattern of life. And to try to live by society's standards always causes me such inner conflict that at times it's unbearable. I don't know whether I'm right or whether society (or some medical authority) is right—I only know how I feel and what makes me happy. This conflict rises up to knock me down at every apex I reach in my career and because the laws of society do not protect me, I'm exposed to any enemy or person who may or may not want to hurt me.[114]

The dangers for Murray seemed greater still—embracing an identity as a member of a "third sex," as her WDL admirer of a few years earlier implored, not only threatened employment prospects but also raised an even more alarming threat of confinement to a psychiatric institution. Such threats encouraged intellectual, political, sexual, and behavioral conformity and inevitably created doubts that she may be a "screwball," not a "pioneer."

In her long letter to Aunt Pauline, Murray began by identifying her hospitalization as stemming from an unknown physiological source and continued:

> Know you think my doings have been strange of late, but that's because my physical stamina has been so low, I just could not get myself together to pack and come home. I'm not ill—just very under weight and run down, and Mildred [sister] had to pour high-powered vitamins into me to keep me from losing weight faster than the food which I ate could give me. There have been all kinds of theories—1) possible ulcer of the stomach, 2) high rate of metabolism which means I burn out the energy [faster] than I can get it in by foods, due to some glandular maladjustment—or just complete physical collapse due to overwork and not enough rest—but I have felt Mildred is afraid to have me examined down at Freedmen's [the hospital where Mildred worked as a nurse], because of the effect high nervous tensions will have in terms of just more talk about the "mad Murrays." She's tried hard to help me over rough places but she has had so many personal problems, that mine just seem to be more than she can bear. We disagree as to my way of life, my emotional attachments and therefore trying to cooperate with her point of view has been extremely difficult for me. So I don't think it wise to pursue the idea of medical attention at Freedmen's any longer.[115]

Murray transitioned through her three deepest anxieties: bodily malfunction, hereditary insanity, and same-sex desires. Two days later, in another letter to Aunt Pauline, Murray expressed confidence that expert attention to her "glandular reactions" would help. She thought she might be able to get the expert treatment from Johns Hopkins Hospital, or Duke University Hospital.[116] Despite dreading falling victim to medical rivalries at Howard, Murray still held faith that the medical profession could resolve her problems, though her respect for medical authority was soon sorely tested.

MURRAY LEFT WARE'S FARM WITH A newly acquired pet dog that she called Toni. She traveled south to visit Aunt Pauline and to consult a doctor at Duke University Hospital on June 17. Although she didn't mention her breakdown in her autobiography, she did describe that her Durham doctor referred her to Duke for "certain tests he wanted." She went on to explain that during the appointment the doctor became increasingly uncomfortable as he questioned her, then suddenly shouted that he was not going to continue and she should put on her clothes and leave. When she asked why, he replied, "I'm not going to have anything to do with Eleanor Roosevelt movements!" His comment referenced a widespread rumor circulating among white southerners: that Black women domestic workers, inspired if not directed by the First Lady, were forming "Eleanor Clubs," whose motto was "A white woman in every kitchen by Christmas."[117]

Murray devoted nearly a paragraph to explaining the fanciful wartime race rumors, but only included one sentence on why Ruffin accused her of involvement. She explained, "Because my bearing was completely at variance with the southern racial stereotype, Dr. Ruffin apparently jumped to the conclusion that I was an organizer of this non-existent 'movement.'"[118] Murray undoubtedly only partially described her encounter with Ruffin, reducing it to an anecdote about racism when the incident was also about her sexuality and gender identity. She mentioned her intention to pursue treatment not only in her letter to Aunt Pauline; she also mentioned to a friend having consulted Ruffin about an "emotional disturbance," though his research area was gastrointestinal.[119] Murray only made some of the personal political in her autobiography, describing the incident to highlight racism and compartmentalizing other aspects (sexuality, gender identity, and mental health) as private.

This is not to suggest her ejection from Ruffin's office had nothing to do with race. It is conceivable that Murray, given her penchant for family history, might have told Dr. Ruffin about Mary Ruffin Smith, Pauli's biological great-aunt who legally owned Grandmother Cornelia after Mary Ruffin's brother raped and impregnated a slave named Harriet. In any case, Dr. Ruffin was a conservative white southerner, and Murray was a fiery activist in the Black freedom struggle, so a clash seemed likely, especially given heightened racial tensions.[120]

Race rumors, such as those concerning "Eleanor Clubs," owed much to the changing circumstances for African Americans during the war years. An upsurge in activism by newly formed groups such as CORE and MOWM, along with labor force changes, fueled belief among some whites about Black political conspiracies. Southern whites were fearful of why their housekeepers were leaving, while urban whites in the North and West were upset by changing neighborhood demographics as African Americans (and whites) flocked to industrial centers for better employment opportunities. The rumors were so common in the South that Howard Odum, the UNC sociologist Murray had applied to study under, compiled them in a book.[121]

Exactly two months had elapsed between the victory over segregation at the Little Palace Cafeteria and the humiliating appointment with Dr. Ruffin, but it must have seemed longer as Pauli made her way back to her childhood home from the Duke University clinic. Aunt Pauline bore the brunt of Pauli's fury. In no uncertain terms—when Pauli became emotional her voice grew high and thin—she told her dour adoptive mother that she would only return to the South to bury her and not for any other reason.[122] Murray returned to New York without the newly acquired puppy, Toni, further displeasing Aunt Pauline, who now had to care for it.

The day after meeting with Dr. Ruffin, Murray wrote to presidential aide Marvin McIntyre to warn him that African Americans were impatient with second-class citizenship.[123] Two days later, a race riot erupted in Detroit. Riots erupted in many other cities in the following days—one contemporary study reported 242 racial battles occurred in forty-seven cities.[124] Murray published an article in *Common Sense* under the title "Negroes Are Fed Up" that virtually predicted the outbreak of riots in Harlem.[125] When Harlem erupted she reported on the riots for *Call*, the Socialist Party newspaper.[126] It wasn't easy to remain a witness, or a pacifist, as her home for over a decade exploded into violence. Her cousin, who had stayed with her when he first came to New York, participated in the riot, and Pauli felt the same "intensely violent urge to strike back against the accumulated hurts, insults, and humiliations" as the rioters did.[127] The police, supported by white vigilantes, violently suppressed the rebellion. Pictures of the carnage appeared in newspapers across the nation; the Black press compared the violence inflicted on African Americans to Nazi attacks on Jews.[128]

More than a month after she had written to FDR's aide warning him about African Americans' impatience with second-class citizenship, the White House had done nothing, further angering Murray. President Roosevelt eventually responded to an inquiry from a New York congressman by stating, "I share your feeling that the recent outbreaks of violence in widely scattered parts of the country endanger our national unity and comfort our enemies. I am sure that every true American regrets this."[129] Murray channeled her dismay at the weak response into her poetry. "Mr. Roosevelt Regrets," published in *Crisis*, asked:

> What'd you get, black boy,
> When they knocked you down in the
> gutter,
> And they kicked your teeth out,
> And they broke your skull with clubs
> And they bashed your stomach in?

An Unknown Negro Girl without Title or Prestige

What'd you get when the police shot you
in the back,
And they chained you to the beds
While they wiped the blood off?
What'd you get when you cried out to
the Top Man?
When you called on the man next to
God, so you thought,
And you asked him to speak out to save
you?
What'd the Top Man say, black boy?
"Mr. Roosevelt regrets . . ."[130]

She combined her passion for creative writing and civil rights into two more poems, "Harlem Riot, 1943" and her magnum opus, "Dark Testament."[131]

Following the Harlem riot, Murray wrote a reflective letter to Caroline Ware. She described feeling less disturbed by this riot than previous violence. Despite her pacifism, she stated her "heart was in it," as it had a purging effect. She also linked it to her recent emotional disturbance: "I begin now to understand the tears I wept in the Spring, the nights of fear and conflict, the apprehensions which hung over me when I was out at the farm. When the hurricane really came I was calm and unafraid. These personal reactions are what I cannot explain—how the intimate and the social were all entwined and the sorrow of one's emotional frustrations merged into the sorrow of a people's frustrations—but what the heck."[132] Murray sometimes sought to separate problems into personal and political ones, but in this instance she wanted to understand the mysterious link between her personal turmoil and the collective upheaval. The riot appeared to be a social manifestation of the conflict existing within herself, a violent eruption of deeply held frustrations that could no longer be contained.

· · · · ·

VI

In the fall of 1943, Murray returned to Howard to take her second-year exams before commencing her final year of law school. War service had thinned class numbers considerably—from her first-year class of thirty students, only seven remained. Two more women had commenced in the law school, but Murray still felt the brunt of gender discrimination—as the top second-year student, school tradition dictated that she should be elected head of the student guild, but the guild decided not to hold elections, and the post remained vacant. Murray had no doubt the election was canceled so her male peers could avoid having to elect a woman to the leadership position for the first time.

More positively, Murray met Betsy Graves Reyneau during this school year. Reyneau—a painter and veteran of the last phase of the suffrage movement—shared inspiring stories of the struggle, such as her arrest in 1917 while picketing the White House with other suffragettes. Murray recalled, "I now realized there was a history of women's efforts to achieve equality, that I was not alone, and that I was not especially excessive in the ways I went about working for change."[133] For someone who worried about the sources of her intense frustrations, befriending people like Reyneau inspired confidence and reassurance that speaking out didn't make her a "screwball."

Although Murray achieved high marks in her first two years at law school, this had more to do with her desire to achieve than her interest in the subject matter. She found many law subjects dry and uninteresting. That changed in her final year, when she got to study civil rights law. For her final term paper, she chose to write about the late nineteenth-century *Civil Rights Acts* and the 1896 *Plessy v. Ferguson* Supreme Court decision.[134] Murray questioned the current NAACP strategy of challenging *Plessy* by attacking the equal side of the "separate but equal" ruling. Instead, she advocated tackling *Plessy* head-on, arguing that separate could never be equal. She believed her argument reflected the thinking among younger law students, whereas older lawyers feared unfavorable rulings would further entrench segregation. The mammoth subject required more time than the school year allowed, so Murray didn't actually complete it until well after she left Howard, but she was justifiably proud of it. She dreamed of one day taking the argument out of the classroom and into the Supreme Court. "Who knows?" she wrote to Ware. "Maybe five years from now I'll be arguing *Plessy v. Ferguson* before the old boys up there."[135] It took twice that long, and Murray didn't get to present the case, but the NAACP did eventually strike at the heart of segregation in 1954 in *Brown v. Board of Education*.

MURRAY'S CONTINUED INVOLVEMENT IN direct-action protests against segregation also delayed her civil rights paper. Howard student activists aimed to repeat their previous year's success in integrating restaurants. Once again, participants were carefully instructed in picketing and public decorum and asked to sign a pledge accepting the philosophy and discipline of the Civil Rights Committee.[136] The action began in the afternoon of April 22, 1944, almost exactly a year since the successful campaign to integrate the Little Palace Cafeteria. This time the protest was even bolder, however, because the students targeted Thompson's, a chain restaurant outside a Black neighborhood in downtown Washington.

Using the same strategy as the previous year, small groups of students entered Thompson's and after being denied service remained seated, reading books. Picketers outside, again careful not to block the busy footpath, carried signs reading, "Are You for HITLER'S Way (Race Supremacy) or the AMERICAN Way (Equality)? Make Up Your Mind!" The only unplanned part of the protest occurred when a group of Black soldiers passing by decided to join the protest. Military police arrived quickly to clear them. As the protestors' designated representative, Murray told the military police that if they were going to ask the Black soldiers to leave the restaurant they should ask all other military personnel to leave too, which the military police then did. Four and a half hours after the audacious protest began, the restaurant served the students.

Thompson's continued to serve African Americans for the next few days before suddenly refusing again.[137] Before the students could take further action, the Howard University Council voted unanimously to forbid further protests because of concerns that southern segregationist politicians, who held the reins to powerful legislative committees, would cut the federal funding on which the university relied if protests continued.[138] The University Council's response supports the arguments of some historians that, following the riots in the summer of 1943, Black leaders, unwilling to risk losing the gains already won, stifled racial militancy.[139]

The University Council's decision particularly pained Murray because many of the Howard staff who voted for the ban were her idols, such as Dean Hastie and Professor Ransom. She recalled, "In the next few days we were to learn that self-inflicted wounds within a group deeply committed to the same objective are often more painful and difficult to bear than hurts imposed by enemies, because they have the effect of dividing one against oneself in ways seldom achieved by an outsider." The experience of a divided self is evident in much of Murray's autobiographical account about the protest ban. She went on to state that the council was concerned not only that government funding might be cut if protests continued, but also that Howard's reputation would be damaged if student actions were associated with "crackpot" movements.[140] This claim had the potential to undermine Murray's confidence and awaken doubts that the radical ways she tried to enact social change might actually expose problems within herself.

The students were not without support. Stories in the Black press criticized the administration's decision, and some Howard staff sided with the students. The Black press also publicized the fact that the students had elected protest leader Ruth Powell as class president, which was widely seen as an endorsement for continuing the protests. The campus seemed set for a showdown after the full membership of the Howard chapter of the NAACP voted unanimously to continue the campaign—its leadership group, headed by Murray, issued a statement describing the administration's decision as a "retreat in the fight for freedom."[141]

A student delegation met with Howard University president Mordecai Johnson, where Murray stated their case. Johnson said they should work with outside groups, not student groups, to protest. It is unclear what else Johnson told the students, but it must have been strongly worded—Murray reported to Aunt Pauline that the students had "taken a terrific pounding today."[142] A week later, the student representatives met with the entire faculty and administration, with no more success. In the end, the students accepted a deal whereby they could campaign with nonstudent groups and appeal the ban to the trustees the next month, by which time the school year would be over. Murray described the students' vote to continue the campaign as brave words of obituary rather than a call to action, attributing the campaign's end to "our own black administrators, held hostage themselves to the forces of bigotry in government."[143]

The Howard administration's protest ban created a dilemma because a protest strategy that emphasized dignified behavior risked getting undignified if it went not only against segregationists but also against established Black leaders. The pledge that protest participants signed included the clause "I further pledge. . . to do or say *nothing* which will embarrass the Committee or the University."[144] Murray understood the protest ban as a wound that divided one against oneself because she did not want to embarrass herself or her cause—she worried already that she might have been too extreme in pushing for change. Yet she also knew the strategy was working. During the dispute she sought spiritual guidance from Howard Thurman, a professor in the Howard School of Religion. Thurman, who had voted for the ban, told her that evil is never fully destroyed—when beaten down in one place, it reemerges in another.

Opposition from the Howard administration and the approach of final-year exams effectively ended the groundbreaking protests. Murray described the campaign's end as "one more bitter defeat," but she also ensured that the lessons from the protests lodged in the collective conscience of Black activists: she published a detailed account of the "stool-sitting" protests, titled "A Blueprint for First Class Citizenship," in the November issue of *Crisis*.[145] The blueprint was put into action fifteen years later in Greensboro, North Carolina, and then elsewhere, with spectacular results. As with other bitter

An Unknown Negro Girl without Title or Prestige

short-term defeats, Murray could later savor the victory of protest strategies she helped develop.

ON JUNE 2, 1944, A FEW WEEKS after the downtown sit-ins, thirty-three-year-old Pauli Murray graduated. The fight with the Howard administration over the protest ban exacted a toll on her grades—her overall grades dropped ten points—but she still finished top of her class. War service had whittled the class to only seven students, yet her ability was clear.[146] She received prizes for achieving the highest grades in numerous subjects, and William Hastie described her as one of the five or six most promising students to come through the school in the past decade.[147] Aunt Pauline came up from Durham for the ceremonies, and Uncle Bubber came from Baltimore. Murray also invited the Roosevelts.

The Roosevelts couldn't attend the ceremony—D-Day was only days away—but ER surprised everyone by sending a large flower bouquet before the commencement ceremony. Murray arranged to have the bouquet placed on the stage without the card, though news of ER's gift still found its way into the Black press. Under the headline "Flowers from the First Lady," the *Pittsburgh Courier* reported, "They were for brilliant, active, strong-willed Pauli Murray, graduate cum laude of the Howard Law School."[148] The magical experience was completed by an invitation to tea with ER at the White House, to which Pauli took along Aunt Pauline, her sister Mildred, and her friend Ruth Powell.[149]

At the ceremony, Howard University president, Mordecai Johnson, urged graduates to move to the South to organize labor and work for the NAACP. Two-thirds of Black lawyers lived in the North, while more than three-quarters of the Black population still lived in the South. Johnson's urging appeared to tempt Murray. Days after the ceremony, several Black newspapers published her "open letter" to the graduating class of 1944 commending Johnson's recommendation.[150] "Have we the courage of our convictions?" she asked. "Shall we move into the relatively freer areas where we may have a little breathing space for ourselves and our children, or shall we go back down into 'Egypt,' so to speak, and rescue our people, both white and black?" She continued, "Shall we leave the South to those who have demonstrated they do not know how to save it, or shall we return to our native land or the land of our grandparents and win it over for democracy inch by inch, with books and ballots, and tolerance and understanding, and love and generosity in place of bullets and the instruments of violent conflict?" Even within this letter, Murray questioned whether she could do it: "I do not have the answer to the questions I have raised, nor can I tell other students to do what I would not do myself. . . . I do not know whether I would have the physical and moral stamina to meet the challenge of President Johnson."[151] Murray concluded that she might if her classmates joined her. One reporter and a letter to the editor expressed confidence she would, but they were wrong.[152]

It would have taken tremendous courage for Murray to strike out on her own in the South as a lawyer. The *Afro-American* dismissed Johnson's call in an article titled "Go South, Commit Suicide."[153] Only a year before Murray had declared she would only return to the South to bury her adoptive mother.[154] Her unwillingness to live in the South, much to the ongoing disappointment of her Aunt Pauline, was often stated. Furthermore, working inch by inch in Black communities in relative anonymity wasn't her preferred strategy for racial uplift. Murray may have been inspired enough by Johnson's words to want simply to publicize and debate the merits of such a move, but even this seems unlikely. Most likely, she was attempting to heal a rift with Johnson following the sit-in dispute. Even years later she held a grudge against Johnson for the "sermons" she took from him during her time at Howard.[155] Murray never planned to go south; she wanted to go farther north, to Harvard University.

MURRAY HOPED TO FOLLOW A pathway undertaken by many of Howard's top students in the past by completing a year of graduate study at Harvard and then returning to Howard to teach. There was one problem with the plan, however: Harvard Law School did not admit women. Murray heard rumors that the ban might be overturned (as the Harvard Medical School ban on women recently had been), which led her to write on a Rosenwald scholarship application — submitted before graduation — that she would use the money to "obtain my master's degree at Harvard University, in the event they have removed their bar against women." Murray then wrote to Harvard Law School inquiring about the ban. A prompt reply simply stated that registration wasn't open to women. Her aspiration became public knowledge when she won a prestigious Rosenwald scholarship (along with such notable recipients as Chester Himes and E. Franklin Frazier). While completing her studies at Howard and dealing with the fallout from the protest ban, the Black press carried news stories that Murray would use the scholarship to study labor law at Harvard.[156]

Murray then found herself in the embarrassing situation of receiving congratulatory letters from people who read about her plan in the newspapers and did not know about the ban on women. Compounding her embarrassment, she recalled being subject to ridicule from Howard men: "The

An Unknown Negro Girl without Title or Prestige

fact that Harvard's rejection was a source of mild amusement rather than outrage to many of my male colleagues who were ardent civil rights advocates made it all the more bitter to swallow."[157] In a letter to Eleanor Roosevelt she wrote, "Dean Hastie and Dean Ransom are kidding me to death about it, but down underneath all the kidding, it hurts not to be able to go to Harvard."[158] Murray felt "mortified" by the publicity, but it didn't destroy her ambition. She believed it "would be a real prize to be the FNW or FW (First Negro Woman or First Woman) to 'darken' dear old Harvard's doors," so she went ahead and applied anyway.[159]

Echoing the University of North Carolina's rejection of her application five years earlier because of race segregation, Harvard Law School responded to Murray's application by informing her that as a woman she was not entitled to admission at Harvard Law School. She wrote to Harvard to appeal the decision, but the conservative governing corporation sidestepped the appeal by stating that faculties set up conditions of admission, therefore the matter of whether women should be admitted was a decision for the Faculty of Law.[160] In a direct appeal to Harvard Law School, Murray concluded that she too would have liked to sidestep the need for an appeal: "Humorously, gentlemen, I would gladly change my sex to meet your requirements but since the way to such change has not been revealed to me, I have no recourse but to appeal to you to change your minds on this subject. Are you to tell me that one is as difficult as the other?"[161] Murray already believed she possessed the personal characteristics positively associated with masculinity—she explained that her "naturally aggressive temperament" meant she wouldn't take Harvard's rejection lying down, but would "put up a clean fight." She also explained, "Very recent medical examination reveals me to be a functionally normal woman with perhaps a 'male slant' on things, which may account for my insistence upon getting into Harvard."[162]

Yet Murray's appeals also reveal a simmering feminist consciousness. She wrote, "I have met a number of women and have heard of many more who wished to attend Harvard and yet were refused. This fight is not mine, but that of women who feel they should have free access to the very best of legal education."[163] Murray believed she fought Harvard on behalf of all women, but she didn't fight with the support of an active social movement. There wasn't a women's equivalent of the NAACP, nor were there women's presses equivalent to the Black press that she could use to appeal for public support. Murray could only challenge the rejection through personal appeal. In addition to her own letters, she called on her ever-growing network of notable contacts for support. From Howard University, William Hastie and Leon Ransom were "quietly supportive," while Caroline Ware—her great-grandfather had been an original Harvard dean—spoke more firmly in support. After Murray appealed to Eleanor Roosevelt, President Roosevelt wrote to the Harvard president in support of her application. Lloyd K. Garrison, a highly credentialed lawyer and a member of the Harvard Board of Overseers, also appealed on Murray's behalf.[164] The appeals were to no avail, however. For all Murray had learned in three years of successful study at Howard, one of the greatest lessons appeared to be that gender discrimination would be no less a barrier to her ambition than racial discrimination.

· · · · ·

VII

Having failed to become the first woman to enter Harvard, Murray looked to Yale, only to discover that it had suspended graduate training because the war had drawn away staff and students. Murray's third choice, the University of California, Berkeley, offered her a place, but she felt ambivalent about relocating to California. Part of her hesitation related to Aunt Pauline and Aunt Sallie. Their letters spoke of loneliness, insecurity, and frailty. Aunt Pauline's frequent ailments and falls had not lessened, yet the now seventy-four-year-old continued teaching purely to bolster the meager pension that had only recently been awarded to Black teachers.[165] Concern for her aunts weighed heavily on Murray, but not so much that she declined the Berkeley opportunity. She resolved to make the move to California, in part because Mildred decided to accompany her. Pauli shared a closer relationship with Mildred than any other sibling; the sisters also shared explosive temperaments.

After hasty preparations, the pair set out driving Mildred's little Chevrolet from Washington to L.A. in late June 1944. They covered four hundred miles on the first day, but also experienced a cracked water pump and two flat tires—having to change tires twice on a 102-degree day provided a foretaste of the taxing journey to come. War rationing proved a major challenge, affecting the availability not only of gas but also of tires and other car parts. In Illinois they agreed to take two young white men on to Denver in exchange for extra tires. This required a major rearrangement to a tiny car already overloaded with an ironing board, turntable, lamps, an electric hotplate, frying pan, cooking utensils, an icebox, bedding, canned food, suitcases, and, of course, Pauli's typewriter. Polaroid sunglasses proved ineffective against the glare: the heat only intensified as they journeyed west through Missouri, Kansas, and Colorado, on highways often made of little more than sandy gravel, the dust plumes created by vehicles passing the other way added a further nerve-wracking edge to driving on tires that wore quickly.

After days of tense driving with little sleep, the weary travelers were only one hundred miles from Denver. With no spare tire remaining and Pauli behind the wheel, the car nudged over sixty miles an hour. Mildred realized this and assailed her sister, ranting that Pauli would tear her car to pieces. Pauli tried to adjust her speed, but Mildred now watched the speedometer like a hawk. Whenever the car pushed past fifty, Mildred would speak up. After one comment too many, Pauli slammed on the brakes, "sailed into" Mildred, got out of the car, slammed the door, and stormed away. An equally enraged Mildred didn't hesitate to jump behind the wheel and speed off, leaving her sister in a dust trial.

Pauli wandered the highway for half an hour, fearful of what looked like an approaching tornado in the distance. An increasingly nervous Pauli looked around for any kind of shelter and saw little. Finally another westbound car picked her up, and she continued on until she spotted Mildred's white Chevrolet coming slowly back down the highway to find her. Pauli recalled the incident in a letter to Mildred written years later: "Remember also how we both almost hurtled over a cliff when we had an argument at the top of the Great Divide? But remember too, that you could not drive on to Denver and leave me on a desolate strip of road although you were angry enough at me to wring my neck?"[166] When Pauli got back in the car the two teenage hitchhikers were no longer in the car—they decided to try for another ride when Mildred turned back to find her sister.[167]

THE DIFFICULT JOURNEY and the pair's fiery temperaments were not the only factors complicating their relationship. Mildred remained disapproving of Pauli's sexual orientation and quests for related medical attention. Before leaving the East Coast, Pauli believed she had found a doctor willing to experiment on her with "male" hormones, but then implicated Mildred as a part of the reason the treatment did not proceed. When she arrived in California, Pauli wrote to a Dr. Mazique: "Have waited to be perfectly calm before writing you, since the trip was exceedingly taxing and hectic. To begin with I was under the apprehension that you and Mildred were going to cooperate and she would give me the male hormone injections along the way. I discovered after leaving Washington that you had said nothing to her. I was disappointed and somewhat resentful. Well, it's all water under the bridge now."

Murray's letter expressed a desire to continue the "experiment as we started it," but it isn't clear whether this meant she had begun receiving hormone treatments, or they had only planned such a treatment. The letter also reveals that Murray had not given up on finding physiological evidence of "maleness," despite previous testing disproving this possibility. She informed Dr. Mazique that she had been experiencing abdominal pain, for which she had a vaginal examination that revealed a uterus displacement and a recommendation of abdominal surgery. She asked if such an operation would help or hinder "our experiment" and continued, "Is there anything they can look for while digging around in my insides, if I decide to have an operation?"[168]

Racial discrimination also made the journey upsetting and potentially further complicated Pauli's relationship with Mildred. Pauli recalled they were denied accommodation in a small Kansas town after the manager, while escorting them to the room, looked more closely at her in the fading light and asked, "Aren't some of you people colored?"[169] Pauli must have found these encounters particularly galling—she was the one being scrutinized and deemed racially unacceptable, while her biological sister stood by her side unnoticed.

Even where all concerned understood the hypocrisy of racism, still it transpired. After Pauli and Mildred arrived in L.A., a Red Cross Blood Bank representative approached them about giving blood for incoming casualties from the war in the Pacific. When Pauli later called to confirm the appointment, she learned that the blood would need to be segregated on instructions from the surgeon general in Washington. Pauli wrote to the local director and the national headquarters of the Blood Bank, as well as the surgeon general's office, stating she wouldn't participate because of her conviction that "it is criminal negligence on the part of any public official . . . to let men die because of a policy which rivals that of Hitler for its official approval of 'racial supremacy.'"[170] She also pointed out that Dr. Charles R. Drew—a leading American authority on blood plasma who helped establish the Blood Bank Plan—was Black. The surgeon general's office responded, agreeing that no scientific basis for blood segregation existed but also plainly stating that disregarding the prejudice or ignorance of many whites would be detrimental to the blood-collecting program. Murray forwarded her correspondence to the NAACP's Roy Wilkins, but beyond boycotting the program and "confrontation by typewriter" there was little more she could do.[171]

Although far from the South, Murray encountered more segregation, this time in housing. The sisters had great difficulty finding a place to live— wartime employment opportunities had resulted in the Black population

An Unknown Negro Girl without Title or Prestige

of L.A. tripling, from 49,000 to 150,000, in the past four years, while the white population grew by nearly 500,000, creating pressure on housing and forcing the boundaries between Black and white neighborhoods to shift. The pair also had no money to pay rent in advance, therefore they were compelled to accept a Black real estate agent's offer of a flat in an extremely dilapidated building he had just purchased in an otherwise neat—white— neighborhood. The sisters moved into an unfurnished railroad flat in the barnlike four-family building that had only cold water. They set up house with only a small single bed—Mildred slept on the bed frame, while Pauli had the mattress on the floor—using their suitcases as seats and eating out of cans heated on a small electric hot plate.[172]

Less than two weeks after beginning life in the less-than-ideal flat, the sisters received a letter addressed to them by name from the "South Croker Street Property Owners' Association." The letter announced that they were living in a property "restricted to the white or Caucasian race only." It continued, "We are quite sure you did not know of this restriction or you would not have rented the flat. We intend to uphold these restrictions, therefore we ask that you vacate the above mentioned flat . . . within seven days or we will turn the matter over to our attorney for action. Thank you."[173] Both sisters no longer felt safe in the rundown ground-floor flat, but Pauli especially so. Her brown skin tone, no doubt, had brought the unwanted attention, and she often remained alone in the flat while Mildred worked nursing shifts until after midnight.[174]

Despite her fear, Pauli took up the fight. Her "confrontation by typewriter" on this issue reached a wider audience because she gained a summer job reporting (sometimes under the pseudonym "Peter Panic") for the Black weekly newspaper, the *Sentinel*. She began investigating the housing issue and soon discovered that her case was one of many conflicts over restricted covenants that forbade the sale or rental of property to any nonwhite person. Murray reported the formation of the Southside Property Owners' Protective League, which had two hundred people at its first meeting and resolved to enforce restriction against "two non-Caucasian families" living in supposed restricted areas. The Murray sisters were one of the two families.[175] Her editor secured police protection for the sisters and published her article, which asserted, "One thing is clear—we do not intend to move."[176]

THE PAIR ONLY MOVED AT THE end of the summer when Mildred decided to return home and Pauli moved on to Berkeley to begin her master's degree. She moved into student accommodation for women and, once again, thrived in the all-women environment—the international students in particular helped broaden her thinking.[177] Murray's labor law study also led her to consider the necessity for legislation outlawing discrimination against women, but she confined her thesis to an examination of employment discrimination on grounds of race, color, creed, national origin, or ancestry.[178] She told Caroline Ware, "I'm beginning to believe strongly the FEPC bill should be amended to include 'sex' along with its other 'race, color, creed or national origin' factors. What do you think? Has anybody done anything along that line? It would be a shame to leave the women out of so broad a statute designed to plug up the holes of present protective legislation re employment."[179] The Fair Employment Practices Committee (FEPC) implemented Roosevelt's executive order banning federal government employment discrimination based on race, color, creed, or national origin. It took another twenty years, but Murray would eventually play a part in having sex added to the list of grounds on which employers could not discriminate.

More immediately, Murray struggled to meet the requirements of her master's degree. She believed the Berkeley law school jealously guarded its reputation and saw her as an oddity because she had been trained elsewhere. She also struggled with the loneliness of independent research and had a particularly difficult relationship with her thesis supervisor, Professor Barbara Nachtrieb Armstrong, an expert in labor law and the first woman appointed to a major law school faculty.[180] Murray described Armstrong as hard driving, strongly opinionated, and merciless in her criticisms: "She also had a disconcerting candor, which pulverized my self-confidence." Numerous drafts were rejected, and "every conference with Mrs. Armstrong became an ordeal, and my anxiety increased as the work dragged on."[181] Murray's correspondence during her time at Berkeley is sparse, something that Murray hinted at in her autobiography when she stated that Aunt Pauline had an uncanny awareness of her troubles even when she did not write.

Murray displayed signs — familiar to previous breakdowns — of taking on too many tasks. While completing her master's, she continued to give considerable attention to discussions around the formation of the United Nations, which she planned to cover for the Black press, and organized her international student roommates to join her in giving talks on diversity in the Bay Area. Although she had often been critical of President Roosevelt, on news of his death she took more time from study to pen a poem in his honor. When she showed the poem to her supervisor, Professor Armstrong commented, "We may be trying to make a second-rate lawyer out of a first-rate writer."[182] As had happened at Howard, Murray's grades began to drop as she focused on extracurricular activities.[183]

Murray didn't complete her thesis on time, forcing her to carry on over the summer without the financial support of the Rosenwald scholarship. It appeared as though she would not finish at all when she decided to enroll in a bar review course so that she could qualify to practice law in California. Professor Armstrong threatened to withhold approval of her thesis unless Murray withdrew from the course—Armstrong didn't believe Pauli had the "mental or physical capacity" to complete her thesis and prepare for the bar exam at the same time. Murray recalled that the hurtful remark turned her from despair to a grim determination to prove her abilities. She canceled the bar review course as Armstrong had insisted, but after finally submitting her thesis she spent the next three weeks studying for the three-day bar exam, passing the notoriously difficult exam without having done the preparation course, much to her supervisor's and her own amazement.[184]

Her thesis, "The Right to Equal Opportunity in Employment," had taken the entire summer to complete, delaying the completion of her master's until October 21, 1945, one month after World War II finally ended. She recalled her thesis as successful, though "produced at great emotional cost."[185] The *California Law Review* published the final product as its lead article, but even this recognition did not revive Murray's spirits from the ordeal of completing it.[186] She had felt constantly frustrated during the writing, believing Armstrong limited her from discussing those issues most important to her—segregation-related cases—and described the article as merely "rubber-stamping" her professor's viewpoint.[187] Murray also attributed the "mortifying experience" to Howard University's lack of a law review, which would have given her greater writing experience before graduate school.

A few years later, she still bemoaned the experience, describing how she had been worn out by her conservative supervisors, "who refused to let me develop my own material."[188] Murray took little pleasure from gaining her master's from Berkeley, a remarkable achievement considering she started her education in a rickety segregated classroom. The lack of enthusiasm for the achievement, even several years later, owes not only to the difficulty with her supervisor, but also to the difficult journey she embarked on to turn her prestigious qualification into lasting employment success.

......

VIII

Murray did not want to remain in California, which makes her determination to take the California bar exam with little preparation all the more remarkable. Thurgood Marshall squashed her dream job of working for the NAACP legal department—he told her there was no possibility of expanding the legal staff beyond the three lawyers and one clerk currently employed. She had no better luck gaining a teaching position at Howard University.[189] She considered further study, but the Berkeley law faculty extinguished that possibility, deciding against recommending her for admission to the doctorate program. Two years later, Murray revealed some of what the law faculty concluded in a less-than-coherent letter to a friend: "They indicated my extracurricula [sic] activities and my 'hectic and tumultous' [sic] year along with 'emotional disturbances' and although they said they did not pass on my ability, their appraisal was based upon actual performance. The performance lacked sufficient 'distinction' to justify recommendation for a higher degree, although the Master's degree apparently was earned. That is that."[190]

Murray would have benefited from a prolonged rest, but she had no source of income. Without work, she would be compelled to once again consider a return to Durham. Murray's ongoing concerns about Aunt Pauline—now in her thirty-ninth year of teaching—had not eased. Pauli had hoped to entice her adoptive mother to California, to visit at first, but Aunt Pauline stated she was too feeble to make the trip. Aunt Pauline's letters frequently referred to worsening health—in addition to falls, she had long suffered "sinking spells"—making Pauli feel suitably concerned and guilty.[191] Uncertainty about her next move is evident in Murray's decision to pack her bags and book a ticket to the East Coast, but then delay traveling to attend the California Bar swearing-in ceremony on December 11, 1945.[192]

At the ceremony, California's attorney general, Robert W. Kenny, surprised Murray with a job offer. Kenny had read her lead article in the *California Law Review* and told her that he wanted her on his staff. What he did not say, but Murray quickly grasped, is that he also wanted her for her race. Kenny planned to run for governor and had been criticized for the lack of African Americans on his staff. Of the forty-five lawyers who worked for him, only seven were women, and none were Black.[193] Race had so long been a barrier to Murray's full participation in society, but in this situation it proved an advantage, which she tried to leverage during salary negotiations. A few days after their meeting, she wrote to Kenny to discuss the job and pay, adding, "I have no doubt but that the Negro community will look upon this appointment with keen interest and I should like to have the opportunity of pioneering with your staff."[194] Murray accepted the position and planned to start in the New Year.

First, she planned to take a break and spend Christmas in L.A. with a friend's family (a decision that cannot have pleased Aunt Pauline). During the bus trip to L.A., Murray experienced "an attack of nausea accompanied

Portrait of Murray
taken in Sacramento,
1946. *(Schlesinger
Library, Radcliffe
Institute, Harvard
University)*

by dull pains" in her side. She recalled experiencing similar attacks during
the bar exam, which she dismissed as nerves, but now she became concerned. Her friend's father, an internist, put her through a series of labo-
ratory tests. According to Murray's autobiography the tests confirmed his
diagnosis of "chronic subacute appendicitis," aggravated by the strain of
completing her thesis and passing the bar. The vague diagnosis and its unclear relationship to her exhausted mental state wasn't greatly reassuring,
but Murray still made the move from Oakland to Sacramento to take up the
position, purely because she believed her status as a "first" made it an important breakthrough.[195]

Black media outlets gave Murray's appointment extensive coverage.
A front-page story appeared in the *L.A. Tribune*, and the *Baltimore Afro-
American* carried both an article and large photo of Murray, copies of which
she ordered for her family.[196] Murray also featured in a newsreel in Black
cinemas, though she and her colleagues could not see it in Sacramento,
where there were no Black cinemas to show it.[197] For someone who had ex-

perienced so much discrimination and marginalization, the positive recognition must have been satisfying, but it also created anxiety about her ability to perform in the new job, especially considering her already-exhausted state.

Letters to Aunt Pauline indicate that concerns about her appendix plagued her from the outset. Aunt Pauline wrote, "Your letter came to me telling me of your first day's work, also of your continued sickness. I am very glad that you are able to be on the job the 1st day. I am very sorry that you have suffered so long and so much. Yes, it will be best to have your ap- removed as soon as you can."[198] Several days later, Pauli assured Aunt Pauline that she was doing better. Aunt Pauline was equally supportive: "I am so glad you are better. I do hope you will not have an operation."[199] Aunt Pauline's own health was poor—in this close pair each woman's health concerns seemingly exacerbated the other's. In the same month Murray began work, January 1946, Aunt Pauline developed bronchial pneumonia, followed by attacks of weakness and drowsiness, for which her physician could not determine the cause.

In resisting a greater role in Aunt Pauline's care, Murray encountered another layer of pressure that affected her health and ability to do the job. If Aunt Pauline could not return to work, then Pauli would be compelled to either quit her prestigious position, return to Durham, and accept the role of dutiful unwed daughter, or increase her income to the point that she would be able to support her adoptive mother from afar. Murray agitated for a higher salary, unsuccessfully, for the second time, despite only just starting the job.[200]

Adding to this family responsibility, Pauli was also hoping to avoid caring for a twenty-year-old male relative who was in trouble and whose mother wanted to send him to stay with her in California.[201] Pauli's sister Grace had also been released from Crownsville, but faced recommitment at any time by her husband. Eager to establish her financial independence, Grace made inquiries to the unwell Aunt Pauline about the possible sale of the small plot of Fitzgerald land that Grandmother Cornelia had originally inherited from her slave-owning forebears. This compounded family and financial worries for Pauli. She thought the family might need to contribute toward a lawyer for Grace in the event she wished to divorce or challenge a future commitment order, but Pauli still owed money to Mildred, among others. In a letter to her uncle in Baltimore, Pauli wrote,

> Now Bubber, we all need to cooperate to pull us all through. We've
> been divided and weak too long. Right now I'm holding up the "dra-

matic" end of the job—but please don't get too elated. I'm only a little deputy attorney general appointed for six months who must take a civil service exam if I want a permanent job and who gets only the minimum pay for attorneys just passing the bar and without experience. The only reason it has any passing significance is that it is a "first." But I'm a little under the weather and trying to hold my end up. I suspect we are all a little under the weather.[202]

Pauli made several plans involving her writing to generate additional income. She told Uncle Bubber,

> I've written the publisher who is holding my manuscript of poetry headed by "Dark Testament" asking him if there is any possibility of publication this year. If the book sells I will get some royalties. I have also written requesting discussion of the possibility of a contract for a book which is inside me and must be written. An advance would be additional income. I am also trying to prepare some articles on the side which may sell, and perhaps a newspaper column. These are merely tentative plans, but if they, or any one of them materialize, I will be able to contribute to whatever may be necessary for Grace's needs. I have one other responsibility—my own private life.[203]

Of these plans, only the newspaper articles came to fruition in the short term.

Murray authored a series of articles for the *Baltimore Afro-American* describing the tremendous conflict for a "militant, aggressive, race relationist" holding public office. In one article she wrote, "I find myself having to think longer before I shoot off at the mouth, of having to pause and consider how much I can say when acting as a State official."[204] California's antimiscegenation laws particularly troubled Murray, since she was under oath to uphold them. Although antimiscegenation laws, her experience with blood donations, and housing in L.A. all exposed her to segregation in California, she still preferred her new state to North Carolina. In another article, she described her "continual nausea" at the thought of having to return to the South. She stated her determination not to live under Jim Crow regardless of inducement or obligations, arguing that other African Americans should also leave the South.[205] Her reference to not returning because of "obligations" seems a public repudiation of the private pleas by her family, particularly Aunt Pauline's.

Uncle Bubber had criticized her move to California, which made her more defensive about her contributions to family problems. She defended the initial move to California by explaining to him that she was focused on broad social and group problems. Trying to advance the condition of the group, she argued, would ultimately serve the family better, especially the generation of her nieces and nephews.[206] The publicity she received for gaining the breakthrough appointment as a deputy attorney general certainly suggested she was advancing the condition of the group, but it was coming at a huge personal cost.

Stark evidence of the unhappiness that lay below Murray's achievement appear in the only two journal entries she made between November and February. On her birthday, November 20, shortly before she accepted the deputy attorney general position, she wrote, "35 years old today. No words come. Perhaps the first stage of my life was the writing stage. Perhaps I pass on to the doing stage."[207] Her next diary entry, written a month into the new job, stated, "Maybe it's the other way around. Perhaps I've passed the doing stage and am in the writing stage."[208] Time and again, when pressures became too great Murray sought to withdraw and focus on writing.[209] In early March she told a friend, "My troubles seemed to start with passing the Bar. I should have flunked and written a novel in peace and 'blessed' ignominity [sic]."[210]

Just as Murray conceived of letter writing as "confrontation by typewriter," creative writing seemed to loom in her mind as self-therapy by typewriter, though she found far fewer opportunities to pursue the latter type of therapy. The stressful effort to achieve the deputy attorney general position, the demands of the job, the pressure and scrutiny associated with being a "first," personal health concerns, and ongoing family problems all contributed to her woes. She had to carry all of these burdens, holding them in to do her job, unless she could somehow escape to focus on creative writing. Barely two months after starting the job, without even packing her belongings, Murray boarded a plane to the East Coast.

MURRAY'S PLANE LANDED IN WASHINGTON in time for her to receive a 1945 "Women of the Year" honor bestowed on her by the National Council of Negro Women. The March 16, 1946, *Washington Evening Star* featured a picture of an emaciated-looking Murray receiving her scroll from Mary McLeod Bethune, along with the other recipients, which included her friend from the Odell Waller campaign, unionist Maida Springer.[211] The next day Murray returned to Durham. Murray's autobiography described finding Aunt Pauline in such an unwell state that she immediately took her back to Washington to have her admitted to Freedmen's Hospital, on the advice of her sister Mildred.[212] The autobiography didn't mention that she too was still unwell and she too entered Freedmen's as a patient. One week after featuring in the press receiving her "Women of the Year" scroll, the March 23 *Baltimore Afro-American* "Behind the Scenes" column revealed, "Pauli Murray, recently appointed an assistant to the attorney in the State of California, is in Freedmen's Hospital in D.C. for a checkup."[213]

Pauli remained in Washington, and in a very depressed mood, through April. She wrote to Morris Milgram, the head of the WDL, expressing her need for $500 to cover the cost of Aunt Pauline's hospitalization. She explained how the hospital staff had forced them to wait in emergency for over four hours before Murray "raised hell" with the staff to get her mother properly admitted. She also reported that Aunt Pauline remained at Freedmen's because of diabetes and a complaint related to complications from a 1942 abdominal operation. Regarding her own health, Murray revealed that she had been suffering glandular problems. She confided to Milgram, "Sometimes I get so thoroughly disgusted with the struggle to stay alive, I wonder why I just don't lie down and die without even bothering." Later in the letter she expressed a familiar desire following periods of extreme duress: "I just want to go away to the country with my dog away from everybody and bury myself for a while."[214]

Another family matter also weighed heavily during her time in Washington. Grace's transition back into the community, after nearly five years in Crownsville, wasn't going well. A month after Grace's release, on May 2, her husband again sought her commitment to the public hospitals. He petitioned to affect a "committeeship" through which Grace's teacher retirement fund could be collected. The petition stated that Grace was unable to care for herself or her property; it included testimony from two white doctors describing Grace as suffering from "progressive paranoia," which they believed would cause "increasing mental deterioration."[215] There is little surviving evidence among Pauli's papers concerning how Grace's plight affected her, though it must have been a contributing, if not primary, worry at this time. Pauli had certainly been involved in trying to assist Grace to adjust to life outside Crownsville — she had made inquiries to get Grace and her husband jobs as camp teachers so they could take their son and live and work somewhere with fresh mountain air, which Pauli herself so often desired in times of crisis.[216]

This private tragedy became public knowledge when the *Baltimore Afro-American* reported that Uncle Bubber and three of Pauli's siblings had filed a counterpetition in the circuit court to prevent Grace's husband from taking control of her assets. They wanted to have Grace removed from the city hospitals and placed in a private institution for a period of approximately two months before later being released into their care.[217] The only two Murray siblings not listed on the petition were Pauli and Bill (who was institution-alized at the time). There could have been multiple reasons why Pauli did not join the petition, including her own ill health, an inability to contrib-ute financially to the court case or Grace's care, or her sensitivity to rumors about the "mad Murrays," which could have made her unwilling to become involved in a publicized court battle.

Although the news story did not mention Pauli, the public airing of this private anguish exacerbated her feelings of being forever on trial. These types of feelings led Murray to strive to prove her capabilities, even when she didn't feel up to the challenge, while also compounding her sensitivity to the fear that she and her loved ones were cursed with hereditary insanity. In the last few months alone, Murray featured in the Black press because of her groundbreaking appointment as a deputy attorney general, her presen-tation with a "Women of the Year" award, and then her hospitalization. Now her family problems were news. Adding further injury to the public wound, the counterpetition failed. On May 8, 1946, Grace returned to Crownsville.

AUNT PAULINE RETURNED TO THE classroom after nearly two months in the hospital to see out her last year before reaching the mandatory retire-ment age of seventy-five.[218] Pauli's guilt over her family obligation could only have worsened as Aunt Pauline approached retirement. Nevertheless, Pauli still refused to return to Durham. She headed back to New York, where she regained some happiness — she confessed feeling better away from "the strain of Washington." Vitamin injections also helped improve her nerves.[219] She described herself to Aunt Sallie as on the way to a new start: "My nerves are unbelievably improved, I have a hearty appetite, am gaining weight, sleeping better and much less jumpy."[220] Soon after returning to New York, Murray must have succeeded in borrowing money, because she had dental work completed. "Naturally," she explained, "$200 is a tremendous amount to pay, but I think just getting my teeth fixed is of psychological value to me." Murray sorely needed some self-care after enduring such a torrid time — and she would also need to regain some confidence to face the struggle of finding professional employment at a time when so many servicemen were flooding back into the civilian workforce.[221]

Feeling better now, Murray made inquiries about how her departure from California had been received and whether there was a possibility of resuming her employment. She wrote to her former employers, describ-ing how she had heard "rumors from the West Coast that she had walked off the job," then going on to provide a lengthy twelve-point explanation of her sudden exit. She explained that on accepting the position on December 17, 1945, she had traveled to L.A. to "rest and gain strength for my duties" and became seriously ill. She then explained how the "chronic appendicitis" diagnosis was revised following a "gastro-intestinal study" to "the normal nervous collapse of students who endure the strain of graduate work and taking the bar." The next four points explain her concern about Aunt Pauline's health and the potential financial strain that placed her under. Point 7 then returns to the issue of her health—Dr. Johnson, at Freedmen's, in consultation with her L.A. doctor, advised she take six months' rest. The remaining five points account for why she did not fully explain her reasons before leaving—Murray stated that she wasn't able to speak to the attorney general before departing and that she didn't formally resign because the attorney general had just announced his candidacy for the governorship. She thought her departure "would have a definite affect upon the Negro community unless it were handled with tact."[222]

Charles W. Johnson, deputy director of the Justice Department, replied to Murray stating that he understood from a telephone conversation he had with her just before her departure that she was resigning. When he did not then receive a formal written resignation, he had no option other than to show her absent without leave on the attendance report.[223] Murray replied warmly, addressing the deputy director as "Dear Charlie." She seemed to be projecting her own experience onto him when she wrote, "I think the various misunderstandings about my leaving the office were due to the terrific pressure under which you were working and our inability to talk the thing through. I did not hand in a resignation because I wanted to return to the office and complete my job. Although it may not be important to the Department of Justice, I feel very strongly about completing a job I start. It is a matter of personal integrity, I think."[224] Murray seemed oblivious to the realities of her departure from California. Or perhaps, once her mood had stabilized, she recognized the precariousness of her situation and was trying to place a more positive spin on her departure.

Further insight into her attempt to return to California appears in a letter to Aunt Pauline. "Mother, I have been reflecting upon the summer and my future plans," she wrote. "In view of the fact that all my clothes, books and personal affects are still out in California I have wondered how I might get back over there to get my things together and complete my job. I have felt that I ought to finish out the four months in the Department of Justice, just for my personal experience record. It will look bad down the line if I don't finish up there, particularly because so much was made of the job by the Negro press and movies etc." She went on to explain, "It seemed to me that if I were going back to California at all, now was the opportune time. School is out and you are on the way to recovery, so that I don't have to worry about additional strains for a while."[225]

It seemed like a fine plan now that she was in a better frame of mind and Aunt Pauline was back on her feet. Her former employers did not agree, though. She was told there was no position for her to go back to, nor would they allow her to sit the public service exam—a requirement for any new appointment—in absentia. With all hope of regaining the job extinguished, Murray now expressed relief to Aunt Pauline that she did not have to go back—revealing that she had inquired only because she felt "duty bound" to make an application for reinstatement.[226]

Becoming the first African American deputy attorney general of California provided title and prestige, which Murray must have hoped could overcome the societally engendered feeling that she was a "nobody" who counted for nothing, but it also created anxieties and sapped already-depleted personal resources. Her return to New York City in the postwar era brought new achievements, but the barriers to her advancement remained significant. Indeed, they became more significant with the onset of the Cold War, when she received a new unwanted marginalizing identity: suspect citizen.

four

SUCH A STATE OF

UNCERTAINTY,

CAUTION, AND FEAR,

1946–1961

. . . . .

I

Murray returned to New York City with a master's degree but still with few encouraging employment prospects. She described her aim on returning to the city: "The main thing right now is to get out of debt, get some money in the bank and get some general legal experience. Of course, being a woman in the field of law is as bad as being a Negro — and the combination is pretty awful."[1] Murray knew when she enrolled at Howard Law School that she was entering a white male–dominated profession — only fifty-nine Negro women attorneys were practicing in the United States at the time.[2] Preferential employment for returned servicemen added another hurdle, as did her ineligibility to practice law in New York.

Despite all the obstacles, in the summer of 1946 Murray gained a position with the Commission on Law and Social Action (CLSA), an agency of the American Jewish Congress. In the work undertaken by the CLSA Murray recognized similarities with the work of her dream employer, the NAACP.[3] Murray essentially performed the duties of a research assistant but still had opportunities to work on significant cases, such as *Mendez v. Westminster*, a case stemming from a lawsuit filed by a group of Mexican American parents challenging the segregation of Southern California schoolchildren based on their surname. The CLSA added a brief to the case, as did the NAACP, and

Murray seated between two women outside International House, New York City, 1947.
(Schlesinger Library, Radcliffe Institute, Harvard University)

Murray's recent employer, the California attorney general. The case never reached the Supreme Court, but NAACP lawyers later studied the briefs when preparing for the *Brown v. Board of Education* case.[4]

In addition to legal work on significant cases, Murray continued her activism to ensure that Supreme Court decisions were enforced. In June 1946, around the time Murray began working for the CLSA, in *Morgan v. Virginia*, the Court ruled segregated interstate transportation unconstitutional. The Congress of Racial Equality (CORE), of which Murray was a member, learned that bus companies planned to simply ignore the Court's decision. CORE's national executive, meeting in Cleveland, decided to organize an interracial bus tour from Baltimore to New Orleans to test the *Morgan* decision. To plan the action, CORE leader Bayard Rustin convened a working group in New York that included Murray. Her commitment to nonviolent direct-action protest and her repeated willingness to test the constitutionality of segregation laws made her an obvious candidate for such a working group. In addition to working with Rustin, on this project Murray also worked with Ella Baker, whom she had first met while on the WPA.

The group made plans for an interracial group to tour the South on

Such a State of Uncertainty, Caution, and Fear

interstate buses, taking up seats that defied segregated seating customs and giving lectures on pacifism along the way. To reduce the likelihood of violence, they decided to confine the "Journey of Reconciliation" to the upper South. Against strong objections from Murray and Baker, the group also decided that only men could participate in the tour, because "mixing races and sexes would possibly exacerbate an already volatile situation."[5] The male-dominated planning group suggested a women's tour at an underdetermined later date, but this token gesture hardly satisfied Murray or Baker, both of whom had challenged segregated bus seating in the past. Compounding Murray's disappointment, few southern men schooled in nonviolent protest could be found for the journey. Murray must have privately lamented the fact that she was a southerner committed to nonviolence and had already been arrested on an interstate bus journey while passing as a man.[6]

It's a remarkable testament to Murray's innovative activism that she carried out, or attempted to carry out, nearly all of the iconic civil rights protests over a decade earlier than the famous versions. Eighteen years before Little Rock, she attempted to integrate southern education. Twenty-two years before Dr. King spoke at the famous demonstration in the nation's capital, she both marched and organized for the March on Washington Movement. Fifteen years before Rosa Parks's bus arrest, Murray experienced the same fate. Seventeen years before the Greensboro lunch counter sit-ins, she helped organize "stool-sitting" protests at segregated restaurants. And thirteen years before the Freedom Rides began, Murray helped organize the Journey of Reconciliation. Although Murray could later take pride in her forward-thinking and daring protests, in the immediate aftermath of each of her protest attempts she felt frustrated and betrayed by the men who failed to support her.

The Journey of Reconciliation went ahead without Murray. Concerns about the dangers were not misplaced. Beginning in Washington, eight Black men and eight white men defied segregated bus seating customs while traveling, without incident, through Virginia—including a stop in Petersburg, where Murray had been arrested—and then into North Carolina, where several of the men were arrested in Chapel Hill and later sentenced to thirty days on a chain gang.[7] A local taxi driver also punched one of the protestors, who had not been arrested, for "coming down here to stir up the niggers." The protestors were then pursued by white taxi drivers to a local minister's house, which the drivers pelted with rocks, breaking several windows. Some UNC students arrived to oppose the mob, but police also arrived to defuse the situation. The protestors carried on through two more states and notched up twelve arrests and extensive coverage in the Black press, but interstate bus segregation continued despite the Supreme Court ruling outlawing it.[8]

MURRAY MADE ONLY A PASSING REFERENCE to the Journey of Reconciliation in a letter to Caroline Ware: "I guess you read of the Reconciliation Tour which tested the *Morgan* decision in North Carolina, Virginia, and Tennessee, and which was brain trusted from this end by a number of us."[9] Her lack of enthusiasm owes not only to her exclusion from the journey, but also to the fact that a week earlier she had quit her job and entered the hospital. The day before the men set out, on April 9, 1947, Murray underwent abdominal surgery. Her autobiography explained, "Although the CLSA dealt with civil rights issues, it did not provide the experience in legal practice I needed, so after nine months I left, entered the hospital for surgery to remove the appendix which had long plagued me, and then set about preparing for the New York bar examinations."[10] Murray didn't indicate what type of legal experience she required, or why she could not have taken sick leave for the operation or studied for the bar while working.

Archival evidence reveals her employers believed she lacked sufficient training and advised her to return to law school.[11] Her employer's dissatisfaction with her performance might in turn have stemmed from her own dissatisfaction with the job. Murray told Aunt Pauline that she had resigned from the CLSA job partly because she was unhappy working for a "cause" organization and had expressed a desire to work in a smaller business office.[12] But she also told a friend that she quit, in part, because she was receiving seventy dollars a week but thought she was worth one hundred.[13] The varying accounts of why she resigned suggest there was more going on in her life at this time than she was willing to acknowledge in her autobiography or the private correspondence she preserved.

There is no direct evidence that the surgery was part of a quest to locate male attributes within her body, though Murray would surely have hoped for such a discovery. Only three years had elapsed since she had asked Dr. Mazique if there was anything surgeons could look for if she ever had a stomach operation.[14] The 1947 operation resulted in the removal of her appendix as well as a fallopian tube and a cystic ovary, but secreted testes were not discovered. If Murray felt devastated by the surgery's failure to confirm her "pseudo hermaphrodite" theory, the remaining evidence doesn't show it. She wrote to the doctor to thank him, joking that if she ever needed her "motor taken apart" again, he would be her first-choice "mechanic."[15]

There is some indirect evidence to suggest that gender and sexuality issues troubled Murray before the operation. The July *Negro Digest* carried an article she wrote titled "Why Negro Girls Stay Single: Negro Males Expose Women to Jane Crow as Well as Jim Crow." She argued that a college-educated Negro woman made a poor match for the average Negro male who left high school for a trade. In addition to economic incompatibility, she described Negro men as emotionally immature and numerically inferior to Negro women. Murray's article may or may not have been inspired by her exclusion from the Reconciliation Tour—it was certainly an expression of her frustration with compounding discrimination. According to her argument, racism inverted traditional gender roles: Negro men lacked employment opportunities but were expected to behave "as if they were lords of creation, bread winners and warriors." Relatively better employment prospects for women, according to her argument, prompted a backlash from emasculated men, who then further oppressed women. The combination of race and gender oppression, she argued, "contributes to a jungle of human relationships, aggravates among Negroes the alienation of the sexes, intensifies homosexuality and often results in a rising incidence of crimes of passion, broken homes and divorces."[16] This is one of the only public comments Murray made about homosexuality—a passing comment that linked it with other negative effects of race and gender oppression.

Problems relating to gender expectations remained evident in other areas of her life. Aunt Pauline's retirement occurred the month before the CLSA employed Murray. The job had given Pauli reason not to return to Durham, but now that she had resigned, the pressure resumed, though she still strongly resisted such a move. "You must not be hurt by the decisions I make," she told Aunt Pauline shortly after her surgery. "Each of us must do what is wisest and best for us, and it seems wisest [at] the moment for me to stay in New York and hold things down here. The South has never been home to me, and a mansion and millions would not make it home. Just as you could not live the kind of life I must lead to follow my own convictions, so I can't live in the South."[17] Only a few weeks earlier, a young man from Baltimore traveling to North Carolina to visit his mother for Easter didn't make it because a railway conductor shot him dead after he resisted segregated seating. After reading about the killing, Murray wasn't even willing to visit, let alone relocate.[18]

Almost from the time Murray returned to New York, she had been resisting the alternative of Aunt Sallie and Aunt Pauline moving to New York to live with her. "You don't know how this problem has worried me," she wrote to Aunt Sallie. "To begin with, I've been holding my breath with reference to my health. It is not so much physical as the nervous strain of getting back to the city."[19] Pauli was also helping their sister, Aunt Marie, who lived alone in New York City despite failing health, leading Murray to describe herself as the "Social Service Bureau for the special benefit of the Fitzgerald family."[20]

In addition to ongoing concerns about her aunts, an even more worrying family crisis developed involving the arrest of her cousin Joshua, whom Pauli and Mac had tried to provide parental-type care for in the prewar period.[21] Pauli had hoped to spend the month of May resting and recuperating from abdominal surgery, but she described to a friend being "shocked out of my lethargy by the knowledge that my godson and cousin was being held at the Federal Detention Headquarters on a charge of mail theft."[22] Murray felt initial reluctance to share the news of the latest family trouble, but her own unemployment and indebtedness meant she could not pay Joshua's initial bail. She wrote to Aunt Sallie, Joshua's mother, saying, "Something has come up on this end and I may need some cash. . . . I'll explain my urgency later."[23] Murray's involvement did not end there.

Given the family's financial hardship, she had little option other than to represent Joshua in court only a month after her operation. Murray's first case as a lawyer required representing her godson who had been charged with a crime that could result in a substantial prison sentence. Because the case was before a federal court, Murray couldn't even draw on her experience as a defendant or witness in earlier criminal trials to guide her, nor was a Berkeley master's thesis in labor law helpful preparation. Since Joshua had confessed, Murray's efforts were directed toward arguing for leniency in sentencing. In private correspondence, she described being "scared to death" and the strain as "terrific."[24] Joshua was sentenced to one year and one day in a federal prison.[25] Pauli described it to Aunt Pauline: "The strain was so great that when the judge finally delivered his sentence (although I fought every step of the way) the tears just welled up and spilled over. I rushed out of the courtroom and up the ladies room and wept."[26] With a little more time, however, Murray reflected positively on her performance—Joshua received half the prison time as one of his coaccused. She also reported receiving praise from court workers for her handling of the case.

Yet more family problems hampered Pauli's recovery from surgery. Grace gained her freedom from Crownsville, against medical advice, on June 21, 1947. Pauli's papers provide little insight into Grace's situation at this time, but it is reasonable to assume that the problems were familiar. "I don't want to be too hard on Grace," Pauli confided to Aunt Pauline the previous year, "but when she is in the hospital she is crazy to get out, and once out she has insisted upon staying with Lewis [her husband] and making herself and everyone miserable."[27] Such ongoing struggles were a source of worry and exasperation, but also a continual reminder of the possibility that mental health problems might have been passed on by her father.

NOW OUT OF WORK, MURRAY AGAIN explored the possibility of pursuing a doctorate degree. She still dreamed of Harvard. Since her initial rejection in 1944, she had inquired again in 1946 while deputy attorney general of California, and again now in 1947, but the ban on women remained in place (it remained until 1950, at which time it became clear to her that she wouldn't be able to meet other admission requirements).[28] Murray learned only now that Berkeley's law faculty had voted last November not to recommend her as a doctoral candidate. She wrote a fiery letter to Berkeley, which she then described to her mentor Caroline Ware: "Actually my shock no doubt led me into so suspicious a frame of mind that I didn't pull my punches, although I tried to end the letter in a friendly tone." She shared a copy of the letter with Ware, who suggested changes to avoid antagonizing the Berkeley faculty, but it was too late, Murray had regretfully already sent off the assertive letter. She wrote a friendlier follow-up letter to the Berkeley law dean urging a reconsideration of the adverse recommendation, which the Boalt Hall Law Faculty duly undertook, but decided against overturning their earlier decision. One Berkeley mentor wrote her a kindly letter suggesting that she pursue a career, or further study, in creative writing.[29]

Murray wanted desperately to pursue a writing career. She borrowed several hundred dollars from a WDL member to whom she sent a thank-you note and receipt, which she joked he would one day be proud of when she won a Pulitzer Prize.[30] Personal loans were not enough to sustain a writing career, however, especially when she made little immediate headway with her writing. Murray's financial situation, which had always been desperate, grew worse in the months after leaving the CLSA job. She had been earning a salary near $4,000 a year, but after her hospitalization she was reduced to working two and a half hours, six mornings a week, in the cafeteria of International House, where she resided, for the pay of only twenty meals a week.[31] The evidence is scare, but it appears that Murray commenced a law doctorate at Columbia University in the months after her departure from the CLSA job.[32] If that is true, it must have been a terribly difficult and short-lived bid to add to her qualifications, undertaken with almost no financial support.

Murray began looking for legal work again. Her difficulty finding any exposes the broader problem faced by Black women seeking professional employment in a society that traditionally excluded them and was still reabsorbing World War II servicemen into the civilian workforce: in the two years before 1947 the number of women workers nationally fell by 4 million.[33] Murray described her appearance during this time as "just shorty of being seedy." She owned only one dress, which she had to keep clean as she traipsed from office to office seeking legal work and facing the "constant dread of rejection." She could never be sure if each rejection was because of her race, gender, downtrodden appearance, or inexperience, and each rejection could only have further eroded her self-belief. Even when she gained law-clerking work, the pay proved so poor that she developed a tapeworm from eating cheap hamburgers.[34]

To improve her employment prospects, Murray sat and passed the New York bar exam in October 1947. In the intervening time between sitting the exam and discovering the results—around Christmastime—she moved to Brooklyn. This move led to a significant delay in gaining admission to the bar, because she needed to reside in the new judicial district for at least six months before she could present her papers for processing. Murray had moved to Brooklyn after a lawyer who also had a real estate business enticed her to accept a law clerk position by also offering her a cheap apartment to rent. The top-floor apartment in a three-story Chauncey Street row house was run-down but still offered a welcome respite from living out of rented rooms.[35] Murray's tumultuous life is starkly illustrated by the number of times she changed accommodation: in the twenty-two years since she had first left Durham, she had lived in at least forty-two different residences.[36]

Murray didn't get to enjoy her own apartment for long. The now-retired Aunt Pauline, who had endured many disappointing festive seasons without her adopted daughter, came to stay with Pauli for a month at Christmas. Shortly after, in early March 1948, Cousin Joshua gained release from prison on the condition that he live with Pauli for the remaining few months of his sentence.[37] Asthmatic and unable to contribute much financially, he also bristled under Pauli's supervision. Joshua moved out at the earliest opportunity, but Aunt Pauline had enjoyed her Christmas stay so much that six months later she and Aunt Sallie sold the Fitzgerald home and moved into Chauncey Street with Pauli. The apartment had three rooms lined up front to back with no internal doors between each room, making privacy a major issue. In an optimistic assessment of the arrangement, Murray took some comfort from having "family problems under one roof."[38]

Murray could also escape Chauncey Street by taking her dog Smokey for walks. She often found it difficult to maintain smooth relationships with people, and dogs had become an increasingly important outlet for affection and companionship. In the early 1940s she had briefly acquired two dogs—Toni, then Petie—but gave both up after short periods because of the ongoing instability in her living arrangements. Once she had settled in at Chauncey Street, she adopted Smokey—a tricolored Shetland sheepdog she named for his black, brown, and white markings. From this point forward, Murray almost always lived with a canine companion.[39]

· · · · ·

II

After six months working as a law clerk, Murray became fed up. She felt like an "errand girl" who received no additional reward or praise for good work and received the blame when things went wrong. She told Caroline Ware, "I'm so tired of being a whipping boy for other people's doings and not be able to answer back."[40] Murray quit and found a slightly higher-paying job as a managing clerk for a Manhattan lawyer. She was able to continue renting the Chauncey Street apartment, however, mercifully ensuring she did not have to move judicial districts again and further delay her application for admission to the New York Bar.

Murray's bar application already faced substantial barriers thanks to the first chill winds of the Cold War that began sweeping through the nation around this time. The long-standing House Un-American Activities Committee started gaining prominence, and in 1947 President Truman initiated a loyalty security program that empowered the FBI to conduct background checks on current and prospective government employees.[41] Just how rapidly Cold War suspicions had escalated became evident to Murray through the differences between her California and New York bar applications: in California, she had needed only an affidavit, but one year later the New York process required listing every place she had lived, every job she had held, every organization she had been associated with, and every publication she had authored. Murray also had to complete a loyalty questionnaire, provide character references from past employers and landlords, and submit to an interview by a Committee on Character and Fitness.[42] Such barriers may have deterred some people, but, typically, Murray became more determined to meet the challenge.

In the application Murray tried to downplay some aspects of her past. To explain her various political involvements between 1936 and 1942, Murray wrote many affidavits and devoted considerable attention to explaining her association with the Lovestoneites, which she described as owing to the curiosity of a student mind. She claimed to have broken with the group over their backing of the Communist Party candidate in the 1936 presidential election and her inability to reconcile her religious convictions with a philosophy of class struggle. She concluded that she did not regret her involvement because the experience gave her a greater appreciation of democracy as well as an ability to identify genuine reformers from "totalitarians."[43]

The list of publications she provided did not include "Three Thousand Miles on a Dime in Ten Days," the short story published in *Negro* that described a boy's adventures riding the rails and included a picture of her dressed as Pete.[44] Murray's autobiography focused on the familiar aspects of the persecution of political leftists during the Cold War, but the Committee on Character and Fitness were judging her on her political and personal past. To overlook the personal is to ignore the persecution of people whose lives were unstable because of impoverishment or mental illness, or because they were marginalized on racial, gender, or sexual grounds or, as in Murray's case, all of the above.

Even answering a basic but scarcely relevant question about her marital status proved troublesome, since Murray remained legally married to Billy Wynn. Ever since studying law at Howard, she had thought the marriage might become a problem and made occasional efforts to find Billy, but only now located him in Virginia.[45] Mildred met with him and reported back: "How did you ever let a fine guy like that loose. Pauli don't be an ASS, keep the guy and try him again." After receiving the letter Pauli asked Aunt Pauline for her thoughts, commenting, "He seems like an intelligent, mature, religious man. Beyond that I don't know."[46] Opinions on her former husband hardly mattered, however, since Billy had remarried—illegally, given that the marriage to Pauli had not been annulled.

Around this time Murray made other occasional, token efforts to conform to heterosexual womanhood. She reluctantly went on an uncomfortable date with a man that her latest employer arranged. Whether she was simply trying to appease her boss isn't certain, but there were no further dates with the gentleman. Murray must have been subjected to ongoing pressure from people wanting to help find her "the right man," even from people familiar with her sexual preference. When Murray praised her new employer's professionalism in a letter to Aunt Pauline, she immediately anticipated her adoptive mother's likely response: her next words were "YES YES YES!! My boss is married."[47]

Murray's personal life came up in other areas of her New York Bar application as well. She feared the committee would learn about her 1940 referral to Bellevue Hospital after Rhode Island police found her disconsolately wandering the streets. Murray consulted Dr. May Chinn, who had treated her during breakdowns in 1934, 1935, and 1940, and possibly other undocumented occasions. Chinn told Murray she would need to get her record from Bellevue and probably get an analyst or psychiatrist to provide a statement as to her present mental and emotional condition.[48] Scholars have identified psychoanalysis as "a veritable fount of homophobia, misogyny, and conservatism, central to the Cold War project of normalization," which must have compounded Murray's family history concerns when consulting an analyst.[49] Bowing to psychoanalytic authority was just one of the ways Murray came to accept the Cold War project of normalization—she had little choice other than to do so if she wanted professional success.

Psychotherapy had long repelled but also intrigued Murray. Any remaining resistance all but disappeared now. Shortly after surgery a year earlier, Murray told a friend that she had attended some analytic sessions and "found them extremely helpful." Murray consulted Dr. Leon Goldensohn— a New York psychiatrist recently returned from working with Nazi defendants awaiting trial in Nuremberg—and continued to consult with him over the next few years. She also reported becoming more "sympathetic to the whole process" of psychoanalysis after attending public lectures by Karen Horney.[50] One of the most famed psychoanalysts of the period, Horney posited childhood experiences as a key determinant of human growth and neurosis. If people have adverse experiences in childhood, Horney argued, they will develop not a feeling of belonging but a profound sense of insecurity and vague apprehensiveness, which she termed "basic anxiety." In the neurotic person, these common tendencies become more rigid and extreme, and the alienation from others and from oneself impairs the individual's inner strength, self-confidence, and coherence. In a quest for a feeling of identity, the individual will search for glory—something that will provide a feeling of power and significance. Horney describes the search for glory as a "neurotic ambition," a drive toward external success, typically success in acquiring power or prestige. If the success is achieved, however, it does not result in banishing the unbearable feelings (feeling lost, anxious, inferior, and divided); rather, the individual comes to realize the futility of the striving and may decide on a new ambition.[51]

There is no way to assess how accurately Horney's ideas applied to Murray's personal psychology, but Murray believed they were helpful. Horney's theories provided an alternative means by which Murray could understand her experiences and impulses—ideas with the potential to ease some of her fear of hereditary insanity. The predominance of psychoanalysis in the postwar period, which could have been disastrous for Murray given that it was a "veritable fount of homophobia, misogyny, and conservatism," seemed beneficial. At least temporarily, she considered that her biology might not be defective—that in fact her traumatic childhood experiences might provide alternative explanations for the patterns of behavior that caused her concern throughout her adult life.

It was well for Murray that she reported benefiting from psychotherapy—had it gone badly, gaining admission to the New York Bar would have become an even more significant test of her resilience and resolve. As historian Rosalind Rosenberg pointed out, Murray had to explain her arrests, hospitalizations, and name changes, as well as her many changes in organizational affiliations, jobs, and residences, in an application that, including appendices, stretched to an exceptional 230 pages. Having submitted the required forms and her accompanying explanations, Murray then had to submit to an interview by the seven-member Committee on Character and Fitness. After the interview, the committee voted 6–1 to admit her. Eight months after she had passed the bar exam, on June 23, 1948, Murray finally gained admission to New York's legal profession, becoming one of only a dozen or so Black women practicing law in the city at the time.[52]

ADMISSION TO THE BAR BETTER positioned Murray to address her mounting financial problems: having sourced loans from ten different friends and friends of friends, she now owed debts totaling over $1,400.[53] She quit her latest clerking position and made an agreement with a successful Harlem attorney, Carson DeWitt Baker. According to this arrangement, Baker would assign her cases and add her name to the door, and in exchange she would pay him a percentage of her fees. Baker mostly assigned her criminal cases—the first of which was defending two Spanish Harlem women charged with prostitution. Murray's autobiography called this her first-ever case (discounting Joshua's case) and described it as embarrassing, infuriating, and insulting to all women. The men who paid the defendants for sex were not charged with any crime—instead they were called as witnesses. When one of the two "witnesses" was asked to point out the woman he had sex with, he pointed at Murray, and the courtroom broke into laughter.[54]

Murray described one other case to highlight the immense challenges confronting Black women trying to survive in a profession from which they were almost entirely excluded. She recounted representing an indebted Black woman attorney brought before the Bar Association's grievance committee on a charge of misconduct because she repaid a loan from a client with a check that bounced. Biographer Rosalind Rosenberg identified the attorney as Urith Josiah, though Murray used the pseudonym "Judith Hinson" in her autobiography.[55] Murray's name choice once again illustrates her flair for pseudonyms—by changing the attorney's real surname, Josiah, into the fake surname Hinson, Murray referenced Josiah Henson, the person whose life story inspired the title character in *Uncle Tom's Cabin*.[56]

Murray described the case as a vivid lesson for her—unsurprisingly, given the striking similarities between the two women attorneys. Both were significantly indebted, both had mothers who were teachers, both had worked on the WPA Adult Education Project, both were thirty-six when admitted to practice law, both had a similar average income, and both had to outlay money for an emergency involving a family member being prosecuted (the other woman in spring 1948 and Murray in spring 1947).[57] Rather than tell her own story in detail, however, Murray chose to explain the hardships of Black women lawyers through the experience of a client in a near-identical position.

Murray stated that the Ethics Committee found her defense so impressive they let Josiah off with a caution and commended her eye-opening presentation of the difficulties confronting Black women lawyers. Of Josiah/Hinson, Murray added, "I do not recall that our paths ever crossed again, but unknowingly she had rendered me a great service by making me realize the pitfalls of trying to practice law on the edge of insolvency."[58] Murray might not have personally crossed paths with Urith Josiah again, but she surely knew what became of her—Black news outlets gave front-page coverage to Josiah's disbarment in May 1953 for issuing worthless checks and converting thousands of dollars of clients' funds to her own use.[59] Whether recounting her own story or the stories of others, Murray's autobiographical recollections emphasized uplifting points, but in doing so she sometimes excluded sad realities and therefore downplayed the full and complex difficulty of surviving systematic oppression.

Murray's problematic first two cases foreshadowed an unhappy experience working with Carson DeWitt Baker. She confessed to not being great at finding clients, and the clients Baker referred to her were usually those least able to pay. After nine months—a typical period of employment for Murray—she had had enough. She believed Baker owed her $400 from cases she had handled for him, and her name still wasn't on the door.[60] Murray decided she would be better off on her own. It was a bold decision when she had few regular paying clients, but alternatives were scarce: few law firms would employ a Black woman, and those that would were potentially exploitative. Working for herself would at least allow her to escape the feeling that others were taking advantage of her and stymieing her chances of success. Since quitting the CSLA job Murray had endured a desperate struggle to earn a living. Now, exactly two years after quitting that job, she opened her own private law practice, complete with an office, on April Fool's Day 1949.

·····

III

Soon after opening the office, in part to build her profile, Murray stood as a candidate in the New York City council elections on the Liberal Party ticket.[61] Established by trade unionists five years earlier, the Liberal Party had a strong civil rights plank—they sought the establishment of a permanent Civil Rights Commission, federal antilynching legislation, fair employment, housing and education legislation, and the abolition of poll taxes, and segregation in the armed forces and on interstate travel. They also called for punishment of police officers convicted of police brutality and advocated for the establishment of a permanent public defender to represent the poor.[62]

The banner on Murray's Liberal Party campaign material, "Good government is good housekeeping," must have caused her some amusement, given her professed difficulty with domestic chores.[63] Supporters also tried to promote her campaign in gendered ways. In a *Pittsburgh Courier* article, a supporter declared that Murray would add "glamour" and brains to a council that lacked both.[64] Murray's friend Ted Poston, writing for the *New York Post*, described her as an "energetic, attractive and articulate young woman who contributed greatly to Harvard University's decision to admit women to its law school."[65] The headline accompanying Poston's article, "Miss Murray Delays Study at Harvard," mischievously implied she had been admitted to Harvard's law school.[66]

Murray later identified her campaign as feminist activism. She wrote, "As a budding feminist I recognized the importance of women actively seeking public office, whatever the outcome, especially Negro women, who were then virtually invisible in politics." Women candidates were scarce—the Republicans and Democrats each named women candidates for only two of the more than sixty-five available seats. Murray added, "The slightly more frequent appearance of women on minor party tickets was largely symbolic, since they had no chance of winning."[67] Presumably, she included her own candidacy among the symbolic women on minor-party tickets, though she ran anything but a symbolic campaign.

Murray campaigned vigorously in Brooklyn's Tenth Senatorial District, speaking at public meetings, seeking endorsements, fundraising, writing press releases and campaign letters, and holding nightly campaign rallies. She recalled with amazement how she and a group of friends, led by campaign manager Maida Springer, an experienced Brooklyn union organizer, campaigned relentlessly: "Night after night we stood on street ladders, shivering in the brisk October air, shouting ourselves hoarse and passing out little blue-and-white fliers containing my photograph, qualifications, and platform."[68] Murray raised nearly $900 in campaign donations, including the maximum twenty-five-dollar donation each from Eleanor Roosevelt, Caroline Ware, and the Brotherhood of Sleeping Car Porters.[69] She kept supporters informed and amused with campaign letters titled "Pixies in Politics." Ware jokingly responded to one update by warning Murray that if she wasn't careful, she might win.[70]

Democrats won the November 1949 elections in a landslide, claiming twenty-four of the twenty-five council seats, including Brooklyn's Tenth District.[71] Murray captured 17 percent of the vote, finishing a mere 102 votes behind the second-place Republican candidate, making her one of the best-performing Liberal Party candidates in New York.[72] Historians have since identified Murray as a link in a chain of Black women's progress in New York governance.[73] Four years after Murray, Ella Baker ran for council, also unsuccessfully on the Liberal Party ticket. Nineteen years after Murray's campaign, Shirley Chisholm, also running for office in Brooklyn, became the first Black woman elected to Congress.[74]

MURRAY HAD RUN A VERY SUCCESSFUL campaign on a minor-party ticket, but it did little to generate clients for her new legal practice.[75] In fact, the dedication with which she had campaigned and another project she had undertaken left little time for practicing law. Murray had opened her office with money from a $500 retainer to undertake a study of race laws for the Women's Division of Christian Service, a Methodist Church group. The Methodist women wanted to understand various states' segregation laws so they could distinguish between custom and legal requirement when carrying out their work. Murray had been interested in such a project since studying at Howard University, but this was her first opportunity since becoming a lawyer to contribute to a Jim Crow–related legal project and be paid for it.[76] The Methodist women wanted a small pamphlet that could be easily printed and distributed to members. With Murray on the job, however, they got a lot more than they initially envisaged.

She visited law libraries, laboriously copying out, in longhand, laws from all over the nation—not just in the South, and not only segregation laws, but all laws relating to race, whether prohibiting discrimination or enforcing separation. She then typed these up in her office. The Methodist women provided extra funding on several occasions as Murray expanded the project.[77] On January 12, 1950, a little over a year after accepting the retainer, Murray delivered not a pamphlet but a 746-page manuscript. The Methodist women were unsure what to do with the enormous tome. They briefly considered printing only the three charts Murray formulated at the beginning of the work—this being much closer to what they had wanted—but ultimately decided to set about raising the money to print the entire manuscript.[78]

COMPLETING THE MANUSCRIPT TOOK away Murray's sense of mission, and one of her only sources of income. After one unprofitable year in private practice—during which time she had devoted considerable energy to running for council and compiling the race laws manuscript—Murray appeared ready to give it up to pursue a job with the American Civil Liberties Union (ACLU). She felt optimistic about her chances of getting the job in April 1950, only to report to Caroline Ware in June that the job "fell through" because her "price tag was too high." The ACLU gave the job to someone, in Murray's words, "with less experience who would be eager to earn what they offered."[79] On two earlier occasions in recent years—at the California attorney general's office and at the CLSA—Murray's wage became a source of discontent. Had she been willing to settle for less, she might have eked out a modest living. The flip side is that the life of diverse achievements for which Murray is celebrated wouldn't have existed.

Murray's unwillingness to settle invariably led to an immediate worsening of her material circumstances. In November 1950, she turned forty. A decade earlier, her birthday reflections described unhappiness with a "grubby existence" on the "fringes of society," prompting her to apply to Howard Law School. During the intervening decade, she had gained two law degrees but had also amassed considerable debts and still struggled for work. Her letters allude to a particularly difficult period in the six months after missing out on the ACLU job. In January 1951, Murray told Caroline Ware, "Need not tell you the terrific pressure and strain of the past six months. Just let me say that I hope that there is never again a period quite like the latter half of 1950. I'll tell you the sad story when it can be mixed with more hopeful things."[80] Murray's reluctance to discuss the "sad story," even privately with the mentor whom she shared so much with, suggests that something particularly awful occurred, but her papers shed no further light.

The extent of her financial woes alone provided considerable cause for pessimism. Personal loans and the help of her two aunts' meager pensions kept Murray going, though the presence of her aunts, cramping her apartment and constantly bickering, came at an emotional cost.[81] In the job market, racism and sexism severely disadvantaged Murray and compounded

Thelma Stevens from the Methodist Church Women's Division
looking over *States' Laws* manuscript with Murray, 1949.
(Schlesinger Library, Radcliffe Institute, Harvard University)

related factors such as her inexperience, patchy employment record, wage demands, and now McCarthyism, which made applying for government jobs frightening. She described two acquaintances as "home front casualties of cold and lukewarm wars" after they were set for government jobs until they failed security checks. She suspected the same might have happened to her when she unsuccessfully applied for a job at the United Nations in January 1951.[82]

Murray had reason to fear that both her personal and her political past might be used against her if she applied for a government job. In February 1950, Senate hearings had revealed that the State Department dismissed nearly a hundred employees for reasons of "moral turpitude."[83] Following the Senate hearing revelations, two senators formed their own subcommittee to investigate homosexuality in government employment. They concluded that homosexuals were a security risk because of "moral weakness" and susceptibility to blackmail.[84] Also in February 1950, Joseph McCarthy launched his crusade to expose and purge the "commies and queers" from government employment.[85] The claims encouraged the populist press to publish sensational stories about homosexual activity.[86] Unsurprisingly, Murray didn't apply for government jobs at this time.

The Cold War context also made Murray concerned about handling po-

liticized legal cases. She told Ware, "All of us are in such a state of uncertainty, caution and fear that we are hesitant in handling unpopular cases,
supporting unpopular causes. . . . Those of us who have been uncompromising in our fight against discrimination are particularly vulnerable because we are not sure that the loyalty experts are careful to distinguish between the 'loyal opposition' and outright subversives."[87] The "uncertainty,
caution and fear" Murray expressed about "handling unpopular cases" related specifically to Ruth Mary Reynolds's case. In January 1951, Reynolds
was charged with sedition for supporting the short-lived, spectacularly unsuccessful Puerto Rican Nationalist Party revolts. The indictment described
two offenses: the first was simply having joined the Puerto Rican Nationalist Party, which the U.S. government deemed communist and dedicated
to achieving independence by violence. The second was that Reynolds had
allegedly traveled in a vehicle transporting weapons in the days leading up
to the revolt.[88] Murray became involved with the case through her activist
contacts: Reynolds, like Murray, had resided at the Harlem Ashram, and
A. J. Muste, who also associated with the Ashram, led the Ruth Reynolds
Defense Committee.[89]

Murray performed some routine preliminary legal work for Reynolds's
defense and then charged a fee of $300 plus expenses for the work. Reynolds
supporter James Peck became outraged. Murray barely knew Peck, though
he had also resided in the Ashram and was an early member of the Congress of Racial Equality (CORE), participating in the men-only 1947 Journey
of Reconciliation that Murray helped plan, during which he was beaten in
Murray's home state of North Carolina.[90] He also edited the Workers Defense League's *News Bulletin*. Through WDL mutual friends, Peck had loaned
Murray $450 back in 1947. Four years later, she had not repaid him a cent
or contacted him to explain why. Peck had not pursued Murray over the
loan either, but now that she had unexpectedly charged a penniless activist
group such a sizable fee, he made the personal loan a political matter. Peck
informed the Ruth Reynolds Defense Committee of the loan because of his
amazement at her "unethicalness." He told Murray what he had done and
informed her that no other lawyer working on the case had asked for a fee.
Even if she was in a "tough spot financially," Peck added, nothing excused
asking for such a large fee.[91]

In responding, Murray tried to draw distinct lines between the personal,
the political, and the professional. She told Peck that she failed to see "any
connection whatsoever between a purely personal indebtedness to you and
my professional services in the Ruth Reynolds case." Murray went on to explain her awareness of lawyers' propensity to handle cases without charge,

telling him she had done so numerous times in criminal cases where she had personal convictions; the Reynolds case did not fall into this category, though, so she had to treat it like a routine office matter. She included a check for ten dollars with the letter and stated an intention to make every effort to make periodic payments until the personal debt was liquidated. It took ten years in total to repay the loan in small increments, but Murray kept her word.[92]

The flare-up between Murray and Peck elucidates the interconnectedness between the personal and the political: one can be shown spilling into the other, and the line of demarcation can shift according to one's perspective. Peck could not understand Murray's insistence on a fee, and to make him understand she would have had to go beyond fully revealing her financial difficulties, enormous enough, and outline the multiple pressures that made handling such a political case so frightening for her at this time. Furthermore, whatever her personal views on the Reynolds case, Murray clearly had political considerations in mind when deciding how to treat it. In an unsent draft reply to Peck, she stated that she had no sympathy for Reynolds, whose case "would have identified me with a cause which would risk my unformed reputation as an attorney who has not yet established a secure financial basis."[93] Murray tried to counter her personal vulnerability during the Cold War era by adopting the role of a strictly professional attorney, yet this made her appear to be a sell-out to former allies while, as will become clear, doing nothing to negate the suspicions of Cold Warriors.

One month after the dispute, the *New York Times* reported that the House Un-American Activities Committee had released a list of 624 organizations and 204 publications deemed subversive.[94] Murray sensed the danger—after checking the full list, she discovered that multiple organizations she had associated with were included.[95] The extent to which Cold War pressures affected her mood is captured in a letter she wrote to Caroline Ware just before the dispute with Peck: "When one looks around one does not see a generation of rebels and revolutionaries to supplant the generation of our youth. It is as if such a generation were non-existent and we who have grown older have become paralyzed. . . . Last Saturday we had an air raid siren test which almost nobody heard. Every time my folks see a flash in the sky (brought on by contact with icy rails of the elevated trains) they wonder if the Atomic Bomb has arrived and demand of me why I don't get out of the Wall Street area before it is too late."[96] Threats seemed to surround her—atomic warfare, nagging aunts, background investigations, financial insolvency, and a white man Pauli scarcely knew aggressively pursuing her over a debt she couldn't pay.

EIGHTEEN MONTHS AFTER MURRAY HAD finished scribbling down and typing up all laws relating to race, the Methodist Church women's group had secured the funds to publish the entire compilation as *States' Laws on Race and Color*. Aunt Pauline attended the launch on April 17, 1951, but Pauli did not. For the past three weeks she had been in Freedmen's Hospital. She reported suffering from intermittent indigestion and weight loss for nearly six months before becoming "totally disabled."[97] Murray believed some kind of glandular imbalance was causing overactivity and weight loss.[98] On the day of the book launch, she wrote to her aunts, "I have what is known as a 'spastic colon' which causes so much digestive difficulty."[99] This diagnosis must have been tentative, however: she later wrote to a friend stating that after five weeks the doctors still couldn't identify the cause of her trouble, but they were sure it was some kind of glandular dysfunction and gave her adrenalin injections.[100] After leaving Freedmen's on April 27 Murray reported feeling better, but "severe tensions" remained in her head, and she didn't expect to resume usual duties for several months.[101]

There were both familiar patterns to this breakdown and one significant difference. Like earlier collapses, this one followed stomach complaints, overactivity, weight loss, and concern about a glandular imbalance. Following hospitalization, Murray again spent time in a remote setting recuperating and again expressed interest in pursuing a writing career, hoping that doctors had "rebuilt the body in preparation for a 'Best Seller.'"[102] Unlike with previous collapses, however, Murray accepted as part of her treatment what she described as a type of "estrogenic" hormone, reversing her earlier refusal to receive such treatment.[103]

There is no evidence among her papers to indicate that she ever again sought treatment with "male hormones" (testosterone) or further physical examination to find evidence of male attributes. Given the Cold War context, it is possible that she continued these efforts in a more secretive manner, but her new acceptance of estrogen makes this seem unlikely. Some combination of psychotherapy, the 1947 abdominal surgery that uncovered no evidence of internal male attributes, and the Cold War context, which made passing the New York bar exam such an ordeal, more than likely ended her quest to transition to male. It is important to note, however, that Murray's concerns about her physical health continued, suggesting that they either manifested in other ways or were never solely related to her sexuality and gender identity.

Murray's hospitalization and period recuperating away from the city restored her physical well-being but also threatened to exacerbate financial woes. Her health insurance initially refused to cover the hospitalization, as her plan didn't cover "diagnostic" studies. She asked her doctor if he could "make a re-interpretation" of his diagnosis, explaining in a follow-up letter that the insurance company would reject any claim involving a "nervous disorder" and therefore requesting that he stress "the gastro-intestinal disturbance."[104] Her doctor complied and the insurance company reversed its decision, sparing her a hospital bill she could ill afford.[105]

Murray's dire financial situation left her physically depleted and therefore less able to face other challenges. Her legal practice had failed to provide an adequate income since its inception. In a period of record income growth for most Americans, Murray's financial situation continually worsened. After three years of private practice, her personal indebtedness had risen to over $3,500. In a letter to James Peck—whose debt worried her the most—she explained that her income had fallen each year since starting her own business. For the years 1949, 1950, and 1951, her average weekly net income was $36.38, $17.91, and $16.22, respectively.[106] The median weekly income for U.S. citizens in 1951 was $57.69, about three and a half times more than Murray received.[107]

The publication of States' Laws could not realistically generate any income for its author. Murray believed the Women's Division had invested at least $2,500 in the book and could not hope to recoup the money from the first edition of two thousand copies. To reissue it, in her view, would also be pointless. She told them, "At the present rate of fluidity in the field, the book may very well be out of date within a year. The cost of revision will add to the cost of re-issue so that it is quite possible the Women's Division will continue to lose money on the book, unless it can find a way of commercializing it at a profit."[108] It would have been a tremendous boost if States' Laws had become the best-seller Murray dreamed of writing, but there was no realistic way for the Women's Division to commercialize it without a substantial rewrite. As it was, the Women's Division donated most copies of the book to law libraries and legal organizations.

Murray still did her best to promote States' Laws. Following her hospitalization, she approached the New York Times Book Review and the law journals of Harvard, Columbia, and the University of California to ask them to review the work. The Harvard Law Review expressed some interest when Murray suggested she might be able to get William Hastie to review it. She wrote to Hastie to ask if he would. His reply, in which he evaded committing to reviewing the tome, suggests that he sensed her anxiety: "I suspect the unexpressed basis of the unwillingness of the Harvard Law Review to review the book is the fact that your work is essentially a compilation, though a painstaking and important compilation of useful material. It is my impression that, except for casebooks and teaching materials, the journal rarely, if ever, reviews this type of publication. I know you have the bad habit of worrying about things and finding in them deeper significance than some of us more credulous souls discover. However, I hope you will take this one in stride."[109] Largely positive reviews appeared in several journals— one reviewer was particularly impressed that Murray had included not only segregation legislation but also civil rights laws.[110] Furthermore, she later claimed that Thurgood Marshall supplied NAACP staff with copies and referred to it as the "Bible" for civil rights lawyers. She also came to interpret the book's limited shelf life as attributable to the legal changes it helped inspire.[111] Once again, however, the immediate impact of her exhaustive efforts wasn't in the positive changes it brought to society, but in the toll it had taken on her health and well-being.

· · · · ·

IV

Murray began 1952 facing more acute versions of the same challenges she had withstood during the previous few years. Her financial problems continued to worsen, Cold War suspicions continued to narrow her employment options, and health concerns remained prominent. In February 1952 she consulted an endocrinologist, reporting to Caroline Ware that her symptoms were less severe than during her hospitalization the previous year, leaving her hopeful that she could get "in under the wire" to get "more security and permit me to function better."[112] Shortly after writing this letter, some light appeared at the end of the tunnel in the form of a job opportunity that would allow her to make use of her legal training and draw on the experience gained through compiling *States' Laws*.

On March 7, 1952, she wrote to Cornell University to express interest in a research position on the Liberian Codification Project, a State Department– funded project to assist the Liberian government in better arranging its legal system. At Murray's request, the next day Caroline Ware sent Cornell a glowing reference, and in the following days Elmer A. Carter from the State Commission against Discrimination, Lloyd K. Garrison, Thurgood Marshall, William Hastie, A. Philip Randolph, and Lester B. Granger all sent recommendation letters.[113] Given her qualifications, relevant experience, and notable referees, Murray appeared well placed to get the job.

She visited Cornell to meet with Professor Milton Konvitz, the project leader, and M. P. Catherwood, dean of the New York School of Industrial and Labor Relations. Catherwood told Murray he had no previous experience with State Department–funded projects and therefore did not know whether a loyalty investigation would be needed. He asked Murray to provide information about her political background in case the matter came up.[114] Following the meeting, Murray sent Konvitz much of the information she had supplied to the New York Bar, documenting her past and present organizational affiliations and publications and adding some information defending her involvement in groups recently deemed subversive by the House Un-American Activities Committee.[115]

Two weeks after the interview, Konvitz telephoned Murray to inform her that, although her references covered her ability and qualifications, they said little about her loyalty to the United States. He suggested that her application would benefit from a referee with a more conservative background. She simply didn't know a notable conservative well enough, so she wrote to her original referees requesting that they write to Konvitz again, specifically addressing the issue of loyalty.[116] Only Hastie's follow-up letter to Konvitz suggested any irritation: "During my fifteen year acquaintance with Miss Murray, I have not known her to conduct or express herself in any way which would indicate lack of loyalty to the United States or its institutions. I assume that, absent evidence of any such conduct, we still have enough confidence in our fellow citizens and in our way of life to trust each other."[117] In thanking Hastie, Murray commented, "What troubles me so about the implications of this type of thing is that the danger to our way of life comes from within—our fear and capacity for being stampeded into silence and inactivity. I do hope that the liberal forces in this country will stand fast and live through this emergency without losing courage."[118]

Murray had serious cause for concern. Six months before she applied for the Cornell job, the government had indicted her old love Peg Holmes on charges of conspiracy to overthrow both the Massachusetts state government and the federal government because of her continuing involvement with leftist groups. In the same month, Ruth Reynolds received a sentence of six years' hard labor. The Supreme Court overturned the conviction in 1954 following a challenge led by famed civil rights attorney Conrad Lynn—another participant in the Journey of Reconciliation. The case against Peg Holmes was also quashed in 1956, but these positive developments were a long way off.[119] In early 1952 Murray's pursuit of employment on a State Department–funded project required considerable bravery. If someone like Peg Holmes—a now-married white New Englander from a very wealthy family—could be charged with sedition, Murray was acutely vulnerable.

On May 5, Konvitz called to inform Murray that Cornell would not employ her because questions about her background might cause bad publicity for the institution. Despite knowing the potential dangers, Murray suggested that he ask the State Department to conduct an investigation to clear up the issue of her loyalty. Konvitz, who seemed keen to have Murray, called the State Department immediately but was told an investigation would take months, and the State Department contracted out work such as the Liberian Codification project in part to avoid the burden of protracted loyalty investigations.[120] Murray told Konvitz she wanted a formal written letter spelling out the reasons for her rejection, which Dean Catherwood provided: it stated bluntly, "There were some questions concerning your past associations which I felt might place the University in a difficult situation."[121] Murray summarized Cornell's position using a health metaphor: "Being well, the University ought not to invite a sick-bed."[122]

Murray had now been rejected from the University of North Carolina on the grounds of race, from Harvard University on the basis of sex, and from Cornell on the basis of past associations. In some ways, Cornell hurt the most. She had applied to UNC and Harvard fully aware of their existing discriminatory policies, but Cornell's rejection surprised her and snatched away potential financial rescue. Ella Baker advised raising the matter with the NAACP, but this led nowhere — unsurprisingly, given the NAACP's complicity with McCarthyism.[123] Lawyer Adolf Berle, a former FDR adviser and founding member of the Liberal Party, informed Murray that there really wasn't a viable legal avenue to challenge the rejection anyway: as a private institution, Cornell could "do what it likes on a pure personnel basis and there is very little one can do except to agitate."[124]

And agitate she did. In a follow-up letter to Konvitz, she wrote, "I have learned that seemingly Dean Catherwood's expressed concern about me is not my organizational background or affiliations so much as his desire to satisfy himself that I am not 'leftish.'" She stated that it would be more accurate to call her "frontish," because she had been in advance of official positions on race and sex. Suspecting that there was more to the rejection, Murray wrote to contacts who knew Konvitz to satisfy herself that the decision wasn't based on gender discrimination. She found evidence that Cornell was a racist institution: according to an NAACP survey conducted a few years earlier, Cornell employed not one African American in a faculty or research position, and department heads and faculty members routinely expressed "lily-white" attitudes.[125] Since many of the groups Murray had associated with were civil rights groups, she questioned whether she was being condemned for caring about social justice. In her words, she was "paying the price that any red-blooded American Negro will pay for having spoken out firmly for justice and for having been associated with unpopular causes like the Odell Waller case."[126] Murray tried to point out the illogical nature of discriminating against someone who cared about the democratic ideals of the nation. In one letter to Konvitz, she argued that in rejecting her on the grounds of past associations, "you also condemn the instrument I have used to enable me to rise above this enforced minority status. This instrument is the Christian ethic which pervaded my writings and my conduct, and which, in my opinion, transcends my political and economic views. Hence, whether it was your intention or not, you have in fact rejected my application on religious as well as racial grounds."[127]

Understandably, given her suitability for the position and desperate financial situation, Murray struggled to comprehend the rejection. Her interest in radical politics had been brief and had taken place in the context of a severe economic depression when many inquiring minds had become interested in Marxist ideology. Furthermore, she had devoted considerable time and energy to opposing communists, such as in the Odell Waller campaign. She told an old friend from the WDL, "What disturbs me about the position taken by Cornell is that, in their fear, they crush the type of person who has been one of the first fighters against Communism, who has said that the best way to combat Communism is to make our own democracy work and cut the arguments from under the Communists."[128]

In other letters Murray went further in expressing strongly anticommunist views, lashing the "termite minds of both the left and the right," who discredit people for being outspoken for social justice. She denounced the "fuzzy-minded and the malicious fellow-travelers and Communists" who unscrupulously linked "fighting liberals" with their cause through mailing lists and "stupid racial groups protesting the lifting of Paul Robeson's passport etc."[129] Murray could have made a case that it shouldn't matter if she was a Marxist, but that wasn't easy to do for a person who struggled to suppress violent thoughts and was living through the torment of being denied an opportunity to rescue herself from financial ruin on the grounds that she had once adhered to beliefs she had long since vehemently opposed.

IN HER AUTOBIOGRAPHY, MURRAY DESCRIBED Cornell's rejection as "infuriating" and leaving her "too bruised and rebellious" to share her aunts' faith that it was all part of "God's plan." She felt caught between her family's faith and the "suspicion" that robbed her of "individuality and discarded me like unwanted refuse."[130] She claimed that, in a flash of insight, she reconceived the taint of "past associations" as meaning her Fitzgerald family, who had endured the degradation of race oppression yet still contributed to the nation, particularly through her grandfather's service in the Union army. It is certainly true that Murray worked furiously following her rejection by Cornell—she wrote ten thousand words in the next two weeks of May alone.[131] Yet she appeared to be taking steps to dedicate herself to writing before the Cornell rejection occurred—she traveled to family history sites in March, and in February her literary agent discussed the hope that Murray would find time to work on a book.[132]

Ever since Hunter College two decades earlier, writing had emerged as Murray's preferred method for working through difficult experiences, and her favorite subject was always her family history. She had written a sketch about the "poor" and "rich" Fitzgeralds in 1933 and had written short stories about her childhood in the 1940s. The poet Stephen Vincent Benét—who regularly read Murray's prose, poetry, and journalism—described the Fitzgerald sketches as "fascinating material" and encouraged her to pursue it as a novel, writing, "It might take you ten years to write a real novel about it. But if you did, and did it well, that would be a book. You see we have had conventional portraits of the dear old mammy and the faithful house-servant of befo' de wa'. We have had revolt things—and very good some of those have been. We have had attempted sketches of Harlem. But nobody as far as I know, has really tried to sit down and do a 'Budden-brooks' or a 'Forsyte Saga' on this particular subject. . . . And it cries to be done—and done from the inside, not the outside."[133] Ten years after Benét's letter, the Cornell rejection provided new impetus and framing for the same project.

After the outpouring of words in the last two weeks of May, progress slowed over the summer. Murray reported to Ware that she was having particular trouble describing her "favorite Fitzgerald," Grandmother Cornelia.[134] Nevertheless, unlike with earlier attempts to focus on writing, Murray didn't abandon the project entirely. She sent a draft chapter to her agent, Marie Rodell, with a note saying, "If you think this is a good piece of writing, then you can thank Cornell for it. . . . Anyway, this writing madness is causing me to neglect what little practice I do have." At Rodell's suggestion, in the fall Murray applied for and won a $2,500 grant established by Harper & Brothers. Murray had long believed that her family history was fascinating story material, and now, crucially, she had the endorsement of a highly regarded book publisher. If Murray could complete the manuscript in a timely manner, the story of her family, which she had aspired to write for nearly two decades, would be published for all the world to read.

Murray's autobiography stated that before she could accept the grant she needed to pay off some debts, so she closed her law office to work for six months as a Department of Welfare social investigator.[135] Yet this seems to be another case of smoothing over the messy complicating aspects of life in an autobiography. Murray didn't close her law office until a month after she had taken the Department of Welfare job, and her deferral of the grant may have had as much to do with self-doubts about her ability to finish the book as it had to do with her debts. If only concerned about her indebtedness, Murray might have closed her office earlier. Rather, it seems that winning the grant prompted something of a crisis: she consulted psychiatrist Edmund Ziman for several months, beginning in November 1952, to help her get "unstuck" from writer's block brought on by the Harper grant. After many rejection slips had amassed (numerous publishers rejected her volume of poetry), she confessed to becoming "panic stricken (something like stage fright)" because she "couldn't take 'success' in stride." Murray claimed she only saw Ziman for a few months and never suffered from writer's block again, though other evidence indicates she continued to struggle.[136]

In January 1953 she noted in her diary, "I did a little revision work on the book today, but nothing new and original. I wonder whether I have anything in me worth saying, or whether I am really capable of saying it. Sometimes I think I am a big fake all around. . . . Is my story important to tell? I think so, yet the burning passion to get it down on paper which I had last spring seems gone from me."[137] Less than a week after wondering if she was a "big fake," Murray finally closed her office. In her autobiography Murray described "suspending" her law practice for four years because of the absorbing research into her family history.[138] In truth, Murray had fallen two months behind in rent and couldn't pay off existing debts, forcing her to close the office.[139]

Privately, she felt that she was at "the end of the line." Her diary included the following "Epitaph to a law practice," written in January 1953:

> I have finished packing my things at the office. I have been at 6 Maiden Lane 3 years, 9 months and 16 days—the longest continuous period I have remained on any job. There were many triumphs and a few shattering defeats, but as I sat there looking at 19 cartons of books and papers—my worldly goods—I could not honestly say I was sorry to leave. That junky little office long ago outlived its usefulness. The past year in it was one of almost continuous pain and turmoil. There was the day to day waiting for clients that did not come, the growing panic of failure, the facing of blank walls, the feeling that I was trapped in a hopeless situation from which I could not escape.[140]

Murray certainly never claimed business success in her autobiography, but she also never wrote so evocatively about what it was like to fail in business as she did in "Epitaph to a law practice." The contrasting descriptions reveal the difficulties any autobiographer faces in deciding how much they are willing to reveal—a problem Murray felt acutely because of fluctuating self-confidence and a related defensiveness about acknowledging the full extent of hardships, which risked appearing to confirm the racist, sexist, and homophobic notions of her inferiority.

Living through McCarthyism also encouraged defensiveness rather than openness about her life. In another diary entry from January, Murray reflected on a friend's experience working at the United Nations and needing to go through a loyalty investigation, describing the process as

> a harassing [sic] experience. One feels frightened, insecure, exposed. One thinks of all the personal errors, the deep secrets of one's life unrelated to political activities. One is apprehensive that all of the details of one's intimate private life will be spread on the record to be read, sifted, weighted, evaluated and judged by strangers—some vicious neighbor with a gossipy tongue will be visited by an investigator and will glibly spread one's goings and comings on the record. One worries over one's private indiscretions and errors of judgment for which one has already paid in regret, remorse, but which may now endanger one's economic security . . .[141]

Since her admission to the New York Bar, the focus on applicants' personal past had only increased. This diary entry appeared just weeks before newly inaugurated President Dwight D. Eisenhower issued an executive order making "homosexuality sufficient and necessary grounds for disbarment from federal employment."[142]

MURRAY'S NEW JOB AS A SOCIAL investigator with the Department of Welfare involved visiting welfare recipients' homes to assess whether their Social Security money was needed and appropriately spent. The dire financial circumstances of her clients, mostly Puerto Rican immigrants, were little different to what she had endured for much of her life; disturbingly, one client was a former social investigator like herself. She worked in an open-plan office with nearly thirty coworkers, which she described as a challenge to her shyness and tendency to withdraw. Two other lawyers worked at adjoining desks, leading Murray to believe that the department was a "corral" for "unsuccessful lawyers."[143] She believed the job lacked any prestige and felt ashamed to have accepted it—a feeling compounded by the knowledge that she had turned down the same position over a decade earlier before entering Howard Law School, making the last ten years of struggle appear to be for nothing.[144]

After accepting the position, Murray hoped "the world would forget her for a while," but quite the opposite occurred. Much to her embarrassment, a coworker came into work one morning excitedly brandishing a copy of *Jet* featuring Murray. The article, titled "Lady Lawyers: Sex No Handicap to Careers," carried a picture of a malnourished Murray, looking, she believed, like a "zombie." She had closed her practice because she was, in her words, "starving—in purse and spirit," yet *Jet* described her as an "eminently successful . . . civil rights attorney whose crusades in that area have caused her to be acclaimed as a 'lawyer's lawyer.'"[145] Just as Murray had received public acknowledgment in the Black press for achieving the position of deputy attorney general of California shortly after leaving the job, she again found herself in the uncomfortable position of receiving accolades for a legal career she had recently abandoned.

Shortly after the *Jet* article, yet another story featuring Murray appeared, this time in *Ebony* magazine. The February 1953 *Ebony* cover story, "Some of My Best Friends Are Negro," authored by Eleanor Roosevelt, included a photograph of Murray. In the article, Roosevelt referred to Murray as a former "firebrand" who was now ready to be "useful."[146] When a coworker also shared this story around the office, Murray tried to look wise and "smile off" the queries.[147] The former First Lady's description of her as a friend flattered Murray—she wrote to Roosevelt to thank her—yet this kind of publicity, which Murray had often sought, proved a mixed blessing, because any satisfaction from the recognition compounded her sense of failure for having accepted routine office work.

This kind of media attention makes it easier to understand why Murray found it difficult to settle for jobs with little prestige, or to fully acknowledge hardships in her memoirs. A few years later, sociologist E. Franklin Frazier published his seminal work, *Black Bourgeoisie*, in which he criticized Black media outlets for creating make-believe accounts of fantastic achievements by African Americans and the recognition accorded them by whites to compensate for feelings of inferiority.[148] Trying to create positive self-images to combat relentless racism created individual pressure to succeed, which made it difficult for Murray to settle for anonymity even when she desired it. She wanted the world to forget her, but she also felt compelled to achieve things in life that would disprove she was in any way an inferior person.

MURRAY QUIT THE WELFARE DEPARTMENT after six months—a decision that had as much to do with a difficult working relationship with her supervisor as it did with any other factor.[149] A financial gift from Caroline Ware allowed Murray to focus full time on the Fitzgerald family memoir. Ware also provided feedback on the manuscript as it progressed, as did Ware's friend

Helen Lockwood, a professor of English at Vassar. Murray also received editorial advice from *Strange Fruit* author Lillian Smith, who told her lover that Murray was a "beginning writer" but a "brilliant girl, really brilliant."[150] Murray's relentless activities and energetic correspondence with so many people over the years had created an impressive network of supporters, who provided not only emotional support but also references, advice, and loans.

Based on the outline and chapters Murray had drafted by the fall of 1953, Harper gave her a contract and a $900 advance.[151] She had been writing sporadically for a year, but plenty of work remained to complete the manuscript. In late 1953 Ware and Lockwood advised Murray to remove the opening prologue, in which Murray rebutted Cornell's rejection based on her "past associations." Although the incident provided impetus for the project, the prologue's defensiveness left both Ware and Lockwood "cold." They urged her to open with Grandfather Robert Fitzgerald's decision to come south following the Civil War.[152] Murray accepted their advice, persevering with the project into the New Year and making several research trips in the first half of 1954. While in Virginia on a research trip, Murray experienced the thrill of meeting the last surviving person to have attended a school in Amelia County that Robert Fitzgerald had established in 1866.[153]

The *Brown v. Board of Education* Supreme Court ruling in May 1954 further buoyed Murray. She had paid close attention to court cases relating to school segregation for two decades, often discussing them in her correspondence. Four years earlier, she virtually predicted the eventual outcome:

> The thrilling thing about these decisions is that for the first time, the Court has faced the psychological implications of segregation—the intangibles—squarely and has not retreated to legal technicalities to reaffirm a simple human right. The decision of the U. of Texas Law School is magnificent. I react to it so strongly because some of the same arguments were used by one Pixie to stress the reason why it was important for a woman to attend Harvard School of Law. . . . All in all, it is a good job and now I feel confident that the Court can't retreat, but must go forward from case to case, until *Plessy* goes down the drain along with the *Dred Scott* decision. I think it is now a matter of timing of strategy to let the cases reach the court when public opinion is ripe. For this is surely as much a political decision as a legal one. It could have been made on legal grounds just as well 50 years ago.[154]

Murray was prescient in her reading of the evolution of Supreme Court rulings. She also believed she had played a role in *Brown*, through the publication of *States' Laws* and her Howard University Law School final paper on

Plessy. Years later, while Murray was visiting Howard Law School, she spoke with Spotswood Robinson, who told her that he had reread her paper while preparing for the *Brown* case. "In fact," she recalled him saying, "it was very helpful to us. We were able to use your paper in the *Brown* briefs."[155]

Following the decision, the *New York Times* published one of Murray's letters. The letter briefly mentioned her own damaging experience of seg-regated public schooling and likened her feelings about the decision to how her enslaved great-grandfather must have felt on hearing news of the Emancipation Proclamation. Otherwise, the letter was an impersonal trib-ute to Justice John M. Harlan, who provided the only dissenting opinion in the 1883 *Civil Rights Cases* and the 1896 *Plessy v. Ferguson* decision.[156] The *Times* also published a joint letter by Aunts Pauline and Sallie, imploring that Black teachers in the South not be overlooked during the integration process.[157] Beginning with Grandfather Robert's efforts to establish a Black school in the post–Civil War South, Murray's maternal family alone could count nearly a century of teaching experience in Black schools.

. . . . .

V

On the day of the historic *Brown* decision, Murray, along with Maida Springer and Springer's adult son, drank a toast to Justice Harlan. Murray and Springer then went to see *Pit of Loneliness*, the only "lesbian-themed" film released in the United States between 1934 and 1961.[158] Panamanian-born Springer shared similarities with Pauli—she too was born in 1910, was short and slight, became politically active through the labor movement in the 1930s, and suffered some health issues—ulcers and bouts of depression—relating to work stress. But Springer and Murray did not share a romantic relationship. Murray once tried to discuss her gender identity struggles with Springer, but Springer dismissed the revelation as "ridiculous!"[159] Never-theless, the friendship, which stretched back to the Odell Waller campaign, certainly benefited Murray. Walking her dog to the Springer home provided Pauli a pleasurable escape after her aunts moved in with her. Pauli spent considerable time at the Springer home, which Maida shared with her law student son and her husband.[160] A month after the *Brown* decision, Springer accompanied Murray on a research trip to visit former Fitzgerald landhold-ings in Pennsylvania.[161]

Four days after returning from the trip, on June 13, 1954, Springer also accompanied Murray to Washington, where Pauli checked in to Freedmen's Hospital. Murray had become totally disabled a few days before admission, and once hospitalized she underwent surgery to remove a growth from her thyroid gland, and small growths from her "chin, face, and neck etc."[162] Murray wrote to her analyst, Edmund Ziman—among many others—during the hospitalization because she wanted to keep him informed about discussions she "had been carrying on with the three medical men at Freedmen's."[163] As with earlier hospitalizations, personal and professional problems appeared to contribute to physical health problems.

Although Murray had been busy with research trips, progress writing about her grandparents remained slow. Her reliance on the memories of her three Fitzgerald aunts, Pauline, Sallie, and Marie, for story details created problems: they were initially apprehensive about the project because they feared that the book would publicize embarrassing details about the family history. Murray's lack of self-confidence also created problems—she routinely panicked and described herself as a "skittish author, easily discouraged by editorial criticism and constantly needing to be rescued from financial difficulties."[164] She also showed familiar signs of taking on too many tasks; in addition to research trips and writing about her family, she took on another paid assignment that created more problems.

Murray negotiated a $1,800 deal with the Methodist Church Women's Division to produce a supplement for *States' Laws*, then negotiated a subsequent fee-sharing deal with a young Black woman attorney to work on it. The young attorney, named Lake, accused Murray of dishonestly claiming too large a share (one-third) of the net fee and misusing project funds to do Fitzgerald family history research. Furthermore, Murray mistakenly believed the Women's Division would be providing a payment installment in June, when in fact the next payment would not be until July. As it was, Murray had already overspent by June, the same month she was hospitalized, compelling her to borrow more money to pay Lake her anticipated share—a check from Murray may have already bounced by then.[165] Lake certainly remained dissatisfied. Murray described Lake as having "emotional problems of her own" and believed Lake's attitude betrayed a doubt about whether Murray was really a "Master of Laws" or just a "hack lawyer." Murray told Caroline Ware that she should simply "absorb this kind of aggressiveness," as she herself had "handed it out in my day," but still felt the affair might be her "swansong" with the law.[166]

The incident illustrates the difficulties confronting Black women trying to survive in a profession from which they had long been excluded. Murray told Ware, "It is a sad commentary on the distrust and suspicion let loose in the world in our time, that two struggling, almost starving, women attorneys who are also Negroes, the most exploited in the legal profession, should not be able to establish a relationship of mutual confidence and trust."[167] Although Murray and Lake eventually resolved their differences well enough to submit the supplement to *States' Laws* for publication in 1955, this incident never made it into Murray's autobiography as an example of the often desperate struggle endured by marginalized individuals in professional occupations.[168]

The hospitalization also occurred at a time of multiple family concerns. In describing the Lake dispute to Ware, Murray stated, "Perhaps if it had come at any other time—when I was well and not too bogged down by my own ill health and family sorrow—I could have taken it in good grace, but my young assistant was well aware of all my family troubles—yet her own inner compulsion to 'lay her cards on the table' and 'speak up for her rights'—something she had not done before, she admits—made it necessary for me to be the victim." One of Pauli's three surviving Fitzgerald aunts, Aunt Marie, seemed close to death when Pauli entered the hospital, but this wasn't the only "family sorrow" weighing on her before hospitalization.[169]

For much of the first half of 1954, trouble had been brewing between the Murrays. Pauli's brother Bill had been institutionalized at St. Elizabeth's Hospital for most of the period between 1935 and 1949. She had visited him there, where she observed him to be incoherent and confused. Sometime before his release, Bill underwent "an experimental pre-frontal lobotomy." Pauli believed the lobotomy improved Bill, for a time—although apathetic, he seemed calm, coherent, and logical following the procedure and his subsequent release—first into Mildred's care then back into his childhood home with Uncle Bubber.[170] Bill and Bubber's relationship deteriorated through early 1954, when Bill initiated court action against Bubber—a move that Pauli took as a bad sign concerning Bill's mental state and that no doubt also created anxiety that the "mad Murrays" would soon be in the public spotlight again.

Less than two weeks before entering the hospital, Pauli tried to mediate the dispute, which seemed to be about money. She wrote to Bubber apologizing on Bill's behalf and asking Bubber to remember that this constituted "the first aggressive action Bill had taken since his discharge," which she interpreted as a hopeful sign of his recovery. She also asked Uncle Bubber to be gentle with Bill and proud of the Murray children: "Not one of them has laid down completely on life—and they all could have, you know."[171] Pauli also wrote to Bill, labeling the dispute a simple "misunderstanding." Despite her own financial difficulties, she included five dollars with the wish that it could be more. She only asked Bill to "remember the Second Commandment—Thou shall love thy neighbor (Bubber) as thyself."[172]

There is no way to know whether this dispute contributed in some way to Pauli's illness, but it is clear that Bill's behavior and the Lake dispute caused her to reflect at length on the sources of her own behavior while she remained hospitalized. She told Caroline Ware, "The problem of self-acceptance and relaxation about the kind of person I really am is still a large one." Pauli believed "the adrenals" caused her very active periods, which could make her "socially productive" but could also, she feared, be responsible for her aggressiveness. She felt in danger of losing all her friends if she could not stop her "pugilistic typewriter barrage."

An example of this pugilism occurred in a "two fisted" letter to Mordecai Johnson—the Howard University president who quashed the sit-in protests—written a short time before her thyroid operation. Concerned that the operation might go badly, Murray didn't want to "cash in" her checks without getting an "eight-year hurt" off her chest. She told Ware, "I am sure one of his graduates never handed it to him clearer and with less mincing of words. I absorbed his sermons well over the three years at Howard and I think he might have felt in the language of my two 'documents' some of his own words coming back at him." After the successful operation, Murray vacillated on how to interpret such eruptions. On the one hand, she considered them her way of "letting off steam," in the same way that others gardened or played golf. On the other, she worried that she couldn't relate to other people at all because of some "tragic flaw," which left her as one of the "lost causes of the world."[173]

Self-acceptance issues, relationship difficulties, family troubles, and physical health concerns were intertwined with the fear of hereditary insanity. From her hospital bed on Independence Day 1954, Murray wrote to Crownsville Hospital to ask for information concerning her father and sister Grace's time there:

> I am particularly anxious to be informed on any peculiar or interesting medical fact on the eyesight or brain reaction of these two members. There is now developing within our sibling range an interesting set of symptoms with reference to our eyesight, which symptoms are now seen in a member of the third generation. It is important that we protect the mental health of our descendants, and therefore, I believe that the widest area of factual findings in our command will help to erase some of the confusions of family legend and the trauma of seeing our father's corpse upon its release from Crownsville in 1923.[174]

She also asked if her father's autopsy revealed anything beyond the blows that killed him—such as evidence of brain tumors. Murray desired physical health information to "protect the mental health" of Murray descendants, because she believed that physical illness precipitated her father's mental deterioration.[175] If Murray feared she had inherited a "fatal flaw" from her father that would first manifest itself in physical illness, then it is little wonder she focused so intently on her health—her body must have seemed like a time bomb that could detonate into insanity.

By writing to Crownsville Murray demonstrated a newfound willingness to confront the specter of hereditary insanity, which is also evident in a letter she wrote to the person she admired above all others, Eleanor Roosevelt. The former First Lady paid Murray a surprise hospital visit, which thrilled Murray. Four days afterward, Murray wrote ER a "personal and confidential" letter that disclosed intimate details about her family history, including her father's death and her two siblings' institutionalization. Murray also revealed that her fear of hereditary insanity prevented her from ever applying for a government job, though she now expressed determination to investigate her family's medical problems.[176]

Yet the pressure to not be open remained immense. While in the hospital, Murray heard a rumor that the FBI had contacted Howard University to obtain a picture of her, though quite why they would be investigating her at this time is unclear. She wrote to J. Edgar Hoover stating that she did not approve of the FBI's "behind the back investigation" and enclosing a portrait photograph and a detailed résumé. She received a reply from the director's secretary stating that no record of any FBI investigation of her could be located. Murray then requested that the FBI come directly to her if they ever did investigate her, so she could furnish them with all the information they wanted.[177] The possibility of being subject to investigation by a powerful government agency would be scary for anyone, but for someone who lived with a deep fear of hereditary insanity and who had been labeled schizophrenic in 1940, it must have been especially unsettling and terrifying.

. . . . .

VI

Murray experienced a "low spell" that continued after she left the hospital. Indeed, she only left the hospital because her Aunt Marie died on July 4. Aunt Marie had been the dressmaking Fitzgerald daughter whose sudden labor had almost derailed Pauli's parents' wedding all those years ago. While growing up, Pauli had had less to do with Aunt Marie, who mostly lived in New York, therefore Marie's death seemed to impact her less, especially when she was so caught up in her own woes. She reported having "no responsibility for Aunt Marie's going and affairs beyond attending the funeral to lend moral support to my ladies." Pauli even hoped some good could come from Aunt Marie's passing: she suggested that her "ladies" go to stay in Marie's vacant Long Island cottage. Aunts Pauline and Sallie "consented without too much resistance," though Aunt Pauline soon reported unhappiness in her new surrounds.[178]

A difficulty with another Black woman compounded Murray's woes. A friend of a friend had moved to New York for work and called on Murray in desperate need of temporary accommodation. Murray accommodated the woman—whom she believed was as "weary" and "disorganized" as herself—but soon regretted it. Pauli felt crowded out of her own place and went to stay at Maida Springer's home, then gave up time to find her houseguest alternative accommodation. After she managed to move the woman on, Pauli had to give up more time to forward mail and packages to the person's new address, all of which led Murray to describe the incident as "another example of the waste, the frustration, of minority status . . ." Despite again recognizing the societal pressures at play in the unhappy affair, Murray then immediately went on to compare herself very unfavorably with Springer, believing her friend put her to "shame" because Springer could educate a son, maintain a household, and contribute to social causes without the same educational advantages as herself. She continued, "I, with the advantage of training, etc., have never been able to carry my own financial burdens, or stick to a job for any length of time, or meet family responsibilities over a long period of time." She believed her friend never imposed on friends, while "I have breezed cheerfully along accepting whatever was given to me, all in the name of the cause. What cause? If I fight for humanity and then am a burden and a problem to my friends and family, of what ultimately good am I?"[179]

In news that wouldn't have arrested the negative thought patterns, Aunt Pauline reported that she would soon be returning to the Chauncey Street apartment—the apartment Pauli had felt unable to stay in until she could remove an unwanted guest.[180] Further unwelcome news appeared when the insurance company—as it had three years early—questioned Murray's hospitalization, especially the recovery time. The usual recovery time for a partial thyroidectomy was six to twelve weeks, and Murray had still not returned to work nearly a month after her expected recovery. The insurance company suspected, correctly, that she might have been engaging in other work. Murray told the insurance company that she still suffered from malnourishment and still needed medical treatment for things such as exhaustion, vision impairment, and sleeplessness.[181]

The insurance company suspected she had resumed working because she had gained a summer residence at the MacDowell Colony for artists. Murray countered, convincingly, that her residence was more for convalescence than for work. Following collapses Murray typically sought writing opportunities and privacy in nature settings. MacDowell's twenty-five individual cabins scattered on 450 acres of New Hampshire woodland offered both. Residents gathered in a common dining hall for breakfast and dinner, while lunch would be left in a basket at each cabin door. Pauli became MacDowell's first resident Black writer, though James Baldwin soon occupied a neighboring cabin.[182]

The pair occasionally socialized in the evenings. Murray reported to Ware, "Jimmy Baldwin and I have gone to the movies, had a beer in the local community 'pub' and the natives are polite, courteous, and do not lift eyebrows—which I thought would be the case."[183] She also told friends that Baldwin experienced "inner conflicts and terrors," which historian Rosalind Rosenberg describes as Murray's code for her sexuality and gender conflicts. Murray and Baldwin shared other similarities—Baldwin did not know his biological father, experienced family violence, and felt torn between responsibility to his family and a desire to pursue creative writing, and his attractions were often to heterosexual-identifying members of the same sex. There were also some notable differences between the two—Baldwin believed he would always be an outsider, he was more open about his sexuality, and although only thirty he was a more established writer when they met, having already published one novel.[184] Murray described herself as blustering about race issues during mealtime while Baldwin remained "silent . . . sweet . . . popular." When the two shared their writing, fellow residents described Baldwin's piece as "disturbing" while only describing Pauli's piece as "interesting," which hurt, though she could hardly have received greater praise when she only shared a biographical essay on the white southern writer Lillian Smith.[185]

Murray met two white women writers at MacDowell who had a greater impact on her than James Baldwin. Henrietta Buckmaster arrived at MacDowell in September and took an immediate interest in Murray's project. Buckmaster was a skilled historical novelist, having already published *Let My People Go*, about the Underground Railway. Murray formed an even more influential relationship with Helen Hanff, then a little-known screenwriter who later published the highly successful *84 Charing Cross Road*.[186] Years after their meeting, Murray wrote to Hanff, "For so long we have been homeless, wandering, square-pegs-in-round holes, unable to hold steady jobs and be solid citizens, and carrying a load of guilt that we don't function like other people—get married, have children, go to Europe, give big parties, etc., etc." Like Murray, Hanff never identified as gay, but Murray's letters suggest the pair were intimate. Pauli referred to her as "Butch," while Hanff called Pauli "Love," "Sugar," and "Cookie." Murray told Hanff later that she felt thankful they had been at MacDowell together, "a place where our 'queerness' is normal, where our bodies and our souls are considered precious."[187]

Although there were still moments of self-doubt and some "blustering" in her interactions with other residents, Murray relished the sustained two-month period of creative freedom at MacDowell. Early in her stay, on August 11, 1954, she told Caroline Ware, "I'm writing more honestly here and with less self-consciousness. I'm able to pull out the hidden fears in my own life and look at them, I've been so anxiety-ridden because of the terrors I live with all the time." Murray didn't feel the need, or perhaps still struggled, to spell out her hidden fears to Ware. She only added, "You know my various terrors . . ."[188] Murray felt heartened by the way some MacDowell resident artists spoke so openly about difficult childhood experiences. She also benefited from an impressive network of supportive women writers that now included Ware, Buckmaster, Hanff, Smith, and Lockwood. With their encouragement, Murray submitted the *Proud Shoes* manuscript—her first substantial piece of writing—in the fall of 1954.

Much to her dismay, the *Harper's* editor was unimpressed. Murray explained to Ware, "I have let facts chain me and have not used my imagination in building scenes or improvising dialogue."[189] In addition to battling her own difficulty loosening up, as Stephen Vincent Benét put it, the past fifteen years of studying and working in the field of law had conditioned Murray to provide evidence rather than invent dialogue. The editor's demand for major revisions badly affected her confidence—once again she experienced writer's block, and once again she turned to her therapist for help getting unstuck.

FURTHER FAMILY TRAGEDIES HAMPERED the revisions. Her brother Bill's hostility toward Uncle Bubber, with whom he lived, had worsened since he had threatened legal action the previous year. Pauli had never been close to Uncle Bubber—in fact, they had clashed several times, beginning when she visited Baltimore as a child and he criticized her appearance. She therefore understood and even shared some of her brother's antipathy toward him. Nevertheless, Pauli had grown increasingly fearful for her elderly uncle over the past year because he suffered heart problems, and she feared Bill

Such a State of Uncertainty, Caution, and Fear

might be becoming violent toward him. Pauli's concerns for Bubber's health weren't unfounded: he died of a heart attack on February 18, 1955.

After traveling to Baltimore for the funeral, Pauli was shocked to witness firsthand Bill's undiminished hostility toward their deceased uncle: Bill openly expressed glee at Bubber's passing. Even more disturbing, Bill's grip on reality appeared dangerously loosened. He talked of chest pain, which he attributed to "devils after my heart," and he shouted things such as "Get out of my face" and "Stop following me around" at imaginary presences. Bill reacted hypersensitively to perceived slights and experienced unpredictable bouts of anger at those around him. His anger found some focus when his siblings tried to make clear to him that Bubber had not bequeathed him the house—Bill paced about the home with a long serving fork tucked in his belt and physically ejected Grace from the property. The night before Bubber's funeral he again ordered Grace out of the house and threatened his younger brother with a carving knife.[190]

On the day of Bubber's funeral, February 21, 1955, police arrested Bill and took him to Crownsville. Pauli signed the commitment papers along with Mildred and Raymond. She had been outraged when Grace's husband had her committed to Crownsville in 1941, but now circumstance had forced the same awful action upon her. Although distraught over Bill's commitment, Pauli also felt great fear over what might happen if Bill were prematurely released. She wrote to Crownsville describing recent events and explaining the circumstances of her older brother's life before concluding, "I stress these facts only because Bill told the police upon his arrest that his 'sisters were railroading him' and that if they succeeded he would never be able to get his share [of Uncle Bubber's estate]. This belief may be so firmly fixed in his mind that he may seek revenge if prematurely discharged."[191] While revising her manuscript, Pauli felt compelled to sign papers committing her partially lobotomized brother to the institution where their father had been beaten to death, and she feared that, if freed, he might attack her. It is hard to conceive of more trying circumstances under which to be writing a positive family history.

But circumstances did in fact become worse. Pauli's sister Mildred solely inherited Bubber's retirement fund, which had a balance of over $30,000, causing consternation among her siblings. The siblings, including Pauli, believed Bubber intended for the money to be shared between them, as with the rest of Bubber's estate. Mildred and Raymond, the coexecutors of Uncle Bubber's will, couldn't resolve the dispute, and a court battle seemed increasingly likely. Fearing public humiliation for everyone, Pauli tried to mediate. On June 1 she wrote to both siblings, stating, "Unless an amicable settlement can be reached, there is no way of settling this issue out of court. If it proceeds to court, no one of us will win and all of us will suffer additional exposure, humiliation and heartache. Knowing the thoroughness of the Murray clan to pursue their claims I can only envision a scandal to end all scandals."[192]

Pauli received no reply from Mildred, prompting her to send a more personal letter three weeks later, appealing to family bonds to avoid a court battle, but also making it clear she thought her sister was in the wrong.[193] She received no reply to this letter either. Matters moved further toward a court battle when Raymond filed suit. Unsure of how to proceed, Pauli wrote to a cousin in September asking the cousin to intervene, repeating her fear that a court battle would "help none of us and hurt us all."[194] The public scandal Pauli hoped to avoid did eventuate: the *Baltimore Afro-American* reported on the court case, divulging details of the family feud. The article named the siblings — mistakenly naming Pauli as Paul — and described some of the siblings as "incompetent."[195]

PAULI GAINED A BRIEF REPRIEVE FROM family tragedies when she celebrated Aunt Pauline's eighty-fifth birthday on September 25, 1955. Murray left New York shortly after the celebration for another period of residence at the MacDowell Colony for artists; however, her plan to finish off the manuscript at MacDowell ended abruptly when she received a disturbing letter from Aunt Pauline. Vision trouble was making Aunt Pauline fearful of permanent blindness. Pauli rushed home to take her to the doctor. The day of the appointment, Aunt Pauline awoke in pain and insisted she was dying: she said, in her matter-of-fact way, "I don't think I'll live to get to the hospital. I've got death rattles in my throat." Pauli had to endure a long day of trying to find a hospital that would admit her mother and then waiting for ambulance transportation. When ambulance officers were finally removing Aunt Pauline from the apartment, the ever-practical Aunt Pauline stopped the paramedics momentarily to point out to Pauli the hatbox that contained her burial undergarments. Once hospitalized, Aunt Pauline improved and told Pauli to go home and rest. Later that night, Aunt Pauline had a massive heart attack and died.[196]

In the past year alone — while trying to complete her family story — Pauli had to deal with the deaths of her adoptive mother, Aunt Marie, and Uncle Bubber, as well as the lawsuit over Bubber's estate and committing her brother to Crownsville. Pauli told her niece, "I believe I have a 'best seller' in the making. I'm about three-fourths through the book. But Aunt Pauline's death following so closely on Bubber's death and the results coupled with this court fight have filled me with so much grief, I find it difficult to write and am not sleeping properly."[197]

Family fallout over Uncle Bubber's estate continued after Aunt Pauline's death. Pauli learned that her niece had issued a "devastating, callous, and heartless assessment" of Pauli and her siblings and their alleged inability to live with others. Pauli tried to explain to her niece the reasons for the Murray siblings' difficulties: "Because of the miserably pitiful lack of knowledge about mental and emotional illness in the first half of the Twentieth Century the Murrays have believed they lived under a hereditary curse of this disease because of their father's illness." This was one of three references to the "curse" of hereditary mental illness in a letter on the troubles of the Murrays, all of whom suffered, seemingly, except for Raymond, who never lived in his parental home. Pauli considered it a miracle that any of the Murrays were functional given the rumors of their mother's suicide and the details of their parents' marriage (which she still refused to discuss). The long-term consequences of these problems, she explained, had manifested themselves in most of her siblings and, to some extent, in Pauli herself—Pauli's "one salvation," derived from the fact that she "grew up among the Fitzgeralds who were solid, farmstock," and molded her "toward some kind of stability as against the hyper-thyroid type the Murrays seem to be."

Pauli's letter went on to assert that Grace might have been spared five years in Crownsville if proper psychiatric care had been available to her when she was suffering from the approaching stage of menopausal depression and the "sapping of her energy through too many contraceptive drastic actions." From her sister's troubles, Pauli moved into a more personal discussion of herself: "Having this history of mental and emotional illness, upon medical advice when I was younger, I decided not to marry and have children." She continued, "I did marry when I was twenty, but it was a mistake and eventually annulled. After that, however, under the misapprehension that our trouble was hereditary, I refrained from allowing myself to get into the position of possible marriage."[198]

The New Year brought no relief from family crises. Aunt Sallie couldn't cope with the loss of her sister—although the sisters had very different personalities and bickered frequently, they had also been devoted to each other. Aunt Sallie now lost her appetite and became listless. In a marked difference with Aunt Pauline or Pauli, Aunt Sallie had not visited a doctor in thirty-seven years. Murray overcame her aunt's opposition, however, and forced Aunt Sallie to see a physician, which led to the discovery of liver cancer. Over the next seven weeks, Pauli visited her aunt in the hospital every day, "watching a life slip away." Each night she returned home to the quiet apartment, empty except for Smokey, where she sustained herself by finalizing revisions to her Fitzgerald family story. Aunt Sallie died in May 1956, less than seven months after her sister had died and just a few days after the *Proud Shoes* manuscript went to press.[199]

Murray's life entered a new period of instability following the tremendous losses. She wrote in her autobiography,

> When it was all over, there was a great void in my life. The manuscript was out of my hands and there was no cushion for my loss. Aunt Sallie was the last of the older generation, and with her passing I was cut adrift, no longer anchored to the ties of my childhood and to those I had always revered as my elders. At the same time, having watched over my aunts for eight years and seen them through to the end, I felt as if I had lost my children. I had now to begin a new life without their faith to lean upon and with only the presence of my little dog Smokey to break the unaccustomed stillness of an empty apartment.[200]

When Pauli looked at the problems of her siblings and the death of her father, she worried about inherited insanity—she tried to view her maternal Fitzgerald ancestry as her positive biological inheritance. The deaths of her Fitzgerald aunts and the completion of *Proud Shoes* severed both physical and intellectual links with her Fitzgerald family history. Murray was alone in the world, her "baby" *Proud Shoes* had gone to press, and the closest people she had to parents, Aunts Pauline and Sallie, were gone too.

THE PUBLICATION OF *Proud Shoes* on October 17, 1956, testified to Murray's perseverance in the face of extreme financial and personal hardships. She dedicated the book to four people: Aunt Pauline; Caroline Ware; her agent, Marie Rodell; and her psychiatrist, Edmund Ziman. In it she wrote, "It had taken me almost a lifetime to discover that true emancipation lies in acceptance of the whole past, in deriving strength from all my roots, and in facing up to the degradation as well as the dignity of my ancestors."[201] Yet Murray wasn't ready to publicly describe all the degradation her family had endured: the book didn't discuss her parents and siblings or acknowledge Grandfather Robert's color complex.

The opening chapter is the strongest in the book, perhaps her best piece of writing ever. This chapter, added after the first draft, is her most successful attempt to address her editor's criticisms that she had "let facts chain" her and had not used "imagination in building scenes or improvising dialogue."[202] The chapter builds beautifully to Grandmother Cornelia's explosion at her neighbors in the Bottoms. After the evocative opening, the narrative turns back to the time before Murray's birth to chronicle her maternal grandparents' lives, particularly her grandfather's. These chapters suffer from the faults earlier identified by Murray's editor: they are more a work of dry history, often relying on impersonal explanations of prevailing attitudes rather than a skillful use of literary and historical imagination to build intimate scenes. The book concluded with an assertion that Grandfather's service to the nation sustained her until she "grew older and found other ways of balancing loyalty with revolt."[203] Murray acknowledged warring tendencies within herself, which she found easier to explore through selective portrayals of the personalities of her maternal grandparents: Grandfather Robert's service to both the nation and his oppressed people and Grandmother Cornelia's vulnerabilities and defiance.

The final book stands in stark contrast to the brief Fitzgerald sketch Murray penned in 1933, which marked the project's early beginnings. The earlier sketch provided a strikingly candid assessment of the Fitzgerald personalities and the circumstances shaping them, which the poet Stephen Vincent Benét encouraged her to make into a novel.[204] By the time Murray came to dedicate herself to the task in the 1950s, she was no longer a youthful Depression-era radical rebelling against the power structure—she was seeking acceptance within a society deeply fearful of perceived disloyalty. Murray's decision to pursue the project as a hybrid history project instead of a pure novel also constrained her. She mined her aunts' memories for material, but they in turn impressed on her concerns about the book's potential to embarrass the family. Their deaths before the project's completion further compelled her to honor the memory of her ancestors.

Though *Proud Shoes* was confined by both national and family issues, Murray also later linked the book to personal and national growth: "The writing of *Proud Shoes* became for me the resolution of a search for identity and the exorcism of ghosts of the past. No longer constrained by suppressed memories, I began to see myself in a new light—the product of slowly evolving process of biological and cultural integration, a process containing the character of many cultures and many peoples, a New World experiment, fragile yet tenacious, a possible hint of a stronger and freer America of the future, no longer stunted in its growth by an insidious ethnocentrism."[205] Murray increasingly saw the personal as political and began conceiving of herself not as a minority American but as a truly representative American.

Proud Shoes received generally positive reviews, but the book didn't become the best-seller Murray longed to write.[206] Initially, fewer than five thousand copies sold, and it made exactly forty-five cents over the publisher's advance.[207] While not an immediate success, as with so many of Murray's endeavors *Proud Shoes* has grown in reputation—it is now a classroom resource, and its continuing availability enables current audiences to reach their own conclusions as to the work's merits.[208] Understanding all that Murray endured while writing it can only increase one's admiration for the work and its author. In *Proud Shoes* she explored the impact of racial oppression on her forebears while enduring the ongoing damaging consequences of multiple forms of oppression. Despite racism, sexism, homophobia, Cold War suspicions, financial hardship, physical and mental health problems, the illnesses and deaths of loved ones, and the consequent lack of self-confidence these experiences engendered, Murray succeeded in adding a Fitzgerald family story to the rich literary tradition of African American life writing.

. . . . .

VII

The 1952 and 1956 presidential election campaigns bookended Murray's work on *Proud Shoes*. Adlai Stevenson's civil rights record as Illinois governor had impressed her so much that she became an enthusiastic, though paid, "Volunteer for Stevenson" during the unsuccessful 1952 campaign, helping him win 83 percent of the Black vote in Harlem. By the 1956 election, however, Murray had become far less enthusiastic about the Democratic candidate. In the wake of the *Brown* decision, the ongoing Montgomery bus boycott, and the beginning of "massive resistance" by white southerners, Stevenson exercised far more caution on civil rights issues. When asked whether he would use the military to enforce desegregation, Stevenson told the *New York Times*, "I think that would be a great mistake. That is exactly what brought on the Civil War. It can't be done by troops, or bayonets. We must proceed gradually, not upsetting habits or traditions that are older than the Republic." Days later Stevenson urged candidates to abstain from discussing integration during the presidential campaign.[209]

Stevenson's timidity infuriated Murray. She believed he would lose the Black vote because African Americans were "weary with those who caution, 'Don't push too fast,'" and claimed she would rather him lose the election than win a campaign that discounted Black citizens.[210] Murray told Eleanor Roosevelt, "It is all very well for Mr. Stevenson to be preoccupied with conciliation and with the dangers involved in upsetting the 'traditions of centuries,' but unless he understands how passionately determined the Negro is that once and for all we will be brought up to par, or die in the attempt, he will underestimate the new situation we are facing in the United States today."[211] In reply, Roosevelt claimed Stevenson had meant something entirely different when he used the term "gradual" than what the word had

Lloyd K. Garrison and Murray launching *Proud Shoes*, 1956.
(Schlesinger Library, Radcliffe Institute, Harvard University)

come to mean to African Americans and described the reporting of Stevenson's comments as garbled. She further argued that it would be a mistake to tear down Stevenson, whom she described as the only hope for African Americans.

Such was Murray's admiration for Roosevelt, and the narrowing of political options during the Cold War, that she continued to work for the New York "Stevenson for President" committee, led by Lloyd K. Garrison, but the campaign held none of the excitement of 1952. Along with other campaigners, Murray felt resigned to defeat before the election. Eisenhower won all but seven states (almost all in the South). Murray's prediction that Stevenson would lose the Black vote proved inaccurate, but his share of the Black vote dropped nearly 20 percent, and in southern cities the majority of Black voters supported Eisenhower.[212]

The campaign had one very positive outcome for Murray. Two weeks after the 1956 election, Garrison found her a job in the New York office of his law firm, Paul, Weiss, Rifkind, Wharton & Garrison. Garrison resembled his famous great-grandfather, abolitionist William Lloyd Garrison, in appearance and commitment to social equality. He also possessed a candor that sometimes felt like "an ice-cold shower" on Murray's ambition, but he combined it with a gentle disposition in a way that made her value his ongoing mentorship.[213] Most lawyers recruited to work at his firm had attended Ivy League colleges and served on law reviews or clerked for judges; consequently, Garrison was only able to persuade his colleagues to offer Murray a part-time librarian position. Despite her years of extreme financial hardship, Murray still hesitated before accepting: she thought settling for an administrative role would be the end of a legal career, although she had already given up on it four years earlier and in the intervening years had accepted far less prestigious jobs, such as typing manuscripts.[214]

Her repeated hesitancy about jobs — often centered on issues of pay and prestige — seems to relate to fluctuating self-confidence, which led her to identify reasons she should not either continue in jobs or enthusiastically accept new ones. The ever-reliable Caroline Ware urged her to accept the position, arguing that working part time for a salary of $5,000 a year, a substantially higher amount than she had ever earned before, would allow time for creative writing while not closing off the future possibility of legal work. The job became impossible to resist when Garrison assured her a position as an associate attorney, though she did not join the firm's litigation department until three months after starting at the firm.[215]

Eleven difficult years after completing her master's degree, Murray became an entry-level attorney at a commercial law firm. None of her experience in private practice, or training in civil rights and labor law, properly prepared her for corporate law. Murray likened it to being "a sandlot player catapulted overnight into major league baseball."[216] When her assigned partner at the firm immediately began asking for memos on mergers, bankruptcies, and the like, Murray panicked. He slammed one of her first attempts, describing the argument as "wavering" and the conclusions as "timid, and uncertain," terms that might well have been applied to her confidence levels. When several more attempts were deemed unsatisfactory, Murray felt ready to quit. Garrison took her to lunch and listened while she confessed her sense of inadequacy. He assured her that her feelings weren't unique, that he too felt overwhelmed when he started at the firm. Murray described the lunch as a turning point, after which she attacked her work with greater confidence, but she also admitted to remaining uncomfortable within a large-scale commercial law practice.[217]

For much of her existence, Murray had struggled just to put food on the table and clothes on her back. It must have been incredibly daunting for Murray—a rookie in corporate law—to walk into a Manhattan office and gaze on a sea of clean-cut young white male lawyers with degrees from Harvard, Yale, and Columbia. Of the more than sixty-five attorneys the firm employed, she was the only Black attorney, and one of only three women attorneys working in the New York office—and she became the sole woman attorney when the other two moved on. Murray struggled with "phantoms lurking in the background, secret fears that gaps in my knowledge or inadequacies in performance would be attributed to my race or sex," which made her feel "on trial on several counts."[218] The age difference also worried her: at forty-six she was the same age as some of the firm's partners. She recalled, "My senior associates who supervised me were ten and fifteen years my junior; our conflicts arose in the fact that while they had the skill, I had the maturity of judgement, but they were the boss."[219] The points of difference and the insecurities they engendered manifested in tense workplace relationships and suggested this job wouldn't last long.

Despite the isolation and self-consciousness entailed with being an older Black woman—a "triple minority"—Murray did not resign within the first year as she had many times before.[220] Her perseverance can be attributed, in large part, to her forming an intimate relationship with the firm's office manager, Irene "Renee" Barlow.[221] Only three years younger than Murray, Renee (pronounced to rhyme with Lenie, Murray's childhood nickname) was also an Episcopalian and, in Murray's eyes, also an "unconscious" feminist. But Renee differed strikingly from Murray in substantial ways—she was English born, white, and tall, and carried herself with quiet self-assurance. Murray described Barlow as "even-tempered, witty, and an able administrator, she made her nerve-racking job look easy, handling a volatile mix of personalities" with skill.[222] For her part, Barlow described Murray as a "frightened rabbit." Murray credited Barlow with helping her manage workplace relationships: "Her constantly urging me to do my best, to be more diplomatic, more graceful in my dress and speech, less the rough diamond and more the sophisticate, was a measure of her anxiety that I make good on the job." Murray described Barlow as a "scourge" who "often flailed" her but who also suffered along with her, helping her survive the painful training period in a "bigtime" law firm.[223] The relationship not only helped Murray endure her initiation into corporate law but also helped her through many more challenges over the years to come.

ACCORDING TO THE UPLIFT IDEOLOGY Murray learned in childhood, proving herself in corporate law was a contribution to advancing the race,

Irene Barlow and Lloyd K. Garrison (*center pair*), ca. 1964 or 1965.
(*Schlesinger Library, Radcliffe Institute, Harvard University*)

but it certainly lacked the drama and excitement of the emerging civil rights struggle. Murray remained in touch with the movement, particularly the "Little Rock Nine" story. She closely followed the young Black students' first year at Central High School and spoke out on behalf of Daisy Bates, the students' mentor throughout the ordeal of integrating the Arkansas high school. The NAACP honored the students, but not Bates, with the Spingarn Award, the NAACP's most prestigious award. The students objected, as did their parents. Murray, a baseball enthusiast, also objected, writing one of her long confrontational letters to the NAACP claiming that leaving Bates off the award list was like trying to think of the New York Yankees without their famed manager, Casey Stengel.[224] In the summer of 1958, the Little Rock Nine and Daisy Bates made a series of appearances in New York City, and Murray trailed them "at a respectful distance all weekend."[225] At a Brooklyn NAACP rally, Murray was particularly struck by Bates's eloquence as she spoke tearfully of the weariness caused by the ordeals of the past eleven months.

The school year at Central High had ended, but the struggle against bigotry continued. Segregationists were trying to force Bates and her husband—who published the *Arkansas State Press*—out of business. Murray's

Such a State of Uncertainty, Caution, and Fear

friend Ted Poston wrote a series of *New York Post* articles on the integration of Little Rock High and told the Brooklyn rally that the White Citizens' Council were close to bankrupting the Bates family through methods such as violent intimidation of newspaper boys and advertising boycotts. Murray felt moved to ask Mr. Bates about the cost of advertising space, then wrote to friends and family to initiate a "Roll Call for Freedom" whereby supporters paid ten dollars to fill the empty advertising space with their names listed in the roll call.[226] The idea was well received, but the NAACP still covered most of the *State Press*'s lost advertising revenue and continued to do so for some time.[227] Bates and Murray became acquainted, to the point that in the following year Murray gave her legal advice concerning a proposed book contract. Murray provided a similar service to Martin Luther King Jr.[228]

Murray also assisted fellow North Carolinian Robert F. Williams, another civil rights activist who shot to national attention in 1959. Williams made provocative comments to the media following a number of outrageous criminal cases. On May 5, two separate criminal trials began in Monroe, North Carolina. In both cases, individual white men stood accused of assaulting Black women. Not only were both men acquitted; the victims were made to suffer further. The victim in the first case, a hotel maid who had been beaten and kicked down the stairs by the acquitted white man, was subject to various forms of harassment, including being arrested for failing to report earnings two years earlier. In the second case, the court allowed a white man accused of attempting to rape a Black woman to have his wife sit by his side during the trial. The defense attorney described the accused's wife as a "pure flower" before asking the all-white male jurors if they thought the accused "would have left this pure flower, God's greatest gift," then pointing toward the victim, "for that." Two other crimes reported in the Black press had already incensed African Americans—the lynching of Mack Parker in Mississippi and the gang rape of a Black woman by white men in Florida, both of which went unpunished.

Robert F. Williams, the president of the Monroe NAACP branch and a World War II veteran, expressed his fury to the media.[229] It was time to "meet violence with violence," he declared, and "we must be willing to kill if necessary." Williams continued, "We get no justice under the present system. If we feel that injustice is done, we must right then and there on the spot be prepared to inflict punishment on these people. . . . Since the federal government will not bring a halt to lynching in the South and since the so-called courts lynch our people legally, if it's necessary to stop lynching with lynching, then we must be willing to resort to that method."[230]

His comments were widely reported—the *New York Times* headline stated, "N.A.A.C.P. Leader Urges Violence," and the *Mississippi State-Times* blared, "Negro Calls for Lynch of Whites." Roy Wilkins, the NAACP national executive secretary, called Williams to ask if the newspaper quotes were accurate. Williams not only confirmed them but added that he had made similar statements in radio interviews that morning and planned to reiterate his points to television crews that afternoon. The phone call ended with Williams only agreeing to clarify that he wasn't speaking on behalf of the NAACP. Realizing that such distinctions would be lost on the broader public, before that day ended Wilkins unilaterally suspended Williams as an NAACP official pending consideration by the group's board of directors at its next meeting. Williams wired back that he would be attending the meeting "with counsel."[231]

Pauli Murray attended the NAACP Board of Directors meeting on June 8, 1959, as one of Williams's two attorneys. She told the board that she didn't think that they should condone violence, but should try to remember the context of Williams's statement and his attempts to qualify it by repudiating revenge attacks on whites in general. "I think that the statement [Williams] made on May 5 was made in anger," Murray insisted, "and there was provocation—the same day that Mack Parker's body was found, and the same day the coed in Florida was raped, the same day the President of the United States of America said he would not call for stronger civil rights legislation. Violence," she argued, "was the order of the day."[232] The NAACP board, however, was not persuaded by Murray's arguments and voted to uphold Wilkins's decision.

Despite her adherence to nonviolence and dignified opposition to racism, Murray's defense of Williams makes sense because she understood the difficulties of containing outrage at injustice. Her childhood fears of rape and lynching must have been awakened by the events Williams spoke out against; that both crimes could still be committed against African Americans with impunity demanded a strong reaction.[233] Representing Williams was also consistent with her commitment to democratic organizing: many activists had growing concerns about the lack of transparency and democracy within the NAACP. The brief for Williams, written by Conrad Lynn, took particular issue with Wilkins's unilateral suspension of Williams.[234]

Rank-and-file activists increasingly criticized the NAACP as unresponsive and in urgent need of new leadership, particularly after the Montgomery Bus Boycott had excited activists about the possibility of broadening the campaign against segregation into a social movement rather than a narrow legal struggle. Murray had written to the NAACP leadership to raise similar concerns a year before she represented Williams. She stated that the NAACP leadership structure needed reform and that the leadership had not done enough to support Daisy Bates during and after the Little Rock crisis. Roy Wilkins wrote a six-page reply repudiating the criticisms: he expressed amazement that Murray gave merit to the organization's critics and asserted that this must be because she hadn't kept abreast of the organization's activities.[235] In a further illustration of the autocratic tendencies of the NAACP leadership, Daisy Bates felt pressured to use her vote on the NAACP national board to uphold Williams's suspension—despite her fierce advocacy of self-defense—because her newspaper business relied on NAACP money.[236]

Wilkins and the NAACP hierarchy maintained a firm grip on the organization, but they couldn't control the civil rights revolution that flourished the following year. On February 1, 1960, four Black university students carried out a peaceful sit-in protest at a segregated Woolworth's lunch counter in Greensboro, North Carolina, sparking a surge in protests against segregation using the nonviolent, direct-action tactics that Murray had helped innovate two decades earlier.[237] By the time news of the Greensboro sit-ins broke, however, Murray was on a boat bound for Africa to begin a new career.

MURRAY'S TIME WORKING AT Paul, Weiss, Rifkind, Wharton & Garrison came to end after three years, her longest-ever stint as an employee during the first fifty years of her life. She had grown less and less engaged in the work assigned to her in the small claims department and had been looking to do more fulfilling legal aid work, like the work she performed for Robert F. Williams.[238] She felt "restless" and couldn't envisage "settling into the career of a desk lawyer in an assembly-line practice" when she saw little opportunity to win promotion and thus little opportunity to win the recognition, prestige, and the personal fulfillment she desired. Africa increasingly interested Murray: her good friend Maida Springer regularly visited the continent as part of her trade union work, and Pauli often met African nationalists staying at Springer's home. Springer alerted Murray to a possible job vacancy at the University of Ghana Law School in early 1959. Murray recalled applying immediately, but it took months of negotiation before she received a formal offer.[239]

Murray didn't leave for Africa until early 1960, yet she appears to have spent much of 1959 doing things other than working in corporate law. Just before taking up Williams's case, Murray had spent April and May at the MacDowell Colony for artists, where she had stayed twice previously when completing *Proud Shoes*. During these two months, she worked on at least five poems, two of which focused on the lynching of Mack Parker, a murder so shocking that it alone might have been enough to make her unwilling to settle for a comfortable existence as an assembly-line lawyer.[240] A mob had entered the Mississippi jail cell where Parker was being held for allegedly raping a pregnant white woman, beat him, dragged him away, shot him dead, and dumped his body in a river.[241] The attack on Parker occurred while he was confined to a white-run facility, which may have reminded Murray of her father's death—America seemed no safer for African Americans thirty-six years on. Murray felt compelled to respond to Parker's lynching. Writing was one response; defending Williams was another.

Not all of the poetry she penned at MacDowell addressed race issues. Murray also revised the poem "Paradox," which she had first written in 1938. It begins with this stanza:

I know a tendril softly twined
About a lofty oak,
Having no power to uproot,
Can gently choke.

The poem goes on to describe a lover's demeanor changing to frosty and remote.[242] The same month she revised this poem, Murray wrote a new love poem, "For Pan," the pet name Pauli had bestowed on her love of two decades earlier, Peg Holmes.[243] Writing so positively about such a distant relationship as well as revising an old poem about the changeability of a lover's heart suggests that problems existed in her relationship with Renee Barlow at this time.

Murray tried to get these new poems, and others written much earlier, published as a collection. The more established poet Leslie Nelson Jennings provided a cover letter in which he referred to Murray as "a young colored girl." The forty-nine-year-old Murray took exception, telling him she reacted "very violently to such a label"; she added that in the present struggle for full equality, African Americans strongly resented stereotypes, and as a "Poet of Rebellion" she was particularly allergic to them. She went on to state: "It is true that I am tense and high-powered, but this is a question of glands, and if I work with you, you will have to accept me as I am. Not even a thyroidectomy has slowed me down and this is a congenital problem with me." Her response illustrates the continual interplay between her identifying problems as external and seeing them as internal. In another draft of the letter, she stated that she had lived with her congenital glandular condition for many years and sometimes forgot that others were "not as high-powered."[244] A correspondence that began full of justifiable annoyance ended with a biological explanation for her behavior: her hurt and anger quickly dissolving into defensiveness and concern about her behavior's sources.

Harper declined to publish her poems, closing off the possibility that she could leave corporate law to write full time anytime soon. Legal aid work with civil rights activists, though more fulfilling than corporate law, could not provide a reliable income. Murray had applied for the University of Ghana job in February but heard nothing until June. When the news did arrive, it wasn't good. The director of legal education in Ghana encouraged her to visit, but no funds existed to employ her; furthermore, he believed any future funds would be inadequate for her salary. Telling Murray she could not do something, however, was a surefire way of making her more determined to do it. She set about lobbying national institutions, including the Ford Foundation, to fund a trip. She asked her employer, Lloyd Garrison, to contact the attorney general of Ghana directly on her behalf. Garrison also provided paid leave for her to attend Columbia Law School in September 1959 to broaden her legal expertise. She had often considered pursuing a PhD, so attending Columbia (this was the third time she had enrolled at Columbia since she first came to New York with the intention of attending the institution) might have been part of a backup plan if Ghana fell through.

That fall she met with both Ghana's foreign minister and attorney general when they visited the United States, and the attorney general at last assured her a job at the University of Ghana on an initial eighteen-month contract as a senior lecturer in law. Her wage would be less than she earned in corporate law, and she suspected the pay offer was less than men in the same position received, but she still withdrew from Columbia in December and packed for Ghana.[245] In her determination to get the position, Murray seemed oblivious to the magnitude of the challenge ahead: she joked about never having traveled farther overseas than Staten Island, yet now she intended to live indefinitely in a recently decolonized tropical African nation.[246] Given her past employment and health troubles, it was a remarkably brave undertaking.

· · · · ·

VIII

Murray and her dog, Smokey, boarded ship for Africa on February 2, 1960.[247] Five days into the voyage, she became homesick. She asked herself, "What is America to me?," and answered that it wasn't places or values but the loved ones she left behind. Tears came at a church service during a stop in Halifax, which reminded her of attending services with aunts as a child and more recently with Renee Barlow.[248] Her first experience of Africa did little to help overcome a longing for home: nothing she had read or heard prepared her for the contrast between the "opulence" of home and the "overwhelming poverty" of the Monrovian masses she encountered during a two-day stop in Liberia.[249]

When the three-week voyage finally ended in Ghana, things didn't improve. Her new residence wasn't ready, forcing her to stay in "dirty, run down" government housing next to the Accra airfield.[250] She found the heat intolerable, the slower pace of life difficult, and the frequent unavailability of basic consumer items frustrating. The insects also bothered Murray—she believed her malaria pills were inadequate and described suffering from malaria frequently. Her first attack proved so violent that Constance E. Stone—a New Englander who directed the United States Information Service libraries in West Africa—took Murray to her own home to care for her until she recovered. Stone remained a close friend throughout Murray's time in Ghana, the latest in a string of women who provided Murray with vital support.[251]

Yaro, a young man Murray reluctantly hired to perform domestic duties, also provided invaluable assistance. Westerners in Ghana referred to their employees by names such as "head boy" or "garden boy" and provided them with uniforms, and for their part, Ghanaians employed by Westerners acted subserviently. Given the overtones of American slavery, all of this made Murray "squeamish," but she accepted that it was an important source of employment for local men. She employed Yaro because, of the stream of people to appear at her door seeking work, he appeared the least obsequious. She referred to him as her "steward" and refused to let him wear a uniform. Instead she bought him casual clothes and raised his pay on the condition that he attend school. Yaro performed domestic chores and tasks requiring native-language skills, such as the purchasing of goods and services, and employing "watchnights" to provide security around the home.[252]

Murray put on a brave front in letters to friends at home, but her diaries express intense loneliness. She had the assistance of Yaro, though he spoke little English, and she had the friendship of Constance Stone and the companionship of Smokey; but these weren't nearly enough to overcome the culture shock and the ensuing depression. Murray believed that the problem might be that she had "no friends of the heart" in Ghana. Renee Barlow had been crucial to the relative stability she experienced in her working and personal life over the last three years, and the pair still corresponded regularly, but this hardly compensated for the physical absence. Murray couldn't even savor Barlow's letters for long—fearful that someone else might read them, she quickly destroyed them.[253]

Loneliness compounded the feeling of being an outsider. Several months after arriving, Murray wrote, "It is the fate of an American Negro to feel far more an American abroad than he does at home. Relieved temporarily of the burden of racial status, the pull and tug of what his country means to him and to millions of others is a powerful emotion."[254] She believed Africans immediately recognized her obvious "Americanness," though she had struggled to have it recognized her whole life at home. Murray likened the feeling to standing on her head: "I discover here if one is not black, one is white, while in America it is just the opposite."[255]

Murray still appreciated having her American identity affirmed, even if only by Ghanaians. The extent to which she embraced Americanness is evident in the dubious distinctions she drew between Americans and the local inhabitants. She wrote, "My American heritage betrays me at every turn— my complexion, the way I walk, my impatience with delay and 'palaver,' my obsession with good plumbing and sanitation, my tendency toward innovation, my belief that the impossible can be done and a stubborn determination to do it in spite of any obstacle in my way."[256] Murray's views reflect the stereotyping prevalent in the world she inhabited, but they also capture the depth of her homesickness and difficulty adjusting to life in Ghana.

As she often did in times of stress, Murray internalized her troubles. In addition to bouts of physical illness, she wondered whether her troubles stemmed from her own inadequacies and whether her abilities did not match her ambitions. Despite noting the differences between herself and Africans, she also felt uncomfortable in the American expatriate social scene.[257] Just as she had felt caught between races in her childhood, between genders as a young adult, between middle-class aspirations and material poverty, between seeking acceptance and rebelliousness, and between the Fitzgeralds and the Murrays, in Ghana she was caught between the expats and the locals. A couple of months into her stay she wrote in her diary, "Part of my problem at the moment is the self."[258] A month later she wrote, "Fighting the trapped feeling again."[259]

AT HOME MURRAY HAD BEEN marginalized for a perceived lack of loyalty to the nation; in Ghana she soon became marginalized because of a fierce loyalty to the United States. In mid-June 1960, Murray traveled to Congo— which had won its independence from Belgium days earlier—to help coordinate the evacuation of a group of South African antiapartheid activists.

She had undertaken the trip in part to establish "good faith" with the Ghanaian government "as a liberal and person of character."[260]

Belgium's ongoing meddling in its former colony created a tense situation that kept Western imperialism prominent in the minds of politically engaged Africans. Soviet support for the Congolese president, Patrice Lumumba, alarmed Belgium and the United States, especially after Cuba's "defection" to communism a year earlier. Just as Murray arrived back in Ghana to prepare for her first semester of teaching, Western powers supported a coup led by Congo's army chief of staff, Joseph Mobutu, on September 14, 1960.[261] Events in Congo resonated deeply in Ghana, which had sent troops as part of an ineffective UN intervention before the coup. Outrage mounted when the new regime executed Patrice Lumumba in January 1961.

Within this context, Murray's attempt to make a positive contribution to a newly independent African country quickly turned into a losing battle to counter anti-American sentiment and the increasingly autocratic tendencies of the Ghanaian government. During the First Conference of African Women and Women of African Descent, held in Accra in July 1960, Murray worked in opposition to a resolution on discrimination that linked the United States with the Union of South Africa. She identified distinctions between the two countries, explaining the history of the U.S. Constitution and the role of the Supreme Court in the Black freedom struggle.[262]

Murray countered common arguments that decried her nation's treatment of African Americans as hypocritical. African Americans embodied the American Dream, she argued, since they had achieved so much against a background of slavery, which she believed demonstrated the "spiritual force of democracy."[263] She also asserted that the heroics of the Black freedom struggle might have contributed in some small degree to the acceleration of independence for African countries.[264] Murray's public optimism concerning her nation's capacity to reform itself may have reflected the coercive Cold War context and a personal defensiveness about her loyalty to the nation, but it also aligned with the uplift ideology of her youth—she had to believe that the United States could and would ultimately deliver equal treatment for Black citizens, or else declare her long-term struggle for full citizenship a lost cause.[265]

Murray joined the American Women's Association of Accra, which among its other activities countered anti-American statements in the state-controlled Ghanaian media.[266] As part of this effort, Murray criticized a pamphlet titled *ABC of Socialism*, which she believed contained distortions about the U.S. economic system, and asserted, "Whether Ghana embraces socialism or not is none of my business, but distortions about my own country are very much my business."[267] Murray also entered into a sharp correspondence with the Ghanaian secretary-general of the Trades Union Congress, John K. Tettegah, concerning a speech he had given in which he claimed capitalist plots against Ghana were being hatched in the United States.[268] Murray again declared no interest in whether Ghanaians chose socialism or capitalism—she only cared about whether the Ghanaian government was authoritarian and hostile to the United States, which she believed was the leading exponent of free and democratic institutions in the world.[269]

WITHIN THIS ALREADY-VOLATILE MIX of cultural alienation, loneliness, and escalating Cold War tensions, Murray began the enormous challenge of teaching law for the first time in a newly independent nation. She recalled feeling overwhelmed—she was the only American and one of only two women on the small staff tasked with training lawyers to work in a barely established legal system. The complete lack of organization and direction within the law school, which Murray perceived, also left her unimpressed.[270] Murray taught constitutional and administrative law, which was considered the most politically delicate subject, as the new constitution granted the Ghanaian president extensive power. Making the task yet more challenging, all twenty of her students were male, none had any prior college education, most worked full time, and Murray had to develop a course for them from scratch with limited resources.

On the first day of class, Murray recalled nervously facing "several rows of young men whose impassive expressions" gave "no hint of their reaction to the unique experience of having a woman professor from the United States."[271] She quickly dispensed with lectures and tried to encourage open discussion of a casebook—a strategy that at first made the students as uncomfortable as the teacher. The students came to embrace the strategy, however; they often stayed after class to debate the issues raised with each other. Murray later recalled that one student, who went on to study at Harvard, praised her teaching methods at the end of the course, and she later helped another former student, Kwaku Baah, get to the United States to further his education by raising money among her contacts. Baah eventually returned to Ghana and was elected to the national parliament.[272]

Even after she began teaching, Murray could not refrain from involvement in national and international political affairs. The day after her fiftieth birthday in November 1960, Murray wrote to President Kwame Nkrumah expressing relief after he made a public statement rejecting dictatorship. She had written to him once before, with typical Murray bravado, to announce her arrival in Ghana. Now she wrote with equal boldness to request an appointment, suggesting that she might be able to help interpret Americans for Africans.[273] Nkrumah's secretary replied, tersely stating that the president would go further than stating dictatorship didn't exist in Ghana — he would argue that it didn't exist in Russia either, a country more democratic than any country in the world, in his view.[274]

Murray largely adopted the U.S. foreign policy line on race relations during the Cold War, telling a story of gradual progress and democracy in action, but resistance to desegregation threatened to make a mockery of the position.[275] In May 1961, the Freedom Rides began to test the government's willingness to enforce desegregation on interstate buses. More than fifteen years had elapsed since the almost-identical Journey of Reconciliation, which Murray helped plan, yet still the federal government urged caution, even though segregation on interstate travel had been unconstitutional all that time. Just as she had used the threat posed by fascism in the 1930s, Murray now used the Cold War to urge the federal government to address race inequality. On a Voice of America broadcast heard by Murray, Attorney General Robert F. Kennedy called on the Freedom Riders to hold off from further actions until tempers cooled. An outraged Murray wrote to Kennedy: "The one weapon which Americans living in developing countries today, and particularly in Africa, can use to counteract attempts to classify the United States with the Union of South Africa is to point to the federal government and say that it is using its full strength to enforce the fundamental law of the land. If the Chief Law Enforcement Officer of the United States shows any ambiguity on this issue, the ground is cut from under our argument and we are helpless in the face of rising anti-American feeling."[276]

Murray continued to fight a war on two fronts by maintaining vocal opposition to authoritarian rule in Ghana. The rhetoric of Nkrumah's government and the use of emergency powers to detain people without charge for up to five years particularly alarmed her. She wrote articles and supplied materials on Ghanaian political developments for friends in the United States to use anonymously. Murray's former employer, Lloyd K. Garrison, wrote to members of the foreign policy establishment to inform them that she had valuable insights into the political situation in Ghana. Murray also renewed her acquaintance with Jay Lovestone, the former leader of the Lovestoneite Marxist group with whom Murray had briefly associated in the 1930s. Lovestone was now a Cold Warrior, a CIA operative, and director of the international free trade union initiative of the American Federation of Labor and Congress of Industrial Organizations (AFL-CIO).[277] Murray also quarreled with old friend Maida Springer over Springer's support of the Ghanaian president; Springer later described Pauli as a "301 percent American" who didn't share her passionate feeling about Africa.[278]

Friends back home urged Murray not to "torture" herself over the political battles taking place all around her.[279] One unidentified correspondent told Murray to confine herself to teaching and bearing witness: "I believe that nothing could contribute more to damaging the USA in Ghana now than for a teacher like you to go behaving like a political propagandist until she finds herself in a situation where she is persona non grata to the government or is herself too tormented by disagreement and frustration to keep realistic about the true nature of her job."[280] Yet Murray remained unable or unwilling to change her ways.

She must have realized that overt criticisms of the government would make her position in Ghana untenable. Ghanaian officials warned Springer that Professor Murray was too critical of the government.[281] Murray suspected her classes were under regular surveillance. On one occasion late in her first semester, all doubt was removed — uniformed members of the Criminal Investigation Department entered her class unannounced and took up seats without saying anything.[282] Murray undertook the daunting challenge of academic teaching for the first time in a foreign country, in an all-male class of students scarcely prepared for college, teaching a politically hot topic, in a classroom under surveillance by a government that could detain people for up to five years without charge.

MURRAY BEGAN LOOKING FOR a way out of Ghana. One year after her arrival, Morris Milgram, whom she worked with on the Odell Waller campaign, wrote to gauge her interest in a job as executive director of the League for Industrial Democracy — a socialist education group whose youth group had broken away to form Students for a Democratic Society the year before. Murray replied, "I have not done any organizational work for almost twenty years. New techniques have grown up in the field since that time. To the degree that I have specialized in anything, it has been law and I'm afraid I'm stuck with it or related work."[283] Murray's lack of interest didn't stem from any desire to stick with her current job in Ghana; she was simply unwilling to go back to activist work. In fact, the right opportunity in the field of law had already presented itself, if she could secure it. In January 1961 she met a visiting scholar from Yale University who suggested that she consider taking a doctorate at Yale.[284] Murray duly applied before setting off to spend the spring break in Europe, where she met up with Caroline Ware and her husband.

During the vacation, Murray acknowledged her alienation in Ghana and how much she appreciated the more-familiar comforts of Europe. She wrote to Renee Barlow, "I have been living in another world entirely, and had I not gone to Africa first, I would not have appreciated Europe as much or recognized what is meant by Western civilization. The people of Holland illustrate so beautifully what industry, tenacity and a sense of order means."[285]

Murray learned that Yale had accepted her shortly after the vacation ended, prompting a scramble to get ready for departure. In addition to teaching, she was also coauthoring a book on Ghanaian law. Murray had already been handing over some of her teaching to a recent Harvard Law School graduate who was in Ghana on a year's grant — she now handed over all her remaining teaching to ensure the completion of *The Constitution and Government of Ghana*.[286] This action meant she left Ghana with barely more than a semester's teaching experience, but she had another publication in the field of law before even beginning a law doctorate.

Murray was also working on an article called "What Is Africa to Me? A Question of Identity," a large chunk of which is quoted in her autobiography.[287] Ware, Springer, Helen Lockwood, and journalist Harold Isaacs, who had encouraged Murray to write about her experiences from the beginning of her Ghana adventure, had provided feedback on earlier drafts. She submitted the finished product to *Harper's* magazine; the editorial staff praised the piece but rejected it because they had too much Africa material already.

Before it could be published elsewhere, the May 13, 1961, *New Yorker* published a similar piece by Harold Isaacs.[288] Murray wrote to both congratulate and "chide" him for "stealing most of my thunder." Caroline Ware, more directly, accused Isaacs of plagiarism. Isaacs responded by pointing out that Murray had called him the "godfather" of her unpublished piece — indeed, Murray went further and told Isaacs that she had used some of his expressions. Isaacs still believed Murray could publish her article with further refinement to make it less vague and impersonal, but Murray felt unenthused and overburdened with other tasks in preparation for her departure and never returned to it.[289] The incident ultimately reveals no wrongdoing on the part of Murray or Isaacs, but it does reveal part of an ongoing pattern — Murray's letters and diaries document a rich array of personal experience and feeling, but her attempts to write for publication often faltered, becoming impersonal in tone and then being abandoned as she shifted focus.

Her departure from Ghana also fits the long-term pattern of quitting jobs after a relatively brief period, though in this case she would surely have been told to leave had she not left voluntarily. Shortly before leaving, she offered unofficial legal advice for a Supreme Court challenge to the detention of a high-profile opposition leader, which undoubtedly would have eventually resulted in her expulsion from Ghana.[290] Furthermore, the American lawyers who replaced her were deported shortly after their arrival.[291] Murray's departure from Ghana was therefore no doubt pleasing to the Ghanaian government and to the Yale-bound Murray.

She later told a friend that during a stopover at a European airport she came to the realization that she really belonged to the "pink and white culture," not the black culture of Africa.[292] On one or two occasions after leaving Ghana permanently, Murray received invitations to tour Africa and write a book on her impressions, but she declined. She frankly acknowledged feeling unsympathetic to Africans because of her severe disillusionment with Ghana.[293] After a year in Ghana she confessed, "I feel that I understand less of all this than I did before I came. In fact, I think Africa has that effect upon one from the West. The longer you stay, the less you understand."[294] Murray didn't form many close attachments with Ghanaians or American expats and missed home terribly. Her staunch defense of the United States in an increasingly hostile environment combined with her criticisms of the Ghanaian government once again put her at odds with the broader society. Wanting nothing more to do with the African continent, Murray returned home to undertake a new challenge.

five

THE PROBLEMS OF

RACE DISCRIMINATION AND

SEX DISCRIMINATION

MEET IN ME, 1961–1973

. . . . .

I

Murray felt a "tremendous sense of relief" to be home, but she did not have to wait long to feel unwelcome. A real estate agent rejected her application for the first New Haven apartment she found: he stated that he could not "risk" renting the apartment to an African American. Nothing, she recalled, prepared one for "those sudden, ruthless psychic blows," which generate an "inner rage" that can fester until it "explodes in indiscriminate violence against white people." When classes began in spring 1961, Murray also felt panicky sitting in classrooms filled with white male students half her age. To keep from feeling overwhelmed, she told herself that if she had to spend three times longer on assignments than classmates, then she should consider the time an "investment in equalizing opportunity." She did, however, enjoy the respect of younger students fresh from participating in civil rights protests once they learned about her earlier efforts.[1]

Her workload increased in April 1962 when she accepted an invitation to work on the President's Commission on the Status of Women (PCSW). President John F. Kennedy had authorized the PCSW "to review progress and make recommendations as needed for constructive action" in the areas of private and federal employment policies and practices, federal social insurance and tax laws, federal and state protective labor legislation, treatment of women under the law, and provision of necessary family services.[2]

Kennedy agreed to the commission because of pressure from women in the labor movement who had supported his presidential campaign.[3] The commission wasn't revolutionary in its intent—Kennedy stated in his remarks at the PCSW's first meeting that women's "primary obligation [is] to their families and to their homes."[4] Nevertheless, feminists quickly recognized the commission's potential significance, because it brought together many influential people to discuss and promote women's rights.

Murray eagerly followed the early stages of the commission's work through friend and PCSW member Dr. Caroline Ware.[5] Just twenty-six people comprised the PCSW initially, and Dorothy Height of the National Council of Negro Women was the only Black woman commissioner.[6] The broad scope of the commission's work, however, soon spurred the creation of seven committees involving more than 120 participants. Dollie Lowther Robinson—Murray's friend who worked for the Labor Department—facilitated her invitation to join the Committee on Civil and Political Rights, which aimed to review and make recommendations on "differences in legal treatment of men and women in regard to political and civil rights, property rights, and family relations."[7]

The Committee on Civil and Political Rights discussed the proposed Equal Rights Amendment (ERA), which had divided feminists for decades. ERA opponents—mainly drawn from the trade union movement—feared that a constitutional amendment granting women equal rights would adversely affect protective labor laws. These laws, gained incrementally over the past five decades, existed to varying degrees in nearly every state and prohibited some exploitative practices with regard to women's wages, hours, and working conditions.[8] ERA supporters—often wealthier, educated women—opposed all protective labor laws, arguing that the proposed amendment would guarantee women's place in society. In 1946 supporters succeeded in having the ERA voted on in the Senate, though senators narrowly voted against the proposal, to the relief of many.[9] A *New York Times* editorial on the vote proclaimed, "Motherhood cannot be amended, and we are glad the Senate didn't try."[10] For different reasons, women in the labor movement were also disturbed that an ERA proposal had progressed to a Senate vote. Consequently, they redoubled efforts to promote alternatives, including a commission to improve the status of women, which they only succeeded in establishing following Kennedy's election.[11]

Murray therefore found herself embroiled in perhaps the PCSW's most important and controversial work.[12] Before the commission was formed, she had not given much attention to the ERA debates; nevertheless, she quickly adopted the view that an ERA was unnecessary and formulated a different approach. On July 24, 1962, the technical secretary to the Committee on Political and Civil Rights, Edward Bershtein, wrote to Murray, "We are very much interested in your theory that unreasonable discrimination against women by state statutes violates the equal protection clause of the 14th Amendment. We do hope that you will develop this theory in writing, and that we may have a copy of your spelled-out thoughts, before our August 24th meeting, if possible."[13]

Murray's approach suggested a way around the ERA debate by pursuing a legal strategy aimed at establishing the Fourteenth Amendment's applicability to women. This approach would attack discrimination against women court case by court case, testing the courts' willingness to see women as people deserving equal treatment before the law—similar to how the NAACP had attacked legal segregation. Murray presented her approach to the Civil Rights Subcommittee meeting in August and then to a meeting of the full commission on October 1. Her presentation impressed commissioners, but the ERA supporters remained unpersuaded, and even ERA opponents expressed some concern that the proposal could invalidate protective labor laws in the same manner as an ERA. Murray promised to provide a detailed memorandum on her views that could be distributed to all commissioners.[14]

Murray worked on the memo over the next two months, though Eleanor Roosevelt's death on November 7 briefly disrupted her work. Less than two weeks before Murray's fifty-second birthday, she and Renee Barlow attended ER's Hyde Park funeral in the pouring rain.[15] Murray coped with the loss of her idol, friend, and mother figure by conceiving of her memo as a way to honor ER, who had been the commission's chairperson.[16] By mid-December, Murray had completed a thirty-eight-page argument on the applicability of using the Fourteenth Amendment to fight discrimination against women, examined at length in Rosenberg's biography.[17] After discussing her proposal with Caroline Ware, Murray removed all reference to the ERA so as not to "draw fire" from ERA supporters.[18] In the final version, she asserted that the Fourteenth Amendment's applicability to women could be carefully tested in the courts on a case-by-case basis to challenge laws that arbitrarily discriminated against women while leaving undisturbed existing laws that protected the rights of women.[19]

Murray never joined the NAACP legal team that pursued legal equality for African Americans using this strategy, but she now led the charge to apply the same legal strategy to advance the struggle for gender equality. She had been likening gender discrimination to racial discrimination since the 1940s, but although she was far from the first person to draw such a comparison, many people remained reluctant to accept that line of thought. One friend wrote to Murray, "While the analogy of the Negro and women is dear to your heart, I think you may get into some trouble carrying it very far. As far as I can see, race is never a valid classification. Whereas . . . discrimination on the basis of sex might be defendable."[20] While even Murray agreed at this stage that some jobs might be better classified by sex, it wasn't long before the race and sex comparison she articulated became widely accepted.[21]

PCSW members widely supported Murray's proposed Fourteenth Amendment strategy, yet it still drew fire from both ERA supporters and ERA opponents outside the commission. The National Woman's Party (NWP) submission argued that Murray's proposal relied on unlikely judicial interpretations when a specific amendment was required.[22] Furthermore, the NWP saw nothing new in Murray's approach—it had been put forward in the 1940s, and the Supreme Court had consistently held that sex was a valid basis for legal classification.[23] ACLU lawyer Dorothy Kenyon lauded Murray's argument but also acknowledged that getting judges to accept it would be the challenge.[24] On the other side of the ERA debate, union groups argued that the proposal was a lesser evil to an ERA but that it still ran the risk of negatively affecting protective labor laws, depending on the wording of any favorable Supreme Court rulings.[25]

The Committee on Civil and Political Rights still backed Murray's proposal. The only member of the fourteen-member committee who supported the ERA, Marguerite Rawalt, predictably disagreed with the proposal. Murray and Mary Eastwood, a young attorney from the Justice Department, spent hours trying to formulate a proposal acceptable to Rawalt.[26] In the end they settled on a sentence that read, "In view of this constitutional approach, the Committee does not take a position in favor of the proposed equal rights amendment at this time." The commission's final report, *American Women*, delivered in October 1963, varied little from Murray and Eastwood's wording.[27]

Murray's work on the commission is significant not only for her intellectual contribution to the debate on how to move the struggle for women's legal equality forward but also for the impact PCSW participation had on her. Only a decade earlier, Murray had felt at a complete loss, her legal career seemingly ended with the failure of her private practice. Two decades earlier, she was experimenting "on the male side" and feeling frustrated by barriers like Harvard Law School's refusal to admit women. Now she had played a critical role on a presidential commission through formulating a legal strategy to break down gender divisions. The PCSW helped focus her attention on gender equality and, as will become clear, introduced her to a well-connected network of feminists who succeeded in dramatically advancing women's legal equality in the United States over the next few years.

MURRAY'S DEEPENING ENGAGEMENT with women's rights intensified her unwillingness to tolerate sexism in the struggle for racial equality. Having been in Ghana during the Greensboro sit-ins and the Freedom Rides, Murray made sure not to miss the next iconic civil rights event—the March on Washington. In fact, she marched twice, both times with interracial organizations—once with the American Civil Liberties Union (ACLU) and then with the New York parish delegation from Saint Mark's-in-the-Bowery, the church she attended with Renee Barlow. Murray described the march as a joyous occasion, likening it to a combination of her childhood imaginings of a jubilee and Judgment Day. She felt even greater joy when she remained in Washington for the week and met with a former classmate from Howard University for lunch in a downtown restaurant. The lunch celebrated the twentieth anniversary of the Howard sit-in protests they carried out to desegregate the type of downtown restaurant in which they now ate unnoticed.[28]

Although the march itself inspired Murray, the exclusion of women from the event's leadership infuriated her. The best-remembered part of the event is Dr. King's "I Have a Dream" speech, but Murray too gave a landmark speech shortly afterward. When addressing the National Council of Negro Women, she stated, "In emerging from an essentially middle-class movement and taking on a mass character, [the movement] has become a vehicle to power and prestige. . . . What emerges most clearly from events of the past several months is the tendency to assign women to a secondary, ornamental, or 'honoree' role instead of the partnership role in the civil rights movement which they have earned by their courage, intelligence, and dedication." Murray wasn't finished there. She went on to assert, "It was bitterly humiliating for Negro women on August 28 to see themselves accorded little more than token recognition in the historic March on Washington. Not a single woman was invited to make one of the major speeches or to be part of the delegation of leaders who went to the White House. This omission was deliberate." Dorothy Height, the National Council of Negro Women's president, described Murray's speech as an "invaluable" turning point for women in the movement. While Height believed the speech made no impression on male civil rights leaders, she stated that Murray's words resonated with Black women in the struggle, who discussed the speech at length. Height believed Murray forced Black women to reflect on their contribution to the movement and galvanized them for further struggle.[29]

Race Discrimination and Sex Discrimination Meet in Me

Murray also took issue with her former hero, A. Philip Randolph, whom she had worked for during the original 1942 March on Washington Movement campaign. Before the march, she wrote to him suggesting that the ten-person delegation scheduled to meet President Kennedy should include five women, two representing national organizations and three representing the grassroots. She also criticized him for agreeing to address the National Press Club despite a picket by women journalists: the Press Club denied women membership, forcing presswomen to sit in the balcony. Murray told Randolph that if she were a journalist she would picket him.[30] Nor did she hesitate to make her criticisms of him public. In her fiery speech to the National Council of Negro Women, she declared, "Mr. Randolph apparently saw no relationship between being sent to the balcony and being sent to the back of the bus."[31] Murray contrasted Randolph's actions with nineteenth-century abolitionists William Lloyd Garrison and Charles Remond, who refused to be seated as delegates at the 1840 World Anti-slavery Convention in London when they learned that women in the American delegation could only sit in the balcony (Garrison highlighted his protest by sitting with the women in the balcony).[32] Murray said of Randolph, "He failed to see that he was supporting the violation of the very principle for which he was fighting: that human rights are indivisible."[33] Through the coming years Murray increasingly referred to the indivisibility of rights, even as rifts grew between social justice movements.

Indeed, Murray's actions even divided her from friends. While in Washington for the march, she had been staying with Maida Springer, whom she had known for over two decades. The pair vehemently disagreed over Murray's opposition to Randolph's decision to cross the presswomen's picket to speak at the National Press Club. Springer recalled the following exchange occurring when she returned home one day:

> We greeted one another; Pauli briefed me on the project: "Maida if need be"—they were going to picket A. Philip Randolph if he spoke at the [National] Press Club. After a passionate exhortation about this unwise decision by our great man Randolph, she asked me, "You will join us, if it comes to that, won't you?" I replied, "No, I will not join in a picket line to picket A. Philip Randolph a week before the March on Washington." Pauli fumed and said something to the effect that she had finally found my "Achilles heel." When I next came home, Pauli had cleared out of my apartment without a "by your leave."

The incident reveals not only the depth of Murray's feeling on the subject but also her explosive temper and urge to escape conflict. The pair had campaigned together as far back as the original March on Washington Movement in the 1940s, but they did not attend the 1963 March on Washington together—and indeed, they didn't speak again for a long time. According to Springer's biographer, this was just one of several strong disagreements that led to "long periods of noncommunication" during the friendship.[34]

Maida Springer clearly prioritized the struggle for racial equality. Murray made no such prioritization. A few months after the President's Commission on the Status of Women delivered its final report, the opportunity to link women's legal equality to the civil rights struggle suddenly presented itself through proposed amendments to the 1964 Civil Rights Act. In a concerted effort to sabotage the proposed legislation, southern white Democrats proposed 122 amendments between January 31 and February 10, 1964, including adding amendments to include "sex" as grounds on which a person could not be discriminated against to many sections of the bill. Most of the amendments were rejected quickly, but the amendment adding sex to Title VII—the section of the bill concerning discrimination in private employment—narrowly passed. The bill moved to the Senate for ratification the following day. If the Senate passed it unchanged, seemingly from nowhere it would suddenly become illegal for private employers to discriminate on the basis of sex.[35]

Before the Senate vote, Republican leader Everitt M. Dirksen announced his intention to remove the amendment adding "sex" to Title VII.[36] Some Civil Rights Act supporters believed the amendment cluttered up a bill designed to end racial discrimination and might divide the bill's supporters, thus destroying the bill altogether. Earlier in the debate Congresswoman Edith Green had argued, "For every discrimination that has been made against a woman in this country there has been ten times as much discrimination against the Negro of this country."[37] Green had authored the 1963 Equal Pay Act and served on the PCSW, chairing the subcommittee on which Murray worked. Nevertheless, she opposed the sex amendment, declaring a willingness to wait for an end to sex discrimination to maximize the bill's chances of success. Politicians less supportive of women's legal equality were receptive to this argument, creating concern among amendment supporters.

The amendment had been added to the bill so hastily that few outside government circles knew much about it. Murray learned of it from PCSW contacts who asked her to prepare a memorandum outlining the importance of the sex amendment.[38] She was well equipped for the task, having raised the possibility of banning sex discrimination in private employment during the PCSW and explored sex discrimination in employment when working on her master's thesis nearly twenty years before.[39] And she had experienced more than enough race and gender discrimination to recognize the inadequacy of addressing one form of discrimination while ignoring the other.

The memorandum she produced pointed to the historical relationship between movements for civil and women's rights and the tragic consequences of ignoring the interrelatedness of rights. She argued that even if racial discrimination had been fiercer than gender discrimination, it "in no way diminishes the force of the equally obvious fact that the rights of women and the rights of Negroes are only different phases of the fundamental and indivisible issue of human rights," and efforts to separate the two "cloaks both timidity and paternalism."[40] Copies were distributed to senators and other influential figures, such as Attorney General Robert F. Kennedy, Vice President Hubert Humphrey, and First Lady "Lady Bird" Johnson.[41]

The response from Murray and others, particularly Senator Margaret Chase Smith, convinced Senator Dirksen to abandon his attempt to remove the amendment. The Civil Rights Act passed on July 2, 1964, with an amendment outlawing sex-based employment discrimination. This achievement has become a prominent feature of biographical accounts of Murray, who championed linking race and sex discrimination when many others recoiled from it. Murray felt proud of her role. In her autobiography she cited a letter from prominent feminist and fellow PCSW member Marguerite Rawalt: "To you comes a real measure of credit for the ultimate successful passage [of the bill]."[42] It is clear why Murray chose to frame her life story as the struggle to overcome Jane Crow. She had undergone a remarkable journey, demonstrating immense fortitude and aptitude to achieve a position whereby she could influence landmark legislation directly affecting her.

· · · · ·

II

Murray campaigned for women's equality while also completing her PhD and working as a tutor at Yale. Despite this hectic schedule and her dismay at sexism in the civil rights movement, she still felt guilty that she wasn't doing more in the struggle for racial equality. Many of her comrades from the late 1930s and early 1940s, such as Bayard Rustin, James Farmer, Juanita Morrow, and Ella Baker, were now leading campaigns with tremendous success using tactics she had helped develop. In the late 1960s she told friends, "I was in turmoil much of 1964–65, torn between the desire to 'witness' in Mississippi, St. Petersburg, Selma, and other places where the battle for civil rights was raging and my responsibility to finish my studies under a

Ford Foundation grant. The hard decision to stick with the thesis and complete my doctoral requirements was not without great emotional cost."[43]

Although a far less exciting contribution than "witnessing" in the South would have been, completing a Yale law doctorate still contributed to African American progress according to the uplift ideology Murray had been imbued with as a young person. The motto printed in her high school yearbook, "The best I can do to help others is to be the best I can myself," still applied and no doubt influenced her feeling of responsibility to finish the doctorate. In the coming years, the understanding of racial uplift that had permeated her upbringing would see her come into increasing opposition with younger Black activists.

Murray tried to combine her responsibility to complete her studies with her desire to participate in the civil rights movement by changing her thesis topic. Halfway through her doctorate, around the time of the March on Washington, she switched from a comparative study of human rights in English-speaking, newly independent African countries to a historical examination of America's race problem, which she completed within two years.[44] Scholar Sarah Azaransky described Murray's thesis as theoretically innovative and belonging to a fourth generation of African American history.[45] Less positively, but no less truthfully, Rosalind Rosenberg wrote, "At 1,300 pages of text and notes, the thesis was a sprawling, often undigested, mass of overly long quotations."[46]

Irrespective of the dissertation's strengths and limitations, Murray's work can be understood not only as a contribution to knowledge but also as another quest to unify the strands of her life by linking historical issues with the personal ramifications. Concerning her topic, Murray described herself as an "involved observer" and the dissertation as "an effort at self-enlightenment, an attempt to achieve intellectual integration of an intensely felt life experience. A conscious process of individual integration may well be necessary to the achievement of genuine racial integration in the United States."[47] In a chapter titled "The Effects of Slavery upon the Personality of the Negro," she explored African American families and communities in the post-Reconstruction period using Erik Erikson's psychoanalytic research into the impact of family life and early experiences on personality development (the two psychoanalytic theorists she seemed most drawn to were Erikson and Karen Horney, both of whom focused their research on identity formation).[48] Azaransky suggested Murray could have had her own family in mind when arguing, in reference to Erikson's work, that "the effects of aggravated family disorganization of Negroes during slavery" are better understood through the knowledge that children who grow up without "clear parental attachments enact similar relationships for future generations."[49] Murray certainly had her family experience in mind—much of her writing, whether creative or academic, was motivated by personal concerns and geared toward self-enlightenment.

Although Murray described completing the dissertation at "great emotional cost" (the exact same words she had used about her Berkeley master's), there is less evidence concerning the tumult this time.[50] No diaries exist among her papers for the period between 1961 and 1965.[51] She continued to correspond with her thesis supervisors well after completing her studies, suggesting that she maintained far better relationships with them than she had with her Berkeley supervisors. Murray was well supported, as ever, by Caroline Ware, who provided encouragement and feedback on her work; she also benefited from the emotional support provided by Renee Barlow, whom she visited in New York regularly throughout her studies.

Barlow attended Dr. Murray's graduation ceremony on June 14, 1965. Murray took great pride in being the first person in her family of teachers to be awarded a doctorate from a prestigious university and, to the best of anyone's knowledge, the first African American, man or woman, to be awarded a law doctorate from Yale Law School.[52] It had been a difficult journey from the rickety segregated primary school in Durham where her formal education began. She had overcome many barriers and hardships to achieve both a notable "first" for her race and a prestigious, highly sought-after degree.

Yet pride in the achievement quickly transformed into hurt when the prestigious qualification didn't translate to employment success. She was disadvantaged in getting a position at a law school because she didn't write her dissertation on a legal subject and no publisher expressed interest in it. In her autobiography, however, she highlighted the social factors behind her lack of employment success, such as her lack of "indispensable contacts" and the reluctance of law faculties to employ women. She discounted the possibility of racial discrimination, since an African American man awarded a Yale master's degree around the same time immediately found a position. Murray described herself as a victim of the stereotyping that positioned men as the chief income earners, which left self-supporting women in a predicament.[53] In crashing through one barrier, becoming possibly the first African American to gain a doctorate from Yale Law School, she came up against another: the lack of employment opportunities for women in academia.

Murray felt embarrassed, though she tried to put that feeling on the institution. She wrote, "Despite Yale Law School's enormous prestige and its reputation for successfully placing graduates holding its higher degrees, I was an embarrassment."[54] Murray had been a senior tutor during her studies and had hoped to gain a permanent position at Yale after completing the dissertation. The shock and disappointment at not achieving a permanent position prompted an angry response, which she vaguely referred to in a diary entry the following year when upset by another job rejection: "Certainly, I learned from Yale. There I had to remain over a period of five months after rejection for a position on the faculty, and during that period certain ways in which I handled various proposals were used against me. This time I was careful to say little and to guard my steps. I got out before there were any incidents or embarrassing moments."[55] Murray's disappointment must have been obvious, at least to her mind, causing her embarrassment at Yale.

Assertiveness, like professional aspirations, was less accepted in women than men. Murray "made a few enemies" at Yale, according to a colleague who described her as having a very fine character, honest, trustworthy, dependable, amenable, and sociable, but also having strong personal convictions regarding civil, women's, and individual rights, which irritated certain people at Yale. Another Yale woman colleague described her as "aggressive," but on the whole, colleagues described Murray in glowing terms.[56] Murray's sensitivity and fluctuating levels of self-assurance made it especially difficult for her to coexist with enemies; instead, she doubted herself and her actions and wanted to flee following displays of anger. When her temper cooled, she believed that she had acted inappropriately and was an embarrassment to the institution that rejected her.

COMPOUNDING THE FRUSTRATION OVER employment problems, the successful campaign to outlaw sex-based employment discrimination was proving to be a hollow victory. Two weeks after Murray received her doctorate, the federal government established the Equal Employment Opportunity Commission (EEOC) to handle employment discrimination complaints arising from the new Civil Rights Act. One-third of complaints made to the EEOC in its first year related to sex discrimination, which the commission failed to handle; instead a temporary staff member's wife, a lawyer, initially handled sex discrimination complaints.[57] Furthermore, the commission could ask the attorney general to sue on victims' behalf, but it had no power to order discrimination stopped, only to investigate it.[58] The EEOC not only lacked resources and enforcement powers; it also showed an unwillingness to take sex discrimination complaints seriously. In November 1965 the EEOC's executive director, Herman Edelsberg, told the press, "There are people on this Commission who think that no man should be required to have a male secretary—and I am one of them."[59]

Yale faculty, 1965. Murray is in the first standing row, sixth from the right.
(Schlesinger Library, Radcliffe Institute, Harvard University)

Newspaper publishers used their considerable voice to mock the new legislation. An August 1965 front-page *New York Times* headline read, "For Instance, Can She Pitch for the Mets?" The article derided the EEOC's deputy counsel by referring to him as "Deputy Counsel on Bunnies"—a reference to a related, derisive story that the new law might require Playboy Clubs to hire male "bunnies," after which the sex discrimination provision became known to opponents as "the bunny law."[60] The *Times* followed up with an even more inflammatory editorial the following day: "Perhaps, it would have been better if Congress had just abolished sex itself," since "this is revolution, chaos. You can't even safely advertise for a wife anymore."[61] The ridicule cloaked a serious backlash that threatened to render the ban on sex discrimination in employment completely irrelevant.

On October 12, 1965, Murray delivered a headline-grabbing speech to a conference of women's organizations responding to the backlash. The speech began as a dry analysis of legal issues arising from sex-based discrimination but culminated with Murray proclaiming that women might have to march on Washington to secure equal opportunity. "If it becomes necessary," she declared, "I hope women will not flinch from the thought." The *New York Times* reported her comments under the headline "PROTEST PROPOSED ON WOMEN'S JOBS; YALE PROFESSOR SAYS IT MAY BE NEEDED."[62] Murray felt embarrassed by the headline's description of her as a Yale professor. Nevertheless, the publicity brought her to the attention of journalist and author Betty Friedan. After reading the article, Friedan telephoned Murray in New Haven to interview her for a follow-up book to the highly successful *Feminine Mystique*.[63] Too busy packing her bags to talk, Murray made tentative plans to meet Friedan in New York.[64]

Murray's speech came at the unhappy end to her time at Yale, where she had felt compelled to remain for the past few months despite the anger and embarrassment she felt over not gaining a permanent position. She recalled returning to New York City permanently as "like coming home again to renew my spiritual resources and get a fresh start."[65] Murray found an apartment overlooking St. Mark's-in-the-Bowery, the Episcopal Church she resumed attending with Renee Barlow. She also replaced her dog Smokey, her companion of the last thirteen years who had been with her in Brooklyn, Ghana, and New Haven before his death in January. She named her new companion Doc, and sometimes Black-and-White-Together-We-Shall-Overcome, for his markings, though it also befitted his large and clumsy nature. Doc's floppy ears obscured a fierce protectiveness that made Murray feel safe wandering the streets of the Lower East Side at night. The pair frequently called on Barlow, who shared a nearby apartment with her housebound mother.[66] At the year's end, Murray and Barlow vacationed in Jamaica, one of several Caribbean Christmas vacations enjoyed by the pair.[67] These moments of joy are less well documented — Murray wrote letters and diaries far more furiously during stressful periods — but they were crucial to her surviving the many battles she waged in opposition to the society that tried to oppress her.

. . . . .

III

In November 1965, the same month Murray turned fifty-five, she joined the national board of the American Civil Liberties Union (ACLU), under the sponsorship of Dorothy Kenyon and James Farmer.[68] Kenyon's broad hats, colorful dresses, and youthful looks masked her seventy-seven years, which entailed a legal career and feminist activism that stretched back to the suffrage struggle. Murray had first met Kenyon two decades earlier when the former desperately sought legal work following her hasty departure from California.[69] Kenyon couldn't help Murray with work then, but she became

Race Discrimination and Sex Discrimination Meet in Me

a mentor, along with Caroline Ware and numerous other independent, intelligent, and politically active women. Like Murray, Kenyon believed the Fourteenth Amendment could ensure women's legal equality.

Murray and Kenyon put their ideas to the courts in a case challenging the exclusion of African Americans from juries in Lowndes County, Alabama. The case originated from the infamous 1965 murder of Viola Liuzzo, a mother of five children from Detroit, murdered by Klansmen following her participation in the Selma-to-Montgomery civil rights marches. Police had no trouble finding the killers — one of the Klansmen present at the murder was an FBI informant who later testified against the accused.[70] Shortly afterward, another civil rights protestor, Jonathan Daniels, was shot dead while shielding a teenager from a white deputy aiming a shotgun at her during a picket of a whites-only store. The deputy only received a manslaughter charge, but as with the killers of Viola Liuzzo, an all-white, all-male Alabama jury still acquitted him.[71]

Black residents from Lowndes County challenged the constitutionality of Alabama's all-white, all-male juries in a case known as *White v. Crook*, discussed at length in Serena Mayeri's book *Reasoning from Race*.[72] The ACLU joined the action, and Murray and Kenyon wrote the section of the ACLU's brief dealing with sex-based exclusion from jury service. Alabama, Mississippi, and South Carolina outright excluded women from jury service while twenty-four other states treated men and women differently in their jury service laws.[73] The case linked the causes of African Americans and women by asserting that both groups were denied equal treatment before the law. Murray believed that if the Supreme Court heard the case and ruled in their favor, women's legal equality would be established without the need for a constitutional amendment. She told a friend that she considered the case the *Brown v. Board of Education* for women.[74]

The *White v. Crook* brief included, as an appendix, an article Murray published in the December 1965 *George Washington Law Review* that further linked racial and gender discrimination.[75] Coauthored with Mary Eastwood, whom Murray had met during the President's Commission on the Status of Women, "Jane Crow and the Law" argued that securing equal employment for women was just as important as securing it for Black men. In a by-now-familiar Murray refrain, they wrote, "The rights of women and the rights of Negroes are only different phases of the fundamental and indivisible issue of human rights."[76] The pair also argued that legal acceptance of classification by sex was akin to "separate but equal."[77]

On February 7, 1966, a federal court in the *White v. Crook* case ruled unanimously in favor of the plaintiffs on both the racial and sex discrimination counts. On the exclusion of women, the court stated, "Jury service is a form of participation in the processes of government, a responsibility and a right that should be shared by all citizens, regardless of sex. The Alabama statute that denies women the right to serve on juries in the State of Alabama therefore violates the provision of the Fourteenth Amendment that forbids any State to 'deny to any person within its jurisdiction the equal protection of the law.' The plain effect of this constitutional provision is to prohibit prejudicial disparities before the law. This means prejudicial disparities for all citizens—including women."[78] Murray and other feminist lawyers, regardless of their views on the ERA, were ecstatic with the decision. The win didn't become the *Brown v. Board of Education* for women, however: the Alabama attorney general didn't appeal the decision, meaning the case never reached the Supreme Court.[79] Nevertheless, the decision amounted to a significant victory for women's legal equality because a federal court had ruled that women were within the equal protection clause of the Fourteenth Amendment, encouraging further legal action in the area and adding to Murray's growing reputation as a leading sex discrimination lawyer.

EACH VICTORY FOR WOMEN'S LEGAL EQUALITY served to further highlight ongoing acts of blatant sexism. The month after the *White v. Crook* ruling, Murray stormed out of a church service, then wandered the streets full of "blasphemous thoughts" after feeling "uncontrollable anger" exploding inside her over the male domination of the Holy Eucharist—the most important service of the week.[80] Murray had no idea why the type of service she had sat through so many times in her life suddenly generated such a rage that day. Once upon her, however, the rage didn't disappear. She wrote to members of the vestry explaining, "Throughout the services I kept asking myself: Why is not one of the candle bearers a little girl? Why cannot the crucifer be a girl or woman? Why cannot the vestmented lay reader be a woman of the church? Why cannot women and men, boys and girls, participate equally in every phase of Church activity?"[81] Murray had found "spiritual renewal" when she returned to New York and resumed participation at St. Mark's, but the church no longer seemed a sanctuary; rather, it had become another source of exclusion. Withdrawal, at least temporarily, seemed the only option.

Murray had further cause for dismay when, in April 1966, the EEOC's weakness became further evident. Title VII of the Civil Rights Act required an end to segregated job advertisements in newspapers. Presumably, if job columns headed "colored" and "white" were banned, then advertising jobs under separate columns for "male" and "female" should also be prohibited. The EEOC, however, agreed to a deal that allowed the American Newspaper Publishers Association total freedom to use sex-segregated job advertisement columns, "to indicate that some occupations are considered more attractive to persons of one sex than the other."[82] The acting EEOC chairman, Luther Holcomb, stated that sex-segregated columns weren't like race classifications, they were simply a way to obtain maximum reader response and didn't prohibit persons of either sex from applying for jobs in either column. On June 20, Representative Martha Griffiths addressed the House citing numerous sources to denounce the EEOC policy, including Murray's coauthored article, "Jane Crow and the Law." EEOC commissioner Richard Graham, along with the only other commissioner sympathetic to women's equality, Aileen Hernandez, both privately believed that the EEOC would respond to organized pressure and urged feminists to consider collective action.[83]

Murray also believed that women needed the same kind of protest strategies and organizations that Black activists had successfully developed if women were to realize the benefits of legal victories. Within this context, Murray finally met with Betty Friedan. Although Friedan had originally wanted to interview her for a new book, the project changed when Murray began introducing Friedan to the network of women that she referred to as Washington's "feminist underground"—women who knew Washington politics and had access to resources and government information that could be used by a women's lobby group.[84] Many of these women had formed close ties during the President's Commission on the Status of Women and maintained contact, in part, through the state-based Status of Women groups that continued its work.[85]

Using a press pass, Friedan attended the third national conference of state Commissions on the Status of Women held in Washington in June 1966. During the conference, Murray, Friedan, and Dorothy Haener of the United Auto Workers union identified potential recruits among the delegates to invite to a discussion about forming a new organization for women. At the conclusion of the conference's penultimate day, about fifteen women gathered in Friedan's hotel room, though Murray knew only five of them. All in attendance agreed to seek resolutions on the final day of the conference urging the enforcement of the sex provision in Title VII and supporting the reappointment of Richard Graham to the EEOC (President Johnson did not intend to reappoint him). However, the majority of women present opposed forming a new women's organization—a move they believed was too radical and unnecessary. Intense arguments continued until after midnight before the meeting finally broke up. Only the moderate proposal of seeking conference resolutions was accepted, half-heartedly by Murray.[86] Friedan believed the women present left her hotel room in "sanctimonious disapproval" of the suggestion for a new independent organization, except for Murray, "the black scholar who'd triggered me first," and one other.[87] Murray felt so disappointed by the meeting that she planned to leave the conference after her presentation the following morning.[88]

Opinions on the need for a new women's group shifted radically during the conference's final morning session. Murray was again instrumental. As a keynote speaker on the "Sex Discrimination—Progress in Legal Status" panel, she delivered an incisive summary of ongoing feminist concerns that, again, stressed the parallels between race and gender discrimination but also described the importance of Title VII for Black women, lamented the "attitude of derision" about sex discrimination, and denounced the EEOC's advertising policy as intimidating and discouraging women. Without mentioning the leaked news of Commissioner Graham's pending termination, Murray's speech noted that his term was due to expire in July and urged the conference to "express its interest in his reappointment." Charles Duncan, the EEOC's general counsel, who followed Murray at the podium, unwittingly aligned himself with Friedan and Murray when he urged women to "put pressure on the EEOC to gain their ends," since government agencies were accustomed to lobbying and the EEOC "welcomes and responds to such pressure."[89] Duncan's comments, among an otherwise moderate speech, undercut the concerns of women who believed forming an independent organization would be too radical. The final push came during the ensuing workshops: in one workshop delegates tried to pass a resolution in favor of Graham's reappointment, only to be told that workshops weren't authorized to pass resolutions; delegates could talk but not act.

The National Organization for Women (NOW) was formed during the luncheon session of the conference, during which Murray and twenty or so other women at the front two tables whispered furiously and passed notes. Friedan wrote the group's mission statement on a paper napkin: "to take the actions needed to bring women into the mainstream of American society, now, full equality for women, in fully equal partnership with men."[90] Before the conference ended that afternoon, twenty-eight women paid a five-dollar membership fee, Kathryn Clarenbach became temporary coordinator, and six women, including Murray, were elected to a "temporary coordinating committee" to develop a framework for a permanent organization.[91]

NOW held its inaugural conference four months later, in October 1966, three years to the month since President Kennedy's Commission on the Status of Women had presented its final report.[92] NOW's inaugural conference agreed on a "Statement of Purpose" that reflected Murray's goal of a civil rights organization for women. The statement specifically noted, "There is no civil rights movement to speak for women, as there has been for Negroes and other victims of discrimination. The National Organization for Women must therefore begin to speak."[93] Murray accepted nomination to the national board at the founding conference and attended NOW's first national board meeting on November 20, 1966, the occasion of her fifty-sixth birthday. Very shortly thereafter, Murray resigned from NOW's leadership, and she never again played a prominent role in the influential organization she had just helped create.

· · · · ·

IV

Since leaving Yale, Murray had only had temporary work, sometimes in Washington, where she boarded with her sister Mildred. The Women's Division of the Methodist Church—the organization that had commissioned her to complete *States' Laws*—commissioned her to write a "Human Rights USA: 1948–1966" report. The report took nearly a year to complete, during which time she continued to seek employment at law schools before giving up entirely.[94] Between June 14 and July 13 she gained a temporary position at the Department of Labor, where colleagues described her as "extremely bright," "intelligent," "very intense," and a "crusader in race matters."[95]

Still in Washington, in fall 1966 Murray gained work as a temporary consultant at the Equal Employment Opportunity Commission—the toothless organization she and others had been criticizing. Her appointment seemed a hopeful sign that the EEOC might begin to take employment discrimination against women more seriously. It also seemed like a hopeful sign for Murray's long-term employment prospects, especially when a permanent position as EEOC general counsel became available. Murray applied just days after attending NOW's first board meeting. Fearful that she might be subject to reprisals at the EEOC if she maintained a leadership role in an organization formed, in part, to put pressure on it, Murray resigned from NOW's leadership.[96]

The Civil Service Commission requested a full FBI background investigation because Murray's job application acknowledged involvement in radical groups during the late 1930s. The investigation proved a torturous ordeal for Murray: FBI agents across the country checked government records and questioned former neighbors and work colleagues. Murray had lived at so many addresses and worked with so many different organizations that it was a long, slow process. FBI agents learned little from former employers or the neighbors that they could locate — they gave up trying to interview all her former neighbors — but following up on information in her 1947 application to the New York Bar, they located the parole officer who remembered escorting Murray from Provincetown to New York in 1940 after police had picked her up wandering the streets hysterically. Thinking back twenty-seven years, the former parole officer recalled Murray saying that she was a "homosexual" receiving hormone treatment at Bellevue to make her a man.[97]

Before the FBI investigation had been finalized, in early April 1967, over three months since Murray had applied, EEOC chairman Stephen N. Shulman announced to a staff meeting that she would be the organization's next general counsel.[98] News of her appointment leaked quickly. Aileen Hernandez, a former EEOC commissioner and future NOW leader who had known Murray since her Howard University days, wrote to Shulman congratulating him: "I am particularly thrilled about Pauli and I am sure that appointment must be some kind of first for a government agency. She has real courage and deep concern and I'm just delighted that at this stage of her life she can begin to get some of the recognition she so richly deserves. . . . I've already started spreading the word and have had great reaction from everyone I've told."[99]

Unbeknownst to Murray or anyone at the EEOC, a month before Shulman's staff room announcement a White House aide called FBI offices to request copies of their investigation on completion. The political landscape had been changing rapidly during the months it took to assess her application: EEOC opponents in Congress had grown substantially following House elections conducted amid race riots.[100] When White House officials saw the FBI report, they promptly vetoed Murray's appointment to the high-profile position, leaving Shulman with the uncomfortable task of telling Murray she wouldn't be appointed to the position he had already said was hers.

He asked the FBI investigators how they thought he should explain it, but they told him their job was only to carry out investigations, not to decide how to act on the information gathered. Shulman told the investigators he would focus on four issues from her past: first, her involvement with "Communist Party organizations" in the 1930s; second, the circumstances of her Bellevue hospitalization after being picked up by police in Provincetown in 1940; third, her "unconsummated marriage and lack of annulment"; and, finally, her two arrests, one for picketing in 1935 and the other stemming

Race Discrimination and Sex Discrimination Meet in Me

from the Greyhound bus incident in 1940.[101] The Greyhound arrest—the most recent event Shulman cited to deny her the job—had occurred over twenty-six years earlier.

MURRAY DESCRIBED THE REJECTION AS "the most crushing blow" of her entire career.[102] Shulman offered her the less high-profile position of deputy general counsel instead, but she was so "angry and hurt over the unnecessary embarrassment" that she not only refused it but also immediately resigned her temporary consultant position.[103] Murray's diary described her embarrassment as acute, requiring "many maneuvers to prevent complete rout and loss of face."[104] The chief maneuver was escape. Murray fled to New York and the support of Renee Barlow within twenty-four hours of her conversation with Shulman.[105] Such was the haste of her departure and the extent of her withdrawal from public life that colleagues remained unaware of her whereabouts; it took the ACLU associate director several months to find her so that he could tell her she had been reelected to the board of directors.[106] Murray felt satisfied that she didn't "crack" during the difficult interviews, believing she conducted herself with dignity and restraint, but still did not feel she could stay on following the rejection. Although concerned that her hasty exit might generate curiosity, she felt the only alternative was open humiliation.[107]

An intense period of self-reflection followed her withdrawal. She expressed far more feelings of humiliation and embarrassment than anger or outrage that an organization tasked with ending employment discrimination denied her a job based on actions she had taken decades earlier and were completely irrelevant to her capacity to do the work. As on earlier occasions when her hopes were crushed and she was left feeling humiliated, she turned her attention from the problems of society to problems of the self. "There must be some reason other than prejudice, lack of opportunity, or bad breaks that have prevented me from advancing along these lines," she wrote in her diary.[108] She filled pages and pages in her diary, sometimes writing multiple long entries in a single day at all hours of the day and night, reflecting on this latest disappointment. On April 22, she wrote and underlined in red pen: "I have faced up to many of my deepest fears and have ridden out the suspenseful period of investigation. This kind of 'inquisition' is behind me."[109] Four days earlier she had confided,

> I have said that we have to live with our choices, whatever they may
> be. When I was younger I made choices which were laden with emotion and in which I could not foresee the outcome. I had few expecta-

tions or hopes of ever overcoming the obstacles which surrounded me. A point in time came when I did have hope and I tried to overcome past mistakes of judgment. It seems that I have gone as far as I could go, but that my best efforts have not been good enough to carry over the wall of earlier choices and their results.[110]

Murray believed the fault lay with her.

Consequently, she expressed no desire to challenge this rejection the way she had challenged Cornell University's rejection a decade earlier. Cornell rejected her purely on her past political associations, which she was willing to defend publicly. The EEOC, however, rejected her on the grounds of her political and personal past—and in 1966 she could not even contemplate publicly defending her sexual orientation and earlier gender passing. Murray now became more intent on concealing her personal past rather than changing prevailing discriminatory attitudes. She purged her personal files, describing the act as a "symbolic shedding of the past" in preparation for a new start. This new start involved "letting go" of civil and women's rights politics for a while—which explains her unwillingness to resume a leading role in NOW—and a renewed desire to write: "If I could only come up with a book worth reading, and a good seller."[111]

Her unwillingness to accept the lower-profile deputy general counsel position stemmed not only from a feeling that she risked open humiliation by staying on but also because unhappiness had set in even before the crushing rejection. After the initial shock had passed, diary entries reveal that Murray felt partly relieved that she did not get the job. She tried to see the rejection not as a disappointment but as a "deliverance."[112] Pauli felt particularly unhappy boarding with Mildred. When she briefly returned to Washington to collect her things, the hot-tempered sisters had a dispute over money, resulting in a particularly angry diary entry in which Pauli described her sister as having a "cruel, sadistic, evil, avaricious streak."[113] She described being an "alien" in her own family, believing nothing had been gained by her closer proximity to her siblings, who had "too many problems of their own" to provide her with support.[114]

Murray's fluctuating self-confidence also affected her enthusiasm for the job. Her diary entries described feeling, at times, out of her depth working at the EEOC. Yet she also believed that if she belonged in the organization, it was as a commissioner and not as a staff member. Her diaries reveal that morale was low among EEOC employees and that in the month before her exit she did little more than push paper around her desk, growing ashamed to submit her "sketchy" weekly activity reports.[115] She did not feel supported by family, and she had few friends at work or in Washington, therefore she believed the rejection provided an "out" at "precisely the right time before I got any deeper."[116] Of the FBI investigation, she wrote, "From the beginning I resented the invasion of privacy, but I was tempted to make the race because of the prestige and the salary."[117]

Her diary entries remained prolific during May. Having fled Washington to New York and the "loving care" of Renee Barlow, her attention gradually shifted from the hurt of the EEOC rejection to what she should do next.[118] She described needing to get a job that wasn't too demanding—a job where she wouldn't have the burden of being a "first" and the associated feelings of being on trial and having "token" status.[119] In the self-analysis carried out in her diary, she described the desire to be an "outstanding success," to "prove to the world and myself that I could rise above all circumstances and triumph," as a "stumbling block." Instead, she critiqued her understanding of what constituted a "successful figure" and a "nobody" as "fake values."[120] Murray also believed a less demanding job might allow her to pursue her interest in writing. In fact, she thought the ordeal might provide the necessary impetus, but this rejection never provided the kind of writing impetus gained from the Cornell rejection.

At times Murray used her personal experiences politically to argue for greater inclusion, particularly personal experiences of racism, sexism, and McCarthyism. She could have used other personal experiences to point out other discriminatory practices, but she feared that these experiences might reflect badly on her, and she knew they could still be used against her. When drafting her autobiography over a decade later, Murray still seemed uncertain as to how to handle the most crushing blow of her career. An early draft included several pages discussing her time working as a consultant for the EEOC, which focused on low employee morale and the lack of women in its leadership. It also described applying to become general counsel, Shulman's announcement that she had gotten the job, and her subsequent embarrassment when later denied the job. She explained that the White House rescinded the appointment because the job was considered a "sensitive position" and the administration feared that her activist background would draw fire from EEOC opponents in Congress. In other words, here she omitted the nonactivist elements of her past that Shulman challenged her on.[121] The published version only stated: "In the fall of 1966, I spent seven months in Washington as a consultant to the Equal Employment Opportunity Commission."[122]

AT THE END OF MAY, MURRAY LEARNED of a job as vice president for curricular development at Benedict College in South Carolina. Despite initially expressing interest in working for a religious organization and a long-held desire for academic work, the opportunity filled her with uncertainty. It didn't resemble her dream job, but she believed it might be the answer to the "jolt" from the EEOC rejection. She flew to South Carolina to visit the campus, which she described as "terrible." The weather was bad, making for a turbulent flight, and once at Benedict she became unnerved by "a reserved group looking me over."[123] A week after visiting South Carolina, Murray recorded in her diary, "I have apparently resolved the job situation in my mind—have felt no anxiety about it. If I take it, I have just about six weeks to pull myself together." After writing prolifically in her diary for over a month, Murray made no further diary entries in the next two weeks, then noted on June 16, "Surgery for I.B."[124]

Irene "Renee" Barlow had been diagnosed with cancer—the surgery was a radical mastectomy. The pair's relationship, which had included long periods of separation since Murray's Ghana adventure in 1960, entered a crisis phase. Renee concealed the diagnosis from most people, including her eighty-seven-year-old mother. Mrs. Barlow had already lost two daughters to cancer, so Renee did not want to put her mother through the ordeal of this cancer treatment. Pauli stayed with Mrs. Barlow during Renee's hospitalization. They told Mrs. Barlow that Renee was having corrective surgery on varicose veins, though Murray found the deception difficult to maintain because she was, by her own admission, "not good at dissembling." Worse still, Renee suffered complications: she was stricken with hepatitis, for example, and had to remain in the hospital for three months. Murray didn't remain in New York for the duration of this hospitalization. She accepted the job at Benedict College and left for South Carolina in late July, while Renee was still only capable of taking one short walk with her along the hospital corridor.[125]

There is little evidence to explain how Murray felt about leaving Barlow. It seems a very curious decision. She left her sick loved one in order to live in the South, where she had not lived since adolescence and had vowed never to live again, to work in a role which offered none of the prestige or pioneering possibilities she usually aspired to and which she expressed great uncertainty about accepting in the first place. The sudden silence in Murray's diaries mean we can do little more than speculate as to how she arrived at this decision. From Murray's descriptions of Renee's independence and character, it is likely that Renee encouraged Murray to go. The difficulty of concealing the illness and the generally closeted nature of their relationship might have also made the situation intolerable for Pauli. Renee's illness may have been more than she could endure when her own resilience was dented by the very recent ordeal with the EEOC. In addition, she had lost loved ones so young that confronting the mortality of her partner, who was at times a substitute mother figure, was perhaps more than she could bear.

· · · · ·

V

The EEOC embarrassment left Murray wondering whether she needed to effect dramatic change. Accepting a job at a small, private, Black Baptist college in Columbia, South Carolina, certainly constituted a dramatic change that would also be, she hoped, not too demanding. Her role at Benedict—securing external funding and developing plans to raise education standards—required embracing a different strategy to racial uplift than the one she had adhered to for much of her working life. The role didn't require her to be a "first" and prove her abilities to a sexist and racist society in the manner of some earlier high-profile quests, but Murray still recognized it as a new challenge in direct service to a Black community.[126] The location also presented a new challenge. She recalled, "Although I had not lived in the South for forty years, I had not conquered the special feeling of unease that assailed me whenever I traveled below Washington."[127]

Murray tried to view the whole venture as a personal test to reidentify herself with an African American community. "This could be the greatest opportunity for service of my entire life," she recorded in her diary, "if I could just see it that way." To see it that way she needed to "overcome any hidden biases in myself toward Negro education and operate on the premise that education in a Negro-led, predominantly Negro institution can achieve excellence."[128] Murray suspected herself of having absorbed societal attitudes, but she also knew the challenge of overcoming long-standing systematic disadvantage. She tried to rouse herself to the challenge by seeing it as a contribution to the Black freedom struggle—a way to shift her involvement in the struggle, as she put it, from the "theoretical and descriptive to the active and involved level."[129] She wrote, "Moreover, it gives me an opportunity to come to terms with the sense of guilt I have had for a number of years that I have not been pulling my weight in the struggle, that I have been more of an observer than a participant and that I have not fully met my responsibilities and fulfilled my mission. I have said that Negroes have been earning this self-respect in the process of the struggle. This self-respect must extend to Negro institutions. We must have confidence in our institutions and our ability to make them competent and creative."[130] The need to rouse herself for the job suggests that Murray had very little confidence the task could be achieved, or at least very little confidence she could meaningfully contribute to it. A lifetime of seeking to prove her capabilities at elite, predominantly white institutions had done little to prepare her for the challenge.

The challenges were significant. *Brown v. Board of Education* had signaled the legal death of segregation in 1954, but in practice the college system remained highly segregated. According to a study published the year before Murray took the job, there were 67,828 Black students registered at colleges located in seventeen southern states, but only 5,388 of these students attended predominantly white colleges.[131] Murray understood that wherever integration occurred it would involve the best-prepared Black college students being drawn to more prestigious, predominantly white schools, further disadvantaging underresourced Black colleges like Benedict.[132]

Once in South Carolina, Murray realized the challenges were as great as she feared. She believed her experience thirty years earlier on the WPA Remedial Reading Project, where she helped Italian immigrant children improve their literacy, was invaluable experience for teaching freshmen at Benedict.[133] She took a strong interest in Benedict's educational programs and student welfare, though her main task involved seeking funding to develop programs that would help close the education gap. Funding opportunities existed, particularly because of an expansion in federal funding, and Murray helped develop Ford Grant proposals that were ultimately successful. Nevertheless, she found the lack of a clear job description frustrating, and she soon came into conflict with the college president.[134]

The challenge of living in the South proceeded far more smoothly. Shortly after arriving at Benedict, Murray attended a late-summer conference near Columbus, Mississippi, where she had the pleasure of meeting Fannie Lou Hamer and reserving a hotel room and eating at Main Street cafeterias without incident.[135] Similarly, Maida Springer visited one weekend, and the pair drove across backcountry roads to a National Council of Negro Women event in rural Georgia. Only three years had elapsed since the passing of the Civil Rights Act, but Murray recalled being treated with southern hospitality when the pair stopped to use the restroom and eat at a roadside diner. These positive experiences were a long way from Murray's disturbing childhood experiences, which included viewing her father's battered corpse following his brutal murder by a white man; living with her grandmother's night terrors, during which Grandmother dragged an ax along the floor raving that the Klan were attacking their isolated house; and observing the dead body of an African American youth, shot through the chest, allegedly for stealing watermelons from a white man. Murray described the consequence of positive experiences in South Carolina as "the gradual exorcism of long-buried childhood terrors of lynching and other forms of racial brutality."[136]

ON THE WEEKEND OF NOVEMBER 18–19, 1967, Murray visited Washington for NOW's second annual conference. Since withdrawing from the leadership after the first national board meeting a year earlier, Murray had played little part in shaping NOW. So much had happened since then. The FBI investigation into her background, her subsequent departure from the EEOC, Barlow's cancer diagnosis and prolonged hospitalization, and her unenthusiastic relocation to South Carolina to take up the Benedict job had all occurred in the year between NOW's founding and its second national conference. Months before the second conference even occurred, Murray noted that she had "soured" on NOW and had no desire to be active in the organization.[137]

While she had soured on NOW, others had embraced it: membership had quadrupled to 1,200 in the first year. NOW's rapid growth created teething problems; in particular, divisions emerged at the second national conference during a discussion on a proposed "Women's Bill of Rights." Two proposed points, one calling for support of the ERA and the other for the repeal of abortion laws, resulted in several women threatening to walk out. Murray found the debate's tone unbearable, confiding in her diary that the conference left her feeling "alien, a stranger in my own household. Moreover I saw displayed at that meeting a kind of ferociousness and blood-letting that filled me with revulsion. I saw a leadership that was so venomous it was painful to try to speak. The only wise thing to do was to withdraw and consolidate my personal resources."[138] Murray's personal resources had taken a considerable battering in this period, and once again the only option seemed to be to withdraw.

Two days after the conference ended and one day after her fifty-seventh birthday, Murray outlined her reasons for withdrawing in a letter to the NOW leadership. She cited the lack of diversity in the organization as one major reason.[139] While the organization had grown substantially, it had diversified little from its founding membership demographic of mostly professional, white, Northeast-based women.[140] The lack of diversity fed into Murray's primary concern: that NOW was splitting away from a broader struggle for human rights and potentially replicating the divisions between nineteenth-century white feminists and abolitionists. She believed the decision to support an ERA was further evidence that NOW was entrenching divisions rather than overcoming them, since an ERA would only address the problems of women. Murray argued for nearly seven pages that NOW should have adopted the Fourteenth Amendment strategy she devised for the President's Commission on the Status of Women. Both strategies aimed to provide women with equal rights, but the Equal Rights Amendment strategy would entrench a gender division, which Murray viewed as a threat to her multiple identities. (At the conference, Murray supported a motion from the floor to change the proposal for an Equal Rights Amendment to a proposal for a Human Rights Amendment, but it was overwhelmingly voted down.) In her resignation letter Murray stated, "And since, as a human being, I cannot allow myself to be fragmented into Negro at one time, woman at another, or worker at another, I must find a unifying principle in all of these movements to which I can adhere." The letter concluded with an acknowledgment of ambivalent feelings about the organization, which stemmed from an open-ended view that she might be wrong; nevertheless, she would not accept a national board position or devote time to the organization, even though it saddened her to the point of being inconsolable.[141]

RENEE BARLOW'S RECOVERY SOMEWHAT cushioned Murray's split with NOW. Barlow had been released from the hospital and returned to work part time in September. At Christmas, the pair took another vacation to Jamaica, where Renee displayed her old gaiety. Murray believed the near-death experience gave Barlow a desire to live each moment to its fullest. Pauli also described the pair's bond as strengthened by the fact that Renee's illness had been kept secret from so many people.[142] The holiday provided a welcome break before the beginning of a tumultuous year for Murray and the nation. In February 1968, violence occurred at South Carolina State College in Orangeburg, just thirty-five miles from Benedict. During the "Orangeburg Massacre," three Black students were shot dead and at least twenty-eight more were wounded, many shot in the back, when police fired on students protesting the ongoing segregation of a local bowling alley.[143] Two months later, Dr. Martin Luther King Jr.'s assassination sparked rioting in many parts of the nation.

Murray observed Benedict students becoming "restless" in the days after King's assassination. From her college residence at midnight, she could see the flashing lights of emergency vehicles and hear the voices of male students running back and forth. Her diaries in the following days also go back and forth, between the civil unrest and increasing personal unrest with her job—the national crisis seemed to exacerbate personal unhappiness. The city of Columbia instated a curfew: from the window of her residence, Murray could see armed National Guardsmen stationed outside the college.

The Benedict administration sent students home early for the Easter break to avoid trouble. Frightened and alone, fearing "another Holocaust," Murray escaped to New York, where she spent the week watching news coverage of the riots and King's funeral with Renee Barlow.[144]

At a King memorial service in Seattle, thousands of attendees heard an excerpt from Murray's poem "Dark Testament." The day after the service, journalist Emmett Watson reported on the Seattle memorial, including the poetry reading. He wrote, "Olivia Cole, a tall, beautiful actress . . . gave a reading from Dark Testament which brought the crowd to its feet in tribute to its eloquence." Watson received so many inquiries about the poem that he reprinted the passages Cole read the following week. Although Murray had never met Olivia Cole, the reading and subsequent reporting of it reached her via an old friend who both heard the recital and read the newspaper report. Murray wrote the poem two decades before King proclaimed, "I have a dream," but the poem's opening line, "Freedom is a dream," and the first line of the closing passage, "Then let the dream linger on," gained new poignancy following King's murder.[145] Morris Milgram, whom Murray had worked with at the Workers Defense League, used a recording of Cole's recitation to persuade Silvermine Publishers to issue a volume of Murray's poetry in 1970.[146]

On the same day that Cole read from "Dark Testament," Murray continued noting her job dissatisfaction. She had gone into the Benedict job with serious reservations that had only worsened over time. Her diary noted, "I have been placed in a role of non-entity, neither consulted or permitted to have any official voice in what is going on. This is what I resent most deeply—being ignored."[147] Anonymity had been a chief attraction of the job, but the kind of inconspicuousness offered by Benedict provided no better contentment than high-status positions did. As she had done in many previous roles, Murray disagreed with her employer. During her first month in the position, she entered into what she considered a "usual spirited discussion" with guests at a college dinner. Afterward she reported that she "received some flak" from the college president about her conduct, which came as a shock. From then on, she did not like him—she believed his cordiality during their initial meeting hid a "dictatorial personality." The accusation seemed justified when he ordered the removal of a private telephone line Murray had paid to have installed in her college residence.[148] By the time of the riots, eight months after starting the job, Murray wrote, "All the evidence points to my leaving as quickly as possible." She did not believe the president could tolerate her "independence, expertise and perhaps warmth of personality."[149]

Fluctuating self-confidence and personal insecurities engendered by a lifetime of being made to feel inferior to others exacerbated difficulties in working and personal relationships. Four months after starting at Benedict, Murray's misery is clear in her negative self-appraisal. She wrote out in her diary a long list of perceived personal faults that included undue sensitivity, fierce outbursts of resentful anger, acquisitiveness in an egotistic way, uncooperativeness with associates, selfishness, deceitfulness, vanity, vindictiveness, a bullying and unscrupulous disposition, slowness to admit error, and a tendency toward plagiarism.[150]

Murray feared professional failure and worried about the sources of her behavior, which made it difficult to take upsets, such as the rebuke by the college president over her argumentativeness at dinner, in her stride. She was also far from her personal support network while living in South Carolina—Murray had no family or friends nearby and took every opportunity to return to New York, where she continued renting an apartment despite having spent most of the past two years working in Washington and then South Carolina.[151] Physical health concerns provided another source of stress that kept Murray on edge—she described her one great fear while living in South Carolina as becoming ill without adequate nearby health facilities or family support.[152] Living in these circumstances created a tenseness that lowered her resilience and increased the difficulty in managing workplace relationships.

In the preceding few years alone she had unhappily parted with Yale, the EEOC, and NOW. Benedict College proved no different. Her varying accounts of why she resigned the position at the end of the school year speak to the ways individuals weave experiences into a broader story of self. In her diary, she described her dissatisfaction with feeling like a "glorified clerk" and needing to get away because of her poor working relationship with the college president.[153] In personal correspondence, Murray explained that her departure would be in Benedict's best interests, since her modest success in securing grants meant that her salary could be better spent on employing someone with greater experience in implementing new programs.[154] In her autobiography, Murray described resigning after a "moderately successful year" feeling convinced that her "talents lay in having direct contact with young minds in classroom situations" and that she was "misplaced in a purely technical, administrative job."[155] In the end, the anonymity and chance to serve a Black community at Benedict provided Murray with even less satisfaction than her previous endeavors. It was time for a new quest for personal fulfillment.

Murray and others listening to Ralph Abernathy, ca. 1968–73.
(Schlesinger Library, Radcliffe Institute, Harvard University)

* * * * *

VI

In the aftermath of Dr. King's assassination, Lawrence Fuchs, chair of the American Civilization program at Brandeis University, urged the university president to employ a Black scholar to introduce courses on the African American experience. Like other higher education institutions, Brandeis was feeling the repercussions of increasingly militant demands for Black Studies programs and additional Black faculty members. The new Brandeis University president, Morris Abram—who learned of Murray via her previous employment in corporate law at Paul, Weiss, where he too had worked—believed Murray could be a "valuable asset in helping ease tensions."[156] Just days after Murray left South Carolina in May 1968, Abram approached Murray to gauge her interest in teaching in the American Civilization program and helping plan an Afro-American Studies program.[157] She briefly visited the Boston campus before leaving the country to attend the Fourth Assembly of the World Council of Churches in Sweden from July 4 to July 20, 1968.

Murray's departure from Benedict had left her in a particularly indecisive mind-set, which included uncertainty about going to the church conference. She told friends she had "grave reservations about going since I am not much of an 'institutional' Christian and am somewhat skeptical about the organized Church."[158] Despite these concerns, Murray thoroughly enjoyed the conference, describing it as the high point of her year. She recalled feeling awestruck by the enormous gathering of Christians from diverse backgrounds and denominations. After the upheavals of King's assassination and the personal turmoil of leaving Benedict, Murray found the services especially affecting and the addresses from famous religious leaders, including Dr. Martin Niemoller, stimulating.[159]

The only trouble during the trip occurred when she received a formal offer from Brandeis for a year's visiting professorship. Already suffering from a summer cold and fever, the offer threw Murray into a terrible turmoil. Her upset at what a more self-assured person would view as an exciting opportunity illustrates a now-familiar pattern of desiring career advancement while doubting her capacity. She recalled feeling, in the words of the Negro spiritual, like a "motherless child, a long way from home." Although it was the kind of career opportunity she had desired since graduating from Howard over two decades earlier, its sudden presentation felt overwhelming. She described "walking the unfamiliar streets, heedless of where I was, trying to weigh the extraordinary challenge."[160]

Before going to Sweden, Murray had been considering returning to legal practice; on returning from Sweden, she suddenly realized she wanted to write a book on Jim and Jane Crow. Murray acknowledged this tendency in her autobiography: the desire to write, she stated, was "a renewal of the conflict that intensified with each career change."[161] In late August 1968, Murray began drafting "Black Power for Whom?" Murray intended to present a personal account of her experiences of race and sex discrimination and began the task by describing an incident involving fellow lawyer and North Carolinian Floyd McKissick, with whom she shared other commonalities. The University of North Carolina had also rejected McKissick on race grounds, nearly a decade after Murray applied. The NAACP, however, pursued McKissick's case and won a legal victory that allowed him to integrate UNC. More recently, McKissick had assumed the leadership of CORE—the once-pacifist organization Murray had worked with two decades earlier—and transformed it into a Black Power organization. Whether this history played any part in her reaction to him now cannot be known, but Murray certainly took offense when she ran into him and he introduced her to another Black Power activist by saying, "This chick really has something on the ball."

Murray explained how she did not see this as complimentary. She drew another race and sex discrimination comparison by equating the label "chick" with that of "Auntie" and "Sambo." She then recalled her earliest years to explain how she developed her sense of universal human rights. The manuscript is only nine pages long, breaking off with incomplete sentences when discussing her ambivalence about the church over its treatment of women and again when discussing her parents' and grandparents' marriages.[162] Not for the first time, Murray tried to make the personal political, but the effort to use her life story to make broader social points broke down when she began discussing childhood events, and the project was abandoned. Murray's attempt to frame her story with the question "Black Power for whom?" also reveals the issue most pressing on her mind when the Brandeis offer arrived. Brandeis wanted her as part of its response to Black Power agitation—yet she identified the same movement as a potential oppressor.

After the siege of nerves and the urge to focus on her writing had passed, Murray finally accepted the visiting fellowship in the fall of 1968. The opportunity to introduce prelaw classes, which were rare at the time, enticed her, as did the brief to help develop an Afro-American program.[163] These opportunities did not, however, negate all her worries. She told friends that she looked forward to the challenge with a blend of eagerness and trepidation: "One of the problems will be finding out how to close the generational gap between the civil rights 'militant' student of the 1940s when I was a 'firebrand' and the 'Militant Black Youth' of the 1960s."[164] She didn't have to wait long before confronting this problem.

Brandeis had been responding to political demands to open college places for African American students—Black student numbers had more than doubled (although they still accounted for only 120 students out of a student body of 2,330), and financial aid for Black students had nearly tripled. President Morris Abram, who brought with him strong civil rights credentials from his native Georgia, authorized a major in Afro-American Studies, to be administered by a committee of student and faculty representatives, which included the newly appointed Murray. Brandeis also introduced a Transitional Year Program (TYP), which aimed to open the college door to local educationally disadvantaged young inner-city residents.

Twenty-six men made up the initial 1968 TYP enrollment—twenty-three were Black, most from Boston's Roxbury neighborhood, and only thirteen had high school diplomas. Murray didn't like the program—she decried the absence of women and believed such opportunities would have been better given to students from Black colleges in the South, like the students she had worked with at Benedict College, since they were better prepared to compete academically with the more privileged white students—though this kind of student ciphering had worried her when she worked at Benedict.[165] Nevertheless, Murray's Benedict experience and her own upbringing made it easier for her to relate to the aspiring Black students of the rural South than young Black men from the urban underclass.

A VERY JITTERY BEGINNER AT THE best of times, Murray had only two nervy weeks to prepare her first course, "Law as an Instrument of Social Change." When Murray stepped into the classroom, she faced fourteen students, including eight seniors, five of whom were honors students, all of whom had strong political science backgrounds. Even more concerning, when Murray looked around the room, she saw four young men from the TYP program. Murray had barely begun outlining the course content when a TYP student interrupted her by asking, "Why do you keep saying 'Knee-grows' when you're talking about *black* people?" Caught off guard, Murray instinctively felt embarrassed and began stammering that "Negro" was a proper noun preferred by many people, including herself. When the student persisted, she answered defensively, referring to the constitutional right of individuals to express themselves freely.[166]

The confrontation went deeper than a simple (though alarming) issue of classroom authority; here class, gender, and generational identity issues intertwined. Murray had striven much of her life to make "Negro" a positive social identity. Now the younger Black generation whom she thought could benefit most from her striving rejected the term and, by implication, her. In the coming years Murray vigorously advocated for the continuing use of "Negro," arguing that it was a proper noun and did not have to do "double duty" as a classification of race and color.[167] Murray didn't see a need to reclaim "black" as a positive affirmation, she asserted, because her generation had had race pride instilled in them from a young age—though this overlooked the Fitzgerald family color complex, which resulted in her ancestors' glorying in the achievements of Negroes while condemning blackness.

Those who preferred "black," like the young man seated in her classroom, equated "Negro" with meekness and aspiring to whiteness. It is perhaps not surprising that participants in a new phase of the freedom struggle should adopt a new name to reflect a new militancy, but Murray didn't emphasize this when explaining the rapid embrace of "black"; rather, she focused on aggressive male advocates who manipulated the media and bullied opponents into silence.[168] The activist most frequently associated with Black Power, Stokely Carmichael, captured both the idea of "Negro" as a lower consciousness and "black" as an assertion of masculinity when he asserted, "Every Negro is a potential black man."[169]

The changing preference among younger African Americans disconcerted many in Murray's generation. Contemporary surveys revealed that the majority of African Americans preferred "Negro," as Murray pointed out in her autobiography. She also shared the sentiments of her old friend Ruth Powell, the woman who chiefly organized the Washington "stool-sitting" protest in 1943 and 1944. Powell had confided, "Pauli, I find it very disconcerting to go to bed one night a Negro and wake up the next morning a 'black.' Nobody gave me any choice in the matter."[170] That the majority appeared to agree confirmed Murray's opinion that Black Power activists spoke for only a minority of African Americans but were nonetheless getting their way by making the most noise in the most macho, aggressive manner.

This belief, however, didn't solve the immediate problem of the challenge presented in her classroom. Murray decided to compromise by using Black at least 50 percent of the time and joking with students when she forgot.[171] Her private correspondence suggests she made some progress in mollifying the students. In late October she told Barlow, "I do not feel the tension-across-lines as I did when the Negro students were throwing their weight around—they've calmed down and are almost as silent as mice—I think it is because they are so transfixed by the presentation of what they don't know about their past, and it rolls out so easy because I'm talking about people and only incidentally about black people and white people." Although Murray saw signs of hope, she also remained aware that she had not won over everyone. In the same letter, she acknowledged that some Black students boycotted her classes, which increased her anxiety about whether she was failing in the role Brandeis brought her in to perform.[172]

In November, the college president asked Murray whether her relations were good enough to invite Black students to her home, but she believed that such an invitation would be premature. Members of the Afro-American Students' Organization had staged a sit-in at the president's office and accused him of stalling on the Afro-American Studies program. As she grew more certain that the administration pinned hope on her to ease tensions, she grew more uncertain she could make a difference. She felt popular with white students and "Negro students," but not "Black students." Her interactions with the leaders of what she called the "Black Consciousness movement" were, in her words, "vigorous, even fierce." She believed her upbringing and lifestyle were completely alien to "Northern Ghetto products" who could not identify with her "as a model of achievement." On one occasion, she described having a "heated exchange" with Black student activists who accused her of disloyalty. She believed they hinted that she owed her employment to them and would remain at Brandeis only because of them.[173]

Although concerning for her hopes of gaining permanent employment at Brandeis, the militant student boycott of her class eased the immediate classroom teaching pressure—until January 8, 1969. Toward the end of an otherwise uneventful Wednesday class, a Black student burst into the room to announce that Black students were taking over the building. The only Black student in the class immediately left to join the action. Murray asked the remaining students what they wished to do, and the students decided to end class.[174] One hour later, the protesting students issued their nonnegotiable demands. The principal demand called for the establishment of an "autonomous" Afro-American Studies Department, with power to hire and dismiss faculty. Other demands included year-round recruitment of Black students under the direction of a Black director, immediate action to hire more Black professors in all departments, and the establishment of ten Martin Luther King or Malcolm X full scholarships for Black students.[175]

Only fifteen Black students launched the takeover, but in the coming days another fifty Black students plus another sixty community members joined the action. Five hundred white students demonstrated in support, and another 150 Black students from other universities protested at Brandeis.[176] The national news media reported on the takeover, which mirrored dozens, possibly hundreds, of protests occurring at other campuses around the country in the late 1960s.[177] Despite the tensions, the action took Brandeis faculty, Murray included, by surprise, though the high rate of absenteeism among her Black students had alarmed Murray. She blamed the action on outside agitators: the night before the takeover, striking students from San Francisco State College had visited Brandeis and urged students to strike.[178] Murray also speculated that the students' fears about looming exams prompted the action—an accusation she would have not have appreciated had it been leveled against her during the 1940s Howard sit-in protests.[179]

Murray strongly opposed establishing an independent Afro-American Studies Department on both practical and principled grounds. She believed—based on the work she had already done trying to help Brandeis recruit staff—that there would be great difficulty finding qualified African Americans to staff an entirely Black department at a time when many universities were urgently trying to address their historic failure to train and employ Black academics. Murray worried that an autonomous Afro-American Studies Department would become a "second rate enclave." Most

Brandeis faculty were similarly resistant to the protest's aims and methods, voting several times to support the college president's refusal to create an autonomous Afro-American Studies Department.[180]

Murray's inability to connect with the protesting students pained her, and that the administration did not seek her input in resolving the dispute was doubly painful. Her well-established activist credentials and standing as the only African American full professor appeared to count for little with either the administration or the protestors. During the takeover Murray reflected, "I am not representative of anybody—so that there was no communication between me and the black Students in any meaningful sense."[181] In her autobiography Murray described her sidelining as gender related, stating that she and the only other Black woman faculty member were "virtually invisible throughout the crisis, which was a struggle for power between white male institutional heads and black male challengers supported by black women students playing a secondary role. . . . We had no real standing with either of the contending parties to the dispute, since no one considered that we might have something to contribute."[182]

Murray's diary reveals that she wasn't even sure she wanted to talk with the protestors. She simultaneously felt an unwillingness to get involved because of a lack of sympathy with the students, while at the same time she felt a responsibility to do something. Four days into the takeover, she recorded in her diary, "In all of this I have had no active role. I did not feel solidarity with the young Blacks and I could not be a hypocrite and go over there. I saw them as a bunch of 'little monsters.' It has bothered me that I could find no role of constructive participation."[183] "Perhaps," she speculated, "I am blinded by my own frustration and feeling that I, too, don't count on grounds of sex. Perhaps my resentment is directed against a group who are potential oppressors and who are unsympathetic to me in my difficulties."[184] Scholars have identified the aggressive masculinity of Black Power activists as a significant force in dividing the Black freedom struggle of the late 1960s. Murray offered a contemporary critical perspective on the movement as it unfolded, though during this incident neither students nor administrators wanted to hear her voice and she herself struggled with what exactly she wanted to say.[185]

Murray grew increasingly concerned that her inability to connect with the protesting students would jeopardize her chances of gaining a permanent position at Brandeis. Her diary reveals anxiety and a sense of isolation: "I cannot help believing that I was being 'used' but that all of this backfired, since there was no clear role or function except to add a 'black professor.'

There is also a loneliness involved because of the lack of easily available like-minded people. Again, the problem of 'token' status."[186] Her recruitment's failure to appease the students—indeed, that it perhaps disgruntled them even further because of what they saw as her lack of Black consciousness—left Murray feeling vulnerable.

She saw further evidence of her expendability in her exclusion from a Brandeis conference convened to consider introducing a Legal Studies program. Although only on a year-long visiting fellowship at this time, she was the only lawyer in the faculty and taught a law-related course. She had suggested the creation of a Legal Studies Department, but only learned during the student takeover that a committee, which didn't include her, had been convened to discuss the proposal. Murray began to see the university president as a powerful enemy: "Now, particularly, that his earlier moves including bringing me here have not prevented a serious demonstration, I am completely expendable."[187]

She experienced further apprehension because the students had taken over the building that housed her office. The possibility that the students could go through her private files left her feeling like a "hostage" and fearful that the takeover could end with the students burning down the building along with her possessions. The protest didn't end in flames: after eleven days, the administration agreed to create a "legitimate" Afro-American Studies Department. Of all the rooms in the occupied building, the students had chosen Murray's office to use as their headquarters and in doing so had "appropriated" personal belongings and left a mess. "When I returned to my office after the takeover ended," she recalled, "I could barely suppress my rage over the violation of my privacy, which I considered just short of a physical violation of my person."[188]

Murray's eventful first semester at Brandeis resulted in familiar responses to stressful situations. As early as Thanksgiving, well before the student takeover, she confessed to having "got off course" and began spending very little time on campus, which she labeled her "withdrawal symptoms." Furthermore, the futility Murray felt about her committee work prompted her to act in ways she regretted during the takeover's uncertainty: "I have probably been aggressive in the wrong way—I should listen more and talk less from here on out." She thought the student takeover disruption might be a "cleansing experience" if people learned from it and were able to find a way of working together.[189] Yet the indications from her turbulent first semester at Brandeis and her familiar responses to situations suggested that Murray's time was destined to be brief.

Murray at work, ca. 1976–77.

(Photo by Milton Williams; Schlesinger Library, Radcliffe Institute, Harvard University)

· · · · ·

VII

Murray's second semester in the classroom proved less dramatic, though life in Boston remained lonely and became lonelier still when her dog Doc died. A short visit from Renee Barlow revived her spirits, though Barlow's departure then compounded her loneliness. "It was a healing process," she wrote, "healing of the loneliness and desolation. Our times together are so few and long spaces between."[190] Murray's new dog, a black Labrador named Roy, provided a valuable outlet. Setting out from her apartment near Massachusetts Avenue, Murray and Roy would take long Sunday walks along the banks of the Charles River.[191] Despite all her fears of expendability, at the end of the academic year Brandeis offered a one-year contract extension. She had hoped a permanent position would be offered and still dreamed of gaining a position at Harvard or Yale Law School, but these dreams remained unrealized, and she accepted the extension. During the 1969 summer Murray spent more time with Renee in New York, where Murray underwent neurological testing after experiencing severe head pains. She told an acquaintance that neurologists couldn't agree on the problem's source, but they did advise avoiding undue pressure.[192] Avoiding undue stress, however, never proved easy.

Murray and Barlow attended St. Mark's Church-in-the-Bowery, where another dramatic takeover by Black Power activists occurred. The activists interrupted a service to issue the Black Manifesto, a 2,500-word document calling for $500 million (later increased to $3 billion) in hardship reparations from the "racist churches and synagogues" to be gained, if necessary, through church seizures, disruptions, demonstrations, and force.[193] James Forman, a former Student Nonviolent Coordinating Committee (SNCC) activist, devised the manifesto and interrupted a Sunday morning service at New York's Riverside Church, one of the nation's most prominent white Protestant churches, to read it out. Following Forman's action, other Black activists presented the manifesto in similar ways in churches around the nation, including St. Mark's. The manifesto presented at St. Mark's included a cover letter calling for the establishment of a "Caucus of Black Communicants to deal only with cultural history, action programs, and the Black revolution."[194]

An outraged Murray wrote to the parish leadership denouncing the Black Manifesto as "riddled with contradictions . . . little short of suicidal rhetoric . . . a hodge-podge of revolutionary quasi-Marxist language." She especially wanted St. Mark's to reject the Black caucus demand, which she equated with reverse racism and fostering separatism. She didn't see Black activists' demands as challenging the white power structure—in fact, she felt so strongly opposed that she threatened to urge white St. Mark's attendees to withhold financial contributions if a Black caucus were formed. In a less threatening manner Murray posed this question: if the Black caucus's aim was to foster greater inclusiveness, "why not broaden it to include all those excluded from full Church participation, i.e. women?"[195]

The St. Mark's parish rector, Reverend Michael Allen, replied promptly. Allen, who had previously been arrested in Baltimore during a civil rights protest, noted in his reply that the congregation had long been divided—white and Black congregations held separate services, the latter using the facilities at the sufferance of the former. Allen recognized the potential trouble a Black caucus could cause but asked, "What is the alternative? A cozy and sleepy church which in its self righteousness knows it has fought the good fight (yesterday's but not today's) and therefore has nothing to do with the present Black battle for freedom? Or perhaps a church which maintains some token Blacks around to keep us from being too brutally attacked by men of good will? It seems to me we have to risk much to be a church of the people run by self determining men and women—by self determining communities learning to live together." He added that this might well fail and the caucus could take over, but still he urged Murray not to panic. "One thing is clear," he concluded. "The present situation of Black powerlessness has to change at St. Marks. Maybe elsewhere as well. Isn't that the problem of the nation?"[196] Murray answered by withdrawing from St. Mark's.[197]

Her relationship with the church had been ambiguous for much of her adult life, and it had become more confrontational in the past few years as second-wave feminism gathered momentum. Three years had passed since she had stormed out of a service in rage at the male domination of the Holy Eucharist, but in the intervening years the church had made only token reforms. Now Black men appeared to be gaining recognition and influence simply by making aggressive demands from the outside, making a mockery of her many efforts to win acceptance within existing frameworks and institutions at a high personal cost—not the least of which was having to continually control or explain her own aggressiveness.

Like Murray's parish church, white Christian churches across the nation responded positively to the manifesto's demands, pledging money that totaled into the millions.[198] The aforementioned money was mostly "earmarked," "invested," "requested," or "set aside," and money that was forthcoming mostly went to community organizations not associated with Black Power, such as the National Committee of Black Churchmen. Nevertheless, by threat and rhetoric alone, Black Manifesto advocates convinced many churches to examine and enlarge existing programs for the disadvantaged, or to institute new programs. When compared with previous proposals such as the "Freedom Budget," the "Domestic Marshall Plan," and the "Economic Bill of Rights for the Disadvantaged," which Murray had supported, it was infuriating to see that the Black Manifesto's forceful language and presentation appeared to be securing more immediate results.[199]

The Episcopal Church's apparent acquiescence to the demands of Black militants contrasted starkly with its resistance to addressing gender inequities. In defiance of Church rules, Californian Episcopalians had selected a woman delegate to represent them at a Special General Convention in September 1969. The convention refused to seat the woman, however, since women were ineligible to be seated as delegates in the House of Deputies, which represented one-half of the Church's ruling body.[200] In response, Murray wrote a twenty-six-point memo to the House of Bishops and the

House of Deputies — subsequently circulated to hundreds of women through the interdenominational Church Women United network — asserting that the male church hierarchy had begun to recognize its failure to fulfill its Christian mission to African Americans but not to women. The Church, according to Murray, "failed to understand the most elementary principle of the present world revolution in human rights; namely, that human rights are indivisible, and that institutions and governments cannot recognize and implement the rights of one disaffected group over another without arousing resentments, creating divisiveness, and exacerbating the very turmoil the Church seeks to resolve."[201] Murray raised the prospect of a women's boycott, in which women would not make financial contributions to the church and organize "stay-at-home Sundays," which would cripple the Church because the overwhelming majority of churchgoers were women.

The month after the convention, while at Brandeis for her second academic year, Murray again tried to contrast the treatment of women in the Episcopal Church with the church's willingness to appease Black Power activists. She wrote to Bishop Stokes in October 1969, after he appealed to Bay State Episcopalians to contribute $22,500 to a Special Fund for Blacks, Indians, and Eskimos. She pointed out that not one word of his appeal referred to women, who represented half the Church's population and had "been treated as second-class citizens for nearly two thousand years." "Since the problems of race discrimination and sex discrimination meet in me," she explained, "I must consider both as equally important." She also reiterated a claim made in her memo to the House of Bishops that, since women were not represented as voting delegates in the House of Deputies and were unable to serve in other capacities, she considered the request analogous to taxation without representation.[202]

IN ADDITION TO CHALLENGING SEXISM in the church, Murray challenged herself and her students in the classroom by designing new courses, such as "Women in American Society," which Brandeis academic Joyce Antler identified as paving the way for the university's eventual Women's Studies program.[203] In course evaluations, students roundly criticized the lack of course structure, though some students described the more successful classes as "consciousness raising sessions," and radicalizing young women sought Murray's advice outside class.[204] Two years on from her tumultuous first semester, Larry Fuchs, who headed the American Civilization program at Brandeis, successfully advocated for Murray to be included in the 1971 edition of Outstanding Educators of America. Murray carried on these innovative teaching efforts despite the isolating effect of being, at the time, the only woman in the American Studies Department.

Murray pushed for tenure during her second year at Brandeis. Colleagues cautioned her to wait—she was still relatively new to academia, and worsening financial circumstances had caused Brandeis trustees to order a tenure freeze—but she was undeterred and, as usual, became more determined. Although thankful that Brandeis had given her an opportunity "at a low ebb" in her career, Murray threatened to resign if Fuchs didn't recommend her for tenure. He acquiesced and then chaired the all-white, all-male Ad-Hoc Committee, which deadlocked on recommending her for tenure. Murray learned that the committee acknowledged that she was a "remarkable person" who had a "remarkable career" but concluded that her published writing lacked "flair, a brilliance, a conceptual power."[205]

The deadlock and critical assessments of her work hurt and infuriated Murray. In correspondence she decried the tenure committee as "BAS-TARDS!" She suspected that race and gender played at least an unconscious role in the deadlock, since those opposed to her tenure were "fixed in established grooves" and couldn't comprehend lateral career pathways to the established "publish or perish" rule. In order to keep her "sanity during the intolerable waiting period," which lasted eight months, she organized countermoves so that if Brandeis decided against tenure, "the whole women's liberation sector of professional and academic women would be in the fight."[206] She also wrote one of her lengthy letters to Fuchs asking him to reconsider the assessment of her work as lacking "flair, brilliance, and conceptual power." As evidence, she explained her foresight in recognizing the legal arguments that others later developed to win greater legal equality for African Americans and women. Fuchs tried again on Murray's behalf, telling the dean she was a visionary with a unique perspective and the leading African American woman academic in the nation.[207]

Murray won tenure and an enhanced reputation for feistiness. Such was Murray's enduring reputation that Joyce Antler, who joined the American Studies Department well after Murray had departed, would still be described by colleagues as "doing a Pauli Murray" when aggressively arguing a position of principle.[208] Murray's evident feistiness masked deeper, hidden insecurities. She only realized how "up tight" she had been when her top student revealed after class, "You always seemed so businesslike and forbidding." In relating the story in private correspondence Murray explained, "Confidentially, I was just plain scared—fear of failure, fear of not meeting my students' expectations, fear of not being relevant, fear of arousing the

Black Students' opposition—fear, fear, fear."[209] The sense of being on trial for her race and sex and perhaps other hidden identities had not gone away despite her successes—it still both motivated her and perpetuated personal insecurities.

Job-related anxieties, the tenure campaign, Black Power's increasing prominence, and the limited role afforded women in the Church contributed to health concerns. She told her literary agent that the tenure campaign "exhausted my physical resources—and, confidentially, I'm a wreck." She also announced to friends and family that during the summer of 1970 she had been "stopped in my tracks with a diagnosis of cardiac irregularity" (she had similar inconclusive medical testing carried out around the time she departed Yale and following the Brandeis takeover).[210] Murray wasn't as prolific a letter writer as she had been earlier in her life, due in part to her workload and the increasing affordability of telephone calls, but there are enough snippets in her papers to indicate that mysterious aliments and physical exhaustion plagued her endeavors as much at age sixty as they had at thirty.

The year 1970 proved especially hectic. Murray's opposition to women's subordination in the Church led to her attendance at the Graymoor Conference in late April. The gathering brought together forty-five Episcopalian women to discuss and formulate a response to gender discrimination in the Church and has been identified as a key event in the Episcopal Church's modern history.[211] One participant recalled that the conference evolved from the women's movement and included "young, militant feminists who felt peripherally connected to the church but very wounded by it."[212] Murray may not have been as young as some participants, or as militant, but her name is still third on the "Graymoor Resolution" list of signatures. The resolution demanded that all roles within the Church be open to women, including full ordination into the priesthood, and began with the forceful statement, "The institutional Episcopal Church is racist, militaristic, and sexist; its basic influence on our lives is negative."[213] Conference attendees established the Episcopal Women's Caucus (EWC) to campaign for women's ordination—a campaign that gained such rapid momentum that many felt optimistic that the Episcopal Church's 1970 triennial General Convention would vote to allow women's ordination.[214]

The 1970 General Convention began promisingly by breaking with tradition and seating women deputies, albeit not without opposition. A successful vote also ensured women could now become deacons, but a vote to allow the full ordination of women as priests narrowly failed.[215] Murray wasn't in Houston for the General Convention; she only later learned that a report she had coauthored making the legal case for women's ordination had been "short-circuited" and never formally presented.[216] Infuriated by what she saw as a half-measure of allowing women to become deacons but not priests, Murray again stopped attending church services, recalling, "My rejection of the church left me floundering in a wilderness of doubt." Instead of attending church on Sundays, she went for long walks with Roy, "while at war" with herself because she wasn't in church.[217] In the past, Murray admitted compartmentalizing aspects of her spiritual and secular life, but that separation no longer seemed possible under the influence of a women's movement that identified the personal as political and a church that seemed more willing to bend to the masculinist demands of Black Power activists than to the feminist demands of women congregants.[218]

Murray continued to take issue with Black male activists. She wrote fellow veteran pacifist activist Bayard Rustin a stinging letter in response to a column he authored criticizing the limited aims of an August 26, 1970, feminist rally. Rustin argued that the demands for free abortions, twenty-four-hour daycare centers, and equal education and employment opportunities, were too limited and isolated from the broader struggle to fundamentally transform society's institutions—limitations that would consign the feminist movement to "just another middle class foray into limited social reform."[219] Murray told Rustin to "descend from [his] lofty masculine height." She agreed that the women's movement should be aligned with other freedom struggles but asserted that the women's movement had emerged because it had been impossible to convince men, including Rustin, to recognize that women's rights were an integral part of the civil rights–human rights revolution. She defended the limited aims of the women's protest, saying it was a necessary tactic to draw in the widest number of women, pointing out that the March on Washington, of which he was a chief planner, had only two demands, "Jobs and Freedom." She also reminded him of the lack of women's representation in the March on Washington leadership and his alleged disregard over women's confinement to balcony seating at the Press Club. Murray could have also mentioned, though she did not, his involvement in the decision to exclude women from the Journey of Reconciliation.[220]

She continued to push the American Civil Liberties Union into advocating for women's legal equality. Before Murray joined the ACLU national board, the organization had paid little attention to issues of women's equality, but by 1970 that had changed dramatically. Murray played an important role in the ACLU's 1970 decision to establish a Women's Rights Project, and under the leadership of future Supreme Court judge Ruth Bader Ginsburg, the project pursued litigation that revolutionized women's legal status.[221] In 1971, Ginsburg wrote an ACLU brief for *Reed v. Reed*, a case in which the Supreme Court finally determined the applicability of the Fourteenth Amendment's equal protection clause to women.[222] In her brief, Ginsburg listed Pauli Murray as a contributor to acknowledge her earlier efforts. Although the ruling vindicated Murray's Fourteenth Amendment strategy, by this time she and most others who had previously opposed an Equal Rights Amendment had dropped their opposition. In September 1970 Murray even testified at Senate hearings in support of an ERA.[223] She was also a much-in-demand speaker all around the nation; the majority of her speeches were about the "new feminism," which she believed was the most significant development of the time.[224]

Murray clearly felt more at home in the women's movement than in the Black freedom struggle. In the summer of 1971, a year after her criticism of Bayard Rustin, Murray again fell out with him. She resigned from the executive board of the A. Philip Randolph Institute, of which Rustin was executive director. Rustin reluctantly accepted her resignation but also strenuously denied her accusation that the institute was a "male oriented organization," nor could he see how her resignation served the struggle for women's equality or reduced the male orientation of the institute.[225] When Murray was confronted like this, her rage quickly subsided. In a striking illustration of her capacity to be both rebellious and eager to please, she replied heartily to Rustin, "Although I threw you a Vida Blue fast ball and resigned from your Executive Committee, this does not mean that I love and admire you any the less or that I do not think your Pamphlet Series is BEAUTIFUL!" She included a small financial contribution and a request to be added to the mailing list.[226]

Murray also furthered the struggle to improve conditions for women academics, launching a campaign over pay and entitlements. She gathered all the information she could about women academics on campus, seeking information about salaries, hiring, and promotion, then collating the information in hand-drawn tables. Her research uncovered a significant wage difference between men and women academics at Brandeis. Furthermore, she found that women comprised only 6 percent of tenured faculty—in the Boston area, only Harvard University had a lower percentage.[227]

Murray wrote to Dean Fuchs to bring the inequities to his attention. In a thinly veiled threat, she expressed hope that a formal complaint, like one recently made at Harvard, could be avoided. In response to the advocacy of the Women's Faculty Group, which included Murray, a Committee on the Status of Women was formed, which also included Murray.[228] Through her involvement with the Committee, Murray learned that she was the second-highest-paid woman faculty member at Brandeis, and the highest-paid woman full professor in the School of Social Science, yet her salary was still $400 below the faculty mean for full professors.[229] The administration responded by informing her that her wage was substantially above that of other faculty in only their second year of tenure. This didn't satisfy Murray, however—and the appointment of three male faculty and no women in the past three years further aggrieved her.[230] The Brandeis Committee on the Status of Women's final report found significant deficiencies in hiring, promotion, and salary patterns at the university.[231]

Perhaps Murray's crowning achievement in this period was the successful campaign she launched over her pay. On April 23, 1973, Murray, with the backing of NOW, the organization she had cofounded, filed a formal complaint to the EEOC, the organization she had lobbied and worked for, alleging that Brandeis had violated the sex amendment to Title VII of the 1964 Civil Rights Act, the amendment she helped retain, by discriminating against women in matters of recruitment, hiring, promotion, salary, benefits, and working conditions.[232] Four years later, the EEOC finally determined that Brandeis had acted unlawfully by violating Title VII of the Civil Rights Act.[233] It was a vindication of Murray's remarkable contributions to furthering workplace equality for women. By the time of the EEOC ruling, however, Murray had left Brandeis to embark on a new quest to enter the Episcopal priesthood.

~~six~~

I AM A CHILD OF GOD,

1973–1985

. . . . .

I

The summer of 1972 marked the fifth anniversary of Renee Barlow's cancer surgery. There were signs, though, that not all was well. Whenever she visited Murray in Boston, Barlow spent most of the time sleeping. She also stopped writing letters because something was wrong with her hand, then she experienced difficulty telephoning because she kept getting the numbers wrong. When Murray visited New York for Thanksgiving, the change in Renee's appearance shocked her. Renee announced that she was planning a two-week trip to Montego Bay. The pair had enjoyed numerous Caribbean vacations in the past few years, but Murray did not plan to go on this trip — instead another friend was meeting Renee in Miami to join her. On the flight to Miami, however, Barlow experienced extreme vertigo and couldn't continue. She returned to New York on the train and tried to resume part-time work, but after one day her leg became paralyzed and she could barely walk. Renee Barlow most likely realized before anyone else what was wrong, but characteristically refused to see a doctor. Murray still had a week of classes to finish before she could go to New York.

During that week, Barlow relented and entered the hospital on January 10, 1973. Murray arrived in New York to find Renee in a dire condition: her right side was paralyzed, affecting her vision, speech, movement, and comprehension. Doctors discovered an inoperable brain tumor. They suggested steroids to reduce the swelling, followed by radiotherapy. The treatment wasn't a cure, but doctors said it could provide between six months and two years of reasonably good life. As Murray held Barlow's power of attorney, doctors informed her and not Barlow. The thought of making a decision on treatment that risked permanent paralysis and blindness stunned Pauli. She didn't feel she could make the decision and insisted that doctors tell Barlow, who consented. Murray also struggled to convince Renee's mother to leave the New York apartment she shared with Renee to go to stay with her other surviving daughter in Philadelphia. But Mrs. Barlow couldn't be convinced to leave until Renee called to tell her mother that she had pressure on the brain and would need to remain in the hospital for a long time.

The treatment began on January 22, Barlow's fifty-ninth birthday. Barlow responded so well to it that doctors planned to release her from the hospital to continue treatment as an outpatient. With this hopeful prognosis in mind, Murray returned to Boston for a few days. While there, she learned that Renee's condition had deteriorated sharply: the tumor had spread to the other side of the brain, and cancer was discovered in a lung. Murray returned to New York on February 5 to find Renee had lost all sight. When conscious, Renee could say Pauli's name and answer yes and no, but she was slipping further and further into unconsciousness for longer and longer periods.

Murray stayed at an apartment for the relatives of terminally ill patients with Renee's sister, who had traveled from Philadelphia. After ten days, Renee's sister returned to Philadelphia because Mrs. Barlow had become gravely ill. Pauli, now alone, sat by the hospital bed holding Barlow's hand, feeling Barlow unconsciously squeezing hers, until Pauli couldn't stand it any longer and had to rush from the room to cry uncontrollably in a linen closet beyond Renee's hearing. Pauli experienced a state of "split consciousness" as the outward part of her tried to act professionally to organize Renee's affairs while the other part of her struggled to understand the "ways of the Lord." On the night of February 20, Renee began to convulse, her breath coming in moaning gasps; Pauli recalled silently pleading, "Take her, God, I can't bear to see her suffer this way." That night a nurse told Murray to leave and not come back. In the early hours of the following morning, Renee Barlow died. Murray's autobiographical recollections of Barlow's death, summarized in the preceding paragraphs, are the most moving parts of her memoir.[1]

MURRAY'S ARCHIVAL WRITING ABOUT Barlow's death is as moving as her published memoirs, but more revealing of the relationship's depth and complexity. Of Barlow, she told friends, "I think she loved me as much because she saw me as identified with 'the despised and rejected' of the earth as because of whatever qualities I had which she admired."[2] Murray credited Barlow with filling the void left by the death of her own mother, pointing out that Barlow was born a month after her mother died from a "cerebral accident." She continued, "I like to think that her [Agnes Murray] beautiful spirit somehow encountered the spirit of a little newly born child in England who ultimately gave me that loving acceptance of which I was suddenly deprived when I was just a little over three years old." Murray had lost not only her lover but also a substitute mother. As Murray sat by the dying Barlow's bed, she asked, "Renee, if you do go on and you meet my parents, will you tell them about me?" In a letter to friends written shortly after Barlow's death, Murray described it as her first experience of inconsolable grief:

> Please forgive me if I was harsh over the telephone to many of you who called Renee's apartment following the sad news of her passing. You had lost a friend—I had lost my silent partner. The difference is only one of degree, but for a "firebrand" like myself involved in public causes and constantly subject to impulsiveness, combativeness, misjudgment of character, the unguarded word which could be used against me and the cause for which I fought—my loss of a guiding hand, a gentle restraint and a loving spiritual embrace in which I was never rejected (remember I am a Negro [not Black] in America, a woman professional in a man's field and a Southpaw in a righthanded world, aside from being a reintegrationist in an increasingly polarized society,) was nothing short of personal disaster. I had not only lost the brakes to a highly sensitive vehicle poised on the top of a steep incline; I had lost a spiritual mate. My relationship to Renee was a deeply spiritual one. Had it not been, we could not have survived the "forces of darkness" which tore at our friendship—racial conflict which invaded even our church, St. Mark's on the Bowerie, a callous society which does not understand the rarity of a Damon-Pythias friendship, jealous friends who feel that they have been displaced when all that has happened is that they were embraced in a larger friendship, a partnership which, in Renee's words "meshed" when necessary and "disengaged" when it was no longer necessary to act as a unit.[3]

Her description of Barlow as a guiding hand and herself without Barlow as a vehicle without brakes poised on a steep hill—elsewhere she used the analogy of a ship without a rudder—suggests that she thought of Barlow, at least since losing her, as having been the force holding her together. She needed a new stabilizing force, and she found it in the Episcopal Church.

The day after Renee's memorial service, Murray wrote to the bishop of Massachusetts asking if he or another priest would be willing to ordain her as a priest in defiance of Church rules prohibiting women's ordination and, if so, could she receive one year's preparation instead of the usual three. Her letter also provided insight as to how this sudden and urgent desire came upon her: "How does one recognize a 'call' to the ministry? Could some cataclysmic event in one's life lead to such a 'call'?" She had been through a "fundamental experience with Death and Resurrection which involved mysteries I do not fully understand."[4] In a follow-up letter, which included a typically lengthy family history and personal biography, she elaborated on these mysteries. At Barlow's funeral, Pauli had placed her hands on the coffin and knelt by it while looking up at the cross, at which time an electric current went through her.[5] She believed the static-electricity shock might be a call—suggesting she was trying to identify a spiritual event, not only a secular concern with human mortality, to legitimize her sudden desire for ordination.

Murray's autobiography didn't mention the electric shock; rather, it emphasized her ministering role. On the final night she spent at Barlow's side, Pauli stood reading the Twenty-Third Psalm, which begins, "The Lord is my shepherd." She continued to play a ministry role through the private funeral and public memorial service, which she planned with little assistance, and recalled that after the service the presiding priest told her that she had performed the duties of a deacon and asked if she had ever considered ordination. As Murray drove back to Boston alone that evening, she witnessed a beautiful sunset that she interpreted as Barlow's smile of approval.[6] The next morning she began her campaign to join the priesthood.

Letter after letter reveals Barlow's death as the primary motivation. In one letter, Murray became defensive about it, writing that she wanted to make clear that her decision was "not an emotional one dependent solely upon my reaction to the death of a very dear friend," but then went on to describe the loss as a "catalytic experience" that compelled her to wrestle with her views on death and resurrection. She continued, "Facing the death of a spiritual sister, friend and partner made me face the implications *of my own death* because I was dealing with the death of a contemporary whose age was close to mine."[7]

Less than five years before Barlow's death, Murray had described herself as "not much of an 'institutional' Christian" and "somewhat skeptical about the organized Church."[8] Her autobiography referred to long-standing "studied indifference," feelings of ambivalence toward the Church, and a tendency to remain "aloof from parish life."[9] Murray told Church leaders, "I have always been a rebellious child of God, a volatile maverick, a supermodel of defiance, stubbornness about the things I believe in, and a perpetual questioner, 'Why'? From the age of about 20, I have had one-foot-in-and-one-foot-out of the Church, in the words of Irene Barlow, 'a frightened rabbit' ready to run at the slightest movement."[10] Renee's strong commitment to the Church—she was one of the first two women elected to the parish vestry—contributed to Pauli's keeping one foot in the Church despite her anger over its treatment of women. Only when Barlow died did Murray decide to make the Church central to her identity. Renee was family, and without her Pauli felt lost. Becoming a priest was a way to honor Barlow and to replace her with something else to hold her "frightened rabbit," "car without breaks," "rudderless ship" side steady.

Barlow's death provided the motivation, but Murray identified other potential positives the priesthood might provide. She told the bishop of Massachusetts, "I would also like to utilize my connection with the Church as a possible priest to carry forward the work of Dr. Martin Luther King to the next stage of development of creative non-violence."[11] Murray later claimed that the political scandal engulfing the nation forced her to reconsider her approach to social change: "Watergate hit me particularly hard because the principals of the scandals were by and large members of my own profession—the legal profession—at the highest levels. I was teaching a class, presenting law as a viable means of social change. And this thing just comes along and just hit me in the face."[12] Murray now seemed less convinced that the law or education could best advance social equality—she told colleagues that she hoped to bring "moral and spiritual concentration upon the vast social problems with which we are faced as individuals, as members of various minorities, and as a nation."[13]

Long ago W. E. B. Du Bois had described the "Preacher and the Teacher" as embodying the race's strivings—a view that accorded with Murray's understanding of racial uplift.[14] She ranked the priesthood alongside law and medicine as the most distinguished employment fields. In addition to occupational prestige, the fact that there were as yet no women Episcopal priests made it potentially a significant "first." This situation, combined with her age, explains her desire to accelerate her training: the Church's triennial convention was only months away, and given that the 1970 convention had only narrowly voted down women's ordination, it seemed likely that women's ordination would be approved this time. If Murray could complete her training in a year, she would be among the first women, and almost certainly the first Black woman, to be ordained. A groundbreaking priesthood, then, might assuage her feelings of instability following Barlow's death, foster a sense of belonging, garner positive social recognition, and provide a new platform from which to challenge social inequality.

Given Murray's increasing unhappiness at Brandeis, she also had little reason to worry about what she might be giving up to pursue the priesthood.

I Am a Child of God

Shortly after Barlow's death she sought and received permission to go to half-time teaching. Murray wrote one of her characteristically long letters to Larry Fuchs assuring him that she could afford to go half time and that the decision was not for health reasons: "My most recent physical examination by Dr. Solomon Fleishman of Harvard Community Health Center on April 5 shows 'not the scintilla of evidence' of any neurological disturbance or brain involvement, as I had feared because of symptoms of dizziness and nausea." Murray displayed another familiar response when she explained to Fuchs that as well as an interest in pursuing a religious vocation, "I just might write a best seller, if I can shake free from Academia."[15]

CHURCH OFFICIALS IN THE DIOCESE OF Massachusetts were less enthusiastic about Murray's sudden desire to become a priest. Their main concern centered on her age — she was sixty-two, and Church pension fund regulations required retirement at sixty-five.[16] Murray countered this by informing the bishop of Massachusetts that she wouldn't be reliant on the Church pension, then added, "You will recall that our Lord Jesus Christ spent 30 years preparing himself for the ministry and only 3 years in the actual ministry."[17] Bishop Arnold suggested, given her age and the already "crowded condition in the ordained ministry," that she might interpret her call as one to follow Jesus Christ in ways other than as an ordained minister, though Murray had already stated in one of her initial letters of inquiry, "I feel that I belong in the Church, not in the pews but in the chancelry [sic]."[18]

Murray interpreted any attempt to discourage her on the basis of her age or the crowded state of the ministry as a disguised attempt to deny her on the basis of sex. Since more people more than ever needed ministering to, she told Bishop Arnold, the clergy's overcrowding indicated the quality of the male-only pool of priests was a greater problem than the quantity.[19] Although she opposed Black Power activists' demands that religious denominations pay reparations, she also argued that the sin of excluding women demanded "restitution" or "rehabilitation."[20] Finally, Bishop Burgess expressed concerns that she might be too independent to "play on the team." It's not known how she responded to that concern, but as ever, attempts to deter Murray only led her to become more determined.[21]

On March 30, 1973, just five weeks after Renee Barlow's death, Murray made a formal application as a Postulate for Holy Orders. Murray explained, "In a long and complex life, in which I have been determined to survive and succeed against all odds — race, sex, lefthandedness, orphaned when quite young, and financial limited means for education — I have experimented with many substitutes and alternatives to the Life of the Church —

the beauty of the outdoors and nature at its finest, law in the highest ethics of the profession, poetry in the best tradition of craftsmanship. Yet, in the ultimate hour of trial — the death of loved ones — only the Church ultimately sustained me."[22] Murray had fought to overcome various barriers in life, but unlike with her previous quests to find fulfillment and contentment, the priesthood offered both occupational satisfaction and spiritual nourishment.

Feminist theologian Mary Daly and Brandeis professor Larry Fuchs provided the application's two written references. Daly described Murray as intelligent, tough minded, and personally warm. She described Murray's weaknesses as those of a poet, who felt deeply and had youthful enthusiasm, which also made Pauli vulnerable.[23] Fuchs described her strengths as courage and absolute commitment to the ideal of individual dignity and worth, and her weaknesses as her temper and tendency to all-too-quickly see discriminatory intent in male colleagues' behavior. He further commented on her tempestuousness in (all-male) American Studies Department meetings: "I have not yet understood her quick temperedness and tension in minor matters of conflict. It may be that this has been her way of letting out some of the deep tension that must be within her as she goes through larger struggles." In a question about the atmosphere of her home, Fuchs stated he had never been there but felt certain it would reflect her personality, then added, "But it also must be a lonely place."[24]

IT IS NOT CLEAR WHETHER MURRAY held concerns that Christianity's traditionally homophobic stances might impede her quest to find fulfillment in the Church. She must have been well aware that the Church condemned the relationship that motivated her to seek the priesthood, yet if this fazed her, she kept it — like her sexual orientation — well hidden. Murray not only continued to compartmentalize her sexual preference, but also recommended that others do the same. At the same time that she began making ordination inquiries, lesbian rights became the source of a rancorous public dispute between NOW members. Betty Friedan published an article in the *New York Times Magazine* in which she expressed opposition to "sexual politics" and a rumored lesbian takeover of NOW. Friedan warned that "proselytizing for lesbianism" would create "a sexual red herring that would divide the movement and lead ultimately to sexual McCarthyism." This created a storm of controversy and a "speak-out" by other feminists, who criticized Friedan as, among other things, a "lesbian-phobe" and a "dyke-baiter."[25]

Despite having little involvement with NOW since the second national conference in 1967, Murray entered this public disagreement on Friedan's side. In a published letter to the *Times*, Murray first outlined her credentials, then asserted, "Friedan and her cohorts are far more of a threat to women's real foes than the so-called revolutionary feminists because Friedan and company know how to organize, to meet the Establishment on its own terms and to utilize the legal system and the democratic process to bring the sexists to justice." She went on to describe Friedan's fears concerning a takeover of the women's movement by radical lesbians as "realistic" and argued that women "are a broad spectrum of humanity of which those who have preference for one's own sex are only a minority. Since the overwhelming majority of women relate to men as daughters, sisters, mothers, wives and fiancées, a lesbian takeover would be comparable to the tail wagging the dog. Problems of equality to lesbians should be handled as civil libertarian problems—as in the American Civil Liberties Union—and not as purely feminist problems."[26]

Julie Lee, a New Jersey branch member of the Daughters of Bilitis, wrote to Murray expressing shock at the *Times* letter. Lee felt deeply offended that Murray didn't think lesbians shared NOW's goal, which Lee defined as enabling women to be independent people. Lee also angrily repudiated the idea of a lesbian takeover of NOW and gave examples from the New Jersey branch where "we up-front Lesbians" carried out the "shitwork" that sustained the women's movement. Lee mentioned "up-front Lesbians" several times, which might have been a deliberate slight on Murray, but even if Lee was oblivious to Murray's sexual preference, Murray must have felt alarmed by the attack. Lee also articulated her suspicions that several closeted Jersey lesbians were trained government agents used to subvert the movement: she explained, "Remember, closet Lesbians have EVERYthing to lose by not cooperating. Up-front Lesbians have NOTHING to lose. So, to fear a Lesbian takeover from up-front Lesbians is nothing short of ridiculous. Maybe you ought to look at your closet cases a bit closer, and do something there." Lee also rejected Murray's claim that the ACLU should handle lesbian rights issues, pointing out that some ACLU branches refused to even grant lesbians an appointment. "So you see," Lee wrote, "not being a Lesbian, you don't know what problems 'they' have." Lee felt disturbed that there even was a "we" and "they" dichotomy in the women's movement. The letter concluded with Lee expressing hurt at now having to "write off" Murray as another women's leader she no longer considered a true sister and coworker.

Murray replied, insisting NOW was about the equality of women in true partnership with men, since women and men were interdependent and indispensable to one another and the goal was to "mesh" on terms of equality. She told Lee, "I support the right of consenting adults to make choices as to the sex they prefer, but I see this as a private personal matter in the same way that I see all sex relationships—personal matters between two people." Many years of hiding her sexuality made it difficult to accept a chief assertion of the women's movement, and a principle she applied to other aspects of her life: the personal is political. In response to Lee's ACLU criticisms, of which Murray was a national board member, Murray retracted her assertion that problems of lesbian equality should be dealt with by the ACLU— she now argued that lesbian issues were not problems for either NOW or the ACLU but, rather, problems best handled by the lesbian rights activist group, Daughters of Bilitis.

Murray conceded that "problems of lesbianism are mixed problems," but still argued that they were not purely feminist problems. Through the 1960s, Murray had consistently and effectively argued that race and gender equality struggles shouldn't be separated, yet she now argued that sexual equality struggles could be compartmentalized. She seemed to recognize the inconsistency in her position, concluding her letter to Lee by suggesting her views were not fixed: "Human Rights are indivisible and the rights of Lesbians to live free of onus and persecution is a legitimate concern of all who believe in human rights. Beyond this I cannot go at this stage of my thinking."[27] Even where Murray could see the contradiction in her position, the habits of a lifetime proved impossible to overcome.

Other women of Murray's generation felt similarly. A former schoolteacher told historian Lillian Faderman, "One reason lesbians of my generation are reluctant to come out is our memory of that time; there is no guarantee that there won't again be a rush to the documents, and a resurrection of our names from somewhere, with who-knows-what-kind of repercussions. I am retired and on pension; presumably nothing can change that. But we didn't believe the stuff McCarthy got away with, either."[28] Murray did not have to think back as far as Joseph McCarthy—she needed only to recall the FBI investigation six years earlier that thwarted her EEOC career ambitions. It is not surprising, then, that Murray remained unwilling to come out in defense of lesbian activists in NOW, but it is difficult to understand why she felt the need to enter the public dispute at all, especially as the *Times* published her letter just sixteen days after Renee Barlow's death.

Intimate relationships remained very much on Murray's mind. Another nine days after her *Times* letter, she wrote to Peg Holmes. Murray's surviving correspondence suggests that Pauli had had limited contact with Peg since the days of the "P-P relationship" in the 1930s, but in the immediate lonely aftermath of Barlow's death, she reached out. Murray revealed that Holmes had inspired a passage in *Proud Shoes*, Murray's 1950s family memoir, which described African Americans searching for loved ones from whom they had been forcibly separated during slavery. For these people, Murray wrote in *Proud Shoes*, "freedom meant an unending quest for loved ones."[29] The passage continued,

> When the parting came, each had carried with him an image of his loved one and the place where he had left him. All his remaining years he would be inquiring of people . . . and trying to get to that place where they had been separated. He would describe the loved one in the intimate way he had remembered him — a charm worn about the neck, a dimple in the cheek, a certain way of walking or smiling. It did not matter that children had grown up and lost childish features or that parents had grown old and white haired. The description remained the same.[30]

Pauli shared one other revelation with Peg that she thought was significant: on the night Barlow died, Pauli made several phone calls to friends; her last call was to Peg at 3 A.M., the approximate time of Barlow's death.[31]

Four months after Renee's death, Murray still struggled from day to day to accept the loss. "I squirm and inwardly squeal," she wrote in her diary, "but I cannot change it. And much of this I must bear inwardly because it is too great a burden of sorrow to impose upon anyone else and much too private a woe to share fully with others." Murray worried that her appreciation of the support of one unnamed woman might lead to complications.[32] She may have formed an attachment to the woman while both were in the process of losing their loved one to cancer at the same hospital. Murray refers to the person as "Dr. A———" in her diary, while in her autobiography she mentioned talking on the telephone with a physician named Grace — the sister of Murray's old schoolmate who was also dying from cancer. Whether the same person or not, according to Murray's diary Dr. A——— had been "warm and supportive" and "obviously wants to continue contact and enjoys communication," but Murray did not want to impose on the woman's privacy or become dependent. "I am so vulnerable in my recent loss that it would be so easy for me to cling to anyone."[33] The same month as this diary entry, June 1973, the Diocese of Massachusetts accepted Murray as a candidate for holy orders.[34]

. . . . .

II

After five years at Brandeis — the longest she had held any job — Murray felt no remorse about resigning. Her diary indicates that she had lost interest in the job, reluctantly attended department meetings, refused to attend faculty meetings, and had difficulty staying on course in the classroom. She had also spent several semesters teaching at Boston College. Murray credited Brandeis with helping restore her self-worth, as well as giving her a reliable income and a pension plan and putting her in a "position to win recognition," but she believed she would have needed to resign soon anyway, as a new administration with which she felt no "simpatico" was taking over. It was better to leave of her own accord and in goodwill because "further years and I might have been so alienated as to blow my stack and resign in bad feeling."[35]

Murray relocated to New York and enrolled at the nation's oldest seminary, General Theological Seminary (GTS).[36] The campus, known as "the Close," had lush green gardens and neo-Gothic buildings that gave it a tranquil appearance. GTS certainly tried to foster a close community—students and faculty could study, worship, and live together at the Close, though this may have been less than ideal for Murray, who lived with a deep fear of being hemmed in ever since the death of her father.[37] It also maintained a strong reputation for adhering to tradition, which, combined with its superior age, led supporters to refer to it as "*the*" seminary.[38] GTS had only begun accepting women as full-time students in the master of divinity program two years before Murray enrolled.[39]

Given the sometimes-tumultuous times she experienced at Hunter, Howard, Berkeley, and Yale, it is a testament to her enduring ambition that she wanted to study at GTS rather than a more liberal seminary.[40] When a fellow seminarian questioned this decision, Murray replied, "Like you, if I am going to become an Episcopal priest, then I want to go to an Episcopal seminary; if GTS represents the heart of Anglican tradition, then I want to be exposed to such tradition. When I graduate from seminary, I want to be prepared and trained in every aspect of Anglican tradition—liturgy, music, theology, biblical history and tradition."[41] This was not simply a concern with the quality of training, however. Later in her studies she admitted, "For all kinds of reasons having nothing to do with self-esteem, but with two of my causes—race and sex—it is important for the GTS record to graduate with top honors, God-willing."[42] Although it is hard to believe this had nothing to do with self-esteem, Murray was still acting consistently with her high school motto, "The best I can do to help others is to be the best I can myself," which for her meant proving her individual abilities at elite institutions.[43]

The year's study began shortly before the 1973 Episcopal Church General Convention convened. Women's ordination advocates were optimistic that this convention would vote in favor of women priests, but they were bitterly disappointed—the 1973 convention again narrowly voted against women's ordination, once again denying Murray an opportunity not because of her ability but because of her physical sex.[44] Murray wasn't at the convention to experience the painful defeat firsthand, which she believed was a good thing, given her volatile temperament.[45]

The failure to approve women's ordination left her angry and worried about what to do. She had resigned her tenured position at Brandeis and moved back to New York for a year of condensed study as a "Special Student" in the expectation that she would then be eligible for the priesthood following the 1973 convention.[46] With no chance of ordination for at least three more years, Murray's special training now seemed pointless. At sixty-three she couldn't be confident of gaining any other employment. The best course of action, she decided, would be to switch into the full three-year academic master of divinity program. If she completed the program on time, she would be qualified for the priesthood on all grounds except for sex at around the time of the Church's next General Convention, when women's ordination would again be put to the vote.[47]

The women's ordination movement in the Episcopal Church began to fracture in the wake of the disappointing 1973 Convention. During the weekend of November 2–4, the Episcopal Women's Caucus of deacons and seminarians, numbering about a hundred women, met to reflect on the convention. Murray sensed that a barrier emerged there between women who attended the convention and those, like her, who had not. As in other struggles, she became acutely conscious of the points of differences between participants. As well as a divide between conference attendees and nonattendees, she also detected a generational divide.[48] The main division, however, was between those willing to wait another three years for ordination and those urging radical action now. While Murray sought acceptance, others in the women's ordination movement questioned the need. One older woman present argued that it had taken a hundred years for women just to be seated at the triennial conventions; in her view another three years was not so long to wait for ordination.[49] Murray could empathize with the younger militants, having been one herself, but on this issue she had demonstrated her willingness to wait by enrolling in the three-year master of divinity. She tried to discuss future steps in the campaign, but the most militant women were too furious to listen.[50] Murray cautioned against leaving the Church, arguing that the angry young women should stay and "raise hell."

The group ultimately decided to engage in what Murray described as

"Godly disobedience."[51] The first action of note occurred a month later, on December 15, 1973. During the ordination of five men at the Cathedral of Saint John the Divine in New York City, five women deacons, dressed in vestments, who met every qualification for the priesthood except the sex qualification approached the altar and knelt alongside the men. Several GTS women, Murray included, attended the ceremony to offer moral and spiritual support. Bishop Moore, the presiding bishop and a liberal supporter of women's ordination, nevertheless refused to defy Church rules. He told the five women deacons who knelt before him, "Go in peace, my sisters."[52] One of the women then read a speech before the five women left silently followed by half the congregation, Murray included. Murray had never been confident engaging in overt public protest, but she stood by those willing to take radical action. Afterward Murray wrote to Bishop Moore praising his dignified handling of the protests and revealing, "Would you believe it Bishop Moore, for all my proven civil rights, civil libertarian, feminist background, I wanted to chicken out and not come on December 15?"[53]

The protest action further divided Episcopalians. Murray became central to debates at General Theological Seminary, despite only commencing study a few months earlier and still experiencing apprehension about participating in organized protests. At least six women seminarians from GTS attended the December protest, but only Murray and one other woman walked out in support of the women deacons.[54] Her diary reveals that she felt hostility from both men and women seminarians at GTS following the action.[55] Heated arguments occurred between supporters and opponents of the protest. By her reckoning the campus was evenly divided over the issue of women's ordination, but even among the half supporting women's ordination, some felt that "civil rights" protests had no place in the solemn liturgy of the Church.[56]

Even without the heightened tensions created by the increasingly militant women's ordination campaign, Murray faced an enormous personal challenge at GTS. Once again, there was the intellectual challenge of proving her academic competence by absorbing a new and large body of learning. In many ways, achieving academic results was the straightforward part—she had always been studious and took pride in academic achievement. The challenge of studying while living in close quarters with people she shared little in common for three years was a less familiar challenge. She had found it difficult to live with anyone for more than a short time—her decision to live in a seminary, and a conservative one at that, for first a year then amended to three, took courage. She recalled,

Seminary subjected me to the most rigorous discipline I had ever encountered, surpassing by far the rigors of my law school training. For most people, I think, seminary is an intensely intellectual and emotional experience of living with others in close quarters while dealing with imponderables and the ambiguities of human existence. . . . One's personality is under the continuous scrutiny of instructors and schoolmates as well as under constant self-examination. . . . Throughout the process [seminarians] have to satisfy various layers of the church hierarchy not only that they are academically competent but also that the spiritual formation essential to a priestly calling is plainly evident in their bearing.[57]

Murray's actions over the early months of 1974 suggest that she felt particularly volatile at this time, as she adjusted to seminary living, experienced her first Christmas without Renee Barlow, and dealt with gender discrimination in the Church.

On January 15 Murray posted an abrasive letter on the GTS Bulletin Board calling the seminary a white male–dominated institution. It was one of a number of open letters to staff and students, on everything from advocating for Nixon's resignation to explaining her financial plight. She also argued for an affirmative action program (there were only nineteen women amid a student body of 133, and only three Black students, in the master of divinity program).[58] Her actions provoked further conflict with seminarians who resented her outspokenness.

As with earlier occasions, Murray's overt political actions appear tied up with hidden personal frustrations. Two weeks after posting on the seminary noticeboard, Murray noted in her diary, "Then there is the complication of a new awareness. It was there almost from the first contact—an awareness and concern. It flared up over the Epiphany term to an active interest. I have kept it under control but it has all the earmarks of a difficult hurdle. I see it as a test of all of my maturity. Have my pop-offs, my encounters and 'fights' stemmed from the frustration of not being able to go all the way with my feelings? How can I reinstate myself with myself and with the community?"[59] Her references to "new awareness," "the first contact," "active interest," and "going all the way with her feelings" indicate concern over an attraction to a woman. She may have been hinting at it in her autobiography when she described how the intensity of living and studying in a community brought to the surface hidden "fears, insecurities, and unresolved problems."[60]

Three weeks later, on February 20, Murray addressed the frustrations by making her feelings known to Page Bigelow—a fellow seminarian, two years ahead of Murray in her studies, who shared a home with her husband of many years. The letter, which Murray called her "True Confessions," explained that when God created her "maybe two got fused into one with parts of each sex—male head and brain (?), female-ish body, mixed emotional characteristics—borderline, marginal type." Bigelow had never met Peg Holmes, but Murray still described a likeness. "There are so many similarities," she confessed, "it almost scares me." Murray left Page Bigelow in no doubt about her feelings: "This had to be said to you, because even though you are mature, perfectly capable of handling yourself, completely absorbed in your family, there is the fatal persuasiveness, the hunt, the chase, the call of nature—'THE FLESH' on my part . . . the intolerable dilemma of 'Admire with your eyes, but don't touch! . . . You said, 'Don't be afraid to touch,' but dear Juliet, this Romeo is not made of angels' stuff, but very, very, human."[61]

Bigelow replied the following day, which happened to be the one-year anniversary of Renee Barlow's death. Bigelow rejected Pauli's advance, explaining, "Being one whose instinct is to hug those I care for, regardless of sex, and also generally having not the slightest sense of any sort of stimulating effect on the hormones in that affectionate embrace, I simply go ahead with my natural sense of wanting to show I care by touching my friends and loved ones. I suppose I should be more guarded but it just is not like me, and perhaps that is not all bad." Murray often told people that she didn't like to be touched, yet it is equally true that Murray also craved love, an apparent contradiction that can only have added to her frustrations and relationship difficulties.[62]

In time Murray and Bigelow went on to become friends, but the rejection's impact on Murray's other actions should not be discounted. Certainly, Murray's actions cannot all simply be attributed to frustrations in her personal life, but nor is the opposite true: not all of Murray's public actions can be simply attributed to purely political motivations. She herself questioned whether her "pop-offs" stemmed from frustrations in her personal life. Indeed, as far back as 1940, over thirty years earlier, she had noted a tendency to create "tension and confusion in the office or at home" because of frustrations in her love life.[63] Murray had ample reason to be angered by the treatment of women in the Church, but some of her responses suggest her passions were inflamed by multiple sources of emotional turmoil.

Three weeks after confessing her feelings to Bigelow, Murray wrote a letter to a male seminarian that illustrates the complexity of her emotional responses at this time. She accused Paul Goranson of making a "crack about

I Am a Child of God

'lipstick' the other morning at breakfast." Murray conceded that he might not have meant it as a sexist remark, "but many liberated women would take it as such—that it is necessary for a woman to wear lipstick to be attractive. To whom? For what purpose? As sex objects?" Murray's letter, which she claimed to have written to raise his consciousness, continued in a manner that suggested frayed emotions. She told Goranson that she was of Chero-kee, African, and European descent and regarded "lipstick as war paint, and wear it when I am either on the warpath or want to protect my lips from chapping. A true woman does not need lipstick to make her attractive, any more than a true man needs it." Murray had stewed on the incident for a number of days before writing this response, which she tried to conclude on a friendly tone: "Glad to see you join us last nite at evensong. And where is that tape of the choral event . . . you promised to let me borrow?"[64] If she had hoped to convey that it was not appropriate to comment on a woman's appearance, the message was convoluted and did more to inflame tempers than to raise consciousness.

Goranson replied to what he called her "attempt at communication," stat-ing that she had misinterpreted his compliment, then went on to accuse her of pettiness and being better at talking than listening.[65] Race and gender separated Murray from the majority of her classmates, as did her age—at sixty-three she was decades older than most classmates and, indeed, many of her instructors. These points of differences cannot have engendered per-sonal security and likely contributed to her behavior, which was the source of dismay to other seminarians. Another male classmate, Earnest Pollock, accused her of dominating classroom discussions, interjecting irrelevant material, and having a rash and authoritarian attitude and a "serious chip on your femenine [sic] shoulder that causes me to say that I do not feel that your best efforts could be used in Holy Orders." He suggested she talk less and listen more, since her "continual badgering and often rude interven-tions" were a "turn off" to a great number of people.[66]

In a measured response, she asked Pollock to imagine what it must be like for a Black woman in an institution dominated by white men who felt threatened by her intellect, achievements, and refusal to be suppressed.[67] Vulnerability and insecurity did not allow her to let the matter end there. As she sometimes did, Murray wrote a second letter, an even longer, six-page, single-spaced letter that included a résumé and biographical statement so he could better understand her. In the letter itself she wrote, "Let me begin by saying that, in spite of ourselves, each of us brings to GTS the baggage of a life lived up to the point of entry. No matter how hard we try to leave the old life behind, it catches up with us and sooner or later we must integrate our past with our new vocation, sloughing off those aspects of the past which hinder our progress and taking on new elements of grace, of Christian love and service. But we must deal with that past; we cannot evade it." She could not, however, be specific about the baggage she lived with, the aspects of the past that caught up with her, or how successfully she integrated them into her current life.

Murray might have further challenged his sexism or ageism, but instead she reverted to biological explanations for her behavior. Her letter continued, "Sixty-three years and four months of struggling to gain self-knowledge of one PM has convinced me that I am one of those multi-faceted personalities, sufficiently complex and sensitive, to react more quickly to situations than most people I know. Medical data, glandular tests, life experience, newspaper profiles, letters of recommendation, etc., etc. all concur on the following descriptives: vulnerability, sensitivity, more highly geared than average although normal within her own biological bounds, a mind which moves quickly, and sometimes so fast that she should wait for her third impulse instead of her first."[68] Murray wasn't content simply to point out the patriarchal institutional values that compelled her into oppositional situations, as she had done in her first letter — she still continually wrestled with the role personality and biological characteristics might play in determining her behavior.

Good relations were proving hard to maintain during this period, even with advocates of women's ordination. After Murray informed another woman seminarian of the frustrations of being a "pugnacious person committed to non-violence," the woman replied to Murray imploring her to be more respectful of people who think and work differently: "I have felt that there's a Murray Program for Women's Ordination and you're frustrated when people don't fall into their places in it."[69] Murray tried to reassure Page Bigelow, two weeks after declaring a romantic interest, that her difficult interpersonal relations were planned experimentation: "Please have faith in me and don't worry about my kooky smokescreens. Of course, I will get hurt, but it is a calculated risk. Of course I will make mistakes, but it just might be that we will begin to evolve something in the nature of a process of conflict and reconciliation which is successful and which can then be applied to larger groups and to society."[70] Given all that was happening in her life at this time, it is hard to believe that Murray's actions were entirely strategic; she appears more like the car without brakes that she felt herself to be in the wake of Barlow's death.

These conflicts nearly ended Murray's quest for the priesthood during her first academic year at GTS. First-term student evaluations praised her

I Am a Child of God

academic ability but also stated that her "adversary approach" had led some to perceive her as "overly argumentative."[71] The end-of-academic-year professorial evaluations changed little, praising her academic abilities while noting her "bristly" personality. An assessment of her as "abrasive" particularly stung.[72] She believed there were only three faculty members with whom she had good relations. She also had poor relations with her sponsoring parish bishop, whom she felt had written her a "blunt and harsh letter," in which he chastised her for writing to the incoming presiding bishop of the Episcopal Church asking him to respond to allegations that he had acted in a racist manner while a bishop in Mississippi. She confided in her diary, "Perhaps time will ease the hurt—time has already done that, and to some extent I have put the whole thing behind me—but it has also increased my wariness and withdrawal—in almost every direction. It would perhaps be better to keep my own counsel in all matters and learn to say what I have to say in the pulpit."[73] Six months later Murray still felt upset over the "letter of discipline" that had "flattened" her and sent her "into a depression for weeks, perhaps months."[74]

Murray acknowledged her reputation for abrasiveness at GTS in her memoirs, attributing it to her legal background, which made her adversarial in class discussions, and to significant hearing loss, which caused her not to realize when others were speaking and therefore to speak over them—at least until she acquired hearing aids.[75] It is true that she had suffered some hearing loss, but she was well aware of this before entering GTS.[76] In private correspondence, she attributed her abruptness to an ongoing thyroid problem, which sometimes prompted hasty and overly intense outbursts.[77] And, as noted, she also wondered about the role of "unrealized desires" in causing her behavior and rationalized it as an experiment aimed at achieving "creative social change."[78] In variously identifying her legal training, hearing loss, an overactive thyroid, sexual frustrations, and creative protest methods as the causes of her behavior, Murray's explanations reflect the different audiences she wrote for, but also an ongoing quest for self-understanding.

· · · · ·

III

Having survived her first year at GTS, in the summer of 1974 Murray undertook the Clinical Pastoral Education (CPE) program at Bellevue Hospital, where she had been hospitalized on at least two occasions following breakdowns.[79] Murray found it difficult to approach patients, especially white male patients—an awkwardness she attributed to her own "highly developed sense of privacy and shyness." She also experienced some difficulty with other participants in the interdenominational program. Her fellow participants—all young white men—considered her uptight, aggressive, and domineering. One participant told her, "It is not what you say which angers me but the way that you say it."[80]

Murray experienced a range of feelings that she could not convey to her young male colleagues. They couldn't have known, for example, that she began the hospital placement the day after returning from her older sister Grace's funeral, her first experience of a sibling dying. Pauli's papers reveal little about the impact of Grace's death on her, but they do reveal the continuing grief she felt over losing Renee Barlow.[81] In a diary entry following a hospital seminar on death and anger she noted, "Perhaps it would be well to let out some of my anger in all of its manifestations." This included "my anger at God because R—— has gone and there is no companion for summer joys—the beach, swimming, movies. I have been in NY all summer and have done nothing as a change of pace from the hospital. And it is summer in NYC which brings back sharply the things we would do. The great gap and no one to fill it. So I rebel and am angry—with myself for letting it get to me."

In the same outpouring, Murray described ongoing anger at the situation involving Page Bigelow, which she had pursued "in a tremendous effort to see and feel a new life ahead, but obviously it couldn't be, and I am angry that I let it happen, angry at myself for letting my feelings develop so strongly." Murray also felt angry with Bigelow for failing to recognize Murray's true feelings "and seeming to encourage that which developed during the year."[82] In a later diary entry, she claimed that this friendship's problems outweighed its joys and it had thrown her off balance. "It helped me over a very rough spot," she reflected, "but also distracted me from studies and I lost some valuable ground."[83]

Murray's Bellevue experience gradually improved. She reported having good relations with the hospital staff, particularly the nursing staff. She evaluated her experiences with the psychiatric staff as less helpful. Despite her own engagement with therapy since the 1950s, in the hospital setting Murray admitted, "Psychiatry still remains mysterious and somewhat frightening to me."[84] (A year later her own early efforts at counseling came in for some criticism—her pastoral counseling evaluation described her as inadequately responding to the counselee's problem by focusing too much on her own formulation of the problem.)[85] Murray reported one particularly pleasing experience during the Bellevue placement: a superficial stab wound victim became hysterical, repeatedly calling her "father" and kissing the cross she wore around her neck.[86]

The women's ordination controversy reignited during the summer, when the more radical advocates again tried to force the issue. Having failed last December in their bid to have a current bishop ordain them, eleven women deacons who met all the other criteria for ordination convinced three retired bishops to ordain them in defiance of Church rules at a ceremony planned for the end of July.[87] Two weeks before Nixon resigned, Murray boarded a train to attend the ceremony in Philadelphia. Despite her feisty defense of women's ordination in the often-hostile environment of GTS, Murray still harbored reservations about attending the irregular ordinations. Murray had been throwing herself into terrifying social situations ever since enrolling in a New York high school with thousands of white kids half a century earlier, yet those accumulated experiences seemed to have done little to diminish the anxiety she felt about challenging the established order. During the first twenty minutes of the journey, her nerves rose to full-blown panic as she contemplated the magnitude of defying two thousand years of tradition. Just when Murray felt ready to get off the train, two joyously enthusiastic clergywomen from the United Church of Christ boarded her carriage and immediately calmed her.[88]

Around two thousand people gathered at the Church of the Advocate, located in Philadelphia's Black ghetto.[89] During the ceremony, after a bishop asked the congregation if anyone objected to the ordination, five male priests stood and read statements denouncing the ceremony as unlawful and schismatic. One priest accused the women of "offer[ing] up the smell and sound and sight of perversion," prompting jeers from many in the audience. In a letter to Bigelow, who didn't attend, Murray described feeling more anxious than outraged until the male priests' speeches ended.[90] Once ordained, the eleven women priests then gave communion, which further horrified the opponents present but inspired Murray—she received a blessing from Jeannette Piccard, an older woman who had already had careers as a leading aviator and a NASA consultant.[91]

In the following days, Murray's panic became joy. She met secretly with a small group for a house communion celebrated by one of "the Philadelphia Eleven." Actions such as these initiated "guerrilla church," where the irregularly ordained women priests held services without church authorities' permission. These experiences revolutionized Murray's feelings toward the Church and its sacraments—she reported feeling more included and better able to enter into the "sacred" experience when a woman presided at the Holy Eucharist.[92]

The irregular ordinations and the subsequent ministering actions of the Philadelphia Eleven deepened divisions within the Church. Some women's ordination supporters were appalled—even some members of the Episcopal Women's Caucus distanced themselves from the action.[93] Following the bishop of Louisiana's death in a plane crash on the way to a meeting to discuss women's ordination, the chairman of GTS's board of trustees told *The Episcopalian* that his fellow bishop wouldn't have died if the Philadelphia Eleven had not defied the Church. Murray responded, "You might just as well have said to Negro slaves and freedmen in 1865, 'Your presence here is the cause of Lincoln's assassination!'"[94] She responded to a letter published in the *New York Times*, which said that those unhappy with the Church should leave it, by again drawing a race analogy: "We feel that we belong to the Church just as native-born Negroes feel that this is their country and they are entitled to all the constitutional rights other citizens possess. To suggest to me, for example, a seventh-generation Episcopalian, that I should leave my church is tantamount to saying to me I should leave the United States."[95] As empowering as Murray found "guerrilla church," initiating a breakaway church wasn't the type of activism that appealed to her—to her mind it seemed another form of segregation. Instead she fought for inclusion within existing institutions, even though, to opponents, reforming the Church using civil disobedience tactics seemed more revolutionary than reformist.[96]

MURRAY MADE A CONCERTED EFFORT to curb her feistiness during her second year at GTS. Her sister Grace's death helped set her on "the long road back," by putting her GTS problems into perspective. The Bellevue Hospital placement's successful conclusion proved another "crucial" turning point.[97] She had entered the program cognizant of concerns expressed by GTS faculty members about "Pauli's abrasiveness and the possible limiting affect that this might have upon her ministry."[98] Yet she believed, as the GTS dean did, that she had made progress toward allaying those concerns during the hospital placement: "by listening more and trying to hear what people are saying, by engaging less in debates on issues of race and sex, by focusing upon studies and the inner life, and by being less anxious about achieving acceptance, I believe that some progress has been made."[99] This statement wasn't a wildly hopeful statement made before beginning her second year of study; rather, it was offered in reflection on a largely incident-free year at GTS.

Second-year student evaluations continued to acknowledge her academic ability and also indicated a less confrontational manner in the classroom. One evaluation described her as "thoughtful and sensitive in class discussion. A delight in every way to have in class. . . . Ms. Murray's examination was the best I can recall reading ever."[100] Privately, she later recalled the "pain and discipline it cost" to curb her "feisty" personality and keep her "mouth shut" during the school year.[101] Despite the conscious and painful struggle to conform to how others wanted her to behave, the year didn't pass without one explosive incident.

Murray had a fierce and ongoing dispute with J. Robert Wright, a conservative younger white male instructor at GTS. The pair clashed on at least three occasions during Murray's two years at GTS. The final heated exchange occurred on July 22, 1975, in the Close lobby in front of shocked onlookers. Murray felt Wright had made vindictive remarks about her competence as a history student, along with her achievements in life more generally, and expressed opposition to her plan to attend another seminary for her final year. Murray gave Wright plenty in return in what quickly became a shouting match. She became so enraged it took a strong act of will to stop herself from punching him in the nose.

The day after the confrontation, still seething, Murray wrote Wright a letter that opened by stating she couldn't bring herself to address him as "father." After defending her abilities for two pages, she wrote, "If I have said things in this letter which hurt and infuriate you, I beg your pardon in advance. Unfortunately, if there is anything to legendary biological traits, yesterday you aroused an African-Irish temper, of which there is no more violent. . . . My temper rarely is out of control, but when it is, I am in a rage murderous! (Don't worry, it subsides as quickly as it blows—the old intellect somehow takes over!)" The strain of biological determinism that had beleaguered Murray's self-perception from a young age emerged as strongly as ever in the crucible of seminary. In the letter's final paragraph, she again linked the altercation to biology and again demonstrated a familiar pattern of trying to end otherwise confrontational letters on a positive note: "Meanwhile, I bear no grudges. My appellation 'Brother Wright' is the most sincere thing I can say to you. You should see the Murray sisters and brothers or nieces and nephews when they have a quarrel."[102]

One issue at stake in the dispute with Wright involved Murray's plan to transfer to Virginia Theological Seminary (VTS) for her senior year while still graduating from GTS. Murray's autobiography stated that attending VTS allowed her to do field education at Saint Philip's Chapel in Prince George's County, Maryland, a church where her uncle (Aunt Sallie's husband) had served as vicar during her childhood.[103] Once again, a different rationale is given in her private correspondence, where she expressed a desire to connect with her siblings. After Renee Barlow and Grace died in consecutive years, Pauli became increasingly concerned with her own mortality and the mortality of her remaining siblings. She told her sponsoring rector that the "physical and spiritual deterioration" of her siblings was a decisive factor in her desire to relocate to the Washington area. Some of her siblings' mental health problems were "too complex and too painful to describe," but all had "lived under the fear of hereditary mental disorder."[104] In a follow-up letter, she reiterated that connecting with her siblings would be mutually beneficial: "Renee was 'family' until her death, and then there was nobody but Roy [her dog] whom I felt responsible to or for."[105] Murray constructed two narratives explaining her motivations for transferring: the publicly stated reason of following in the proud shoes of a forebear and the private reason of wanting to help her siblings while filling the lonely void in her own life.

In addition to connecting with siblings, Murray buttressed her case for transferring from GTS to VTS by outlining other potential advantages. She cited a "calling" to work in the Washington area because there were Black women in positions of authority and prestige who needed Black women role models before they would be attracted to the clergy. Murray also expressed a desire to work as a mission priest at rural churches in southern Maryland, cited a desire to study at VTS to receive the "Evangelical approach" to complement the "Anglo-Catholic approach" she received at GTS, and expressed enthusiasm for working in a diocese that had a Black bishop—Reverend John T. Walker. At the end of the four-page letter, Murray briefly outlined one further "practical consideration": Massachusetts would require her to go through physical exams and psychological exams before becoming a deacon and then before ordination to the priesthood, whereas in D.C. she only needed to go through the procedure once before ordination to the priesthood.[106] Given her history of physical and mental health concerns as well as her age—she was nearly sixty-five—she was eager to avoid unnecessary examination.

Murray gained permission for the transfer. There is little evidence to indicate how the move affected her relationship with her siblings, though it must have been challenging. The previous summer, in August 1974, shortly after Grace's death, Pauli had taken care of her brother Bill for three weeks while their sister Mildred vacationed. For most of his adult life, Bill had shuttled between psychiatric institutions, the family home, foster homes for the nonpsychotic mentally ill, and finally Mildred's home. Bill, now legally blind, cared only about getting three meals a day on time; if he did not get them he would wander out into the streets. According to Pauli, Bill would "slip in and out of our world," occasionally recognizing voices then immediately becoming lost again, talking to himself about some earlier life incident, often relating to his time in mental hospitals. Pauli had trouble handling

Bill, describing him as alternating between the "passiveness of an animated vegetable" and an assertiveness that yielded only to Mildred's "iron hand."[107]

After the experience of looking after Bill for three weeks, Pauli told Mildred she would never again care for Bill. It wasn't just the physical side of caring for Bill that disturbed Pauli, but her own resemblance to him. "I couldn't take it," she confided. "It was like looking into a mirror and seeing my ghost (we almost look like twins)."[108] Pauli had also become increasingly concerned about her younger sister Rosetta, who experienced a protracted depression that became progressively worse in the second half of each school year (until she left her teaching post in 1977 because of what Pauli described as "possible glandular difficulty").[109] Rosetta's episodes of what Pauli termed "disintegration-anxiety," which were treated with electroshock therapy, drove those around Rosetta out of their "collective mind with worry."[110]

There wasn't much Pauli could do for Rosetta, but even if there had been, study demands left her little opportunity. During periods of crisis, she talked with her sister twice a day on the telephone and advocated to doctors on Rosetta's behalf. Pauli concluded one letter to Rosetta's doctor by stating, "Our family has suffered so much from gossip and distortions about our mental health, it would be the answer to our prayers if Rosetta could throw off the 'hex' and be her true, loveable, affectionate, productive self."[111] Pauli identified character similarities between Rosetta and herself: "We both have similar tendencies—manic-depressive, high creativity followed by uncommunicative states of silence and withdrawal, the need for community—an institution of some sort, school, church, university, or seminary, refusal to eat, keeping odd hours, running on a few hours of 'sleeping hard and fast,' literally unconscious when we sleep and thus vulnerable to any accident or emergency—hence the dog."[112] Pauli's close physical resemblance to Bill combined with the behavioral traits she recognized in Rosetta made it hard to ignore biology as a potential contributing factor to the problems endured by family members.

In an interview conducted a year earlier, Pauli described her life history as "being pulled between my family and other things."[113] This assertion's full meaning is not evident in her autobiography, where she felt constrained from revealing too much. Pauli wanted to pursue fulfilling, self-affirming goals, such as the priesthood, that would also counter notions of inferiority, but she also felt responsible to the family she could never fully embrace because of her early separation and the specter of hereditary insanity. Rather than addressing her loneliness and sense of responsibility, connecting with her siblings often served to exacerbate Pauli's own concerns about her physical and mental well-being. Although she often saw the relationship between the personal and the political, Pauli never fully and consistently blamed a maddening, oppressive society for family mental health problems. Instead, she absorbed the "mad Murrays" tale, which encouraged her to fear a genetic flaw.

Understanding these private struggles makes it easier to understand Murray's insecurities and eagerness to prove her abilities, as well as making her achievements all the more admirable. Murray successfully completed the master of divinity. Her final-year thesis, "Black Theology and Feminist Theology: A Comparative View," identified some similarities between the two theologies, notably the critiques of oppression, striving for self-definition and empowerment, and strong emphasis on the social rather than individual character of sin and salvation, which required action in the present.[114] Murray left readers in no doubt about which of the two theologies she preferred. As with Black Power, Murray identified an exclusiveness bordering on arrogance in Black Theology, arguing that its preoccupation with racism ignored the interrelatedness of other structures of oppression and exploitation.[115] This contrasts with Murray's assessment of Feminist Theology, which she credited with "an inclusive approach and a capacity for self-critical reflection which, if taken seriously, can be a powerful force for humanizing the entire spectrum of liberation movements." Through coalitions, Murray argued, women could "transcend barriers of race, class, and nationality."[116] She studied under one of the leading exponents of Black Theology at VTS but appeared to maintain good relations with him and completed the final stages of her master's degree without incident. Murray was now ready to become an Episcopal priest, if the Church was ready to accept women priests.

· · · · ·

IV

In September 1976, the Episcopal General Convention met in Minneapolis and once again revisited the question of women's ordination. Murray found the months leading up to the convention "intolerable" because her faith wasn't "robust enough to hazard the possibility of still another rejection in my life."[117] She didn't attend the convention for this reason—and because spells of "bad equilibrium," which she'd suffered since the late 1960s, made her reluctant to travel (the same letter reveals she lived with the fear that she might develop cancer ever since her 1954 partial thyroidectomy).[118] The Church's sole Black woman deacon remained at home in Maryland praying for a positive outcome.[119] Her prayers were duly answered: the convention's

Murray, Page Bigelow, and Reverend Jerr at Murray's ordination party, 1977. *(Schlesinger Library, Radcliffe Institute, Harvard University)*

approval of women's ordination into the full priesthood would go into effect on January 1, 1977. Murray described the timing as providential in her auto-biography, since her training would be complete by early December.[120] It is little wonder that Murray ascribed a role to divine intervention. After three years of preparation and having so many of her earlier dreams thwarted, often for spurious reasons, the victory for women's ordination felt exhila-rating.

Her ordination was scheduled for January 8 in Washington's National Cathedral.[121] Murray experienced ongoing anxiety that she might be par-ticipating in a monstrous wrong, but not to the point that she could not help publicize her ordination.[122] She invited newly elected President Carter and the First Lady, even though Pauli had met neither and Carter was pre-paring for his own inauguration twelve days later. She issued press releases, writing to Barbara Walters specifically to let the newswoman know that she was a significant person worthy of an interview.[123] The press, minus Barbara Walters, concurred that Murray's story was newsworthy—stories appeared in newspapers around the world.[124]

Murray was the last person to be consecrated on a wintry day in Washing-ton Cathedral. In her autobiography she recounted that just as the bishop placed his hands on her forehead, "the sun broke through the clouds out-side and sent shafts of rainbow-colored light down through the stained-glass windows. The shimmering beams of light were so striking that members of the congregation gasped."[125] Murray took it as a sign of God's will, for which she had been praying, just as four winters earlier she had interpreted the sun's emergence as a sign of Renee Barlow's approval of her decision to seek ordination.

A month after ordination, on February 13, 1977, Murray celebrated her first Holy Eucharist at the Chapel of the Cross, in North Carolina, next door to where her enslaved Grandmother Cornelia Fitzgerald had been baptized in 1854. Murray also publicized this occasion, and the press responded again — Charles Kuralt's popular "On the Road" segment on *The CBS Evening News with Walter Cronkite* televised the event. In her sermon, Murray declared, "A victim of the University's rejection stands before you today in Chapel Hill, the site of that rejection, to proclaim the healing power of Christ's love who paid the ultimate cost of crucifixion." She paraphrased the hymn "In Christ There Is No East or West" to emphasize a message of reconciliation: "My entire life's quest has been to spiritual integration. There is no black Christ, no white Christ or red Christ; there is only one Christ, the spirit of love."[126] Murray asserted that Christ is all things and all identities, then applied this idea to her own life to suggest that the priesthood provided the unifying thread to her identities.

Her autobiography concluded with the scene of her celebrating the Holy Eucharist at the Chapel of the Cross. She saw this event not just as the crowning achievement of a life filled with notable accomplishments but also as the realization of her true and whole self. In the final sentences, she described having achieved long-sought identity unification: "Whatever future ministry I might have as a priest, it was given to me that day to be a symbol of healing. All the strands of my life had come together. I have already been called poet, lawyer, teacher, and friend. Now I was empowered to minister the sacrament of One in whom there is no north or south, no black or white, no male or female — only the spirit of love and reconciliation drawing us all toward the goal of human wholeness."[127]

The autobiography's conclusion indicates that she had achieved human wholeness through religion, with her ministry offering the opportunity to use her own story as a symbolic example of how society might also overcome differences and achieve unity. Like Murray, historians Patricia Bell-Scott and Rosalind Rosenberg both elected to end their accounts of Murray's life at the same point, Rosenberg dealing with the remaining years of Murray's life in an epilogue.[128] The powerful symbolism of Reverend Murray returning to the site of her enslaved grandmother's baptism to deliver a televised sermon about the strands of her life finally coming together provides both an uplifting crowning achievement and a neat unifying conclusion to a life

I Am a Child of God

story. The inclination to end Murray's life story at this point, however, reveals as much about the need for auto/biography to impose meaning and direction on a life as it does about Murray, who lived for another eight years.[129]

MURRAY IDENTIFIED ORDINATION AS her life's unifying thread in other public forums. In numerous speeches and sermons, she interpreted personal experience through biblical texts. When only starting out her training at GTS, in the aftermath of Barlow's death, she reflected on her own emotional suffering: "I do not want to suffer silently. When someone is unjust to me, I want to scream and yell and tell them off. I do not want to be despised and rejected. I do not want to be humiliated. When things get too tough, I want to run and hide."[130] While Murray held doubts about how to respond to suffering, she nevertheless thought it inevitable, likening it to a "sickness of our common history."[131] In another sermon, Murray took heart from seeing Jesus as one of the despised and rejected—she described his life as a failure by worldly standards, since he wielded no institutional power and had no visible means of support.[132] She made this point repeatedly—clearly, she saw parallels with her own struggles. "Having been on the losing side for so much of my life," she sermonized, "I find it significant that I come out on the winning side in the one decision I made to put God in the center rather than on the periphery of my existence."[133] Such feelings encouraged Murray to view the conflicts she had wrestled with as resolved through the priesthood.

Murray also used the pulpit to argue for an androgynous god. In a Father's Day sermon she challenged the need to begin the Lord's Prayer with the phrase "Our Father." She argued, "In the late twentieth century, the theologian must also speak to his or her own era, and it is my understanding as a student of theology that God is not limited by any man's notion of sex, or gender, or race or ethnic origin, or status—God is all-inclusive."[134] In a 1979 Mother's Day sermon, she stated, "When we pay tribute to the essential qualities of motherhood, is it so unthinkable to enlarge our admittedly inadequate human symbolism of the Infinite to include the concept of the *Motherhood of God?* Test yourselves. Does it bring you closer to Divine Love when you think of God as both Mother and Father?"[135] In 1975, Murray sermonized, "When I say that I am a child of God—made in his image . . . I imply that 'Black is beautiful,' that White is beautiful, that Red is beautiful, or Yellow is beautiful. I do not need to make special pleading for my sex—male or female, or in-between—to bolster self-esteem."[136] Using the aegis of God, and not just personal experience, she now argued for the removal of barriers to social inclusion.

Her achievement as the first Black woman to be ordained as an Episcopal priest led her to see her multiple identities not as a source of division and isolation, but as an example of unification. "The contribution I hope to make as one of the successors to Martin Luther King Jr. is to address myself to the possibility of reconciliation," she said.[137] Having suffered childhood trauma, grown up in a family divided by color and class, come of age in a world that condemned desires outside the heteronormative framework, struggled for career advancement in a society that limited opportunities for Black women and political activists, and weathered the strains of aggressive Black Power, Murray thought she could educate her fellow citizens. The priesthood provided a platform from which to present her struggles for identity cohesion as symbolic of the nation's struggles for social cohesion — her inclusion in the priesthood pointed the way forward to social inclusion.

MURRAY REGULARLY DEPLOYED HER life story to make political points, but only some of the personal ever became political, even though sexuality also became widely discussed in the Church at this time. The historic 1976 Episcopal General Convention that approved women's ordination also passed a resolution declaring, "Homosexual persons are children of God who have a full and equal claim with all other persons upon the love, acceptance, and pastoral concern and care of the Church."[138] The resolution caused controversy, which immediately widened because of Ellen Barrett's ordination. Barrett refused to conceal her sexual preference, believing that God made her who she was and that the same God called her to ordination. Intense scrutiny, both in the Church and in the wider media, followed Barrett's ordination, since she was only the second openly gay person and first gay woman to be ordained in any Christian denomination.[139]

Conservative Episcopalians greeted Barrett's ordination with dismay. The bishop who ordained Barrett received forty-two letters from fellow bishops regarding the ordination — thirty-two of them were negative. The bishop of Albany wrote to him, "This hurts the whole Church. To be personal, I shall be sharing the priesthood with a lesbian. Is this fair?" Church officials tried to maintain a unified public position, informing the media that sexuality had "not been a test of the validity of ordination," but one priest, Reverend Wattley, attended Barrett's ordination and read a protest statement. Barrett's ordination occurred at the same time as Murray's, and the media clamor to cover it was comparable. Three television networks wanted to cover Barrett's ordination live, but only one was allowed into the small New York church where it occurred.[140] Murray relished such media attention, but she was far from willing to be identified as the first Black lesbian to be ordained.

I Am a Child of God

Murray writing, 1977. *(Schlesinger Library, Radcliffe Institute, Harvard University)*

Murray must have received quite a shock when she saw the Saturday morning front-page headline "Episcopals to Ordain Black Woman, Lesbian" in her hometown paper, the *Baltimore News-American*. The ambiguity of the comma in the headline could have led readers to believe that a single Black lesbian was to be ordained. The article itself explained that a Black woman (Murray) was to be ordained as well as a lesbian (Barrett); nevertheless, a clarification appeared in the following edition, stating that it had been called to the paper's attention that some readers might have misinterpreted the headline. The clarification doesn't reveal who called it to the paper's attention, or exactly how the headline might be misinterpreted, but it is highly likely that Murray had asked for the clarification, since she retained both the article and the clarification among her papers.[141]

The Church's resolution stating that "homosexual persons are children of God," combined with Barrett's openness and the growth of the gay liberation movement, made it increasingly difficult to compartmentalize sexuality as a private, personal issue. Barrett was a leader of Integrity, a network established in November 1974 to campaign for gay rights within the Church.[142] Everyone active in the Episcopal Church knew of Integrity—the group seemed to have a disconcerting effect on women's ordination activists, not dissimilar to the disconcerting effect lesbian activists had on NOW.

Murray's papers include some Integrity newsletters and a summary from the "Homosexuality Issue Group" that met during the January 20–22, 1977, Open Conference on the Ministry of Women.[143] Murray didn't attend the conference, but her preservation of the working group's summary reveals her interest in the subject.[144] The group discussed Bible passages condemning homosexuality and questioned what authority these passages still had, since the Church had moved away from so many negative passages about women. They recognized that women's ordination, especially the ordination of Barrett, raised the issue of homosexual ordination, yet the group acknowledged the issue of "sexual identity" was where they individually felt "most disturbed and uneasy about homosexuality." This vague concern led the group to adopt a final position of "creative ambiguity" until further (unspecified) information could be gathered. In the meantime, the group recommended treating individual homosexuals with "sensitivity and warmth."[145] The phrase "creative ambiguity" neatly encapsulates Murray's own position on gay rights, suggesting that her reasons for unease weren't unique. Indeed, historian Heather Huyck confirmed this, revealing that several women's ordination activists admitted to her confidentially that they were gay; some of them later came out.[146]

Murray discussed the issue with friends, formulating a more publicly supportive view of gay rights while keeping her own sexual preference off-limits. Privately she wrote to one friend, "It was you, Jim, who taught me that we bring our total selves to God, our sexuality, our joyousness, our foolishness, etc. etc."[147] Publicly she told a church congregation, "When confronted with controversial issues, such as desegregation, affirmative action, ERA, capital punishment, homosexual rights, abortion, and so on, do we ask ourselves, 'What would Jesus do?' Or are our decisions determined by our own self interests, group loyalties, and the notion of 'we' and 'they'?"[148] For Murray, the widening campaign for social inclusion and reform was a visible sign of a "second American Revolution," a revolution marked by healing and reconciling groups alienated by race, religion, gender, and sexual practice.[149] Murray made a public plea for tolerance of homosexuality under the aegis of Jesus's love and God's creation, although only in conjunction with other forms of oppression, and her own sexual orientation remained a troublesome subject.

Murray came into conflict with the bishop of Washington, John Walker, whom she had previously identified as a reason for transferring to the area. She had enjoyed her time as a deacon at St. Philip's Chapel, Maryland— a small, rural, predominantly Black church led by a white priest, Reverend Jerr. Her autobiography attributed her departure from the parish to a fire

I Am a Child of God

that destroyed St. Philip's toward the end of 1976.[150] Even before the fire, however, Murray had concerns about staying on. On September 15 Bishop Walker had removed Reverend Jerr—a decision Murray opposed and one that revived racial tensions among congregants. Once Murray became ordained into the priesthood, she didn't offer herself as a candidate for vicar-in-charge. The reason she gave was that it was impractical for an aging woman living alone to be isolated thirty-two miles from Washington. In a letter explaining the decision, however, Murray hinted at a deeper conflict prompting her exit. "Sometimes," she wrote, "when one is emotionally involved in a situation one's withdrawal removes a disturbing set of vibrations and helps to clear the air."[151] Only slightly less vaguely, Murray continued, "Typical of rural communities, but not limited to them, Aquasco and environs was a hotbed of rumors, some of them vicious, and I wanted to dissociate myself from the entire scene and maintain silence so that I would do nothing to influence members of the congregation in their choices."[152] Her vagueness might be explained by a letter written a few months later, which reveals her belief that rumors were being spread about her.

Two months after her ordination, Murray accused Bishop Walker of gossiping about her sexuality. She confronted him in a letter: "I hear you have been making 'tut' 'tut' remarks about my sexuality. 'It's unfortunate that she's a 'so-and-so.'" Such was the extent of her discomfort that she couldn't even repeat the label she accused him of applying to her. She could express her fury, however. She explained that even though it was in her racial interest for him to be successful—Walker was the first African American bishop of the Washington, D.C., diocese and had a notable civil rights record—she contemplated a full range of responses, ranging from civil legal action to blackening both his eyes. In two different drafts of the letter, she concluded by posing different questions to Walker. The final draft asked what he knew about sexuality, "hetero, bi, homo, trans, or uni," and "What do you know about metabolic imbalance? Endocrine imbalance? The varieties of approach to mental health?"[153] In the first draft, however, Murray posed a third question: "God made me as I am. Are you, a Bishop of the Church, questioning God's handiwork?"[154] This question, which Murray later removed, suggests she was getting closer to self-acceptance regarding her attractions. That she removed it from the second draft is unsurprising given the time and energy she had previously devoted to questioning, worrying about, and even attempting to alter medically, God's handiwork.

Murray ended her autobiography by asserting that becoming a priest unified the strands of her life, but ongoing sensitivity to rumors about her sexual orientation and the silences concerning her love life in the same memoir suggest this area remained a somewhat loose thread. Indeed, if the omissions from her autobiography are a measure, several life strands remained troublesome beyond Murray's ordination. This does not mean that Murray achieved no self-acceptance—she may have achieved something like a "working coexistence" between her identities, compartmentalizing things such as her sexual identity from other aspects of her life that she put on the public record.[155] To question Murray's autobiographical conclusion is not to indict her but to question the circumstances that led her to exclude some significant experiences from her memoirs. Murray's reluctance to disclose, for example, the extent to which mental health problems affected her life must owe to the still-prevalent stigmatization of mental illness as a shameful personal weakness. Irrespective of how much personal fulfilment the priesthood brought Murray, the world she inhabited remained far from perfect and therefore ensured she would face further battles over the final few years of her life.

·····

V

Reverend Murray's ministry faced significant challenges, not least because many Episcopalians remained opposed to women priests. Newspaper reports reveal some of what Murray omitted from her autobiography—about fifteen Episcopalians opposed to women's ordination picketed her ordination at the Washington Cathedral. The protesters carried signs and distributed leaflets critical of the "priestesses."[156] Those opposed to women priests called a meeting at St. Louis in September to consider options for fighting the reform and possibly breaking away from the Church.[157] At least three male priests in Murray's diocese resigned. The bishop of West Missouri refused to recognize Katrina Swanson's ordination, prompting some women deacons to hold off their own ordinations in solidarity.[158] Murray and her bishop received letters objecting to her ordination from Reverend James C. Wattley—the priest who had read a statement of protest at Ellen Barrett's ordination. Wattley wrote on behalf of the Coalition for the Apostolic Ministry (CAM), a newly formed coalition to fight women's ordination. He argued that the tradition of male priesthood was theologically validated by "the Father's" choice of gender for "His Son." Consequently, Wattley considered Murray's ordination theologically dubious and expressed concern that the questionable nature of her priesthood might cause her unnecessary anguish.[159]

Murray's reply to Wattley, published in the *Episcopal Times*, pointed out that she was a seventh-generation Episcopalian who had achieved much

I Am a Child of God

in her life—to which God was due some credit—and she did not choose to become a priest; God had called her. Furthermore, she explained, she had met all the requirements for the priesthood according to church rules. She continued, "I am deeply sympathetic to the anguish you and the members of your coalition must feel to have overturned one of your most deeply held articles of faith, comparable to the belief in racial superiority which has brought our nation to bloodshed and grief all too often in its short history." Murray went on to express support for his right to oppose women's ordination through peaceful protests, but as a lawyer she could not abide any overt act that would discredit her ministry or bother those in her pastoral care. Finally, she informed Wattley that his intention not to "accept the sacramental acts of this ministry" placed him in danger of violating his ordination vow.[160]

Insurgent Christian conservatism more broadly hampered her aspiration to be a reconciliation symbol. After noticing her clerical collar, a train conductor took the liberty to inform Murray that he had left the Episcopal Church because of women's ordination.[161] Acknowledging that women's ordination resulted in declining participation and a schism in the Episcopal Church would have complicated the autobiographical conclusion of her life journey's neat completion with the achievement of her priesthood. Murray positioned ordination into the priesthood as the final unifying event of her life that pointed the way to broader social unity, but such is the artificiality of selecting and interpreting life events that one might just as easily posit her activist ministry as another difficult struggle—this time against the rising tide of conservative evangelism.

The same year that the Episcopal Church voted to allow women's ordination, 1976, a Gallup poll found that one in three Americans identified as evangelical, and *Newsweek* dubbed it "the year of the evangelical."[162] Just as Murray understood her ministry as a tool for social progress, millions of conservative Americans, alienated by the upheavals of the 1960s and early 1970s, understood the opposite.[163] Furthermore, the year of Murray's historic ordination, 1977, has since been identified by historians as a symbolic date in the emergence of the modern culture wars.[164] Gender was at the center of this developing war—the Hyde Amendment, which prohibited the use of Medicaid funds for abortion except where the woman's life was at stake, passed Congress and was upheld by the Supreme Court. The amendment prompted Murray to write to a presidential adviser stating that, though she had concerns about the ethical and religious problems of abortion, they were matters between a woman and her god; removing federal funding would only further disadvantage the poor.[165]

Opposition to the Equal Rights Amendment became another rallying point for conservatives. By 1977, only three more states were needed for ratification of the constitutional amendment, which had been passed by Congress in 1972, but only two more years remained before the period for state ratification expired.[166] During her much-publicized first celebration of the Holy Eucharist in Chapel Hill, Reverend Murray did not shy away from making political statements. She prayed for ratification of the ERA, urging any North Carolina legislators present in the congregation to "please take note."[167] Despite the coverage given to Murray's sermon, her voice was ultimately drowned out by the clamor of conservative opposition. Led by Republican Party lawyer Phyllis Schlafly, ERA opponents made emotional attacks, variously asserting that the amendment would lead to unisex bathrooms and showers, force women into military combat, deny women alimony, and lead to gay marriage and adoption. Such suggestions horrified conservative Christians, contributing to the rise of the Moral Majority and the failure of North Carolina and the other remaining state legislatures to ratify the ERA.[168]

DURING HER FINAL YEARS, Murray remained as active and combative as ever. Her sermons touched on all the major events of the period, including the threat of nuclear annihilation, environmental destruction, Andrew Young's sacking as a United Nations representative for talking with the Palestinian Liberation Organization, the Jonestown Massacre, and the Iranian hostage crisis. She also prayed for President Reagan after he was shot, while in the next breath she wondered if the assassination attempt might be reflective of the proliferation of handguns.[169] Her concerted opposition to the conservative trends during the late 1970s and early 1980s took a personal toll, contributing to long-familiar behavior patterns that her priesthood had done nothing to end. She still experienced employment difficulties, financial hardships, relationship problems, family troubles, and physical and mental health concerns, and battled the psychological harm inflicted by entrenched discrimination.

One month after her historic ordination, Pauli wrote to Peg Holmes. The letter was written on February 21, 1977, the fifth anniversary of Renee Barlow's death. Not for the first time, Barlow's death led her to think of her earlier, seminal love interest. Murray's letter raised another matter that she had trouble integrating into her life story: mental illness. She shared some of her concerns regarding whether mental illness was biological, social, or spiritual, telling Holmes, "We might ask ourselves: How much of mental illness is some chemical deficiency (glandular or otherwise)? How much is the fragility of personality which succumbs when the living problems become too massive? Is religion an 'opium' or 'a vitamin pill' or 'the water of life?' How much of mental illness is a 'sickness of the spirit'? A lack of integration of the personality? A lack of a vital center? A lack of 'getting it all together.'"[170] Murray hoped the priesthood could provide the "vital center," but continued to wonder about her body as a site of trouble. She developed an interest in holistic medicine, but that interest did not alleviate her tendency to become physically unwell during stressful periods.

Employment problems also remained. After leaving rural Maryland to quell the "disturbing vibrations," Murray expressed some initial interest in teaching at a seminary. She wrote to GTS, where she had spent two tumultuous years as a student, pointing out the lack of women and nonwhite faculty, though she insisted she wasn't seeking a job for herself, joking that such a move would raise the blood pressure of current faculty and her own.[171] She remained as ambitious as ever, holding out hope for a position at Harvard University Divinity School that didn't eventuate.[172] Her age often counted against her, especially with seminaries, since she either had already reached, or was about to reach, their mandatory retirement age. She was similarly disadvantaged in obtaining a parish priest position, though she searched in Massachusetts, New York, and Washington before settling for supply-priest work in and around Washington, performing services, weddings, and funerals.[173] By far the most demanding of these was serving as priest at the January 1980 funeral of her niece June, Grace's daughter. Again, Pauli used her professional capacity to manage a challenging family situation, as she had done when she represented her cousin at the outset of her legal career.

Shortly after, on January 31, 1980, Murray entered Howard University Hospital, formerly known as Freedmen's Hospital, where she had been hospitalized several times before. Doctors tentatively diagnosed a myocardial infarction and released her on February 12. She wasn't convinced by the diagnosis, however, as she explained to her bishop: "There is some doubt in my mind as to whether I did in fact suffer a heart attack, or whether some angina is involved, or the results of a hiatal hernia under extreme stress are also involved—since this ambiguity has long been part of my medical history."[174] She also wrote to a niece, explaining, "I believe Carl's diagnosis of 15 years ago may be still valid. It may now be modified through possible angina, as he pointed out to me in the hospital, but I think the alimentary system may reveal the seat of my medical trouble."[175] Whatever the physiological cause of her recent illness, Murray took it as a warning to modify her living habits, limit her workload, and avoid stressful situations.[176]

The emotional strain included a mix of personal and professional problems. She had no doubt that June's death was "the final straw that put me in the hospital."[177] Pauli had developed a closer relationship with her niece following Grace's death. June aside, Pauli believed her family was alienated from the Episcopal Church and had not visibly supported her ministry, which created another wedge between Pauli and her kin. In line with her understanding of some of the personal being political, Pauli told another niece that resolving family problems was key to solving broader social problems: "It is my conviction that if we can just learn to communicate among members of the same blood-related family, we have taken an important first step toward keeping the peace of the world."[178] Statements like this acknowledge not only the magnitude of family disputes but also the significance she placed on them. Knowing full well the damage social divisions inflicted on individuals and families, Pauli understood unity as something that needed to occur on an individual, family, and national level; achieving unity on one level would point the way forward for achieving it on other levels.

Following June's death, Pauli moved back to Baltimore, the city of her birth seventy years earlier.[179] Her work as a supply priest wasn't enough to live on. For additional income, she relied on Social Security, her retirement fund from Brandeis, and paid lectures. She couldn't purchase a home; instead she moved into an apartment above the dental surgery owned by June's son-in-law, shortly after her niece's death. Pauli lived alone with her dog in the apartment for the next four years, though she eventually fell out with June's son-in-law: she wrote in her diary that he had accused her of "doing the devil's work disguised as a priest!"[180]

Her dispute with June's son-in-law related to affairs at the Church of the Holy Nativity, where he was a parishioner and she became a supply priest in July 1981.[181] Church attendance was in rapid decline; of those still attending, half were white and half were Black. According to Murray, the church was also "almost top heavy with clergy 'types.'" This created tensions over finances, race issues, and church leadership. She told Page Bigelow, "They could use me as co-rector, but I do not know whether the active whites will accept black leadership, and the infusion of aggressive blacks to make the parish truly interracial."[182]

To the very end of her working life, Murray's health remained problematic and connected to external events. After much debate, Murray was appointed the priest-in-charge of the struggling Church of the Holy Nativity. A month later, in June 1982, she was again hospitalized, this time at Johns Hopkins Hospital. With the usual level of detail, she wrote to her bishop de-

I Am a Child of God

scribing that she had suffered "adhesions," which she called "pesky things." She continued, "Fortunately, we were able to pump out stomach acids, allow the intestines to relax and unkink themselves. I feel fine, but obviously must be prudent with diet and digestive management."[183] In further personal correspondence with Peg Holmes, Murray described her illness in far more serious terms—she revealed that a friend had found her on the floor in unbearable pain. Murray believed her sudden collapse was the result of a "messed up diagnosis that had me being treated for intestinal flu instead of an intestinal obstruction, and I was literally dying, turning green."[184]

Murray returned to her duties at Holy Nativity, where things were set to become even more "bumpy," as she explained to a congregant who severed her relationship with the church after Murray bluntly accused her of lobbying. At one planning meeting, "gloves were taken off, heads, fists and bodies, symbolically were knocked together, bloodied."[185] Murray hoped the meeting had had a cathartic effect but feared, correctly, that it was only temporary. At the year's end, the seventy-two-year-old reached the church's mandatory retirement age but still worried about the underlying causes of disputes with the senior warden. She speculated that the warden envied her, but also wondered, "How much of it was my fault?" Murray didn't worry so much about her interpersonal skills; rather, she worried that perhaps the warden judged her "style of dress" and "freedom from the 'cannons of respectability.'"[186] Although Murray craved respectability for much of her life, she still appeared to both want to be free of it and worried that she might not be worthy of it.

THIS IS NOT TO SUGGEST THAT Murray derived no satisfaction from life during her final years. The widespread coverage of her ordination provided her with more public recognition than she had ever received. Given all the attention, the first year of her ministry was somewhat unorthodox, as people of all faiths across the country reached out to her. She had a kind of 1970s phone counseling service or, as she described it, a "telephone ministry," where she tried to make callers feel stronger and connect them with whatever resources she knew of in their area. Murray came to rue the publicity to a certain extent, describing it as "a cross."[187] Although her ministry and paid speaking engagements kept her too busy to complete an autobiography for Harper and Row by the January 1, 1979, deadline, Murray continued to absorb herself in the project. Her fame combined with the success of Alex Haley's *Roots* led the publishers of her 1950s Fitzgerald family memoir, *Proud Shoes*, to reverse their earlier decision not to reissue the book.

Murray with Maida Springer, 1979. *(Schlesinger Library, Radcliffe Institute, Harvard University)*

She sent a copy of the new paperback edition to Katherine Hepburn, who replied, praising the work—which prompted Murray to write again to tell Hepburn that she would be perfect for the role of Grandmother Cornelia.[188]

The year after her historic ordination, Murray learned that the University of North Carolina wanted to confer an honorary doctorate on her at their commencement ceremony in 1978. She wrote a delighted acceptance letter to the chancellor, Ferebee Taylor, who had been a first-year student when Pauli applied to UNC in 1939. Murray saw the award as an important gesture for African Americans who had suffered the indignity of hearing, "Members of your race are not admitted to the University," and for the Fitzgeralds specifically. "To me," she explained, "it was more than an academic honor; it was a symbol of acceptance stretching back to my Grandmother Cornelia and her relationship to the Chapel Hill Smiths, whose position as benefactors of the university from which I was excluded had intensified my feeling of being disinherited."

An honorary doctorate from the institution that received Grandmother's expected inheritance and rejected Murray's application all those years ago could have been another uplifting, unifying event with which to end her life story, but it wasn't to be. A few weeks after sending her acceptance letter, the press began reporting on a federal government threat to cut funding

I Am a Child of God

to UNC for failing to address the legacy of segregation on all its campuses. Murray urged mediation, hoping the dispute could be resolved before the ceremony. When it wasn't, she sorrowfully withdrew from accepting the honorary doctorate. To accept, she believed, might be interpreted as acquiescence with the failure to fully desegregate the institution.[189]

Murray's adventurous life and priesthood made her the subject of numerous newspaper and magazine profile pieces. She often recalled events from her past in a relaxed manner, joking about her insatiable ambition—she told one interviewer that she had written to President Nixon in 1971 to nominate herself for a vacant position as Supreme Court justice.[190] In another interview she compared *Proud Shoes* to the more recent and successful *Roots*. "It had to be a man and the willingness of America to listen," she told *The Sun*. "Alex Haley was there at the right time. I was 21 years ahead of myself, but I am not too early to become the first Anglican pope."[191]

She was less carefree about putting aspects of her personal life on the record. One article explained, "Murray was married once, quite briefly, when she was very young. It is the one subject about which she is clearly reticent. 'I'm not at all sure marriage is for everyone,' she begins carefully. 'My marriage probably wouldn't have lasted, because I wasn't going to settle for a derivative status, being Mrs. so-and-so. I missed companionship, but so do many wives.'"[192] In another feature article, she admitted to having led a lonely life, then added, "But I suppose I have been conditioned to a lonely life. It's not necessarily the one I would choose again, but I find that if you have convictions and operate on principle, and if you do it often enough, then you learn to accept the consequences. It doesn't change the loneliness. It doesn't change the pain. But somehow one is given the strength to live with it."[193]

Murray also discussed contemporary issues in interviews. She still routinely made the case for the term "Negro" and claimed to be adopting a wait-and-see approach to the Reagan administration, yet at the same time she expressed concern at the rise of the radical right. She also expressed concern at the proliferation of retirement homes: "I am really troubled by these retirement homes. It is just another kind of segregation," she said, demonstrating her awareness of ageism as another marginalizing practice.[194]

Murray was spared from ending her days in a retirement home, she passed her final days with her old friend Maida Springer in Pittsburgh. Springer initiated the move to Pennsylvania following the death of her husband because her son and his family lived there. Pauli and Maida eventually moved into an older two-story home converted into two apartments—Pauli occupied the upstairs—an arrangement that Murray described as "a joint venture in cooperative yet autonomous living." Murray remained as active as ever, walking her latest dog, Christy, in the park, taking a cross-country train trip to Seattle with Springer, revising her autobiography, delivering the odd sermon, and speaking at a conference commemorating the centennial of Eleanor Roosevelt's birth. Murray was due to accept an honorary doctorate from Hunter College, but illness prevented her from attending.[195]

In December 1984, doctors began treating Murray for another stomach complaint. A battery of tests found nothing, but Murray told friends that her doctors suspected pancreatic cancer. In late January she returned to the hospital for more tests. As staff prepared to insert an illuminating dye into her, Murray's heart stopped. It started again after ten seconds. Murray opened her eyes and asked, "Did you get the tube in?" then fell into a comatose state for eight days. Her old dog Christy passed away in her absence. Doctors gave Murray forty-eight hours to live. Never one to conform to expectations, Murray regained consciousness and began a slow recovery. She hung a sign over her hospital bed that read, "Please refer to this patient as the Reverend Dr. Pauli Murray."[196] By early March she was back at home, back to smoking cigarettes, and back at the typewriter, working on her memoirs and keeping up her correspondence. But the recovery didn't last. Her seventy-four-year-old, eighty-five-pound body could take no more. On the eighty-second anniversary of her parents' wedding, July 1, 1985, with Maida Springer by her side, the Reverend Dr. Pauli Murray died at home.[197]

I Am a Child of God

EPILOGUE

Pauli Murray's funeral took place at the Washington Cathedral, where she had been ordained as a priest eight years earlier. She also requested that her ashes be interred there, though this plan did not come to pass. Murray's remains went, as she had earlier planned, into a family plot in Brooklyn's Cypress Hills Cemetery — one of New York's most integrated cemeteries — where Renee Barlow, Aunt Pauline, and Aunt Sallie were already laid to rest.[1]

In her final few years, Murray gave increased attention to burial sites, particularly through periodic efforts to get the private Fitzgerald family graveyard restored and heritage marked. Six months before her death she learned that the burial ground where her grandparents lay was completely overgrown — in stark contrast to the pristine and once-segregated Maplewood Cemetery located beside it. Murray must have been concerned that her grandparents' final resting place would go the way of her parents' burial site. Years earlier Pauli had visited Baltimore's Laurel Cemetery, where her parents shared a plot, but she couldn't find the grave amid the undergrowth and vandalism. Before she had an opportunity to do anything further, the land was sold off and a shopping center built over it.[2]

In trying to prevent her grandparents' graves suffering the indignity inflicted on her parents and in seeking interment at the Washington Cathedral, Murray was doing what she had done for much of her life: insisting, in the face of uncaring and unrelenting forces, that her life and the lives of her loved ones mattered. Tending her grandparents' burial grounds and seeking interment at the Washington Cathedral capture something of the lifelong two-front battle she waged against her oppressors. Murray asserted her own significance in conventional ways, such as her quests to break down barriers and achieve notable firsts. But she also did it through documenting so much of her lived experience and the experiences of her loved ones, which when taken together testify that, for oppressed people, survival is a political act.

Buried in the middle of *Proud Shoes* — Murray's story of her Fitzgerald ancestors — a couple of lines capture these two strands of resistance. Murray wrote, "There were the heroic words and deeds which kept hope alive among people of color during the riptide of those years and which brought emancipation nearer. Then there were the small, persistent, unheroic acts of obstinate folk like my Fitzgerald great-grandparents and their neighbors who never dreamed of making history."[3] Murray's writings, published and unpublished, combine to assert that all people, not just those who hold prominent positions in society, have the right to occupy the historical record and that humanity benefits from recording all of these voices. And in applying Murray's lines to her own life, her "heroic words and deeds" as well as her "small, persistent" acts can keep hope alive for people continuing to resist oppression.

Murray's attentiveness to the preservation of the Fitzgerald burial grounds in the last months of her life has a poignancy because this site is the setting for the final scene in *Proud Shoes*. The book described how, following Grandfather's death, she would tend to the gravesite, especially around Memorial Day, when Maplewood Cemetery was littered with Confederate flags. Murray would take the Union flag the family received for Grandfather's Civil War service, walk through Maplewood and beyond the iron fence that separated it from the private Fitzgerald burial grounds. She would place the flag over Grandfather's grave—and, soon enough, Grandmother's grave too—and stay for hours tending this patch of ground.[4]

Over sixty years later, as her own death approached, Murray's discovery that the site had fallen into neglect signals a simple and inescapable truth: nothing is permanent. A gravesite, like any other part of a legacy, can be diminished or obliterated entirely. Today Murray's legacy seems strong. Her lifetime contributions to making the world a more equitable place are rightly recognized and celebrated. But that doesn't mean her achievements are immune to threats. Gains won can be wound back, and histories of oppression can be downplayed or denied by the peddlers of narrow-minded agendas. Fortunately for us, in preserving the stories of her life, Murray provided an incredible resource to tend and expand the historical record and, in turn, inspire efforts to protect and advance human rights.

The story of a young Pauli caring for the Fitzgerald burial grounds is but one example. It's an arresting image of her childhood self—who had already suffered incomprehensible losses at the hands of oppressive forces—working away, alone and insistently, to protect the memory of her ancestors and show the world that she and her loved ones mattered. Murray recalled, "I spent many hours digging up weeds, cutting grass and tending the family plot. It was only a few feet from the main highway between Durham and Chapel Hill. I wanted the white people who drove by to be sure to see this banner and me standing by it."[5]

Acknowledgments

Writing about Pauli Murray has been an immense privilege for which I feel an enormous debt of gratitude to the entire universe. More specifically, my thanks to Roger Markwick and Marguerite Johnson for guiding me through my Ph.D. Roger was there from the beginning, wading through clunking drafts of my work with good humor and helpful feedback. Marguerite also provided great feedback as well as boisterous enthusiasm for Murray's life. I can still hear Marguerite's voice echoing down the McMullin Building corridor, "I love Pauli Murray!"

Many excellent University of Newcastle people — too many to mention — have provided me with friendship, feedback, and employment over the years. Special thanks to Caragh Brosnan, who had the particularly wonderful habit of bobbing up with work offers at crucial times. I'm also grateful to Robbert Duvivier not only for giving me work, but also for showing me great kindness when I really needed it.

I am immensely thankful to all my friends and family who have supported me through the writing of this book. Foremost among them is my beautiful Mum, Carolyn Lorna Kent, to whom I owe everything. My big sister Tracey and her boys Harry and Charlie Duggan have been opening their home in the Ridge to me for nearly two decades. My best friend and brother Glenn and his two girls, Charlotte and Juliette Saxby, provided lots of laughs and a Bayside getaway. Glenn even read this manuscript twice, so if there are errors in it, they are his responsibility.

I am certain that this book would have never gotten finished without the million and one things Adrian Bernard has done for me over the years. I might have led him into believing that me finishing this book would result in him getting a holiday to the United States, and for that I apologize. I also want to thank Stacey, Sonny, and Alice Bernard. During a time while writing this manuscript when I was particularly prosperous, the Bernards let me live in their garage like some strange uncle, though they never made me feel that way.

On the subject of strange, I would like to thank Sean Durbin. Sean is like a stray pet that you find on the street and you have to take it home because you can't just leave it there. But then the creature grows on you and you come to depend on it. The Railway Street years were crucial years to finishing this book, and Sean was a great sounding board, a tidy housemate, an excellent cook, a true friend, and a loyal pet.

Vanessa Whitehead not only lived with this project for several years but also read manuscript drafts and believed in me and supported me through the best and worst times I have known. My old friend Alison Dellit read the entire manuscript in three days and provided a host of helpful feedback. The Pickham family made my life so much easier by providing me a home away from home in the United States. David Pickham also took on the role of unpaid research assistant with great zeal.

My thanks to Schlesinger Library and its friendly staff, who helped me find my way around Pauli Murray's papers. I also owe a huge debt of gratitude to Barbara Lau for showing me around Pauli Murray's childhood home in Durham and for providing feedback on a draft of the childhood chapters. The work that Barbara and the Pauli Murray Project have done in getting the Fitzgerald home restored and listed as a National Historic Landmark, among other things, is incredibly inspiring.

I am eternally grateful to everyone at UNC Press for supporting this project from the first day. I'm especially thankful to Chuck Grench for reading drafts, organizing reviews, lots of other stuff I will never know about, and buying me lunch that time. I also really appreciate Cate Hodorowicz's insight and great advice, which undoubtedly improved this book.

Some people who were very important to me passed away during the writing of this book. I want to acknowledge the profound impact that the following people had on me: my father, Robert Saxby; my stepfather, William Kent; the wise Aubrey Patch; the fun-loving Barbara Arnold; the beautiful Jayne Kauffman; and all of my hopes and dreams, Luke and James Saxby.

Finally and most importantly, I thank Dr. Emma Hamilton—aka Hammo, Hammy, Hambo, Hamster, Ham Bone, the Brick with Eyes, and occasionally, Emma. Throughout the life of this project, Emma has acted as an unofficial editor, unofficial therapist, and official most amazing friend. And her eyes never glazed over once during the countless times I started on about how I couldn't do this and it was all too hard. This book only exists because I had such great support from good people like Emma.

Notes

PREFACE

1. "Killing Insane Principal," *Baltimore Afro-American*, June 22, 1923, 1.

2. Murray didn't describe traveling to her father's funeral in her autobiography beyond stating that she traveled alone. Her memories of the journey to Croom, visiting Baltimore, seeing her father at Crownsville, and attending his funeral are in Murray, *Pauli Murray*, 50–57, 39–45.

3. Murray proudly identified as "Negro" throughout her life, even after the term "Negro" fell out of favor. For a contemporary readership, however, Negro seems jarring. I have primarily used the term "Black" as a compromise because Murray's main objection to "black" was that it lacked the dignity of a proper noun—an approach suggested by Caldbeck, "Religious Life," 22.

4. Height, "'We Wanted the Voice,'" 89–90; Murray, "Negro Woman in the Quest for Equality," November 14, 1963, B84, F1459, Pauli Murray Papers, the Arthur and Elizabeth Schlesinger Library, Radcliffe Institute for Advanced Study, Harvard University, Cambridge, Mass. (hereafter cited as PMP).

5. For a sample of Murray literature, see Azaransky, "Jane Crow"; Cooper, *Beyond Respectability*; Drury, "Boy-Girl"; Drury, "Love, Ambition"; Gilmore, *Defying Dixie*; Mack, *Representing the Race*; Mayeri, *Reasoning from Race*; Peppard, "Poetry, Ethics, and the Legacy."

6. Azaransky, *Dream Is Freedom*; Bell-Scott, *Firebrand*.

7. Rosenberg, *Jane Crow*, 9–30, 167–72.

8. Murray, *Pauli Murray*, 153.

9. Murray to Rodell, August 5, 1970, B99, F1777, PMP.

10. Ware to Murray, August 15, 1971; Murray to Ware, August 19, 1971, B106, F1898, PMP.

CHAPTER 1

1. Birth certificate; baptism certificate; Murray to Superintendent of Schools, December 15, 1966; Murray to the Rector, December 15, 1966, B1, F1, Pauli Murray Papers, the Arthur and Elizabeth Schlesinger Library, Radcliffe Institute for Advanced Study, Harvard University, Cambridge, Mass. (hereafter cited as PMP).

2. Murray, *Pauli Murray*, 1.

3. Murray, *Pauli Murray*, 2–8.

4. Rosenberg, *Jane Crow*, 12–13.

5. Agnes Murray to Robert and Cornelia Fitzgerald, August 24–26, 1905, B10, F226, PMP; "Personal Notes," *Baltimore Afro-American*, August 26, 1905, 7.

6. Murray, *Pauli Murray*, 31.

7. Family Tree, B12, F331, PMP.

8. Murray to June Gwynn, December 10, 1955, B10, F245, PMP.

9. Murray, *Pauli Murray*, 3.

10. Agnes Murray to Dame, October 21, 1912, B10, F264, PMP.

11. Murray, *Pauli Murray*, 12.

12. Agnes Murray certificate of death, March 13, 1967, B10, F227, PMP; Murray, *Pauli Murray*, 1, 11.

13. Except where otherwise indicated, the preceding discussion of Murray's first three years is summarized from chapter 1 of her autobiography. Murray, *Pauli Murray*, 1–13.

14. Murray, *Pauli Murray*, 12.

15. Interview with Pauli Murray, Documenting the American South, http://docsouth .unc.edu/sohp/G-0044/G-0044.html, accessed October 12, 2011.

16. "Problem Child," B84, F1457, PMP.

17. Raggatt, "Multiplicity and Conflict," 16.

18. "Beginning of Proud Shoes," July 18, 1933, B76, F352, PMP.

19. Murray, *Pauli Murray*, 3.

20. Leslie Brown, *Upbuilding Black Durham*, 78, 344.

21. Rosenberg, *Jane Crow*, 13.

22. "Beginning of Proud Shoes," July 18, 1933, B76, F352, PMP; Murray, *Pauli Murray*, 14–15.

23. Murray, *Pauli Murray*, 13, 16.

24. Murray, *Pauli Murray*, 15.

25. hooks, *Where We Stand*, 21.

26. Murray, *Pauli Murray*, 15.

27. Dear Uncle Harry and Aunt Mildred, April 8, 1946, B102, F1844, PMP; Murray, *Pauli Murray*, 16; Murray, *Proud Shoes*, 251, 55.

28. Murray, *Pauli Murray*, 1, 27.

29. "Beginning of Proud Shoes," July 18, 1933, B76, F352, PMP.

30. Murray, *Pauli Murray*, 16–17.

31. Murray, *Proud Shoes*, 1–2.

32. Murray, *Pauli Murray*, 127.

33. "Autobiography of Pauline F. Dame," Summer 1944, B11, F275, PMP.

34. Murray, *Proud Shoes*, 10.

35. Interview with Pauli Murray, Documenting the American South, http://docsouth .unc.edu/sohp/G-0044/G-0044.html, accessed October 12, 2011.

36. Murray, *Pauli Murray*, 23.

37. Murray, *Pauli Murray*, 62.

38. "The Well," B77, F1366, PMP.

39. Murray, *Proud Shoes*, 7.

40. Murray, *Proud Shoes*, 13.

41. Murray, *Proud Shoes*, 14.

42. Murray, *Proud Shoes*, 20.

43. Murray, *Proud Shoes*, 48–53.

44. Murray, *Proud Shoes*, 16.

45. Murray, *Pauli Murray*, 19.

46. Murray, *Proud Shoes*, 217.

47. Murray, *Proud Shoes*, 56.

48. Murray, *Proud Shoes*, 70.

49. "Beginning of Proud Shoes," July 18, 1933, B76, F352, PMP.

50. And other memoirs. See Harris, "African American Autobiography," 181.

51. "Beginning of Proud Shoes," July 18, 1933, B76, F352, PMP.

52. "Beginning of Proud Shoes," July 18, 1933, B76, F352, PMP; Murray, *Pauli Murray*, 14–15.

53. "Beginning of Proud Shoes," July 18, 1933, B76, F352, PMP.

54. Murray to Rodell, August 5, 1970, B99, F1777, PMP.

55. "Beginning of Proud Shoes," July 18, 1933, B76, F352, PMP.

56. Murray, *Pauli Murray*, 35.

57. Murray, *Pauli Murray*, 32.

58. Murray, *Pauli Murray*, 28.

59. Murray, *Proud Shoes*, 270.

60. "The Well," B77, F1366, PMP.

61. Interview with Pauli Murray, Documenting the American South, http://docsouth .unc.edu/sohp/G-0044/G-0044.html, accessed October 12, 2011.

62. Leslie Brown, *Upbuilding Black Durham*, 12, 16.

63. Leslie Brown, *Upbuilding Black Durham*, 1–8.

64. Anderson, *Durham County*, 134.

65. "Beginning of Proud Shoes," July 18, 1933, B76, F352, PMP.

66. A pellagra epidemic occurred in the first half of the twentieth century; at its peak produced more than 250,000 cases and 7,000 deaths a year in the southern states alone. Bollet, "Politics and Pellagra"; Anderson, *Durham County*, 137; Murray, *Proud Shoes*, 252.

67. "Beginning of Proud Shoes," July 18, 1933, B76, F352, PMP.

68. Anderson, *Durham County*, 218, 190.

69. Leslie Brown, *Upbuilding Black Durham*, 14.

70. Murray, *Pauli Murray*, 267.

71. Gaines, *Uplifting the Race*, 14; Frazier, *Black Bourgeoisie*, 20; Wilder and Cain, "Teaching and Learning," 577–78.

72. Frazier, *Black Bourgeoisie*, 26.

73. Gaines, *Uplifting the Race*, 3.

74. Murray, *Pauli Murray*, 30.

75. Murray, *Pauli Murray*, 23–24.

76. Murray, *Pauli Murray*, 61.

77. https://paulimurrayproject.org/ https://paulimurrayproject.org/becoming-involved, accessed September 24, 2019.

78. Murray, *Pauli Murray*, 19.

79. Anderson, *Durham County*, 137.

80. Murray, *Proud Shoes*, 26–27.

81. Interview with Pauli Murray, Documenting the American South, http://docsouth .unc.edu/sohp/G-0044/G-0044.html.

82. O'Dell, *Sites of Southern Memory*, 1; Anderson, *Durham County*, 512.

83. Murray, *Proud Shoes*, 27.

84. Murray, *Proud Shoes*, 25–29.

85. Murray, *Proud Shoes*, 27.

86. Murray, *Proud Shoes*, 30; "Auntie," September 10, 1944, B77, F1366, PMP.

87. Wilder and Cain, "Teaching and Learning," 577–78.

88. Murray, *Pauli Murray*, 30.

89. Murray, *Pauli Murray*, 108–9.

90. Fairclough, *Class of Their Own*, 137.

91. Murray, *Pauli Murray*, 302.

92. Murray, *Proud Shoes*, 6.

93. Murray, *Proud Shoes*, 244.

94. Murray, *Pauli Murray*, 17–18.

95. Leslie Brown, *Upbuilding Black Durham*, 150.

96. Murray, *Proud Shoes*, 269.

97. Fairclough, *Class of Their Own*, 48, emphasis in original.

98. Interview with Pauli Murray, Documenting the American South, http://docsouth .unc.edu/sohp/G-0044/G-0044.html, accessed October 12, 2011.

99. Murray, *Proud Shoes*, 271.

100. Murray, *Proud Shoes*, 271; Frazier, *Black Bourgeoisie*, 227.

101. Murray, *Pauli Murray*, 25–27.

102. Murray, *Proud Shoes*, 263.

103. Interview with Pauli Murray, Documenting the American South, http://docsouth .unc.edu/sohp/G-0044/G-0044.html, accessed October 12, 2011.

104. Murray, *Pauli Murray*, 32–34.

105. Interview with Pauli Murray, Documenting the American South, http://docsouth .unc.edu/sohp/G-0044/G-0044.html, accessed October 12, 2011.

106. Murray, *Pauli Murray*, 32–34.

107. Murray, *Pauli Murray*, 40–42.

108. Interview with Pauli Murray, Documenting the American South, http://docsouth .unc.edu/sohp/G-0044/G-0044.html, accessed October 12, 2011.

109. Murray, *Pauli Murray*, 39.

110. Autobiography draft, B81, F1426, PMP.

111. Murray, "Problem Child," B84, F1457, PMP.

112. Autobiography draft, B81, F1426, PMP.

113. Murray, *Pauli Murray*, 39.

114. Murray, *Pauli Murray*, 4.

115. Murray, *Pauli Murray*, 41.

116. Murray, *Pauli Murray*, 42–43.

117. Autobiography draft, B81, F1426, PMP.

118. The published autobiography only attributes these traits to her former husband. Autobiography draft, B81, F1426, PMP; Murray, *Pauli Murray*, 3.

119. Murray, *Pauli Murray*, 94.

120. Murray, *Pauli Murray*, 41.

121. Phillips, "If You Ask Me," *Baltimore Afro-American*, March 5, 1955, 8.

122. Murray to Gwynn, December 10, 1955, B10, F245, PMP.

123. Pauli discussed it with her older sister Mildred at some point. Mildred—who would have been seven at the time—remembered being on the way out the door to school with her sibling Willie and their father when they heard their mother fall upstairs, which prompted their father to rush upstairs. "Mil's memory of her mother," undated, B76, F1352, PMP.

124. Murray, *Pauli Murray*, 12–13.

125. Tom Marquardt, "Tragic Chapter of Crownsville State Hospital's Legacy," *Capital Gazette*, June 5, 2013.

126. Marquardt, "Tragic Chapter of Crownsville State Hospital's Legacy"; Jackson, "Separate and Unequal."

127. "Crazy Guards," *Baltimore Afro-American*, September 28, 1923, A8.

128. De Vise, "Studying a Relic," *Washington Post*, August 12, 2005.

129. Skloot, *Immortal Life of Henrietta Lacks*, 275–76.

130. "Dear Miss Murray," September 22, 1954, B10, F231, PMP.

131. "Mil's memory of her mother," undated, B76, F1352, PMP.

132. Meng to Murray, September 22, 1954, B10, F231, PMP.

133. Murray, *Pauli Murray*, 43.

134. Murray, *Pauli Murray*, 43–45.

135. Murray, *Pauli Murray*, 45, 37–38.

136. Murray, *Proud Shoes*, 272–73.

137. Murray, *Proud Shoes*, 8.

138. Murray, *Proud Shoes*, 272–76.

139. Murray, *Proud Shoes*, 274.

140. Murray, *Pauli Murray*, 47.

141. Murray, *Proud Shoes*, 17, 20.

142. Superior Court, "Letters of Adoption," September 12, 1919, B10, F249, PMP.

143. Murray, *Pauli Murray*, 48.

144. Murray, *Pauli Murray*, 22–23; "What Is Africa to Me?," December 1960, B85, F1480, PMP.

145. "Auntie," September 10, 1944, B77, F1366, PMP.

146. Murray, *Pauli Murray*, 22.

147. "Beginning of Proud Shoes," July 18, 1933, B76, F352, PMP.

148. Murray, *Pauli Murray*, 49–50.

149. Murray, *Pauli Murray*, 51–53.

150. "Killing Insane Principal," *Baltimore Afro-American*, June 22, 1923, 1; "Crazy Guards," *Baltimore Afro-American*, September 28, 1923, 1.

151. "Crazy Guards," *Baltimore Afro-American*, September 28, 1923, 1; "Killing Insane Principal," *Baltimore Afro-American*, June 22, 1923, 1; Murray, *Pauli Murray*, 56–57.

152. Murray, *Pauli Murray*, 57–58.

153. Murray, *Pauli Murray*, 62.

154. Murray, *Proud Shoes*, 33.

155. Murray, *Proud Shoes*, 251.

156. Murray, *Pauli Murray*, 62.

157. Leslie Brown, *Upbuilding Black Durham*, 14, 252; Fairclough, *Class of Their Own*, 171, 43.

158. Mack, *Representing the Race*, 209.

159. Murray, *Pauli Murray*, 60.

160. Murray, *Pauli Murray*, 61.

161. Rosenberg, *Jane Crow*, 30.

162. Interview with Pauli Murray, Documenting the American South, http://docsouth .unc.edu/sohp/G-0044/G-0044.html, accessed October 12, 2011; Murray, *Pauli Murray*, 64.

163. Murray to Dame and Cornelia Fitzgerald, June 24, 1921, B10, F252, PMP.

164. Murray, *Pauli Murray*, 65.

165. Murray, *Pauli Murray*, 2–3.

166. Murray, *Pauli Murray*, 70.

167. Murray, *Proud Shoes*, 271.

CHAPTER 2

1. Arnesen, *Black Protest*, 1.

2. Gallagher, *Black Women*, 15.

3. Murray, *Pauli Murray*, 65.

4. Murray, *Pauli Murray*, 67.

5. Murray, *Pauli Murray*, 66–68.

6. Murray, *Pauli Murray*, 69.

7. Murray, *Pauli Murray*, 66, 69.

8. Murray, *Pauli Murray*, 67–69.

9. Interview with Dr., Tuesday morning, December 16, 1937, B4, F71, Pauli Murray Papers, the Arthur and Elizabeth Schlesinger Library, Radcliffe Institute for Advanced Study, Harvard University, Cambridge, Mass. (hereafter cited as PMP); Rosenberg, *Jane Crow*, 57; Murray, *Pauli Murray*, 68–70; undated notes, B76, F1352, PMP.

10. Murray, *Pauli Murray*, 70.

11. FBI, "Subject File"; Leslie Brown, *Upbuilding Black Durham*, 14.

12. Murray, *Pauli Murray*, 67, 71.

13. Murray, *Pauli Murray*, 88; Faderman, *Odd Girls*, 19; Ware, *Holding Their Own*, 57.

14. Murray, *Pauli Murray*, 71–73.

15. Ware, *Holding Their Own*, 64.

16. Gibson, "Masculine Degenerate," 89.

17. Leslie Taylor, "'I Made Up My Mind,'" 250–86; Kennedy and Davis, *Boots of Leather*, 34.

18. Rosenberg, *Jane Crow*, 35.

19. Murray, *Pauli Murray*, 74–75.

20. Chauncey, *Gay New York*, 155–58.

21. Summary of symptoms, March 8, 1940, B4, F71, PMP.

22. Faderman, *Odd Girls*, 32, 74–75.

23. Murray, *Pauli Murray*, 74, 84.

24. Murray, *Pauli Murray*, 74, 23.

25. Wehnert, *Passing*, 5.

26. Hedgeman to Murray, November 17, 1983, B96, F1703, PMP.

27. Gates, "Trope of a New Negro," 136, 148.

28. Murray, *Pauli Murray*, 72, 131.

29. Murray, "Working Student," *Hunter College Echo*, December 1932, B83, F1449, PMP.

30. Murray, "Working Student"; Murray, *Pauli Murray*, 76.

31. Chauncey, *Gay New York*, 254; Drury, "Experimentation," 135.

32. Rosenberg, *Jane Crow*, 38; Murray, *Pauli Murray*, 73.

33. Murray, *Pauli Murray*, 76–77.

34. Autobiography draft, B81, F1429, PMP.

35. Interview with Dr., Tuesday morning, December 16, 1937, B4, F71, PMP.

36. Murray to Burgess, March 9, 1973, B95, F1667, PMP.

37. Murray, *Pauli Murray*, 77.

38. Rothschild to Murray, April 24, 1948, B28, F553, PMP.

39. D'Emilio and Freedman, *Intimate Matters*, 227.

40. Murray, *Pauli Murray*, 77; Drury, "'Experimentation,'" 66.

41. See Devor, *FTM*, 468–71; Garber, *Vested Interests*, 14; Cavanagh, *Queering Bathrooms*, 1–2; Halberstam, *Female Masculinity*, 20–22.

42. Rosenberg, *Jane Crow*, 39; Drury, "'Experimentation,'" 66; Azaransky, *Dream Is Freedom*, 11; Bull to Murray, March 20, 1931, B4, F84, PMP.

43. Bull to Murray, March 20, 1931, B4, F84, PMP; Drury, "'Experimentation,'" 66.

44. Murray, *Pauli Murray*, 77; Faderman, *Odd Girls*, 63.

45. Autobiography draft, B81, F1429, PMP.

46. Murray, *Pauli Murray*, 78.

47. Klarman, "Scottsboro," 379-81.

48. Murray, *Pauli Murray*, 78–81.

49. Murray, *Pauli Murray*, 79.

50. Cresswell, "Embodiment, Power," 186.

51. Cunard, *Negro*.

52. Murray to Holmes, March 18, 1973, B96, F1688, PMP.

53. Cunard to Murray, January 15, 1934, B4, F84, PMP.

54. Murray, "Three Thousand Miles," in Cunard, *Negro*, 68; Drury, "'Experimentation,'" 75–76.

55. Cunard to Murray, January 15, 1934, B4, F84, PMP; Drury, "'Experimentation,'" 72.

56. Murray, *Pauli Murray*, 83–84.

57. Autobiography draft, B81, F1429, PMP; FBI, "Subject File."

58. Murray, *Pauli Murray*, 90.

59. Murray, *Pauli Murray*, 89.

60. Autobiography draft, B81, F1429, PMP.

61. Murray, *Pauli Murray*, 89.

62. Gilmore, *Defying Dixie*, 136, 148.

63. Murray, *Pauli Murray*, 85–87, 92; Murray, "Working Student," *Hunter College Echo*, December 1932, B83, F1449, PMP.

64. FBI, "Subject File."

65. Poole, *Segregated Origins*, 18.

66. Murray, *Pauli Murray*, 76.

67. Murray, *Pauli Murray*, 75–76, 83; Azaransky, *Dream Is Freedom*, 14; Whitaker, "Restaurateurs," August 11, 2008, http://restaurant-ingthroughhistory.com/2008/08/11/restaurateurs-alice-foote-macdougall/.

68. FBI, "Subject File."

69. "Contradictions," June 6, 1938, B83, F1451, PMP.

70. "Beginning of Proud Shoes," July 18, 1933, B76, F352, PMP; Murray, *Pauli Murray*, 93–94; Rosenberg, *Jane Crow*, 47.

71. Murray, *Pauli Murray*, 94–95.

72. Application for admission, May 7, 1948, B28, F554, PMP.

73. Murray, *Pauli Murray*, 95.

74. Interview with Dr., Tuesday morning, December 16, 1937, B4, F71, PMP.

75. Murray, *Pauli Murray*, 96.

76. See Kornbluh, *New Deal*, 79.

77. Murray, *Pauli Murray*, 95.

78. Kornbluh, *New Deal*, 88–89.

79. Murray, *Pauli Murray*, 96.

80. Drury, "'Experimentation,'" 91.

81. "TERA Times," Christmas 1934, B83, F1448, PMP.

82. Murray, *Pauli Murray*, 96.

83. Murray, *Pauli Murray*, 97.

84. Drury, "'Experimentation,'" 88.

85. Murray, *Pauli Murray*, 98; Ware, *Holding Their Own*, 33–34.

86. Diary, April 27, 1935, B1, F25, PMP.

87. Diary, April 28, 1935, B1, F25, PMP.

88. Diary, May 7, 1935, B1, F25, PMP.

89. Diary, April 27 to May 23, 1935, B1, F25, PMP; interview with Dr., Tuesday morning, December 16, 1937, B4, F71, PMP.

90. Murray to Dame, June 4, 1943, B10, F253, PMP.

91. Murray to Bellevue, May 5, 1948, B28, F554, PMP.

92. "Contradictions," June 6, 1938, B83, F1451, PMP.

93. Interview with Dr., Tuesday morning, December 16, 1937, B4, F71, PMP.

94. Murray to Meng, February 23, 1955, B10, F240, PMP; Murray to Holmes, February 21, 1977, B96, F1688, PMP.

95. Drescher, "Out of DSM."

96. Dowbiggin, *Keeping America Sane*, 32; Lombardo, *Century of Eugenics*, ix.

97. Murray to Meng, February 23, 1955, B10, F240, PMP.

98. Murray to Holmes, February 21, 1977, B96, F1688, PMP.

99. Murray, *Pauli Murray*, 89.

100. Murray, *Pauli Murray*, 99.

101. Jason Scott Smith, *Building New Deal Liberalism*, 87.

102. Memorandum, July 13, 1942, B4, F71, PMP.

103. Rosenberg, *Jane Crow*, 52; Sketch, 1935, B83, F1451, PMP.

104. FBI, "Subject File."

105. Murray, *Pauli Murray*, 100–101.

106. Murray, *Pauli Murray*, 98–101.

107. FBI, "Subject File."

108. Altenbaugh, "Children," 400.

109. Altenbaugh, "Children," 397; Murray, *Pauli Murray*, 93.

110. Murray, *Pauli Murray*, 105–6.

111. Altenbaugh, "Children," 397–406.

112. Fine, *Sit-Down*; Shogun, "Labor Strikes Back," 40.

113. Murray, *Pauli Murray*, 106.

114. Rosenberg, *Jane Crow*, 136.

115. Gilmore, *Defying Dixie*, 254; Altenbaugh, "Children," 400.

116. Alexander, *The Right Opposition*, 7.

117. Murray, *Pauli Murray*, 103.

118. Application, May 7, 1948, B84, F1463, PMP; FBI, "Subject File."

119. FBI, "Subject File."

120. Kornbluh, *New Deal*, 98–99.

121. Murray, *Pauli Murray*, 104.

122. Drury, "'Experimentation,'" 96; Drury, "Boy-Girl," 146–47.

123. Faderman, *Odd Girls*, 99–105.

124. Terry, *American Obsession*, 271–76.

125. Long Island Rest Home notes, December 14, 16, 17, 1937, B4, F71, PMP.

126. Interview with Dr., Tuesday morning, December 16, 1937, B4, F71, PMP.

127. Rosenberg, *Jane Crow*, 50.

128. Drury, "'Experimentation,'" 146–49.

129. Drury, "'Experimentation,'" chap. 3; O'Dell, *Sites of Southern Memory*, 146–48; Ordover, *American Eugenics*, 107–8; Mack, *Representing the Race*, 215; Rosenberg, *Jane Crow*, 59.

130. Murray to Doctors, December 17, 1937, B4, F71, PMP.

131. Summary of symptoms, March 8, 1940, B4, F71, PMP. For discussion of the social construction of "male" and "female" hormones, see Fausto-Sterling, *Sexing the Body*, chap. 6.

132. Rosenberg, *Jane Crow*, 63; Ella Baker, Harlem Advisory Committee, December 12, 1938, B72, F1236, PMP; Class Report, October 1939, B72, F1239, PMP; Organization and Courses, B72, F1236, PMP.

133. Murray to Holmes, September 1938, B83, F1451, PMP.

134. Murray to Thomas, January 26, 1939, B102, F1836, PMP.

135. Friess, "Review: War without Violence," 247.

136. Slate, *Colored Cosmopolitanism*, 206–7; Murray to Shulman, April 18, 1967, B72, F1246, PMP; Murray, *Pauli Murray*, 58.

137. Gilmore, "Admitting Pauli Murray," 62.

138. Murray, *Pauli Murray*, 108.

139. FBI, "Subject File."

140. Gilmore, *Defying Dixie*, 260–61.

141. Gilmore, *Defying Dixie*, 264; Gilmore, "How Anne Scott and Pauli Murray," 150; Murray, *Pauli Murray*, 115; Murray to Shepard, December 6, 1938, B15, F380, PMP.

142. Murray to Shepard, December 6, 1938, B15, F380, PMP; Gilmore, *Defying Dixie*, 265–66.

143. Bell-Scott, *Firebrand*, 26–29.

144. Gilmore, *Defying Dixie*, 266.

145. Bell-Scott, *Firebrand*, 30.

146. Murray, *Pauli Murray*, 115.

147. Murray, *Pauli Murray*, 125.

148. Murray to Graham, December 17, 1938, B15, F380, PMP.

149. Gilmore, "Admitting Pauli Murray," 63; Murray to Graham, December 17, 1938, B15, F380, PMP.

150. Murray to "Lisha," December 17, 1938, B15, F380, PMP; Gilmore, *Defying Dixie*, 267–68.

151. Gilmore, *Defying Dixie*, 268.

152. "Colored Tries," January 6, 1939, *Daily News*, B15, F382, PMP.

153. Clipping, January 5, 1939, B15, F382, PMP.

154. "Negress Applies," January 6, 1939, *Durham Morning Herald*, B15, F382, PMP.

155. "Grinding Slowly," January 12, 1939, *Daily Tar Heel*, B15, F380, PMP.

156. "Negress Applies," January 6, 1939, *Durham Morning Herald*, B15, F382, PMP.

157. Glenn Hutchinson, "Jim Crow Challenged in Southern Universities," *Crisis* 46, no. 4 (1939): 104.

158. Murray to Greedy, March 6, 1939, B15, F381, PMP.

159. Hutchinson, "Jim Crow Challenged," 104.

160. "Only One Negro," *Durham Morning Herald*, January 10, 1939, B15, F382, PMP.

161. Murray, *Pauli Murray*, 119.

162. Gilmore, *Defying Dixie*, 285–86.

163. Dame to Murray, December 17, 1938, B10, F257, PMP.

164. Summary of symptoms, March 8, 1940, B4, F71, PMP.

165. Dame to Murray, January 6, 1939, B15, F380, PMP.

166. Murray, *Pauli Murray*, 120–21.

167. Murray, *Pauli Murray*, 117.

168. Murray to Austin, January 18, 1939, B15, F381, PMP; *Amsterdam News*, February 11, 1939, B15, F383, PMP; Gilmore, *Defying Dixie*, 280.

169. Berg, "Black Civil Rights," 88, 93.

170. Marable, *Race, Reform*, 26–32.

171. Gilmore, *Defying Dixie*, 285–86.

172. Murray, *Pauli Murray*, 126.

173. Interview with Pauli Murray, Documenting the American South, http://docsouth .unc.edu/sohp/G-0044/G-0044.html, accessed October 12, 2011.

174. Gilmore, *Defying Dixie*, 287–88; Mack, *Representing the Race*, 219; Bell-Scott, *Firebrand*, 37–39.

175. Murray to DeVane, February 22, 1939, B15, F381, PMP.

176. Murray, "Who Is to Blame," *Black Dispatch*, 1939, B15, F383, PMP.

177. Murray, *Pauli Murray*, 126–27.

178. "The Raw Stuff of Democracy," 1940, B83, F1453, PMP; Murray, *Pauli Murray*, 108, 130–32.

179. Harold Garfinkel, "Color Trouble," 144.

180. Notes, November 28, 1939, B83, F1451, PMP.

181. Murray to Dame and Small, October 6, 1939, B10, F252, PMP.

182. Murray to Dame and Small, August 13 and 28, 1939, B10, F252, PMP.

183. Murray to Dame, August 28, 1939, B10, F252, PMP; Murray to McBean, August 22, 1939, B83, F1451, PMP.

184. FBI, "Subject File."

185. Murray to Thyra, September 28, 1939, B72, F1244, PMP.

186. Rosenberg, *Jane Crow*, 79.

187. Murray to Dame and Small, September 11, 1939, B10, F252, PMP.

188. Murray, *Pauli Murray*, 57.

189. Murray to William Murray, October 9, 1939, B10, F238, PMP.

190. Murray to Wong, October 9, 1939, B10, F240, PMP.

191. Murray to Dame and Small, September 11 and 28, 1939, B10, F252, PMP.

192. Murray to Dame and Small, November 11, 1939, B10, F252, PMP.

193. "Pill 'Planted,'" *New York World-Telegram*, November 11, 1939, B4, F71, PMP.

194. "To the Editor," November 9, 1939, B4, F71, PMP.

195. Fausto-Sterling, *Sexing the Body*, 170.

196. Summary of symptoms, March 8, 1940, B4, F71, PMP.

197. To the Editor, December 6, 1939, B102, F1836, PMP; Murray to Eleanor Roosevelt, December 6, 1939, B99, F1779, PMP.

198. Murray to Pauline Dame, January 10, 1940, B10, F253, PMP.

199. Murray, *Pauli Murray*, 134–35.

200. Murray to Agnes, undated, B72, F1251, PMP.

201. Bell-Scott, *Firebrand*, 52.

202. Murray, *Pauli Murray*, 135.

203. Bell-Scott, *Firebrand*, 153–54; Murray, *Pauli Murray*, 136–37.

204. Murray to Pauline Dame, January 10, 1940, B10, F253, PMP.

205. Summary of symptoms, March 8, 1940, B4, F71, PMP.

206. Murray, *Pauli Murray*, 137.

207. Natalie Gordon, "Gracious Ladies," *Boston Traveler*, November 7, 1945, B96, F1688, PMP; Rosenberg, *Jane Crow*, 80. Provincetown also had an emerging gay scene; see Krahulik, *Provincetown*.

208. FBI, "Subject File."

209. Drury, "'Experimentation,'" 209.

210. Murray to Agnes, undated, B72, F1251, PMP.

211. Summary of symptoms, March 8, 1940, B4, F71, PMP.

212. Murray to Rogers, March 8, 1940, B4, F71, PMP.

213. Bell-Scott, *Firebrand*, 57–58; Murray to Roosevelt, March 15, 1940, B4, F85, PMP.

214. Murray to Rogers, March 11, 1940, B4, F71, PMP.

215. Murray, *Pauli Murray*, 109.

216. Diary, March 26, 1940, B84, F1861, PMP.

217. Murray to Trailways, April 17, 1939; Trailways to Murray, April 26, 1939, B102, F1836, PMP.

218. Murray, *Pauli Murray*, 138; diary, March 26, 1940, B84, F1861, PMP.

219. Murray to Dame, June 2, 1943, B10, F253, PMP.

220. Murray to Rogers, March 11, 1940, B4, F71, PMP.

221. Murray, *Proud Shoes*, 113.

222. Murray, *Pauli Murray*, 141.

223. Murray, *Pauli Murray*, 142.

224. Notebook, March 25, 1940, B4, F85, PMP; Gilmore, *Defying Dixie*, 319.

225. Notebook, March 25, 1940, B4, F85, PMP.

226. Murray to Jean and Pan, April 9, 1940, B4, F87, PMP; Murray, *Pauli Murray*, 145.

227. Gilmore, *Defying Dixie*, 317; Western Union, March 23, 1940, B4, F85, PMP.

228. Bell-Scott, *Firebrand*, 66.

229. Rosenberg, *Jane Crow*, 88.

230. Murray to Robinson, March 24, 1940, B4, F85, PMP.

231. Murray to Clendenin, March 29, 1940, B4, F86, PMP.

232. Murray to Cooley, April 2, 1940, B4, F86, PMP.

233. Valentine and Cooley to Murray and McBean, April 8, 1940, B4, F85, PMP.

234. Murray to Dame, April 25, 1940, B10, F253, PMP.

235. Murray, *Pauli Murray*, 149.

236. Murray to Dame, May 17, 1940, B4, F88, PMP.

237. Murray to Milgram, May 14, 1940, B4, F88, PMP; telegram, May 16, 1940, B4, F85, PMP.

238. Murray to Dame, April 25, 1940, B10, F1253, PMP.

239. Murray to Dame, April 25, 1940, B10, F1253, PMP; Murray to Dame, May 17, 1940, B4, F88, PMP.

240. Rosenberg, *Jane Crow*, 90–91.

241. Murray, *Pauli Murray*, 149.

242. Gilmore, *Defying Dixie*, 322–25.

243. Murray, *Pauli Murray*, 93, 147.

244. Harold Garfinkel, "Color Trouble," 144.

245. Harold Garfinkel, "Color Trouble," 144–45.

246. Harold Garfinkel, "Color Trouble," 149.

247. Dickens, *Oliver Twist*.

248. Harold Garfinkel, "Color Trouble," 150.

249. Dame to Murray, August 10, 1940, B10, F257, PMP.

250. Murray to Valentine and Cooley, undated, B4, F88, PMP.

251. Harold Garfinkel, "Color Trouble."

252. Bell-Scott, *Firebrand*, 65.

253. Harold Garfinkel, *Studies in Ethnomethodology*, 13.

254. Doubt, "Garfinkel before Ethnomethodology."

255. Gilmore, *Defying Dixie*, 536.

256. Weber, "Harold Garfinkel."

CHAPTER 3

1. Sherman, *Case of Odell Waller*, 17–19.

2. Notes 1940, B83, F1452, Pauli Murray Papers, the Arthur and Elizabeth Schlesinger Library, Radcliffe Institute for Advanced Study, Harvard University, Cambridge, Mass. (hereafter cited as PMP).

3. *All for Mr. Davis*, 15, B72, F1250, PMP.

4. Sherman, *Case of Odell Waller*, 3.

5. Sherman, *Case of Odell Waller*, 19–20.

6. *All for Mr. Davis*, 15, B72, F1250, PMP.

7. Sherman, *Case of Odell Waller*, 19–20.

8. Sherman, *Case of Odell Waller*, 17.

9. Notes 1940, B83, F1452, PMP; Murray, *Pauli Murray*, 152.

10. Murray, *Pauli Murray*, 152.

11. Notes 1940, B83, F1452, PMP.

12. Murray, *Pauli Murray*, 152.

13. Notes 1940, B83, F1452, PMP.

14. Notes 1940, B83, F1452, PMP; Murray, *Pauli Murray*, 157.

15. Murray, *Pauli Murray*, 162–63; Murray to WDL, November 12, 1940, B72, F1253, PMP; diary, January 9, 1941, B1, F26, PMP.

16. Murray to Milgram, April 29, 1940, B4, F85, PMP.

17. Notes 1940, B83, F1452, PMP; Murray, *Pauli Murray*, 160.

18. Murray, *Pauli Murray*, 161–62.

19. Murray, *Pauli Murray*, 163–64.

20. Sherman, *Case of Odell Waller*, 40.

21. Murray, *Pauli Murray*, 162–63.

22. Sherman, *Case of Odell Waller*, 41–42.

23. Stack, "John Dewey."

24. Sherman, *Case of Odell Waller*, 42–43.

25. Murray, *Pauli Murray*, 166.

26. Murray to Shulman, April 18, 1967, B72, F1246, PMP.

27. Diary, January 6, 1941, B1, F26, PMP; Slate, *Colored Cosmopolitanism*, 209–10.

28. FBI, "Subject File."

29. Sherman, *Case of Odell Waller*, 44–46.

30. Sherman, *Case of Odell Waller*, 43–44.

31. Murray, *Pauli Murray*, 165,

32. Sherman, *Case of Odell Waller*, 56.

33. Sherman, *Case of Odell Waller*, 56–57.

34. Murray, *Pauli Murray*, 167.

35. Sherman, *Case of Odell Waller*, 57–58.

36. Sherman, *Case of Odell Waller*, 16–17.

37. Murray and Kempton, *All for Mr. Davis*, B15, F41, PMP; Sherman, *Case of Odell Waller*, 52–53; Brewer, "Poll Tax," 268, 76–79; Newman, *Civil Rights Movement*, 40–41.

38. Sherman, *Case of Odell Waller*, 67–69.

39. "Night and Day," *Daily News*, March 24, 1941; "Sharecropping," *Baltimore Afro-American*, June 1, 1941; "Mother of Sharecropper," *Louisville Courier-Journal*, May 30, 1941, all in B72, F1256, PMP.

40. Murray, *Pauli Murray*, 168.

41. Waller notes, May 9, 1941, B84, F1462, PMP, emphasis in the original.

42. Unknown to Murray, January 8, 1941, B4, F71, PMP. For the use of "this life" in gay culture, see Chauncey, *Gay New York*, 15.

43. Diary, February 15, 1941, B1, F26, PMP.

44. Waller notes, May 7, 1941, B84, F1462, PMP.

45. Murray to McCall, June 16, 1941, B83, F1453, PMP.

46. Diary, July 8, 1941, B1, F26, PMP.

47. Murray, *Pauli Murray*, 177–78.

48. See "The Ice-House," "Leaving Home," "The Clinic," and "Auntie," July–August 1941, B83, F1453, PMP.

49. Murray, *Pauli Murray*, 179–80.

50. Bertram, "Making a Gay Identity," 151; Raggatt, "Multiplicity and Conflict," 16; Barresi, "The Identities of Malcolm X," 203; Caruth, "Recapturing the Past: Introduction," 152.

51. Murray, *Pauli Murray*, 181.

52. Murray to McCall, August 11, 1941, B83, F1454, PMP.

53. Murray to McCall, August 11, 1941, B83, F1454, PMP.

54. "Leaving Home," August 29, 1941, B83, F1454, PMP.

55. Murray to Mildred, August 25, 1941, B10, F238, PMP.

56. Crownsville to Murray, September 22, 1954, B10, F231, PMP.

57. Murray to Mildred, August 25, 1941, B10, F238, PMP.

58. Murray to Holmes, February 21, 1977, B96, F1688, PMP.

59. Murray to Mildred, August 25, 1941, B10, F238, PMP.

60. Drury, "'Experimentation,'" 246.

61. Murray, *Pauli Murray*, 5.

62. Hunter, "Howard University," 55; Murray, *Pauli Murray*, 200.

63. Murray, *Pauli Murray*, 183–84.

64. Murray to Dobbins, November 7, 1941, B102, F1838, PMP.

65. Murray, *Pauli Murray*, 183.

66. Murray, *Pauli Murray*, 183.

67. To the Editor, October 1, 1942, B87, F1810, PMP; Murray, "Negro Youth's Dilemma," *Threshold*, B84, F1458, PMP; Murray, *Pauli Murray*, 187–88.

68. Herbert Garfinkel, *When Negroes March*, 89.

69. Murray, *Pauli Murray*, 172.

70. Murray, *Pauli Murray*, 173–74.

71. Murray, *Pauli Murray*, 174; Sherman, *Case of Odell Waller*, 173.

72. Richards, *Conversations with Maida Springer*, 124, emphasis in original.

73. Memorandum, July 13, 1942, B4, F71, PMP.

74. Hamilton to Murray, July 16, 1943, B102, F1839, PMP.

75. Murray to Randolph, July 24, 1942, B72, F1265, PMP; Herbert Garfinkel, *When Negroes March*, 100.

76. Herbert Garfinkel, *When Negroes March*, 100.

77. Herbert Garfinkel, *When Negroes March*, 102.

78. Murray, *Pauli Murray*, 176.

79. Herbert Garfinkel, *When Negroes March*, 100; W. E. B. Du Bois, "Crow Flies," *Amsterdam News*, August 29, 1942, B72, F1257, PMP; Murray to Randolph, July 24, 1942, B72, F1265, PMP.

80. Murray, *Pauli Murray*, 128, 149, 228.

81. Jacquelyn Dowd Hall, "Long Civil Rights Movement."

82. Sherman, *Case of Odell Waller*, 177.

83. Murray, *Pauli Murray*, 189–95.

84. Murray to Eidelsberg, July 13, 1942, B4, F71, PMP.

85. Memorandum, July 13, 1942, B4, F71, PMP.

86. Eidelsberg to Murray, July 22, 1942, B4, F71, PMP.

87. Murray to Fox, July 25, 1942, B4, F71, PMP.

88. Fox to Murray, July 31, 1942, B4, F71, PMP.

89. Murray to Farmer, August 12, 1942, B102, F1839, PMP.

90. Randolph to Winters, July 31, 1942, B4, F73, PMP.

91. Hunter, "Howard University," 62.

92. Drury, "'Experimentation,'" 264.

93. Murray, *Pauli Murray*, 201.

94. Drury, "'Experimentation,'" 262; Azaransky, *Dream Is Freedom*, 27–28; Murray and Babcock, "Alternative Weapon."

95. Dominy, "Reviewing the South," 29; Murray and Babcock, "Alternative Weapon," 54.

96. Rosenberg, *Jane Crow*, 125.

97. Murray, "Blueprint," B84, F1457, PMP.

98. Murray, *Pauli Murray*, 205.

99. Murray, "Blueprint," B84, F1457, PMP.

100. Murray, *Pauli Murray*, 208.

101. Murray, "Blueprint," B84, F1457, PMP; "Howard Students Picket," *Chicago Defender*, April 24, 1943.

102. Murray, *Pauli Murray*, 208.

103. Dalfiume, "'Forgotten Years,'" 106.

104. Murray, *Pauli Murray*, 208–9.

105. Gilmore, "Am I a 'Screwball,'" 277.

106. Beside notes, May 13, 1943, B4, F71, PMP.

107. Murray to Ethel, June 29, 1943, B83, F1455, PMP; Murray to Overholt, June 9, 1943, B98, F1762, PMP.

108. "Should Negro Graduates Go South?," *Chronicle*, June 24, 1944, B72, F1262, PMP; Murray to Dame, June 2, 1943, B10, F253, PMP.

109. Rosenberg, *Jane Crow*, 127.

110. Bell-Scott, *Firebrand*, 118–19; Murray, *Pauli Murray*, 195–97.

111. Murray, *Pauli Murray*, 198–99.

112. Murray to Dame, June 2, 1943, B10, F253, PMP.

113. Drury, "'Experimentation,'" 256.

114. Murray to Dame, June 2, 1943, B10, F253, PMP.

115. Murray to Dame, June 2, 1943, B10, F253, PMP.

116. Murray to Dame, June 4, 1943, B10, F253, PMP.

117. Odum, *Race and Rumors*.

118. Murray, *Pauli Murray*, 211.

119. Murray to Ethel, June 29, 1943, B83, F1455, PMP.

120. Tyor, "Memorial: Julian M. Ruffin," http://europepmc.org/articles/PMC2279491/pdf/tacca00097-0076.pdf.

121. Odum, *Race and Rumors*.

122. Murray, *Pauli Murray*, 210–11; memorandum, July 13, 1942, B4, F71, PMP.

123. Sitkoff, "Racial Militancy," 670.

124. Sitkoff, "Racial Militancy," 661–63.

125. Murray, "Negroes Are Fed Up," 274–76.

126. Murray, *Pauli Murray*, 212; Murray, "And the Riots Came."

127. Murray, *Pauli Murray*, 214

128. Gilmore, *Defying Dixie*, 372–73.

129. Murray, *Pauli Murray*, 212.

130. Murray, "Mr. Roosevelt Regrets," *Crisis* 50 (1943): 252.

131. Murray, *Dark Testament*.

132. Murray to Ware, 1943, B102, F1840, PMP.

133. Murray, *Pauli Murray*, 217–18.

134. Rosenberg, *Jane Crow*, 147–50; Mack, *Representing the Race*, 230–32.

135. Firor Scott, *Pauli Murray and Caroline Ware*, 33.

136. Murray, "Blueprint," B84, F1457, PMP.

137. Murray, "Blueprint," B84, F1457, PMP.

138. Murray, *Pauli Murray*, 226.

139. Sitkoff, "Racial Militancy"; Finkle, "Conservative Aims."

140. Murray, *Pauli Murray*, 226.

141. Murray to Ransom, May 2, 1944, B18, F396, PMP; Murray, *Pauli Murray*, 227–28.

142. Gilmore, *Defying Dixie*, 393.

143. Murray, *Pauli Murray*, 228.

144. "Civil Rights Committee," April 25, 1944, B18, F395, PMP, underlined in original.

145. "Blueprint," B84, F1457, PMP; Murray, *Pauli Murray*, 228.

146. Murray, *Pauli Murray*, 228.

147. FBI, "Subject File"; "Student Fights," *New York Amsterdam News*, August 19, 1944, 8A.

148. McAlpin, "Mrs. F. D. R. Sends Posies," June 10, 1944, B72, F1262, PMP.

149. Murray to Roosevelt, May 4, 1944, B18, F398, PMP; Bell-Scott, *Firebrand*, 137.

150. "Should Negro Graduates Go South?," *Chronicle*, June 24, 1944, B72, F1262, PMP; "Shall I Go South?," *Baltimore Afro-American*, June 10, 1944, B72, F1262, PMP.

151. "Open Letter," May 29, 1944, B18, F396, PMP.

152. "Should Negro Graduates Go South?," *Chronicle*, June 24, 1944, B72, F1262, PMP; "From the Readers," *New York City PM*, June 25, 1944, B72, F1262, PMP.

153. "Go South, Commit Suicide," *Baltimore Afro-American*, June 24, 1944, B73, F1270, PMP.

154. Murray, *Pauli Murray*, 211.

155. Murray to Ware, July 21, 1954, B100, F1819, PMP.

156. Murray, *Pauli Murray*, 238–39.

157. Murray, *Pauli Murray*, 240; Murray to Smith, June 24, 1944, B18, F415, PMP.

158. Bell-Scott, *Firebrand*, 133.

159. Murray to Hastie, August 5, 1944, B96, F1698, PMP; Murray to Smith, June 24, 1944, B18, F415, PMP.

160. Murray to Smith, June 24, 1944, B18, F415, PMP.

161. Murray to Harvard Law, July 20, 1944, B18, F415, PMP; Murray, *Pauli Murray*, 243.

162. Murray to Smith, June 24, 1944, B18, F415, PMP.

163. Murray to Smith, June 24, 1944, B18, F415, PMP.

164. Murray, *Pauli Murray*, 240–42.

165. Murray, *Pauli Murray*, 246.

166. Murray to Mildred, June 20, 1955, B10, F245, PMP.

167. Murray, *Pauli Murray*, 247–51.

168. Murray to Mazique, July 29, 1944, B4, F73, PMP.

169. Murray, *Pauli Murray*, 249.

170. Murray, *Pauli Murray*, 252.

171. Murray to Wilkins, August 2, 1944, B98, F1752, PMP.

172. Murray, *Pauli Murray*, 251–52.

173. Murray, "Pauli Murray," *Baltimore Afro-American*, September 2, 1944, B72, F1262, PMP.

174. Murray, *Pauli Murray*, 253.

175. Murray, *Pauli Murray*, 254.

176. Murray, "Pauli Murray," *Baltimore Afro-American*, September 2, 1944, B72, F1262, PMP; Gilmore, *Defying Dixie*, 401.

177. Murray, *Pauli Murray*, 261.

178. Murray, "Right to Equal Opportunity," 389.

179. Firor Scott, *Pauli Murray and Caroline Ware*, 36.

180. Rosenberg, *Jane Crow*, 140.

181. Murray, *Pauli Murray*, 262–63.

182. Murray, *Pauli Murray*, 263.

183. Rosenberg, *Jane Crow*, 159.

184. Murray, *Pauli Murray*, 262–63.

185. Murray, *Pauli Murray*, 262.

186. Murray, "Right to Equal Opportunity."

187. Murray to Hastie, November 13, 1945, B96, F1698, PMP.

188. Rosenberg, *Jane Crow*, 160.

189. Murray to Marshall, November 4, 1945, B73, F1279, PMP; Murray, *Pauli Murray*, 268.

190. Murray to Garcia, May 23, 1947, B102, F1845, PMP.

191. Murray to Dame, May 22, 1940, B10, F253, PMP; Dame to Murray, September 11, 1939, B10, F257, PMP; Murray, *Pauli Murray*, 263.

192. Murray to Duveneck, March 4, 1946, B102, F1844, PMP.

193. Murray to Griffith, January 26, 1946, B102, F1843, PMP; Murray to Glucksman, February 8, 1946, B102, F1843, PMP.

194. Murray to Kenny, December 14, 1945, B28, F544, PMP.

195. Murray, *Pauli Murray*, 264.

196. Murray to Dame, June 12, 1946, B10, F254, PMP; "Pauli Murray Named," *Baltimore Afro-American*, January 19, 1946, 14; "Attorney General," *Baltimore Afro-American*, February 2, 1946, 15.

197. Murray to Glucksman, February 8, 1946, B102, F1843, PMP.

198. Dame to Murray, January 8, 1946, B10, F258, PMP.

199. Dame to Murray, January 13, 1946, B10, F258, PMP.

200. Murray to Kenny, April 19, 1946, B28, F544, PMP.

201. Murray to Johnson, April 8, 1946, B102, F1844, PMP.

202. Murray to Lewis Murray, January 25, 1946, B10, F244, PMP.

203. Murray to Lewis Murray, January 25, 1946, B10, F244, PMP.

204. Murray, "Progress Report," *Baltimore Afro-American*, March 9, 1946, 5.

205. Murray, "Progress Report," *Baltimore Afro-American*, March 9, 1946, 5; Murray, "We Need a Blitzkrieg," *Baltimore Afro-American*, March 16, 1946, 14; Murray, "New Western Frontiers," *Baltimore Afro-American*, March 23, 1946, 5.

206. Murray to Lewis Murray, September 26, 1944, B13, F338, PMP.

207. Diary, November 20, 1945, B1, F26, PMP.

208. Diary excerpts, 1940–42, B1, F26, PMP.

209. Cohler, "Making a Gay Identity."

210. Murray to Duveneck, March 4, 1946, B102, F1844, PMP.

211. *Washington Evening Star*, March 16, 1946, B102, F1844, PMP.

212. Murray, *Pauli Murray*, 265.

213. "Behind the Scenes," 2.

214. Murray to Milgram, April 5, 1946, B98, F1741, PMP.

215. "Family Answers Gwynn Petition," ca. 1945, B10, F243, PMP.

216. Murray to Duveneck, March 4, 1946, B102, F1844, PMP.

217. "Family Answers Gwynn Petition," ca. 1945, B10, F243, PMP.

218. Murray, *Pauli Murray*, 268–69.

219. Murray to Dame, June 12, 1946, B10, F254, PMP; Murray to Milgram, April 5, 1946, B98, F1741, PMP.

220. Murray to Small, June 5, 1946, B11, F294, PMP; Murray to Dame, June 12, 1946, B10, F254, PMP.

221. Rosenberg, *Jane Crow*, 167.

222. Murray to Kenny, April 19, 1946, B28, F544, PMP.

223. Johnson to Murray, May 1, 1946, B28, F544, PMP.

224. Murray to Johnson, June 6, 1946, B28, F544, PMP.

225. Murray to Dame, June 12, 1946, B10, F254, PMP.

226. Murray to Dame, June 25, 1946, B10, F254, PMP.

CHAPTER 4

1. Murray to Dame, June 18, 1946, B10, F254, Pauli Murray Papers, the Arthur and Elizabeth Schlesinger Library, Radcliffe Institute for Advanced Study, Harvard University, Cambridge, Mass. (hereafter cited as PMP).

2. Murray to Dobbins, November 7, 1941, B102, F1838, PMP.

3. Murray to Dame, June 25, 1946, B10, F254, PMP.

4. Rosenberg, *Jane Crow*, 167–72.

5. Arsenault, *Freedom Riders*, 21.

6. D'Emilio, *Lost Prophet*, 133–34.

7. Meier and Rudwick, "First Freedom Ride," 218, 222.

8. D'Emilio, *Lost Prophet*, 136–40.

9. Firor Scott, *Pauli Murray and Caroline Ware*, 39.

10. Murray, *Pauli Murray*, 270.

11. FBI, "Subject File."

12. Murray to Dame, June 17, 1947, B10, F254, PMP.

13. Murray to Eva, March 10, 1948, B100, F1790, PMP.

14. Murray to Mazique, July 29, 1944, B4, F73, PMP.

15. Murray to Mason, April 19, 1947, B4, F73, PMP; Mason to Murray, April 20, 1947, B4, F73, PMP.

16. Murray, "Why Negro Girls," 5–9; "Pauli Murray Shows Why Men Make Poor Husbands," *Baltimore Afro-American*, June 14, 1947, 11; Cooper, *Beyond Respectability*, chap. 3; Rosenberg, *Jane Crow*, 175.

17. Murray to Dame, May 14, 1947, B10, F254, PMP.

18. Murray to Ware, May 3, 1947, B100, F1816, PMP.

19. Murray to Small, August 28, 1946, B11, F294, PMP.

20. Murray to Dame, June 23, 1947, B10, F254, PMP.

21. Murray to Dame, June 11, 1947, B10, F254, PMP.

22. Murray to Garcia, May 23, 1947, B102, F1845, PMP.

23. Murray to Small, May 15, 1947, B11, F294, PMP.

24. Murray to Garcia, May 23, 1947, B102, F1845, PMP.

25. Application for admission, May 7, 1949, B28, F554, PMP.

26. Murray to Dame, June 17, 1947, B10, F254, PMP.

27. Murray to Dame, June 18, 1946, B10, F254, PMP.

28. Murray to Handy, February 28, 1946, B77, F1360, PMP; Griswold to Murray, January 24, 1947, B18, F415, PMP; Freund to Murray, October 14, 1949, B18, F415, PMP.

29. Murray to Ware, May 3, 1947, B100, F1816, PMP.

30. Murray to Peck, May 20, 1947, B7, F211, PMP.

31. Murray to Dame, July 5, 1947, B10, F254, PMP.

32. FBI, "Subject File."

33. D'Emilio, "Homosexual Menace," 236.

34. Murray, *Pauli Murray*, 270–72.

35. Murray, *Pauli Murray*, 273.

36. FBI, "Subject File."

37. Application for admission, May 7, 1949, B28, F554, PMP.

38. Murray, *Pauli Murray*, 278–79, 272; Rosenberg, *Jane Crow*, 176.

39. Murray, *Pauli Murray*, 278.

40. Rosenberg, *Jane Crow*, 179.

41. Dean, *Imperial Brotherhood*, 73–74; D'Emilio, *Lost Prophet*, 176.

42. Murray, *Pauli Murray*, 294–95.

43. Application, May 7, 1948, B84, F1463, PMP.

44. Application, May 8, 1948, B73, F1286, PMP.

45. Murray to Wynn, May 26, 1943, B3, F70, PMP; Rosenberg, *Jane Crow*, 181.

46. Murray to Dame, May 6, 1948, B10, F255, PMP.

47. Rosenberg, *Jane Crow*, 179–80.

48. Murray to Dame, May 6, 1948, B10, F255, PMP.

49. Zaretsky, "Charisma or Rationalization?," 328.

50. Murray to Garcia, May 23, 1947, B102, F1845, PMP.

51. Horney, *Neurosis*, 18–26.

52. Rosenberg, *Jane Crow*, 182; FBI, "Subject File."

53. Rosenberg, *Jane Crow*, 182.

54. Murray, *Pauli Murray*, 274.

55. Rosenberg, *Jane Crow*, 183.

56. Henson, *Uncle Tom's Story*.

57. Murray to Dame, May 14, 1947, B10, F254, PMP; Murray to Ware, July 21, 1954, B100, F1819, PMP; Murray, *Pauli Murray*, 274–76.

58. Murray, *Pauli Murray*, 276.

59. "Disbar 2 Harlem," *Jet*, May 21, 1953, 7; "Disbar Lawyers," *New York Age: Defender*, May 9, 1953, 1.

60. Murray, *Pauli Murray*, 277.

61. Zimmerman, *Government and Politics*, 60; Firor Scott, *Pauli Murray and Caroline Ware*, 47.

62. "Liberal Party Platform," October 23, 1949, B87, F1516, PMP.

63. Murray to voters, October 28, 1949, B73, F1273, PMP.

64. "Pauli Murray Would," *Pittsburgh Courier*, October 29, 1949, B73, F1273, PMP.

65. Ted Poston, "Miss Murray Delays Study at Harvard," undated newspaper clipping, B18, F415, PMP.

66. Poston, "Miss Murray Delays Study at Harvard."

67. Murray, *Pauli Murray*, 280.

68. Murray, *Pauli Murray*, 280–81.

69. Statement of contributions, 1949, B73, F1275, PMP; "Pauli Murray Would," *Pittsburgh Courier*, October 29, 1949, B73, F1273, PMP.

70. Firor Scott, *Pauli Murray and Caroline Ware*, 47.

71. Azaransky, *Dream Is Freedom*, 37; Murray, *Pauli Murray*, 282.

72. Springer to friend, December 1, 1949, B73, F1273, PMP.

73. Gallagher, *Black Women*, 84.

74. Murray, *Pauli Murray*, 280–82; Ransby, *Ella Baker*, 158.

75. Firor Scott, *Pauli Murray and Caroline Ware*, 47.

76. Murray, *Pauli Murray*, 285–87.

77. Murray, *Pauli Murray*, 285–86.

78. Rosenberg, *Jane Crow*, 187; Murray, *States' Laws*.

79. Rosenberg, *Jane Crow*, 189.

80. Murray to Ware, January 5, 1951, B100, F1817, PMP.

81. Murray to Peck, October 6, 1952, B7, F211, PMP.

82. Murray to Ware, February 1, 1951, B100, F1817, PMP.

83. Braukman, *Communists and Perverts*, 8–10; D'Emilio, "Homosexual Menace," 227.

84. Dean, *Imperial Brotherhood*, 76–77.

85. Dean, *Imperial Brotherhood*, 71.

86. Dean, *Imperial Brotherhood*, 81–83; D'Emilio, "Homosexual Menace," 227.

87. Murray to Ware, February 1, 1951, B100, F1817, PMP.

88. Morales Carrion, *Puerto Rico*, 276–77; Indictment: *Puerto Rico v. Reynolds*, B32, F615, PMP.

89. Murray to Muste, January 24, 1951, B32, F615, PMP.

90. Catsam, *Freedom's Main Line*, 29.

91. Peck to Murray, February 5, 1951, B32, F615, PMP.

92. Murray to Peck, February 7, 1951, B32, F615, PMP; Murray to Peck, December 24, 1959, B7, F211, PMP.

93. Murray to Peck, February 7, 1951, B84, F1456, PMP.

94. "624 Groups," *New York Times*, March 8, 1951, B73, F1282, PMP.

95. Murray to Konvitz, April 16, 1952, B73, F1283, PMP.

96. Murray to Ware, February 1, 1951, B100, F1817, PMP.

97. Statement of attending physician, May 28, 1951, B4, F72, PMP; Murray to Stevens, April 17, 1951, B75, F1327, PMP.

98. Murray to Mason, April 10, 1951, B4, F73, PMP.

99. Murray to Dame and Small, April 17, 1951, B77, F1360, PMP.

100. Murray to Leatherman, June 11, 1951, B94, F1639, PMP.

101. Murray to Johnson, May 7, 1951, B4, F73, PMP; statement of physician, May 28, 1951, B4, F72, PMP; Murray to Stevens, April 17, 1951, B75, F1327, PMP.

102. Murray to Johnson, May 7, 1951, B4, F73, PMP.

103. Murray to Leatherman, June 11, 1951, B94, F1639, PMP.

104. Murray to Johnson, June 23, 1951, B4, F73, PMP; Murray to Johnson, May 25, 1951, B4, F73, PMP.

105. Pilger to Johnson, August 10, 1951, B4, F73, PMP.

106. Murray to Leatherman, June 11, 1951, B94, F1639, PMP.

107. Department of Commerce, "Current Population Reports."

108. Murray to Stevens, May 23, 1951, B75, F1327, PMP.

109. Hastie to Murray, June 6, 1951, B75, F1328, PMP.

110. Davis, "Review," 328; Mangum, "Review"; Mahoney, "Review," 283.

111. Murray to Fuchs, December 7, 1971, B45, F800, PMP; Murray, *Pauli Murray*, 289.

112. Murray to Ware, February 28, 1952, B100, F1818, PMP.

113. All in B73, F1282, PMP.

114. Murray to many, May 6, 1952, B73, F1283, PMP.

115. Murray to Konvitz, April 16, 1952, B73, F1282, PMP.

116. Murray to many, May 6, 1952, B73, F1283, PMP; Murray to Thompson, April 29, 1952; Murray to Thurgood Marshall, April 29, 1952; Murray to William Hastie, April 29, 1952, all in B73, F1283, PMP.

117. Murray to Konvitz, April 30, 1952, B73, F1283, PMP.

118. Murray to Hastie, May 2, 1952, B73, F1283, PMP.

119. Murray to Ware, February 1, 1951, B100, F1817, PMP; "Otis Hood Indictment," *Boston Traveler*, May 3, 1956, B96, F1688, PMP.

120. Murray to many, May 6, 1952, B73, F1283, PMP.

121. Catherwood to Murray, May 21, 1952, B73, F1284, PMP.

122. Murray to Konvitz, May 9, 1952, B73, F1283, PMP.

123. Murray to Johnson, May 13, 1952, B73, F1283, PMP; Marable, *Race, Reform*, 26–32.

124. Berle to Murray, May 22, 1952, B73, F1284, PMP.

125. Murray to Konvitz, May 9, 1952, B73, F1283, PMP; Marcuse, "Some Attitudes."

126. Murray to Overholt, May 17, 1952, B73, F1284, PMP.

127. Murray to Konvitz, May 9, 1952, B73, F1283, PMP.

128. Murray to Overholt, June 2, 1952, B73, F1285, PMP.

129. Murray to Robinson Morrow, May 17, 1952, B73, F1284, PMP.

130. Murray, *Pauli Murray*, 297–98.

131. Murray to Overholt, June 2, 1952, B73, F1285, PMP.

132. Murray, *Pauli Murray*, 297–98; Murray to Rodell, February 1, 1952, B83, F1448, PMP; Rosenberg, *Jane Crow*, 194.

133. Murray, *Pauli Murray*, 132.

134. Rosenberg, *Jane Crow*, 195.

135. Murray, *Pauli Murray*, 299; Murray to Overholt, June 2, 1952, B73, F1285, PMP.

136. Item 28, appendix (9), July 28, 1966, B74, F1294, PMP; Murray to Rodell, February 1, 1952, B83, F1448, PMP.

137. Diary notes, January 10, 1953, B1, F27, PMP.

138. Murray, *Pauli Murray*, 299; Murray, *Proud Shoes*, xi.

139. Murray to Peck, May 18, 1952, B73, F1284, PMP; diary notes, February 15, 1953, B1, F27, PMP.

140. Diary notes, January 16, 1953, B1, F27, PMP.

141. Diary, January 31, 1953, B1, F27, PMP.

142. D'Emilio, "Homosexual Menace," 229.

143. Diary, January 23, 1953, B1, F27, PMP.

144. Diary, January 30, 1953, B1, F27, PMP.

145. Murray to Ware, January 21, 1953, B100, F1818, PMP.

146. Eleanor Roosevelt, "Some of My Best Friends Are Negro," *Ebony* 8, no. 4 (1953): 16.

147. Murray to Ware, January 21, 1953, B100, F1818, PMP.

148. Frazier, *Black Bourgeoisie*, 194.

149. Diary, February 10, B1, F27, PMP.

150. O'Dell, *Sites of Southern Memory*, 146; Lillian Smith, *Strange Fruit*.

151. Rosenberg, *Jane Crow*, 194.

152. Rosenberg, *Jane Crow*, 203.

153. Murray, *Pauli Murray*, 302.

154. Firor Scott, *Pauli Murray and Caroline Ware*, 61–62.

155. Bryant, "Examination of the Social Activism," 65; Murray, *Pauli Murray*, 255.

156. "Justice Harlan's Contribution," *New York Times*, May 19, 1954, B84, F1466, PMP.

157. "Role of Negro Teachers," *New York Times*, May 30, 1954, B11, F266, PMP.

158. Diary, May 17, 1954, B1, F27, PMP; Noriega, "Something's Missing," 26.

159. Rosenberg, *Jane Crow*, 179; Richards, *Conversations with Maida Springer*, 1–2.

160. Murray, *Pauli Murray*, 278.

161. Diary, June 7, 1954, B1, F27, PMP.

162. Murray to Johnson, July 14, 1954, B4, F73, PMP; statement of attending physician, July 10, 1954, B4, F72, PMP; diary, June 14, 1954, B1, F27, PMP.

163. Firor Scott, *Pauli Murray and Caroline Ware*, 164; Drury, "'Experimentation,'" 277; Murray to Ziman, July 7, 1954, B4, F73, PMP.

164. Murray, *Pauli Murray*, 299–300.

165. Murray to Ware, July 26, 1954, B100, F1819, PMP.

166. Murray to Ware, July 21 and 26, 1954, B100, F1819, PMP.

167. Murray to Ware, July 26, 1954, B100, F1819, PMP.

168. FBI, "Subject File."

169. Murray to Ware, July 21 and 26, 1954, B100, F1819, PMP.

170. Murray to Meng, February 23, 1955, B10, F240, PMP.

171. Murray to Lewis Murray, June 2, 1954, B10, F238, PMP.

172. Murray to Lewis Murray, June 2, 1954; Murray to William Murray, June 2, 1954, both in B10, F238, PMP.

173. Murray to Ware, July 21 and 26, 1954, B100, F1819, PMP.

174. Murray to Crownsville, July 4, 1954, B10, F231, PMP.

175. Murray, *Pauli Murray*, 10.

176. Bell-Scott, *Firebrand*, 228–30; Murray to Ware, July 21, 1954, B100, F1819, PMP.

177. FBI, "Subject File."

178. Murray to Ware, July 21 and 26, 1954, B100, F1819, PMP.

179. Murray to Ware, July 21 and 26, 1954, B100, F1819, PMP.

180. Murray to Ware, July 21 and 26, 1954, B100, F1819, PMP.

181. Murray to Hauptman, September 15, 1954, B4, F73, PMP.

182. Murray, *Pauli Murray*, 299–300; Rosenberg, *Jane Crow*, 200.

183. Rosenberg, *Jane Crow*, 200.

184. Leeming, *James Baldwin*.

185. Rosenberg, *Jane Crow*, 201.

186. Buckmaster, *Let My People Go*; Hanff, *84, Charing Cross Road*.

187. Rosenberg, *Jane Crow*, 201–3.

188. Murray to Ware, August 11, 1954, B100, F1819, PMP.

189. Rosenberg, *Jane Crow*, 203–4.

190. Murray to Meng, February 23, 1955, B10, F240, PMP.

191. Murray to Meng, February 23, 1955, B10, F240, PMP.

192. Murray to Mildred and Raymond, June 1, 1955, B10, F245, PMP.

193. Murray to Mildred, June 20, 1955, B10, F245, PMP.

194. Murray to Susie, September 4, 1955, B10, F245, PMP.

195. "Brother, Sister in 54G Fight," *Baltimore Afro-American*, B10, F245, PMP.

196. Murray, *Pauli Murray*, 303–5.

197. Murray to Gwynn, December 10, 1955, B10, F245, PMP.

198. Murray to Gwynn, December 10, 1955, B10, F245, PMP.

199. Murray, *Pauli Murray*, 305.

200. Murray, *Pauli Murray*, 305.

201. Braxton, *Black Women*, 141.

202. Rosenberg, *Jane Crow*, 203–4.

203. Murray, *Proud Shoes*, 275.

204. Murray, *Pauli Murray*, 132.

205. Murray, *Proud Shoes*, xx.

206. Toppin, "Review"; Williams, "Review."

207. Murray, *Pauli Murray*, 311.

208. Murray, *Proud Shoes*, ix.

209. Murray, *Pauli Murray*, 306–8.

210. Murray to Fleeson, February 11, 1956, B100, F1800, PMP.

211. Murray, *Pauli Murray*, 308.

212. Murray, *Pauli Murray*, 309–10.

213. Murray, *Pauli Murray*, 242.

214. FBI, "Subject File."

215. Rosenberg, *Jane Crow*, 209.

216. Murray, *Pauli Murray*, 311.

217. Murray, *Pauli Murray*, 312.

218. Murray, *Pauli Murray*, 314.

219. "What I Have Learned," March 12, 1973, B6, F174, PMP, underlined in original.

220. Murray, *Pauli Murray*, 312.

221. Murray to Green, February 28, 1973, B97, F1727, PMP.

222. Murray, *Pauli Murray*, 314.

223. "What I Have Learned," March 12, 1973, B6, F174, PMP.

224. Stockley, *Daisy Bates*, 180.

225. Murray to many, June 16, 1958, B93, F1620, PMP.

226. Murray to unknown, June 16, 1958, B93, F1620, PMP.

227. Stockley, *Daisy Bates*, 194.

228. Stockley, *Daisy Bates*, 193; Bell-Scott, *Firebrand*, 281.

229. Tyson, *Radio Free Dixie*, 148–65.

230. Tyson, *Radio Free Dixie*, 149.

231. Tyson, *Radio Free Dixie*, 151–52.

232. Tyson, *Radio Free Dixie*, 160.

233. For rape fears, see Murray to Mother and Grandmother, June 24, 1921, B10, F252, PMP. For lynching fears, see Murray, *Pauli Murray*, 375.

234. "Brief for the Respondent," B98, F1755, PMP.

235. Wilkins to Murray, July 18, 1958, B102, F1828, PMP; Tyson, *Radio Free Dixie*, 161.

236. Tyson, *Radio Free Dixie*, 159–60.

237. Hogan, *Many Minds*, 26–27.

238. Murray to Kleinbard, January 29, 1959, B103, F1860, PMP.

239. Murray, *Pauli Murray*, 318.

240. Murray, *Dark Testament*, 38, 39.

241. Smead, *Blood Justice*, xi–xiv, 107–9.

242. Murray, *Dark Testament*, 85.

243. Murray, *Dark Testament*, 86–87.

244. Murray to Nelson Jennings, May 18, 1959, B83, F1448, PMP.

245. FBI, "Subject File"; Rosenberg, *Jane Crow*, 220–21.

246. Murray to Stevenson, March 18, 1959, B100, F1800, PMP.

247. Murray to Stevenson, March 18, 1959, B100, F1800, PMP.

248. Ghana diary, February 7, 1960, B41, F710, PMP.

249. Murray, *Pauli Murray*, 321.

250. Rosenberg, *Jane Crow*, 223.

251. Murray, *Pauli Murray*, 324–26.

252. Murray, *Pauli Murray*, 326.

253. Rosenberg, *Jane Crow*, 224.

254. American in Ghana, July 3, 1960, B5, F138, PMP.

255. "What Is Africa to Me?," December 1960, B85, F1480, PMP.

256. "What Is Africa to Me?," December 1960, B85, F1480, PMP.

257. Ghana diary, June 3, 1960, B41, F710, PMP.

258. Ghana diary, June 5, 1960, B41, F710, PMP, underlined in original; Gaines, *American Africans in Ghana*, 120.

259. Ghana diary, July 2, 1960, B41, F710, PMP.

260. Rosenberg, *Jane Crow*, 230.

261. Kent, *America, the UN*, chaps. 1–2.

262. Gaines, *American Africans in Ghana*, 123.

263. Murray to *Washington Post*, August 29, 1960, B41, F713, PMP.

264. Murray to *New York Times*, August 28, 1960, B5, F138, PMP.

265. Gaines, *American Africans in Ghana*, 117.

266. Gaines, *American Africans in Ghana*, 131.

267. Murray to Dove, October 25, 1960, B41, F714, PMP.

268. Tettegah to Murray, October 27, 1960, B41, F714, PMP.

269. Accra, Ghana, October 6, 1960, B41, F714, PMP.

270. Rosenberg, *Jane Crow*, 231.

271. Murray, *Pauli Murray*, 335–36.

272. Murray, *Pauli Murray*, 346.

273. Murray to Nkrumah, November 21, 1960, B41, F715, PMP; Nkrumah to Murray, March 18, 1960, B41, F712, PMP.

274. Office of President to Murray, November 28, 1960, B41, F715, PMP.

275. Dudziak, *Cold War Civil Rights*, 13.

276. Murray to Kennedy, May 25, 1961, B41, F717, PMP.

277. Gaines, *American Africans in Ghana*, 120, 131–32; Morgan, *Covert Life*.

278. Richards, *Conversations with Maida Springer*, 227.

279. Rosenberg, *Jane Crow*, 231.

280. Helen to Murray, December 11, 1960, B41, F715, PMP.

281. Richards, *Conversations with Maida Springer*, 227–28.

282. Murray, *Pauli Murray*, 339.

283. Milgram to Murray, February 10, 1961; Murray to Milgram, February 20, 1961, B41, F716, PMP.

284. Murray, *Pauli Murray*, 340.

285. Murray to Barlow, April 10, 1961, B5, F138, PMP.

286. Murray, *Pauli Murray*, 342; Rubin and Murray, *Constitution and Government of Ghana*.

287. Murray, *Pauli Murray*, 328–33; "What Is Africa to Me?," December 1960, B85, F1480, PMP.

288. Isaacs, "Back to Africa," *New Yorker*, May 13, 1961, 105.

289. Rosenberg, *Jane Crow*, 236–37.

290. Murray, *Pauli Murray*, 342–43.

291. Murray, *Pauli Murray*, 339.

292. FBI, "Subject File."

293. FBI, "Subject File."

294. Murray to Milgram, February 20, 1961, B41, F716, PMP.

CHAPTER 5

1. Murray, *Pauli Murray*, 344–45; Rosenberg, *Jane Crow*, 244.

2. "Executive Order 10980," December 14, 1961, B50, F890; Kennedy, "Remarks," February 12, 1962, B50, F890, Pauli Murray Papers, the Arthur and Elizabeth Schlesinger Library, Radcliffe Institute for Advanced Study, Harvard University, Cambridge, Mass. (hereafter cited as PMP).

3. Harrison, "'New Frontier,'" 634.

4. Kennedy, "Remarks," February 12, 1962, B50, F890, PMP; Hartmann, *From Margin to Mainstream*, 52.

5. Murray, *Pauli Murray*, 347.

6. Gallagher, *Black Women*, 124.

7. Peterson to many, undated, B49, F875, PMP; Murray, *Pauli Murray*, 347.

8. Harrison, "'New Frontier,'" 632–33.

9. Rosenberg, *Divided Lives*, 180–81.

10. Harrison, *On Account of Sex*, 23.

11. Harrison, "'New Frontier,'" 632–33; Brauer, "Women Activists," 40–41; Rupp and Taylor, *Survival*, 166–71.

12. Harrison, "'New Frontier,'" 639.

13. Bershtein to Murray, July 24, 1962, B49, F875, PMP.

14. Murray, *Pauli Murray*, 349–52.

15. Bell-Scott, *Firebrand*, 316.

16. Murray, *Pauli Murray*, 351.

17. Rosenberg, *Jane Crow*, 249–61.

18. Murray to Ware, October 23, 1962, B49, F878, PMP.

19. "Proposal to Reexamine," December 12, 1962, B89, F1542, PMP.

20. Pam to Murray, January 16, 1963, B49, F878, PMP.

21. Mayeri, *Reasoning from Race*, especially the introduction.

22. Holden, "Argument in Favor," March 23, 1963, B49, F883, PMP.

23. Zelman, *Women, Work*, 34.

24. Kenyon to Murray, April 4, 1963, B49, F878, PMP.

25. AFL-CIO to PCSW, March 13, 1963, B49, F883, PMP.

26. Murray, *Pauli Murray*, 348.

27. Murray, *Pauli Murray*, 352.

28. Murray, *Pauli Murray*, 353–54.

29. Height, "'We Wanted the Voice,'" 89.

30. Murray to Randolph, August 21, 1963, B94, F1644, PMP.

31. "Negro Woman," November 14, 1963, B126, F2282, PMP.

32. Lois A. Brown, "William Lloyd Garrison," 68.

33. "Negro Woman," November 14, 1963, B126, F2282, PMP.

34. Richards, *Conversations with Maida Springer*, 263; Rosenberg, *Jane Crow*, 266.

35. Zelman, *Women, Work*, 63.

36. Bird, *Born Female*, 11; Brauer, "Women Activists," 54–55.

37. Brauer, "Women Activists," 50.

38. Murray, *Pauli Murray*, 356–57; Bird, *Born Female*, 11; Azaransky, "Jane Crow," 156.

39. Murray to Ellickson, March 20, 1964, B49, F877, PMP; Murray to Thacher, January 30, 1963, B49, F878, PMP.

40. Gallagher, *Black Women*, 137.

41. Murray, *Pauli Murray*, 357; Bird, *Born Female*, 11; Azaransky, "Jane Crow," 156.

42. Murray, *Pauli Murray*, 358.

43. Murray to many, August 27, 1968, B81, F1420, PMP.

44. Murray, *Pauli Murray*, 347.

45. Azaransky, *Dream Is Freedom*, 73–74.

46. Rosenberg, *Jane Crow*, 281.

47. Azaransky, *Dream Is Freedom*, 73.

48. Erikson, *Identity*; Horney, *Neurosis*.

49. Azaransky, *Dream Is Freedom*, 72.

50. Murray to many, August 27, 1968, B81, F1420, PMP; Murray, *Pauli Murray*, 262.

51. Rosenberg, *Jane Crow*, 432.

52. Murray, *Pauli Murray*, 360.

53. Murray, *Pauli Murray*, 360.

54. Murray, *Pauli Murray*, 360.

55. Diary, 2:15 p.m., April 26, 1967, B2, F30, PMP.

56. FBI, "Subject File."

57. Bird, *Born Female*, 12.

58. Bird, *Born Female*, 12.

59. Harrison, *On Account of Sex*, 187.

60. Bird, *Born Female*, 5, 13.

61. Zelman, *Women, Work*, 99.

62. Edith Evans Ashbury, "Protest Proposed on Women's Jobs," *New York Times*, October 13, 1965, 32.

63. Friedan, *Feminine Mystique*.

64. Murray, *Pauli Murray*, 365.

65. Murray, *Pauli Murray*, 363.

66. Murray, *Pauli Murray*, 363.

67. FBI, "Subject File."

68. Hartmann, "Pauli Murray," 75.

69. Murray, *Pauli Murray*, 271; Weigand and Horowitz, "Dorothy Kenyon," 126.

70. May, *Informant*, ix.

71. Eagles, *Outside Agitator*.

72. Mayeri, *Reasoning from Race*, 27–29.

73. Murray, *Pauli Murray*, 363–64.

74. Mayeri, *Reasoning from Race*, 29.

75. Murray and Eastwood, "Jane Crow."

76. Zelman, *Women, Work*, 100.

77. Murray and Eastwood, "Jane Crow," 239–40.

78. Murray, *Pauli Murray*, 364.

79. Mayeri, *Reasoning from Race*, 28–29.

80. Murray, *Pauli Murray*, 370.

81. Murray to Vestry, March 27, 1966, B69, F1194, PMP.

82. Zelman, *Women, Work*, 93, 102.

83. Zelman, *Women, Work*, 104.

84. Friedan, *It Changed My Life*, 77.

85. Zelman, *Women, Work*, 105.

86. Murray, *Pauli Murray*, 367; Friedan, *It Changed My Life*, 82.

87. Friedan, *It Changed My Life*, 82.

88. Murray, *Pauli Murray*, 368.

89. Zelman, *Women, Work*, 106–7.

90. Friedan, *It Changed My Life*, 83.

91. Murray, *Pauli Murray*, 368.

92. Harrison, *On Account of Sex*, 192.

93. Friedan, *It Changed My Life*, 87–91.

94. Murray, *Pauli Murray*, 360–61.

95. FBI, "Subject File," 17.

96. Murray to Friedan, December 21, 1966, B50, F896, PMP; untitled notes, B81, F1424, PMP; Murray to Shulman, November 23, 1966, B74, F1299, PMP.

97. FBI, "Subject File."

98. Autobiography draft, B81, F1424, PMP.

99. Hernandez to Shulman, April 11, 1967, B74, F1300, PMP.

100. Norrell, *House I Live In*, 248.

101. FBI, "Subject File."

102. Diary, 4:30 p.m., May 11, 1967, B2, F30, PMP.

103. Autobiography draft, B81, F1424, PMP.

104. Reitman to Murray, March 28, 1967, B59, F1001, PMP.

105. Autobiography draft, B81, F1424, PMP.

106. Reitman to Murray, August 2, 1967, B59, F1001, PMP.

107. Diary, 9 a.m., April 26, 1967, B2, F30, PMP.

108. Diary, April 18, 1967, B2, F30, PMP.

109. Diary, 8 p.m., April 22, 1967, B2, F30, PMP.

110. Diary, April 18, 1967, B2, F30, PMP.

111. Diary, 9 a.m., April 26, 1967, B2, F30, PMP.

112. Diary, April 18, 1967, B2, F30, PMP.

113. Diary, 7:30 a.m., May 13, 1967, B2, F30, PMP.

114. Diary, 6 a.m., April 28, 1967, B2, F30, PMP.

115. Diary, 6 a.m., April 28, 1967, B2, F30, PMP.

116. Diary, 2:30 p.m., April 27, 1967, B2, F30, PMP.

117. Diary, 9 a.m., April 26, 1967, B2, F30, PMP.

118. Diary, 9 a.m., April 26, 1967, B2, F30, PMP.

119. Diary, 7:30 a.m., May 13, and 9 a.m., May 24, 1967, B2, F30, PMP.

120. Diary, 8:30 a.m., April 27, 1967, B2, F30, PMP.

121. Autobiography draft, B81, F1424, PMP.

122. Murray, *Pauli Murray*, 373.

123. Diary, May 23, 1967, B2, F30, PMP.

124. Diary, June 1 and 16, 1967, B2, F30, PMP.

125. Murray, *Pauli Murray*, 374.

126. Murray, *Pauli Murray*, 373; Caldbeck, "Religious Life," 188.

127. Murray, *Pauli Murray*, 375.

128. Diary, 11 a.m., May 23, 1967, B2, F30, PMP.

129. Diary, 9 a.m., May 24, 1967, B2, F30, PMP.

130. Diary, 11 a.m., May 23, 1967, B2, F30, PMP.

131. Bullock, *History of Negro Education*, 262, 81.

132. Hi Blanket, September 5, 1967, B17, F138, PMP.

133. Murray, *Pauli Murray*, 101.

134. Murray to Payton, September 19 and 26, 1967, B44, F777, PMP; Unknown to Murray, September 6, 1968, B45, F788, PMP.

135. Report on Conference, August 9–10, 1967, B44, F776, PMP.

136. Murray, *Pauli Murray*, 375.

137. Diary, 2:30 p.m., April 27, 1967, B2, F30, PMP.

138. Diary, 5:45 a.m., November 21, 1967, B2, F30, PMP.

139. Murray to Clarenbach, November 21, 1967, B51, F899, PMP.

140. Freeman, *Politics of Women's Liberation*, 55–56.

141. Murray to Clarenbach, November 21, 1967, B51, F899, PMP.

142. Murray, *Pauli Murray*, 375.

143. Shuler, *Blood and Bone*, 2; Murray, *Pauli Murray*, 377.

144. Diary, April 6, 7, and 9, 1968, B2, F30, PMP.

145. Murray, *Pauli Murray*, 378.

146. Murray, *Dark Testament*, 4.

147. Diary, April 7, 1968, B2, F30, PMP.

148. Rosenberg, *Jane Crow*, 313–14.

149. Diary, April 10, 1967, B2, F30, PMP.

150. Diary, December 4, 1967, B2, F30, PMP.

151. Murray, *Pauli Murray*, 373.

152. Diary, May 31, 1968, B2, F30, PMP.

153. Diary, May 31, 1968, B2, F30, PMP.

154. Murray to Emerson, April 28, 1968, B104, F1879, PMP.

155. Murray, *Pauli Murray*, 379.

156. Murray, *Pauli Murray*, 380; "Black" Professor, July 1969, B85, F1479, PMP.

157. Antler, "Pauli Murray," 78.

158. Murray to many, August 27, 1968, B81, F1420, PMP.

159. Murray, *Pauli Murray*, 381–85.

160. Murray, *Pauli Murray*, 386–87.

161. Murray, *Pauli Murray*, 388.

162. "Black Power for Whom?," August 26, 1968, B2, F30, PMP.

163. Murray, *Pauli Murray*, 387.

164. Murray to many, August 27, 1968, B81, F1420, PMP.

165. Murray, *Pauli Murray*, 398–99.

166. Murray, *Pauli Murray*, 401–4.

167. "Explanation of Use," B90, F1567, PMP.

168. Murray, *Pauli Murray*, 402–3.

169. Van Deburg, *New Day*, 55.

170. Murray, *Pauli Murray*, 402.

171. Murray, *Pauli Murray*, 420

172. Murray to Barlow, October 24, 1968, B5, F139, PMP.

173. Diary, November 1, 1968, B2, F30, PMP.

174. Murray, *Pauli Murray*, 408.

175. "15 Negroes Seize Brandeis Center, Students Press Demands for Wider Recognition," *New York Times*, January 9, 1969, 17.

176. "Sit-In at Brandeis," 33.

177. "15 Negroes Seize," 17; Rojas, *From Black Power*, 4.

178. Diary, January 9, 1969, B2, F30, PMP.

179. Murray, *Pauli Murray*, 409.

180. Murray, *Pauli Murray*, 412–13.

181. Diary, 10 p.m. Sunday, January 12, 1969, B2, F30, PMP.

182. Murray, *Pauli Murray*, 410–11.

183. Diary, 8:30 a.m., January 12, 1969, B2, F30, PMP.

184. Diary, 11:30 p.m., January 10, 1969, B2, F30, PMP.

185. hooks, *Yearning*, 16.

186. Diary, 8:30 a.m., January 12, 1969, B2, F30, PMP.

187. Diary, January 10, 1969, B2, F30, PMP.

188. Murray, *Pauli Murray*, 410.

189. Diary, 10 p.m., January 12, 1969, B2, F30, PMP.

190. Rosenberg, *Jane Crow*, 328.

191. Murray, *Pauli Murray*, 419.

192. Murray to Rustin, August 13, 1969, B99, F1770, PMP.

193. Lecky and Wright, *Black Manifesto*, 4; Van Deburg, *New Day*, 182–87.

194. Garcia to many, August 12, 1969, B62, F1045, PMP.

195. Murray to Garcia, August 26, 1969, B62, F1045, PMP.

196. Allan to Murray, September 8, 1969, B62, F1045, PMP.

197. Murray to Burgess, March 9, 1973, B95, F1667, PMP.

198. Frye, "'Black Manifesto,'" 68–70.

199. Frye, "'Black Manifesto,'" 75.

200. Oppenheimer, *Knocking on Heaven's Door*, 134–35.

201. Murray to Bishops and Deputies, September 5, 1969, B62, F1045, PMP.

202. Murray to Stokes, October 19, 1969, B62, F1045, PMP.

203. Antler, "Pauli Murray," 78.

204. "Women in American Society," B45, F800, PMP; Murray to Feinberg, March 8, 1973, B45, F795, PMP.

205. Murray to Emerson, June 30, 1970, B45, F802, PMP; Rosenberg, *Jane Crow*, 346.

206. Murray to Emerson, June 30, 1970, B45, F802, PMP.

207. Rosenberg, *Jane Crow*, 244.

208. Antler, "Pauli Murray," 79.

209. Murray to Rodell, August 5, 1970, B99, F1777, PMP; Murray to many, August 16, 1971, B106, F1898, PMP.

210. Murray to Rodell, August 5, 1970, B99, F1777; Murray to many, August 16, 1971, B106, F1898; Murray to Bonnie, February 23, 1980, B13, F339; Murray to Rustin, August 13, 1969, B99, F1770, all PMP.

211. Caldbeck, "Religious Life," 86; Chaves, *Ordaining Women*, 78.

212. Chaves, *Ordaining Women*, 78.

213. "Graymoor Resolution," April 24–26, 1970, B95, F1666, PMP.

214. Oppenheimer, *Knocking on Heaven's Door*, 139.

215. Hein and Shattuck, *Episcopalians*, 140.

216. Murray to Burgess, March 9, 1973, B95, F1667, PMP; Murray, *Pauli Murray*, 418–19.

217. Murray, *Pauli Murray*, 419.

218. Murray, *Pauli Murray*, 373.

219. "Feminism and Equality," August 27, 1970, B99, F1784, PMP.

220. Murray to Rustin, September 9, 1970, B99, F1770, PMP.

221. Hartmann, "Pauli Murray," 75–76.

222. Rosenberg, *Divided Lives*, 214–15.

223. ERA Statement, September 16, 1970, B56, F966, PMP.

224. Antler, "Pauli Murray," 80.

225. Rustin to Murray, September 17, 1971, B99, F1784, PMP.

226. Murray to Rustin, September 19, 1971, B99, F1784, PMP. For the youthful description of herself as rebellious and eager to please, see "Sketches: Contradictions," June 6, 1938, B83, F1451, PMP.

227. Antler, "Pauli Murray," 80.

228. Antler, "Pauli Murray," 80.

229. Murray to Fuchs, December 7, 1971, B45, F800, PMP.

230. Murray to Fuchs, April 17, 1973, B45, F806, PMP.

231. Antler, "Pauli Murray," 80.

232. "Charge of Discrimination," April 23, 1973, B45, F806, PMP.

233. Ginsburg to Murray, January 19, 1977, B45, F806, PMP.

CHAPTER 6

1. Murray, *Pauli Murray*, 420–25.

2. "What I Have Learned," March 12, 1973, B6, F174, Pauli Murray Papers, the Arthur and Elizabeth Schlesinger Library, Radcliffe Institute for Advanced Study, Harvard University (hereafter cited as PMP).

3. Murray to many, March 7 and March 13, 1973, B6, F167, PMP.

4. Murray to Burgess, February 28, 1973, B95, F1667, PMP.

5. Murray to Burgess, March 9, 1973, B95, F1667, PMP.

6. Murray, *Pauli Murray*, 424–25.

7. "Supplemental Statement," April 29, 1973, B95, F1668, PMP, emphasis in original.

8. Murray to many, August 27, 1968, B81, F1420, PMP.

9. Murray, *Pauli Murray*, 369.

10. Murray to Burgess, March 9, 1973, B95, F1667, PMP.

11. Murray to Burgess, February 28, 1973, B95, F1667, PMP.

12. Clipping from *Ebony*, September 1979, B63, F1068, PMP.

13. Murray to Fuchs, April 18, 1973, B45, F806, PMP.

14. Gaines, *Uplifting the Race*, 42.

15. Murray to Fuchs, April 18, 1973, B45, F806, PMP.

16. Burgess to Murray, March 7, 1973, B95, F1667, PMP.

17. Murray to Burgess, March 9, 1973, B95, F1667, PMP.

18. Arnold to Murray, March 14, 1973, B95, F1667, PMP; Murray to Burgess, February 28, 1973, B95, F1667, PMP.

19. Murray to Arnold, March 29, 1973, B95, F1667, PMP.

20. Murray to Garcia, August 26, 1969, B62, F1045, PMP; Murray to Burgess, March 9, 1973, B95, F1667, PMP.

21. Murray to Esther, December 19, 1982, B93, F1629, PMP.

22. Murray to Burgess, March 30, 1973, B95, F1667, PMP.

23. Murray to Arnold, May 25, 1973, B95, F1668, PMP.

24. Fuchs to Arnold, May 7, 1973, B95, F1669, PMP.

25. "Feminists Score Friedan," *New York Times*, March 8, 1973, 40.1, B95, F1681, PMP.

26. "To the Editor," March 9, 1973, B95, F1681, PMP.

27. Lee to Murray, March 25, 1973; Murray to Lee, April 3, 1973, B95, F1681, PMP.

28. O'Dell, *Sites of Southern Memory*, 145.

29. Drury, "Love, Ambition," 307; Murray, *Proud Shoes*, 167; Murray to Holmes, March 18, 1973, B96, F1688, PMP.

30. Murray, *Proud Shoes*, 167–68.

31. Murray to Holmes, March 18, 1973, B96, F1688, PMP.

32. Murray, *Pauli Murray*, 424; Diary, June 23, 1973, B2, F30, PMP.

33. Diary, June 23, 1973, B2, F30, PMP.

34. Murray, *Pauli Murray*, 427.

35. Diary, August 25, 1973, B2, F31, PMP.

36. Murray to Creighton, August 8, 1975, B63, F1072, PMP.

37. General Theological Seminary, http://gts.edu/the-close, "Welcome Home to the Close," June 4, 2019; Murray, *Pauli Murray*, 58.

38. Oppenheimer, *Knocking on Heaven's Door*, 137; "GTS Detailed History," General Theological Seminary, "GTS Detailed History," http://gts.edu/index.php?option=com_content&view=article&id=1030%3Agts-detailed-history&catid=35&Itemid=52, accessed November 11, 2013.

39. "An Episcopal Glossary of the Church," https://www.episcopalchurch.org/library/glossary/general-theological-seminary, accessed June 4, 2019.

40. Murray to Foster, February 4, 1977, B63, F1078, PMP; Ruether, "Emergence of Feminist Theology," 9.

41. Murray to Pollock, March 22, 1974, B23, F466, PMP.

42. Caldbeck, "Religious Life," 213.

43. Rosenberg, *Jane Crow*, 30.

44. Oppenheimer, *Knocking on Heaven's Door*, 140.

45. Murray, *Pauli Murray*, 429.

46. Murray to Creighton, August 8, 1975, B63, F1072, PMP.

47. Murray to Creighton, August 8, 1975, B63, F1072, PMP; Murray to Burgess, June 6, 1973, B63, F1071, PMP.

48. Murray to Moore, December 26, 1973, B26, F517, PMP.

49. Caldbeck, "Religious Life," 89.

50. Murray, *Pauli Murray*, 429.

51. Murray to Creighton, August 8, 1975, B63, F1072, PMP; Murray to Moore, December 26, 1973, B26, F517, PMP; Caldbeck, "Religious Life," 89–90.

52. Murray, *Pauli Murray*, 429; Oppenheimer, *Knocking on Heaven's Door*, 142–43.

53. Murray to Moore, December 26, 1973, B26, F517, PMP.

54. Murray to Anderson, December 19, 1973, B67, F1159, PMP.

55. Diary, 12:45 a.m., February 1, 1974, B2, F31, PMP.

56. Murray to Anderson, December 19, 1973, B67, F1159, PMP; Murray, *Pauli Murray*, 430.

57. Murray, *Pauli Murray*, 427–28.

58. Murray to Trustees, January 15, 1974, B23, F467, PMP; Murray to Pollock, March 21 and 22, 1974, B23, F466, PMP; Pollock to Murray, March 19, 1974, B23, F466, PMP; Caldbeck, "Religious Life," 219.

59. Diary, 12:45 a.m., February 1, 1974, B2, F31, PMP.

60. Murray, *Pauli Murray*, 427–28.

61. Rosenberg, *Jane Crow*, 363–64.

62. Rosenberg, *Jane Crow*, 364.

63. Summary of symptoms, March 8, 1940, B4, F71, PMP.

64. Murray to Goranson, March 11, 1974, B22, F463, PMP.

65. Rosenberg, *Jane Crow*, 359.

66. Pollock to Murray, March 19, 1974, B23, F466, PMP.

67. Murray to Pollock, March 21, 1974, B23, F466, PMP.

68. Murray to Pollock, March 22, 1974, B23, F466, PMP.

69. Blacklock to Murray, undated, B67, F1159, PMP.

70. Murray to Bigalow, March 5, 1974, B22, F463, PMP.

71. Evaluation, Michaelmas, 1973, B22, F463, PMP.

72. Murray to Arnold, June 8, 1975, B63, F1071, PMP; Caldbeck, "Religious Life," 222.

73. Diary, June 6, 1974, B2, F31, PMP.

74. Diary, December 21, 1974, B2, F31, PMP.

75. Murray, *Pauli Murray*, 428.

76. Murray to Fuchs, April 18, 1973, B45, F806, PMP.

77. Caldbeck, "Religious Life," 217.

78. Murray to Foster, January 27, 1974, B23, F467, PMP.

79. Caldbeck, "Religious Life," 240.

80. Final evaluation, August 2, 1974, B24, F495, PMP; pastoral evaluation, Summer 1974, B26, F516, PMP.

Notes to Pages 262–70

81. Murray to Ruth, June 23, 1974, B96, F1689, PMP.

82. Diary, July 2, 1974, B2, F31, PMP.

83. Diary, December 21, 1974, B2, F31, PMP.

84. Final evaluation, August 2, 1974, B24, F495, PMP.

85. Pastoral counseling, April 5, 1975, B26, F516, PMP.

86. Murray to Ruth, June 23, 1973, B96, F1689, PMP.

87. Oppenheimer, *Knocking on Heaven's Door*, 144.

88. Murray to Bigalow, August 4, 1974, B67, F1156, PMP; Murray, *Pauli Murray*, 430.

89. Murray, *Pauli Murray*, 430–32.

90. Murray to Bigalow, August 4, 1974, B67, F1156, PMP; Oppenheimer, *Knocking on Heaven's Door*, 147.

91. Oppenheimer, *Knocking on Heaven's Door*, 144.

92. Caldbeck, "Religious Life," 92.

93. Oppenheimer, *Knocking on Heaven's Door*, 147.

94. Murray to Wolf, August 27, 1975, B68, F1175, PMP.

95. Murray to Ennis, September 2, 1975, B68, F1175, PMP.

96. Murray to Editors, September 3, 1975, B68, F1175, PMP.

97. Diary, December 21, 1974, B2, F31, PMP.

98. Foster to Burgess, May 17, 1974, B26, F516, PMP.

99. Personal statement, March 26, 1975, B26, F518, PMP; Foster to Burgess, April 14, 1975, B26, F516, PMP.

100. Student course evaluation, June 12, 1975, B63, F1071, PMP.

101. Murray to Foster, February 4, 1977, B63, F1078, PMP.

102. Murray to Wright, July 23, 1975, B26, F516, PMP.

103. Murray, *Pauli Murray*, 431.

104. Murray to Kershaw, June 14, 1975, B63, F1071, PMP.

105. Murray to Kershaw, June 25, 1975, B63, F1071, PMP.

106. Murray to Burgess, June 6, 1973, B63, F1071, PMP; Murray to Creighton, August 8, 1975, B63, F1072, PMP.

107. Murray to Holmes, February 21, 1977, B96, F1688, PMP.

108. Murray to Holmes, February 21, 1977, B96, F1688, PMP.

109. Stevens to Mitchell, February 25, 1977, B100, F1798, PMP.

110. Murray to Holmes, February 21, 1977, B96, F1688, PMP.

111. Murray to Clark, March 14, 1977, B97, F1728, PMP.

112. Murray to Holmes, February 21, 1977, B96, F1688, PMP.

113. Interview with Pauli Murray, Documenting the American South, http://docsouth.unc.edu/sohp/G-0044/G-0044.html, accessed October 12, 2011.

114. Murray, "Black Theology," 3–4.

115. Murray, "Black Theology," 11.

116. Murray, "Black Theology," 23.

117. Murray, *Pauli Murray*, 432.

118. Murray to Caldwell, April 9, 1976, B89, F1556, PMP.

119. Murray, *Pauli Murray*, 432.

120. Murray to Lewis, January 19, 1977, B69, F1194, PMP.

121. "Episcopal Women's Ordination," *Washington Afro-American*, January 15, 1977, B63, F1068, PMP.

122. Murray, *Pauli Murray*, 434.

123. Murray to Walters, December 31, 1976, B63, F1078, PMP; Caldbeck, "Religious Life," 228–29.

124. "History as Black Woman Ordained," *West Australian*, January 10, 1977, B63, F1070, PMP.

125. Murray, *Pauli Murray*, 435.

126. "1st Negro Woman Priest," *Washington Post*, February 25, 1977, B87, F1506, PMP.

127. Murray, *Pauli Murray*, 435.

128. Bell-Scott, *Firebrand*, 360; Rosenberg, *Jane Crow*, 379.

129. Bourdieu, "Biographical Illusion," 297–98.

130. Pinn, *Pauli Murray*, 8.

131. Azaransky, *Dream Is Freedom*, 108.

132. Pinn, *Pauli Murray*, 39.

133. Pinn, *Pauli Murray*, 85.

134. Pinn, *Pauli Murray*, 14.

135. Pinn, *Pauli Murray*, 74, emphasis in original.

136. Pinn, *Pauli Murray*, 15.

137. Pinn, *Pauli Murray*, 91.

138. Caroline Hall, *Thorn in the Flesh*, 53.

139. Caroline Hall, *Thorn in the Flesh*, 152–54; Hein and Shattuck, *Episcopalians*, 143.

140. Caroline Hall, *Thorn in the Flesh*, 54–55.

141. "Episcopals to Ordain," *News American*, January 8, 1977, B63, F1068, PMP.

142. Caroline Hall, *Thorn in the Flesh*, 48–49; Hein and Shattuck, *Episcopalians*, 143.

143. Integrity, B125, F2254, PMP, n.d.

144. Murray to Lewis and Havens, January 19, 1977, B69, F1194, PMP.

145. Summary of Homosexuality Issues Group, January 22, 1977, B69, F1194, PMP.

146. Oppenheimer, *Knocking on Heaven's Door*, 163.

147. Murray to Jim and Mary, February 4, 1977, B68, F1078, PMP.

148. Pinn, *Pauli Murray*, 33.

149. Pinn, *Pauli Murray*, 82.

150. Murray, *Pauli Murray*, 431–32.

151. Murray to Kershaw, December 28, 1976, B63, F1078, PMP.

152. Murray to Kershaw, December 28, 1976, B63, F1078, PMP.

153. Murray to Walker, March 14, 1977, B97, F1728, PMP.

154. Azaransky, *Dream Is Freedom*, 98.

155. Halbertal and Koren, "Between 'Being' and 'Doing,'" 39.

156. "Episcopal Priests Ordained," *Washington Post*, January 9, 1977, B63, F1068, PMP.

157. "Episcopals to Ordain," *News American*, January 8, 1977, B63, F1068, PMP.

158. Notice of Renunciation, February 4, 1977, B62, F1050, PMP.

159. Caldbeck, "Religious Life," 261–62; Wattley to Creighton, January 13, 1977, B62, F1050, PMP; Wattley to the Diocese of Washington, January 13, 1977, B63, F1078; Wattley to *Episcopal Times* Editor, April 28, 1977, B63, F1078, PMP.

160. Murray to Wattley, January 21–22, 1977, B69, F1194, PMP.

161. Simmons and Thomas, *Preaching with Sacred Fire*, 787.

162. Caroline Hall, *Thorn in the Flesh*, 13.

163. Caroline Hall, *Thorn in the Flesh*, 15–18.

Notes to Pages 277–85

164. Jenkins, *Decade of Nightmares*, 108.

165. Murray to Costanza, March 30, 1977, B94, F1634, PMP.

166. Caroline Hall, *Thorn in the Flesh*, 13.

167. "1st Negro Woman Priest," *Washington Post*, February 25, 1977, B87, F1506, PMP.

168. Caroline Hall, *Thorn in the Flesh*, 13.

169. Pinn, *Pauli Murray*, 131, 40–42, 32, 44–45, 55.

170. Murray to Holmes, February 21, 1977, B96, F1688, PMP.

171. Murray to Foster, February 4, 1977, B63, F1078, PMP.

172. Murray to Arnold, February 12, 1977, B62, F1050, PMP.

173. Rosenberg, *Jane Crow*, 380.

174. Murray to Coburn, February 19, 1980, B62, F1052, PMP.

175. Murray to Bonnie, February 23, 1980, B13, F339, PMP.

176. Murray to Coburn, February 19, 1980, B62, F1052, PMP.

177. Murray to Bonnie, February 23, 1980, B13, F339, PMP.

178. Murray to Bonnie, February 23, 1980, B13, F339, PMP.

179. Murray to Coburn, February 19, 1980, B62, F1052, PMP.

180. Rosenberg, *Jane Crow*, 384.

181. Murray to Coburn, February 19, 1980, B62, F1052, PMP.

182. Rosenberg, *Jane Crow*, 383.

183. Murray to Coburn, December 31, 1982, B62, F1053, PMP.

184. Murray to Holmes, December 6, 1985, B96, F1688, PMP.

185. Murray to McIntyre, September 27, 1982, B98, F1039, PMP.

186. Rosenberg, *Jane Crow*, 384.

187. Murray to Coburn, January 30, 1978, B62, F1051, PMP.

188. Bell-Scott, *Firebrand*, 339.

189. Murray, *Pauli Murray*, 128–29.

190. "Why Me?," *Gainesville Sun*, B63, F1069, PMP.

191. "Pauli Murray," *The Sun*, April 24, 1977, B63, F1069, PMP.

192. "The Poet," *D.C. Post*, February 14, 1977, B63, F1068, PMP.

193. "Lifestyle," *Ebony*, September 1979, B63, F1068, PMP.

194. "Minority Priest," *Lynchburg News*, February 16, 1981, B63, F1069, PMP.

195. To many, December 1984, B99, F1783, PMP; Rosenberg, *Jane Crow*, 384–85; Bell-Scott, *Firebrand*, 355–60, 433.

196. Bell-Scott, *Firebrand*, 359.

197. Murray to family and friends, March 10, 1985, B99, F1783, PMP; Bell-Scott, *Firebrand*, 358–60; Murray to Engle, March 18, 1985, B95, F1665, PMP; Murray to Greenfield, April 1, 1985, B87, F1566, PMP.

EPILOGUE

1. O'Dell, *Sites of Southern Memory*, 135–38; Bell-Scott, *Firebrand*, 360.

2. Murray, *Pauli Murray*, 57.

3. Murray, *Proud Shoes*, 100.

4. Murray, *Proud Shoes*, 275–76.

5. Murray, *Proud Shoes*, 276.

Bibliography

ARCHIVAL SOURCES

Pauli Murray Papers, 1827–1985. The Arthur and Elizabeth Schlesinger Library, Radcliffe Institute for Advanced Study, Harvard University.

NEWSPAPERS AND MAGAZINES

Baltimore Afro-American

Capital Gazette

Carolina Times

Crisis

Ebony

Jet

Negro Digest

New York Age: Defender

New York Amsterdam News

New York Times

Opportunity

Pittsburgh Courier

Washington Post

OTHER PRIMARY SOURCES

Cunard, Nancy, ed. *Negro: An Anthology.* New York: Frederick Ungar, 1970.

Davis, John A. "Review." *Journal of Negro History* 37, no. 3 (1952): 327–29.

Duke Human Rights Center, Pauli Murray Project at the Franklin Humanities Institute, http://paulimurrayproject.org. Accessed June 30, 2014.

Federal Bureau of Investigation. "Subject File: Anna Pauline Murray." Washington, D.C.: U.S. Department of Justice, 1967.

Firor Scott, Anne, ed. *Pauli Murray and Caroline Ware: Forty Years of Letters in Black and White.* Chapel Hill: University of North Carolina Press, 2006.

Garfinkel, Harold. "Color Trouble." In *Best Short Stories of 1941*, edited by Edward J. O'Brien, 97–119. New York: Houghton Mifflin, 1941.

Henson, Josiah. *Uncle Tom's Story of His Life: The Autobiography of the Reverend Josiah Henson.* Chapel Hill: University of North Carolina Press, 2011.

Isaacs, Harold R. "Back to Africa." *New Yorker,* May 13, 1961, 105.

Mahoney, Mildred H. "Review." *New England Quarterly* 26, no. 2 (1953): 283–84.

Mangum, Charles S., Jr. "Review." *Journal of Southern History* 18, no. 4 (1952): 531.

Marcuse, F. L. "Some Attitudes toward Employing Negroes as Teachers in a Northern University." *Journal of Negro Education* 17, no. 1 (1948): 18–26.

Murray, Pauli. "And the Riots Came." *The Call,* August 13 (1943): 1, 4.

———. "Black Theology and Feminist Theology: A Comparative View." *Anglican Theological Review* 60 (January 1978): 3–24.

———. *Dark Testament and Other Poems.* Norwalk, Conn.: Silvermine, 1970.

———. "Interview." February 13, 1976. Interview G-0044. Southern Oral History Program Collection (#4007) in the Southern Oral History Program Collection, Southern Historical Collection, Wilson Library, University of North Carolina at Chapel Hill. Published by Documenting the American South [accessed 12 October 2011]. http://docsouth.unc.edu/sohp/G-0044/G-0044.html.

———. "Male and Female He Created Them." In *Preaching with Sacred Fire: An Anthology of African American Sermons, 1750 to the Present*, edited by Martha Simmons and Frank A. Thomas, 782–89. New York: W. W. Norton, 2010.

———. "Negroes Are Fed Up." *Common Sense* 12 (1943): 274–76.

———. *Pauli Murray: The Autobiography of a Black Activist, Feminist, Lawyer, Priest, and Poet*. Knoxville: University of Tennessee Press, 1989.

———. *Proud Shoes: The Story of an American Family*. Boston: Beacon, 1999.

———. "The Right to Equal Opportunity in Employment." *California Law Review* 33, no. 3 (1945): 388–433.

———. *States' Laws on Race and Color*. Cincinnati: Methodist Church, 1951.

———. "Why Negro Girls Stay Single: Negro Males Expose Women to Jane Crow as Well as Jim Crow." *Negro Digest*, July 1947, 5–9.

Murray, Pauli, and Henry Babcock. "An Alternative Weapon." *South Today* (Winter 1942–43): 53–57.

Murray, Pauli, and Mary O. Eastwood. "Jane Crow and the Law: Sex Discrimination and Title VII." *George Washington Law Review* 34, no. 2 (1965): 232–56.

Odum, Howard W. *Race and Rumors of Race*. 1943; repr., Baltimore: Johns Hopkins University Press, 1997.

Pinn, Anthony B., ed. *Pauli Murray: Selected Sermons and Writings*. New York: Orbis Books, 2006.

Rubin, Leslie, and Pauli Murray. *The Constitution and Government of Ghana*. London: Sweet & Maxwell, 1964.

Simmons, Martha, and Frank A. Thomas, eds. *Preaching with Sacred Fire: An Anthology of African American Sermons, 1750 to the Present*. New York: W. W. Norton, 2010.

Toppin, Edgar Allan. "Review." *Journal of Negro History* 42, no. 1 (1957): 67–69.

U.S. Department of Commerce. "Current Population Reports: Consumer Income." September 26, 1952, http://www2.census.gov/prod2/popscan/p60-010.pdf.

Williams, McDonald. "Review: Walking toward Freedom and Respect." *Phylon Quarterly* 18, no. 1 (1957): 90–91.

SECONDARY SOURCES

Alexander, Robert J. *The Right Opposition: The Lovestoneites and the International Communist Opposition of the 1930s*. Westport, Conn.: Greenwood, 1981.

Altenbaugh, Richard J. "The Children and the Instruments of a Militant Labor Progressivism: Brookwood Labor College and the American Labor College Movement of the 1920s and 1930s." *History of Education Quarterly* 23, no. 4 (1983): 395–411.

Anderson, Jean Bradley. *Durham County: A History of Durham County, North Carolina*. Durham, N.C.: Duke University Press, 2011.

Antler, Joyce. "Pauli Murray: The Brandeis Years." *Journal of Women's History* 14, no. 2 (2002): 78–82.

Arnesen, Eric. *Black Protest and the Great Migration: A Brief History with Documents*. Boston: Bedford/St. Martin's, 2003.

Arsenault, Raymond. *Freedom Riders: 1961 and the Struggle for Racial Justice*. Pivotal Moments in American History. New York: Oxford University Press, 2006.

Azaransky, Sarah. *The Dream Is Freedom: Pauli Murray and American Democratic Faith.* Oxford: Oxford University Press, 2011.

———. "Jane Crow: Pauli Murray's Intersections and Antidiscrimination Law." *Journal of Feminist Studies in Religion* 29, no. 1 (2013): 155–60.

Barresi, John. "The Identities of Malcolm X." In McAdams, Josselson, and Lieblich, *Identity and Story,* 201–22.

Basile, Mary Elizabeth. "Pauli Murray's Campaign against Harvard Law School's Jane Crow Admissions Policy." *Journal of Legal Education* 77, no. 57 (2007): 77–101.

Bell-Scott, Patricia. *The Firebrand and the First Lady: Portrait of a Friendship: Pauli Murray, Eleanor Roosevelt, and the Struggle for Social Justice.* New York: Knopf, 2016.

Berg, Manfred. "Black Civil Rights and Liberal Anticommunism: The NAACP in the Early Cold War." *Journal of American History* 94, no. 1 (2007): 75–96.

Bird, Caroline. *Born Female: The High Cost of Keeping Women Down.* Rev. ed. New York: Pocket Books, 1971.

Black, Allida M. "A Reluctant but Persistent Warrior: Eleanor Roosevelt and the Early Civil Rights Movement." In *Women in the Civil Rights Movement: Trailblazers and Torchbearers 1941–1965,* edited by Vicki L. Crawford, Jacqueline Anne Rouse, and Barbara Woods, 233–49. Bloomington: Indiana University Press, 1993.

Bollet, Alfred Jay. "Politics and Pellagra: The Epidemic of Pellagra in the U. S. In the Early Twentieth Century." *Yale Journal of Biology and Medicine* 65, no. 3 (1992): 211–21.

Bourdieu, Pierre. "The Biographical Illusion." In *Identity: A Reader,* edited by Paul Du Gay, Jessica Evans, and Peter Redman, 297–303. London: Sage, 2000.

Brauer, Carl M. "Women Activists, Southern Conservatives, and the Prohibition of Sex Discrimination in Title VII of the 1964 Civil Rights Act." *Journal of Southern History* 49, no. 1 (1983): 37–56.

Braukman, Stacy. *Communists and Perverts under the Palms.* Gainesville: University Press of Florida, 2012.

Braxton, Joanne M. *Black Women Writing Autobiography: A Tradition Within a Tradition.* Philadelphia: Temple University Press, 1989.

Brett, Judith. "The Tasks of Political Biography." In *History on the Couch: Essays in History and Psychoanalysis,* edited by Joy Damousi and Robert Reynolds, 73–83. Melbourne: Melbourne University Press, 2003.

Brewer, William M. "The Poll Tax and Poll Taxers." *Journal of Negro History* 29, no. 3 (1944): 260–99.

Brown, Leslie. *Upbuilding Black Durham, N.C.: Gender, Class, and Black Community Development in the Jim Crow South.* Chapel Hill: University of North Carolina Press, 2008.

Brown, Lois A. "William Lloyd Garrison and Emancipatory Feminism in Nineteenth-Century America." In *William Lloyd Garrison at Two Hundred,* edited by James Brewer Stewart, 41–76. New Haven, Conn.: Yale University Press, 2008.

Bryant, Flora Renda. "An Examination of the Social Activism of Pauli Murray." Ph.D. diss., University of South Carolina, 1991.

Buckmaster, Henrietta. *Let My People Go: The Story of the Underground Railroad and the Growth of the Abolition Movement.* New York: Harper & Brothers, 1941.

Bullock, Henry. *A History of Negro Education in the South: From 1619 to the Present.* Cambridge: Harvard University Press, 1967.

Caldbeck, Elaine Sue. "The Poetry of Pauli Murray, African American Civil Rights
Lawyer and Priest." In *Gender, Ethnicity, and Religion: Views from the Other Side*, edited
by Rosemary Radford Ruether, 45–65. Minneapolis: Fortress, 2002.

———. "A Religious Life of Pauli Murray: Hope and Struggle." Ph.D. diss.,
Northwestern University, 2000.

Caruth, Cathy. "Recapturing the Past: Introduction." In *Trauma: Explorations in Memory*,
edited by Cathy Caruth, 151–57. Baltimore: Johns Hopkins University Press, 1995.

Catsam, Derek Charles. *Freedom's Main Line: The Journey of Reconciliation and the
Freedom Rides*. Lexington: University Press of Kentucky, 2009.

Cavanagh, Sheila. *Queering Bathrooms: Gender, Sexuality, and the Hygienic Imagination*.
Toronto: University of Toronto Press, 2010.

Chauncey, George. *Gay New York: Gender, Urban Culture, and the Makings of the Gay Male
World, 1890–1940*. New York: Basic Books, 1994.

Chaves, Mark. *Ordaining Women: Culture and Conflict in Religious Organizations*.
Cambridge: Harvard University Press, 1999.

Cohler, Bertram J., and Phillip L. Hammack. "Making a Gay Identity: Life Story and the
Construction of a Coherent Self." In McAdams, Josselson, and Lieblich, *Identity and
Story*, 151–72.

Cooper, Brittney C. *Beyond Respectability: The Intellectual Thought of Race Women*.
Urbana: University of Illinois Press, 2017.

Crenshaw, Kimberlé. "Mapping the Margins: Intersectionality, Identity Politics, and
Violence against Women of Color." *Stanford Law Review* 43, no. 6 (1991): 1241–99.

Cresswell, Tim. "Embodiment, Power and the Politics of Mobility: The Case of Female
Tramps and Hobos." *Transactions of the Institute of British Geographers* 24, no. 2 (1999):
175–92.

Dalfiume, Richard M. "The 'Forgotten Years' of the Negro Revolution." *Journal of
American History* 55, no. 1 (1968): 90–106.

Dean, Robert D. *Imperial Brotherhood: Gender and the Making of Cold War Foreign Policy*.
Amherst: University of Massachusetts Press, 2001.

D'Emilio, John. "The Homosexual Menace: The Politics of Sexuality in Cold War
America." In *Passion and Power: Sexuality in History*, edited by Kathy Peiss, Christina
Simmons, and Robert A. Padgug, 226–40. Philadelphia: Temple University Press,
1989.

———. *Lost Prophet: The Life and Times of Bayard Rustin*. Chicago: University of Chicago
Press, 2004.

D'Emilio, John, and Estelle B. Freedman. *Intimate Matters: A History of Sexuality in
America*. 2nd ed. Chicago: University of Chicago Press, 1997.

Devor, Holly. *FTM: Female-to-Male Transsexuals in Society*. Bloomington: Indiana
University Press, 1997.

Dickens, Charles. *Oliver Twist, or, the Parish Boy's Progress*. London: Penguin Classics, 2003.

Dominy, Jordan J. "Reviewing the South: Lillian Smith, *South Today*, and the Origins of
Literary Canons." *Mississippi Quarterly* 66 (2013): 29–50.

Doubt, Keith. "Garfinkel before Ethnomethodology." *American Sociologist* 20, no. 3
(1989): 252–62.

Dowbiggin, Ian Robert. *Keeping America Sane: Psychiatry and Eugenics in the United States
and Canada, 1880–1940*. Ithaca, N.Y.: Cornell University Press, 1997.

Drescher, Jack. "Out of DSM: Depathologizing Homosexuality." *Behavioral Sciences* 5, no. 4 (2015): 565–75.

Drury, Doreen M. "Boy-Girl, Imp, Priest: Pauli Murray and the Limits of Identity." *Journal of Feminist Studies in Religion (Indiana University Press)* 29, no. 1 (2013): 142–47.

———. "'Experimentation on the Male Side': Race, Class, Gender, and Sexuality in Pauli Murray's Quest for Love and Identity." Ph.D. diss., Boston College, 2000.

———. "Love, Ambition, and 'Invisible Footnotes' in the Life and Writing of Pauli Murray." *Souls* 11, no. 3 (2009): 295–309.

Dudziak, Mary L. *Cold War Civil Rights: Race and the Image of American Democracy.* Princeton: Princeton University Press, 2000.

Eagles, Charles W. *Outside Agitator: Jon Daniels and the Civil Rights Movement in Alabama.* Chapel Hill: University of North Carolina Press, 1993.

Episcopal Glossary of the Church. https://www.episcopalchurch.org/library/glossary /general-theological-seminary. Accessed March 14, 2019.

Erikson, Erik H. *Identity, Youth and Crisis.* New York: W. W. Norton, 1968.

Faderman, Lillian. *Odd Girls and Twilight Lovers: A History of Lesbian Life in Twentieth-Century America.* New York: Columbia University Press, 1991.

Fairclough, Adam. *A Class of Their Own: Black Teachers in the Segregated South.* Cambridge, Mass.: Belknap Press of Harvard University Press, 2007.

Fausto-Sterling, Anne. *Sexing the Body: Gender Politics and the Construction of Sexuality.* New York: Basic Books, 2000.

Fine, Sidney. *Sit-Down: The General Motors Strike of 1936–1937.* Ann Arbor: University of Michigan Press, 1969.

Finkle, Lee. "The Conservative Aims of Militant Rhetoric: Black Protest During World War II." *Journal of American History* 60, no. 3 (1973): 692–713.

Frazier, Edward Franklin. *Black Bourgeoisie.* Glencoe, Ill.: Free Press, 1957.

Freeman, Jo. *The Politics of Women's Liberation: A Case Study of an Emerging Social Movement and Its Relation to the Policy Process.* New York: Longman, 1975.

Friedan, Betty. *The Feminine Mystique.* New York: W. W. Norton, 1963.

———. *It Changed My Life: Writings on the Women's Movement.* New York: Random House, 1976.

Friess, Horace L. "Review: War without Violence. A Study of Gandhi's Method and Its Accomplishments by Krishnalal Shridharani." *Social Research* 8, no. 2 (1941): 247–50.

Frye, Jerry K. "The 'Black Manifesto' and the Tactic of Objectification." *Journal of Black Studies* 5, no. 1 (1974): 65–76.

Gaines, Kevin Kelly. *American Africans in Ghana: Black Expatriates and the Civil Rights Era.* Chapel Hill: University of North Carolina Press, 2006.

———. *Uplifting the Race: Black Leadership, Politics, and Culture in the Twentieth Century.* Chapel Hill: University of North Carolina Press, 1996.

Gallagher, Julie A. *Black Women and Politics in New York City.* Urbana: University of Illinois Press, 2012.

Garber, Marjorie B. *Vested Interests: Cross-Dressing & Cultural Anxiety.* New York: Routledge, 1992.

Garfinkel, Harold. *Studies in Ethnomethodology.* Englewood Cliffs, N.J.: Prentice-Hall, 1967.

Garfinkel, Herbert. *When Negroes March: The March on Washington Movement in the Organizational Politics for Fepc.* New York: Atheneum, 1969.

Gates, Henry Louis, Jr. "The Trope of a New Negro and the Reconstruction of the Image of the Black." *Representations*, no. 24 (1988): 129–55.

General Theological Seminary. http://gts.edu/the-close. Accessed March 13, 2019.

Gibson, Margaret. "The Masculine Degenerate: American Doctors' Portrayals of the Lesbian Intellect, 1880–1949." *Journal of Women's History* 9, no. 4 (1998): 78–103.

Gilmore, Glenda Elizabeth. "Admitting Pauli Murray." *Journal of Women's History* 14, no. 2 (2002): 62–67.

———. "'Am I a "Screwball" or Am I a Pioneer?': Pauli Murray's Civil Rights Movement." In *Profiles in Leadership: Historians on the Elusive Quality of Greatness*, edited by Walter Isaacson, 261–80. New York: W. W. Norton, 2010.

———. *Defying Dixie: The Radical Roots of Civil Rights, 1919–1950.* New York: W. W. Norton, 2008.

———. "How Anne Scott and Pauli Murray Found Each Other." In *Writing Women's History: A Tribute to Anne Firor Scott*, edited by Elizabeth Anne Payne, 142–71. Jackson: University Press of Mississippi, 2011.

Ginsberg, Elaine K. "Introduction: The Politics of Passing." In *Passing and the Fictions of Identity*, edited by Elaine K. Ginsberg, 1–19. Durham, N.C.: Duke University Press, 1996.

Halberstam, Judith. *Female Masculinity.* Durham, N.C.: Duke University Press, 1998.

Halbertal, Tova Hartman, with Irit Koren. "Between 'Being' and 'Doing': Conflict and Coherence in the Identity Formation of Gay and Lesbian Orthodox Jews." In McAdams, Josselson, and Lieblich, *Identity and Story*, 37–61.

Hall, Caroline J. Addington. *A Thorn in the Flesh: How Gay Sexuality Is Changing the Episcopal Church.* Lanham, Md.: Rowman & Littlefield, 2013.

Hall, Jacquelyn Dowd. "The Long Civil Rights Movement and the Political Uses of the Past." *Journal of American History* 91, no. 4 (2005): 1233–63.

Hall, Stuart. "Introduction: Who Needs Identity?" In *Questions of Cultural Identity*, edited by S. Hall and P. du Gay, 1–17. London: Sage, 1996.

Hamilton, Nigel. *Biography: A Brief History.* Cambridge, Mass.: Harvard University Press, 2007.

Hancock, Ange-Marie. *Intersectionality: An Intellectual History.* New York: Oxford University Press, 2016.

Hanff, Helen. *84, Charing Cross Road.* New York: Grossman, 1970.

Harris, Trudier. "African American Autobiography." In *The Cambridge Companion to Autobiography*, edited by Maria DiBattista and Emily O. Wittman, 180–94. Cambridge: Cambridge University Press, 2014.

Harrison, Cynthia E. "A 'New Frontier' for Women: The Public Policy of the Kennedy Administration." *Journal of American History* 67, no. 3 (1980): 630–46.

———. *On Account of Sex: The Politics of Women's Issues, 1945–1968.* Berkeley: University of California Press, 1988.

Hartmann, Susan M. *From Margin to Mainstream: American Women and Politics since 1960.* New York: McGraw-Hill, 1989.

———. "Pauli Murray and the 'Juncture of Women's Liberation and Black Liberation.'" *Journal of Women's History* 14, no. 2 (2002): 74–77.

Height, Dorothy I. "'We Wanted the Voice of a Woman to Be Heard': Black Women and the 1963 March on Washington." In *Sisters in the Struggle: African American Women in the Civil Rights-Black Power Movement*, edited by Bettye Collier-Thomas and V. P. Franklin, 83–91. New York: New York University Press, 2001.

Hein, David, and Gardiner H. Shattuck Jr. *The Episcopalians*. Westport, Conn.: Praeger, 2004.

Hewitt, Nancy A. "Feminist Frequencies: Regenerating the Wave Metaphor." *Feminist Studies* 38, no. 3 (2012): 658–80.

Hogan, Wesley C. *Many Minds, One Heart: SNCC's Dream for a New America*. Chapel Hill: University of North Carolina Press, 2007.

Holmes, Richard. *Footsteps: Adventures of a Romantic Biographer*. London: Penguin, 1985.

hooks, bell. *Where We Stand: Class Matters*. New York: Routledge, 2000.

———. *Yearning: Race, Gender, and Cultural Politics*. Boston: South End, 1990.

Horney, Karen. *Neurosis and Human Growth: The Struggle toward Self-Realization*. New York: W. W. Norton, 1950.

Humez, Jean M. "Pauli Murray's Histories of Loyalty and Revolt." *Black American Literature Forum* 24, no. 2 (1990): 315–35.

Hunter, Gregory. "Howard University: 'Capstone of Negro Education' during World War II." *Journal of Negro History* 79, no. 1 (1994): 54–70.

Jackson, Vanessa. "Separate and Unequal: The Legacy of Racially Segregated Psychiatric Hospital." https://www.patdeegan.com/sites/default/files/files/separate_and_unequal.pdf. Accessed February 4, 2014.

Jeffers, Trellie. "A Personal Viewpoint: The Black Black Woman and the Black Middle Class." *Black Scholar* 12, no. 6 (1981): 46–49.

Jenkins, Philip. *Decade of Nightmares: The End of the Sixties and the Making of Eighties America*. Oxford: Oxford University Press, 2006.

Kennedy, Elizabeth Lapovsky, and Madeline D. Davis. *Boots of Leather, Slippers of Gold: The History of a Lesbian Community*. New York: Routledge, 1993.

Kent, John. *America, the UN and Decolonisation: Cold War Conflict in the Congo*. Hoboken, N.J.: Taylor and Francis, 2010.

Kessler-Harris, Alice. "Why Biography?" *American Historical Review* 114, no. 3 (2009): 625–30.

Klarman, Michael J. "Scottsboro." *Marquette Law Review* 93 (2009): 379–432.

Kornbluh, Judith L. *A New Deal for Workers' Education: The Workers' Service Program 1933–1942*. Chicago: University of Chicago Press, 1987.

Krahulik, Karen Christel. *Provincetown: From Pilgrim Landing to Gay Resort*. New York: New York University Press, 2005.

Lecky, Robert S., and H. Elliott Wright, eds. *Black Manifesto: Religion, Racism and Reparations*. New York: Sheed and Ward, 1969.

Leeming, David A. *James Baldwin*. New York: Random House, 1996.

Little, Graham. "Using Childhood." *Eureka Street* 4, no. 7 (1994): 28–32.

Lombardo, Paul A. *A Century of Eugenics in America: From the Indiana Experiment to the Human Genome Era*. Bloomington: Indiana University Press, 2011.

Lueptow, Lloyd B., Lori Garovich, and Margaret B. Lueptow. "The Persistence of Gender Stereotypes in the Face of Changing Sex Roles: Evidence Contrary to the Sociocultural Model." *Ethology and Sociobiology* 16, no. 6 (1995): 509–30.

Mack, Kenneth Walter. *Representing the Race: The Creation of the Civil Rights Lawyer.* Cambridge, Mass.: Harvard University Press, 2012.

MacKinnon, Neil J., and Tom Langford. "The Meaning of Occupational Prestige Scores: A Social Psychological Analysis and Interpretation." *Sociological Quarterly* 35, no. 2 (1994): 215–45.

Mann, Susan. "Scene-Setting: Writing Biography in Chinese History." *American Historical Review* 114, no. 3 (2009): 631–39.

Marable, Manning. *Race, Reform and Rebellion: The Second Reconstruction and Beyond in Black America, 1945–2006.* Updated ed. Basingstoke: Palgrave Macmillan, 2007.

May, Gary. *The Informant: The FBI, the Ku Klux Klan, and the Murder of Viola Liuzzo.* New Haven, Conn.: Yale University Press, 2005.

Mayeri, Serena. "A Common Fate of Discrimination: Race-Gender Analogies in Legal and Historical Perspective." *Yale Law Review* 110, no. 6 (2001): 1045–87.

———. "Constitutional Choices: Legal Feminism and the Historical Dynamics of Change." *California Law Review* 92, no. 3 (2004): 755–839.

———. "Pauli Murray and the Twentieth-Century Quest for Legal and Social Equality." *Indiana Journal of Law and Social Equality* 2, no. 1 (2013): 80–90.

———. *Reasoning from Race: Feminism, Law, and the Civil Rights Revolution.* Cambridge, Mass.: Harvard University Press, 2011.

McAdams, Dan P., Ruthellen Josselson, and Amia Lieblich, eds. *Identity and Story: Creating Self in Narrative.* Washington, D.C.: American Psychological Association, 2006.

McCall, Leslie. "The Complexity of Intersectionality." *Journal of Women in Culture and Society* 30, no. 3 (2005): 1771–1800.

Meier, August, and Elliott Rudwick. "The First Freedom Ride." *Phylon* 30, no. 3 (1969): 213–22.

Morales Carrion, Arturo. *Puerto Rico: A Political and Cultural History.* New York: W. W. Norton, 1983.

Morgan, Ted. *A Covert Life: Jay Lovestone, Communist, Anti-Communist, and Spymaster.* New York: Random House, 1999.

Nasaw, David. "Introduction." *American Historical Review* 114, no. 3 (2009): 573–78.

Newman, Mark. *The Civil Rights Movement.* Edinburgh: Edinburgh University Press, 2004.

Noriega, Chon. "'Something's Missing Here!': Homosexuality and Film Reviews during the Production Code Era, 1934–1962." *Cinema Journal* 30, no. 1 (1990): 20–41.

Norrell, Robert J. *The House I Live In: Race in the American Century.* Oxford: Oxford University Press, 2005.

Norwood, Kimberly Jade. *Color Matters: Skin Tone Bias and the Myth of a Postracial America.* Hoboken, N.J.: Taylor and Francis, 2013.

O'Dell, Darlene. *Sites of Southern Memory: The Autobiographies of Katharine Du Pre Lumpkin, Lillian Smith, and Pauli Murray.* Charlottesville: University of Virginia Press, 2001.

Oppenheimer, Mark. *Knocking on Heaven's Door: American Religion in the Age of Counterculture.* New Haven, Conn.: Yale University Press, 2003.

Ordover, Nancy. *American Eugenics: Race, Queer Anatomy, and the Science of Nationalism.* Minneapolis: University of Minnesota Press, 2002.

Oshinsky, David M. *A Conspiracy So Immense: The World of Joe McCarthy.* New York: Macmillan, 1983.

Peppard, Christiana Z. "Poetry, Ethics, and the Legacy of Pauli Murray." *Journal of the Society of Christian Ethics* 30, no.1 (2010): 21–43.

Pinn, Anthony B. "Pauli Murray's Triadic Strategy of Engagement." In *Journal of Feminist Studies in Religion* (Indiana University Press), 160–64. Bloomington: Indiana University Press, 2013.

———. "Religion and 'America's Problem Child': Notes on Pauli Murray's Theological Development." *Journal of Feminist Studies in Religion* 15, no. 1 (1999): 21–39.

Poole, Mary. *The Segregated Origins of Social Security: African Americans and the Welfare State.* Chapel Hill: University of North Carolina Press, 2006.

Raggatt, Peter T. F. "Multiplicity and Conflict in the Dialogical Self: A Life-Narrative Approach." In McAdams, Josselson, and Lieblich, *Identity and Story*, 15–35.

Ransby, Barbara. *Ella Baker and the Black Freedom Movement: A Radical Democratic Vision.* Chapel Hill: University of North Carolina Press, 2003.

Richards, Yevette. *Conversations with Maida Springer: A Personal History of Labor, Race, and International Relations.* Pittsburgh: University of Pittsburgh Press, 2004.

———. *Maida Springer: Pan Africanist and International Labor Leader.* Pittsburgh: University of Pittsburgh Press, 2014.

Rojas, Fabio. *From Black Power to Black Studies: How a Radical Social Movement Became an Academic Discipline.* Baltimore: Johns Hopkins University Press, 2007.

Rosenberg, Rosalind. *Divided Lives: American Women in the Twentieth Century.* American Century Series. New York: Hill and Wang, 1992.

———. *Jane Crow: The Life of Pauli Murray.* New York: Oxford University Press, 2017.

Ruether, Rosemary Radford. "The Emergence of Feminist Theology." In *The Cambridge Companion to Feminist Theology*, edited by Susan Frank Parsons. Cambridge: Cambridge University Press, 2002.

Rupp, Leila J., and Verta Taylor. "Pauli Murray: The Unasked Question." *Journal of Women's History* 14, no. 2 (2002): 83–87.

———. *Survival in the Doldrums: The American Women's Rights Movement, 1945 to the 1960s.* New York: Oxford University Press, 1987.

Sartain, Lee. *Border of Equality: The NAACP and the Baltimore Civil Rights Struggle, 1914– 1970.* Jackson: University of Mississippi Press, 2013.

Sherman, Richard B. *The Case of Odell Waller and Virginia Justice, 1940–1942.* Knoxville: University of Tennessee Press, 1992.

Shogun, Robert. "Labor Strikes Back." *American History* 45, no. 5 (2006): 36–42.

Shuler, Jack. *Blood and Bone: Truth and Reconciliation in a Southern Town.* Columbia: University of South Carolina Press, 2008.

Sitkoff, Harvard. *A New Deal for Blacks: The Emergence of Civil Rights as a National Issue*, vol. 1: *The Depression Decade.* New York: Oxford University Press, 1978.

———. "Racial Militancy and Interracial Violence in the Second World War." *Journal of American History* 58, no. 3 (1971): 661–81.

Skloot, Rebecca. *The Immortal Life of Henrietta Lacks.* New York: Broadway, 2010.

Slate, Nico. *Colored Cosmopolitanism the Shared Struggle for Freedom in the United States and India.* Cambridge, Mass.: Harvard University Press, 2012.

Smead, Howard. *Blood Justice: The Lynching of Mack Charles Parker.* New York: Oxford University Press, 1986.

Smith, Jason Scott. *Building New Deal Liberalism: The Political Economy of Public Works, 1933–1956*. New York: Cambridge University Press, 2006.

Smith, Lillian. *Strange Fruit*. New York: Harcourt, Brace & World, 1944.

Stack, Sam F. "John Dewey and the Question of Race: The Fight for Odell Waller." *Education and Culture* 25, no. 1 (2009): 17–35.

Stockley, Grif. *Daisy Bates: Civil Rights Crusader from Arkansas*. Jackson: University Press of Mississippi, 2005.

Stryker, Susan. *Transgender History*. Berkeley: Seal Press, 2008.

Taylor, Clarence. *Black Religious Intellectuals: The Fight for Equality from Jim Crow to the 21st Century*. Hoboken, N.J.: Taylor and Francis, 2013.

Taylor, Leslie A. "'I Made Up My Mind to Get It': The American Trial of 'The Well of Loneliness,' New York City, 1928–1929." *Journal of the History of Sexuality* 10, no. 2 (2001): 250–86.

Terry, Jennifer. *An American Obsession: Science, Medicine, and Homosexuality in Modern Society*. Chicago: University of Chicago Press, 1999.

Tyor, Malcolm P. "Memorial: Julian M. Ruffin." http://europepmc.org/articles/PMC2279491/pdf/tacca00097-0076.pdf. Accessed October 31, 2013.

Tyson, Timothy B. *Radio Free Dixie: Robert F. Williams and the Roots of Black Power*. Chapel Hill: University of North Carolina Press, 1999.

Van Deburg, William L. *New Day in Babylon: The Black Power Movement and American Culture, 1965–1975*. Chicago: University of Chicago Press, 1992.

Walker, Alice. *In Search of Our Mothers' Gardens: Womanist Prose*. London: Women's Press, 1984.

Ware, Susan. *Holding Their Own: American Women in the 1930s*. Boston: Twayne, 1982.

Weber, Bruce. "Harold Garfinkel, a Common-Sense Sociologist, Dies at 93." *New York Times*, May 3, 2011.

Wehnert, Kathleen. *Passing: An Exploration of African-Americans on Their Journey for an Identity along the Colour Line*. Hamburg: Diplomica GmbH, 2010.

Weigand, Kate, and Daniel Horowitz. "Dorothy Kenyon: Feminist Organizing 1919–1963." *Journal of Women's History* 14, no. 2 (2002): 126–31.

Whitaker, Jan. "Restaurateurs: Alice Foote MacDougall." 2008. http://restaurantingthroughhistory.com/2008/08/11/restaurateurs-alice-foote-macdougall/. Accessed July 10, 2014.

Wilder, JeffriAnne, and Colleen Cain. "Teaching and Learning Color Consciousness in Black Families: Exploring Family Processes and Women's Experiences with Colorism." *Journal of Family Issues* 32, no. 5 (2011): 577–604.

Woolf, Virginia. *Moments of Being: Autobiographical Writings*. New ed. London: Pimlico, 2002.

Zaretsky, Eli. "Charisma or Rationalization? Domesticity and Psychoanalysis in the United States in the 1950s." *Critical Inquiry* 26, no. 2 (2000): 328–54.

Zelman, Patricia G. *Women, Work, and National Policy: The Kennedy-Johnson Years*, Studies in American History and Culture; No. 33. Ann Arbor: UMI Research Press, 1982.

Zimmerman, Joseph F. *The Government and Politics of New York State*. 2nd ed. Albany: SUNY Press, 2008.

Index

Note: the initials "PM" refer to Pauli Murray. Works listed are by Pauli Murray unless otherwise indicated. The recipients of quoted letters are not indexed. *Page numbers appearing in italics refer to illustrations.*

of Women, 250–51; wage differences, 250–51

Bridgeport, Conn., incident, 47–48

Brookwood Labor College, 61–63

Brown v. Board of Education, 144, 146, 174–75, 230

Buckmaster, Henrietta, 181

Burgess, John M., 257

Burton, Lula, 43

California Law Review, 135

Call (Socialist Party newspaper), 122

Camp TERA (Temporary Emergency Relief Assistance), 55–57

Carmichael, Stokely, 238

Carolina Times (newspaper), 42, 74

Carter, Elmer E., 166

Case-by-case basis as legal strategy, PM's argument for, 208

Cathedral of Saint John the Divine (New York), 264

Catherwood, M. P., 166, 168

Chapel of the Cross (North Carolina), 278

Chase Smith, Margaret, 213

Chinn, May, 55, 154–55

Chisholm, Shirley, 159

Church of the Advocate (Pennsylvania), 271

Church of the Holy Nativity, 288–89

Church Women United network, 246

Civil Rights Act (1964), 212–13, 216, 220, 230, 251

Civil Rights Committee (Howard University students), 116, 124–25

Clayton Powell, Adam, 45, 103

Coalition for the Apostolic Ministry (CAM), 284

Cold War: climate of suspicion, 153–55, 161–62, 163, 172; investigation of homosexuality, 161, 172. *See also* House Un-American Activities Committee

Cole, Olivia, 233

"Color Trouble" (Garfinkel), 92–93

Columbia University, 39, 54, 63, 151, 165, 191, 197

Commission on Law and Social Action (CLSA), 145–46, 148–49, 151, 160

Committee on Civil and Political Rights (part of PCSW), 207–8, 209

Common Sense, 122

communist organizations, 47, 63, 77. *See also* Trotskyist organizations

Communist Party, 52; PM's feelings toward, 57, 63, 68, 77, 78, 98, 169

Congo, coup in, 199–200

Congress of Racial Equality (CORE), 116, 117, 121, 146, 162, 236

Constitution and Government of Ghana, The, 204

Cornell University Liberian Codification Project, PM's job application for, 166–69

Crisis (NAACP magazine), 73, 122, 126

Croom, Md., xi, xii, 35, 36, 38

Crownsville State Hospital for the Negro Insane, xi, xii, 28–30, 35, 77, 108, 138, 141–42, 150, 178–79, 183, 184, 185

Cunard, Nancy, 51

Daily Tar Heel (UNC student newspaper), 70–72

Daly, Mary, 258

Dame, Morton (uncle), 9–10

Dame, Pauline (née Fitzgerald, aunt), 4–5, 34, 40), 180; character, 9–10, 15, 45; relationship with PM, 10, 11, 19, 32, 73, 90, 152; teaching, 10, 130, 142, 175; visits to PM, 39, 127, 152; PM's visits to, 51, 76, 88, 106, 122; illness, 51, 136, 138, 140–41, 184; PM's sense of obligation to, 69, 77, 81, 85, 107, 130, 136, 138, 149

Daniels, Jonathan, 219

Das Kapital (Marx), 57

Daughters of Bilitis, 259–60

Davis, Oscar, 94

Decosta, Maysie "Tom Thumb," 51

Dewey, John, 99

Diocese of Massachusetts, 261

Dirksen, Everitt M., 212, 213

Drew, Charles R., 132

Drury, Doreen, 50, 57

Du Bois, W. E. B., 16, 18, 256
Duke University Hospital, 120
Duncan, Charles, 222
Durham Morning Herald (newspaper), 71

Eastwood, Mary, 209, 219
Ebony, 173
Edelsberg, Herman, 216
Eidelsberg, Joseph, 113–14
"Eleanor Clubs," 121
Elliot, Susie (cousin), 115
Ellis, Havelock, 43, 67
employment discrimination: PM's thesis
    on, 134; amendments to Civil Rights
    Act, 212–13; women in academia, 215
Episcopal Church: and demands of Black
    militants, 245–46; and gender dis-
    crimination, 245–46, 248–49; ordi-
    nation of women, 256, 263–64, 271,
    276–77, 284, 285; ordination of homo-
    sexuals, 280–82
Episcopal Church General Convention:
    1969, 245; 1973, 262–63; 1976, 276–77,
    280
Episcopal Women's Caucus (EWC), 248,
    263, 272
Equal Employment Opportunity Com-
    mission (EEOC), 216, 226; press re-
    sponse to, 217; PM's speech on, 217–18;
    weakness of, 220; PM's position with,
    223–25
Equal Rights Amendment (ERA), 207–9,
    250, 286
Erikson, Erik, 214

Faderman, Lillian, 260
Fair Employment Practices Committee
    (FEPC), 134
Farmer, James, 100, 115, 213, 218
FBI: request photo of PM, 179; back-
    ground check of PM for EEOC role,
    223–25
Fellowship of Reconciliation (FOR), 115
Feminine Mystique (Friedan), 218
Feminist Theology, PM's attitude toward,
    276

"feminist underground" (Washington,
    D.C.), 221
Finerty, John F., 101, 102
First Conference of African Women and
    Women of African Descent, 200
Fitzgerald, Bertie (aunt), 3, 4
Fitzgerald, Cornelia (grandmother), 8,
    12–13, 14, 17, 18, 20–24, 31–32, 36–37,
    70, 121, 138, 170, 186–87, 230, 278, 290,
    294
Fitzgerald, Marie (aunt), 149–50, 179–80
Fitzgerald, Pauline. *See* Dame, Pauline
    (née Fitzgerald, aunt)
Fitzgerald, Richard (grandfather's
    brother), 3, 18
Fitzgerald, Robert (grandfather), 8, 11–15,
    17, 18–22, 27, 31, 43, 86, 174–75, 186–
    87
Fitzgerald, Sadie (cousin), 2, 97
Fitzgerald, Sallie (aunt), xi, 8, 10–11, 15,
    16, 19, 25, 31–36, 34, 76–77, 80–81, 88,
    118, 119, 130, 149–50, 152, 175, 176, 180,
    185–86, 293
Fitzgerald, Tommie (uncle), 15, 31
Forman, James, 244
Fourteenth Amendment, PM's strategy
    for, 208–9, 219, 220, 232, 250
fourth generation African American his-
    tory, 214
Fox, Ruth, 114–15
Frazier, E. Franklin, 19, 109, 128, 173
Freedmen's Hospital, 120, 140–41, 143,
    164, 175, 287
Freedom Rides, 147, 202, 210
Friedan, Betty, 218, 221–22, 258–59
Fuchs, Lawrence, 235, 246–47, 250, 257,
    258

Gaines, Lloyd, 69
Gaines Supreme Court decision, 70
Gandhi-inspired nonviolent protest, 68,
    116
Garfinkel, Harold, 90–93
Garrison, Lloyd K., 130, 166, *189*, 190, *192*,
    197, 202
Garrison, William Lloyd, 211

General Theological Seminary (GTS), 262, 264, 265, 267–69, 271–74, 287
Gersh, Harry, 56
Gilmore, Glenda, 90, 93
Ginsburg, Ruth Bader, 249–50
Goldensohn, Leon, 155
Goranson, Paul, 266–67
Graham, Frank P., 70–71, 73, 74
Graham, Richard, 221–22
Granger, Lester B., 166
Graymoor Conference and Resolution, 248
Great Depression, the, 45, 57
Green, Edith, 212
Greensboro sit-ins, 126, 147, 195, 210
Greenwich Village (New York), 61
Griffiths, Martha, 221
"guerrilla church," 271–72
Gwynn, June (niece), 287–88

Haener, Dorothy, 221
Hamer, Fanny Lou, 230
Hanff, Helen, 181–82
Harlan, John M., 175
Harlem, 44, 51, 60, 68, 76, 78, 106, 115, 122–23, 156, 170, 188
"Harlem Ashram," 100, 162
Harper & Brothers, 170–71, 174, 182, 197
Harper and Row, 289
Harper's (magazine), 204
Harvard Law Review, 165
Harvard Law School admissions campaign, 128–30, 151, 158
Hastie, William, 89, 92, 125, 127, 129, 165–66, 167
Hayden, Dorothy "Toni," 47, 51, 64
Hayti district (Durham, N.C.), 37
Height, Dorothy, 44, 207, 210
Hepburn, Katherine, 290
Hernandez, Aileen, 221, 224
Holcomb, Luther, 221
Holmes, Margaret "Peg," 56–58, 64, 64–65, 77, 82, 167, 196, 260–61, 266, 286, 289
Holy Eucharist: PM's objection to the male domination of, 220, 271; PM's first, 278, 286
homophobia, 45–46, 65, 67

homosexuality, 57, 66, 149; "treatment" of, 67, 78–79, 113
Hoover, J. Edgar, 65, 179
Horney, Karen, 155, 214
House Un-American Activities Committee, 153, 163, 167
Houston, Charles Hamilton, 74, 88
Howard University, 109–10, 115, 123–24, 136; student sit-ins, 116–18, 124–27; council decision to ban protests, 125–26
Howard University Hospital. *See* Freedmen's Hospital
human rights, PM's belief in the indivisibility of, 211, 213, 219, 231–32, 246, 260
"Human Rights USA: 1948–1966" (report), 223
Humphrey, Hubert, 213
Hunter College (New York), 39–43, 51, 53, 54, 71, 73, 170, 262, 292
Huyck, Heather, 282
Hyde Amendment, 285

Innes, Margaret "Pee Wee," 51, 55, 56
Integrity (network), 281–82
Interracial organizations, 112–13
Isaacs, Harold, 204

Jane Crow, 110, 149, 213, 219, 236
"Jane Crow and the Law" (PM and Eastwood), 219, 221
Jefferson, Louise "Lou," 51
Jennings, Leslie Nelson, 196
Jerr, William, 277, 282–83
Jet, 173
Jim Crow, 10, 30, 97, 103, 110, 111, 139, 149, 159, 236
job advertisements, sex-segregation of, 221
Johns Hopkins Hospital, 120, 288
Johnson, Charles W., 143
Johnson, Mordecai, 126–28, 178
Josiah, Urith, 156–57
jury service, sex-based exclusion from, 219

Kempton, Murray, 103
Kennedy, John. F., 206–7, 211

over pay and entitlements for women academics, 250; speeches on the "new feminism," 250

—appearance: skin color, 23, 41, 91; as "tomboy," 25, 33, 40; dress, 25, 47, 51, 60, 64, 152; physique, 66, 73, 83, 91, 111

—arrests: detainments/questioning, 47–48, 58, 82, 86; arrests, 59, 60, 87–88; imprisonment, 89

—campaigns: Tarrytown automobile workers strike, 62; UNC admission campaign, 70–75; Sharecroppers Week, 80–82; Greyhound bus incident, 88–93; Waller campaign, 96–99, 101–5, 110–11; "Journey of Reconciliation," 146–48, 162; feminist activism, 158; pay campaign at Brandeis University, 251; PCSW, 206–9

—childhood and early life: birth, 1; memories of parents, 1, 3, 5–6, 7, 26, 30; early stay with Aunt Pauline, 4–5; move to Durham and life with Fitzgerald family, 8–12, 16, 18, 19–21, 24, 31–32; at West End School, 22–23; early experience with racial violence, 23; visit to Baltimore, 24–25; Murray and Fitzgerald acrimony, 26–27; visit to father at Crownsville, 28–30; death of grandfather and time alone with grandmother, 31–32; death of father, 35; summer visits to Croom, 35; death of grandmother, 36; at Hillside High School, 37–38; wins scholarship to Wilberforce, 38; at Richmond Hill High (New York), 41–42

—education: at Hunter College, 42–46, 47, 51, 53; at Brookwood Labor College, 61–63; at New Workers School (Lovestoneites), 63; at Howard University, 109–10, 115–18, 123–27; at Berkeley, 133–36; at Columbia University, 151, 197; at Yale, 203–4, 206, 213–14, 216, 218; PhD thesis, 214–15; at General Theological Seminary (GTS), 262–63, 264–65, 267, 268–69, 272–73; Clinical Pastoral Education (CPE) program,

269–70, 272; at Virginia Theological Seminary (VTS), 273–74; master of divinity thesis, 276; offer of honorary doctorate by University of North Carolina, 290–91; offer of honorary doctorate by Hunter College, 292

—employment: Bankers Fire Insurance Company, 42; *Carolina Times*, 42; North Carolina Mutual Life Insurance, 42; early short-term work, 42, 47, 51, 53–54, 54–55; general instability of, 42, 53–54, 223; Open Road Inc., 47; as waitress, 51; Alice Foote MacDougall, 53–54; National Urban League, 54–55; WPA, 60–61, 68, 69, 77; WEP 63; Negro People's Committee to Aid Spanish Democracy (NPC), 77, 78; Annual National Sharecroppers Week, 80–82, 83–84; Workers Defense League, 94, 96–99, 101–5; as deputy attorney general, 136–37, 139, 142–44; Commission on Law and Social Action, 145, 148; law clerk, 152, 153; for Carson DeWitt Baker, 156–57; own private law practice, 158, 159, 170–71; social investigator at Department of Social Welfare, 170–71, 172–73; attorney at Paul, Weiss, 189–91, 195; Senior Lecturer in Law at University of Ghana, 195, 197, 201, 203, 205; Department of Labor, 223; Equal Employment Opportunity Commission, 223; at Benedict College, 228–30, 232–34; Brandeis University, 235–43, 246–47, 250–51, 257, 261–62; supply-priest work, 287; priest-in-charge Church of the Holy Nativity, 288–89

—financial issues, 78, 136, 145, 151, 156, 157, 160, 162–63, 164–75, 176, 288

—health and body anxieties: belief in "hereditary insanity," 35, 36, 59, 115, 119–20, 142, 178–79, 185, 274, 286; beliefs regarding "hidden male attributes," 66–67, 83, 114, 132, 148; beliefs regarding "mental conflict," 113, 114; beliefs regarding "glandular" issues, 66–67, 114, 120, 164, 178, 196; interest in psychoanalysis/psychotherapy, 154–56; biological determinism, 273

— health and medical treatment, 45, 47, 54–55, 73, 78, 132, 136–38, 142, 234, 288–89, 292; breakdowns, 58, 66, 82, 118; physiological tests, 66–68, 73, 78, 79, 83, 114–15; periods of convalescence, 118–19, 164, 180–81; hormone treatments, 131–32, 164; appendix removal, 148; thyroid issues, 166, 175–76, 196, 269; malaria, 198; neurological testing, 244; cardiac issues, 248, 287

— hospitalizations: Camp TERA, 55–57; Bellevue Hospital, 58, 82; Long Island Rest Home, 65–66; Rogers Hospital, 82–84; Howard University infirmary, 118, 120; Freedmen's Hospital, 140–41, 164–65, 175, 287; appendix removed, 148; Johns Hopkins Hospital, 288

— identity formation, 7, 9, 20, 51, 106, 214, 215; personal uncertainty, 1, 7, 20, 117–18, 125, 234, 241, 247–48; as Native American, 23, 58; feeling of being an outsider, 25, 199; rejection of gender roles, 33, 50; providential view of self, 38, 42, 229; burden of being a "first," 227, 256; search for "prestige," 227, 256; "token" status, 227, 242

— legal career: bar admittance, California, 135, 136; deputy attorney general, L.A., 136–37, 139, 142–44; first case (Joshua Small), 150; bar admittance, New York, 152, 153–54, 156; first case (prostitution), 156; representing Urith Josiah, 156–57; private law practice, 158, 171–72; Ruth Mary Reynolds case, 162–63; as attorney, corporate law, 189–91; Robert F. Williams defense, 193–95. See also Fourteenth Amendment, PM's strategy for

— names (other than Pauli Murray): Annie/Anna, 1; Lenie, 6, 51; "Pete," 51, 64; Agnes, 51; "the dude," 51; Paul, 51; Oliver Fleming, 91–92

— opinions: feelings toward the South, 107, 116–17, 128, 139, 142, 149, 228–29, 230–31; lesbian rights, PM's stance on, 260. See also uplift ideology, racial

— personal life: family "color complex," 11, 15–16, 23, 25, 59; loneliness, 20, 21, 31, 41, 46, 79, 115, 134, 198–99, 241–42, 243, 258, 291; personality, 23, 37, 49, 54, 104, 129, 176, 178, 234, 265, 268; pastimes, 44, 84; emotional strain, 44, 114–15, 288; marriage, 46, 154, 185, 291; "Women of the Year" award (1945), 140; dates with men, 154; journey to Africa, 197–98; homesickness, 198–99; spring break in Europe, 203–4; graduation, 215; vacations in Jamaica, 218, 232; rejection by Page Bigelow, 265–66, 270

— pets: Petie, 105, 106; Toni, 120, 122; Smokey, 152–53, 186, 197, 198, 218; Doc, 218, 243; Roy, 243, 249, 274; Christy, 292

— places of residence: Baltimore, 4, 288; Durham, N.C., 5, 6, 8, 16, 19, 37; New York, 39, 40, 44, 76, 106–7, 142, 152, 218, 225, 234, 262; Katonah, 61–63; Washington, D.C., 109, 115–17, 226, 287; Los Angeles, 132–33; Oakland, 133–37; Sacramento, 137; frequency of moves, 100, 152, 224; Ghana, 198–99; New Haven, 206; Columbia, S.C., 228–29, 232; Boston, 243; Pittsburgh, 291

— press coverage of, 71, 74, 90–92, 103–4, 127, 128, 137, 140–41, 173, 277–78, 281, 291

— relationships, 44, 47, 48, 83; with Peg Holmes, 56–58, 64–65, 82; with Adelene "Mac" McBean, 76, 82, 85, 106–7, 119; with Helen Hanff, 181–82; with Irene "Renee" Barlow, 191, 196, 198–99, 232, 253–57, 260–61, 270, 286, 293

— religion, 46, 169, 236, 245, 249, 255; "call" to the ministry, 255; formal application as a Postulate for Holy Orders,

257–58; ordination, 277–78; first Holy
Eucharist, 278, 286; spiritual integration, 278; androgynous god, 279; tolerance of homosexuality, 282; sermons,
286; "telephone ministry," 289
—teaching: for Sunday school at St
Philip's Church, 46; for WPA 61, 68,
230; for WEP, 63; family's experience
of, 175; for University of Ghana Law
School, 201, 203, 204; as tutor at Yale,
213; at Brandeis University, 238–43,
247, 257; inclusion in 1971 edition of
Outstanding Educators of America,
246; Boston College, 262
—writing: as expression of grievance, 56,
70; pamphlets, 103; autobiographical short stories, 106, 107; political
articles, 116, 122, 126, 133, 139, 219;
poetry, 122–23, 139, 233, 196; open letters, 127–28, 175; as self-therapy, 140;
desire to write, 151, 226, 235; *States'
Laws on Race and Color*, 159–60, 164,
165–66; challenges with, 171, 204; attempts to publish poems, 196–97; *The
Constitution and Government of Ghana*,
204; autobiography, 227, 278, 289, 292;
"Black Power for Whom?" manuscript,
236–37; memo to Episcopal Church,
245–46. See also *Proud Shoes*
Murray, Raymond (brother), 5, 27, 183–85
Murray, Rose (aunt), xii, 25–27, 29–30,
33, 35
Murray, Rosetta (sister), 5, 85, 108, 275
Murray, William (brother), 4, 36, 59,
77–78, 108, 119, 142, 177–78, 182–83,
274–75
Murray, William H. (father), xi–xiv, xvii,
xx, 1–9, 21, 24–25, 28–30, 35, 45, 59,
61, 65, 76–78, 108, 151, 178–79, 183
Muste, A. J., 61, 100, 162

NAACP, xvi, 38, 69, 98, 107, 111, 124, 126,
127, 132, 135, 145–46, 166, 192, 208,
236; involvement in UNC case, 70–71,
73, 74–75; involvement in Petersburg
case, 86, 88–90, 91, 92; complicity
with McCarthyism, 168; involvement in Little Rock case, 192–93; involvement in Monroe cases, 193–95;
unresponsive, 194–95
Nachtrieb, Barbara. *See* Armstrong,
Barbara Nachtrieb
National Cathedral (Washington, D.C.),
277, 284, 293
National Council of Negro Women, xiii,
140, 207, 210, 211, 230
National Guard, 232
National Legal Committee, 89
National Organization for Women
(NOW): formation, 221–23; growth,
231; PM's withdrawal from, 231–32;
and lesbian rights debate, 258–60
National Press Club, picket of, 211, 249
National Urban League, 38, 54–55, 90
National Woman's Party (NWP), 209
Negro: An Anthology (Cunard), 50–51
"Negro," PM's advocacy of term, 43, 238–
39, 291
Negro Digest, 148
New Deal programs, 55–56, 60, 64, 79
New Negro, The (Locke), 44
Newport, R.I., 47
New York Public Library, 60
New York Times, 43, 44, 83–84, 93, 163,
165, 175, 188, 194, 207, 217–18, 258, 272
Niemoller, Martin, 236
Nkrumah, Kwame, 201–2
nonviolent resistance, practice of, 68
North Carolina College (North Carolina
Central University), 69
North Carolina Mutual Life Insurance, 42

Odum, Howard, 72, 121
Open Conference on the Ministry of
Women, 282
Opportunity (National Urban League
magazine), 54, 90, 92
"Orangeburg Massacre," 232
ordination of women. *See* Episcopal
Church: ordination of women

"Paradox" (poem), 196
Parker, Mack, 193–94, 196
"passing": racial, 15, 41, 58, 97; gender, 50, 58, 91; as Cuban, 65
Peck, James, 162–63, 165
personal as political, 121, 123, 162–63, 187, 214, 237, 260
Petersburg, Va., 86–89, 92, 147, 213
Petersburg City Prison, 87
"Philadelphia Eleven," 271–72
Phillips, Gene, 96–97
Piccard, Jeannette, 271
Pit of Loneliness, 175
Plessy v. Ferguson, PM's term paper on, 124, 174, 175
Pollock, Earnest, 267
poll tax, 103
Poston, Ted, 59–60, 110, 158, 193
Powell, Ruth, 116, 126, 127, 239
President's Commission on the Status of Women (PCSW), 206–9; Civil Rights Subcommittee, 208. *See also* Committee on Civil and Political Rights
Price, James H., 99
"Problem Child" (short story), 6–7
Proud Shoes (family history), 12, 16, 21, 31, 170, 186–87, 260–61, 291, 293–94; writing of, 170–71, 173–76; grant for, 170–71; editorial guidance, 173–74; contract, 174; manuscript submitted, 182; publication, 186; reception, 187–88, *189*; reissue, 289–90
psychoanalysis, 155, 214
public bathrooms, 47–48, 85
Puerto Rican Nationalist Party, 162

Queens, N.Y., 41

race and gender equality, PM's argument for similarities between, 208–9, 213, 219, 237
race relations, as gradual progress, 202
race riots: Detroit, 122; Harlem, 122–23
racial uplift ideology. *See* uplift ideology, racial

racism/racial discrimination, 62–63, 106, 132; as inverting gender roles, 149
Randolph, A. Philip, 68, 110–11, 166, 211; A. Philip Randolph Institute, 250
Ransom, Leon A., 98–99, 109, 110, 118, 125, 129
Rawalt, Marguerite, 209, 213
Reed v. Reed, 250
relief, 79
Remedial Reading Project, 61, 230
Remond, Charles, 211
returned servicemen, 142, 145, 152
Revolutionary Workers League (RWL), involvement in Waller case, 95–96, 98, 101–2
Reyneau, Betsy Graves, 124
Reynolds, Ruth Mary, 162–63, 167
Richmond Hill Episcopal Church, 46
"Right to Equal Opportunity in Employment" (PM's thesis), 135
Riverside Church (New York), 244
Robinson, Spotswood, 175
Rodell, Marie F., 170, 186
Roosevelt, Eleanor, xiii, xv, 55, 57, 88, 121, 159, 292; PM's correspondence with, 70, 79, 80, 84, 99, 113, 129, 130, 173, 179, 188; PM's meetings with, 81, 113, 118, 127, 179; funeral, 208
Roosevelt, Franklin D., 53, 110, 122, 127, 134; PM's letters to, 69–70, 113
Roots (Haley), 289, 291
Rosenberg, Rosalind, xv–xvi, 156, 181, 208, 214, 278
Rosenwald Scholarship, 128, 135
Ruffin, Julian M., 121
Rustin, Bayard, 100, 115, 146, 213, 249, 250

Satyagraha, practice of, 68, 86, 88, 90
Schlafly, Phyllis, 286
Scottsboro case, 49
segregation: of movie theaters, PM's attitude toward, 24, 25; of public transport, PM's attitude toward, 24, 54, 84–85, 96, 103; PM's awareness of, 24, 75, 110; education, 69, 71–72, 74, 174–

75, 230; Petersburg incident, 85–90; direct-action protests in D.C., 116–17, 124; blood plasma, 132; housing, 132; relationships (antimiscegenation), 139; "Journey of Reconciliation," 146–48, 162; Freedom Rides, 147, 202

Sentinel (newspaper), 133

separate but equal: disparity of, 22, 69, 85; PM's term paper on, 124

sex, interracial, 72

"sex criminals," treatment of, 65

"sexual inversion," 43, 65, 67, 78

Sharecroppers Week, Annual National, 80–82

sharecropping, 94, 103

Shepard, James, 69–70, 72–73, 75

Shridharani, Krishnalal, 68

Shulman, Stephen N., 224–25, 227

Silvermine Publishers, 233

sit-ins, D.C. campaign as forerunner of, 117, 126

slavery, 13, 14, 200, 214–15

Small, James (cousin), 34, 76–77, 80

Small, John Ethophilus Grattin (uncle), xi, 33–35, 34, 76, 273

Small, Joshua (cousin), 34, 76–77, 80, 81, 150, 152, 156

Smith, Frank, 13

Smith, Harriet (great-grandmother), 13, 151

Smith, James S., 70

Smith, Lillian, 174, 181

Smith, Mary Ruffin, 13, 70, 121

Smith, Sidney (great-grandfather), 13, 70, 109

Socialist Party, 62, 68, 80, 94

Song in a Weary Throat (autobiography), xvi, 15, 227, 278, 289, 292

South Africa, 200, 202

Southern Tenant Farmers' Union (STFU), 80

Springer, Maida, 111, 140, 158, 175, 180, 195, 202–3, 204, 211–12, 230, 290, 291–92

States' Laws on Race and Color, 159–60, 164, 165–66, 174–75; supplement, 176–77

Status of Women groups, 221

St. Elizabeth's Hospital (Washington, D.C.), 77

Stevens, Thelma, *161*

Stevenson, Adlai, 188–89

St. Mark's-in-the-Bowery (New York), 210, 218, 220, 244–45

Stokes, Anson P., 246

Stone, Constance E., 198

Stone, Maysie, 51, 60

Stone, Thomas H., 96, 98, 99, 103, 112–13

St. Philip's Chapel (Maryland), 273, 282–83

St. Philip's Church (New York), 46

strikes, automobile industry, 62

Students for a Democratic Society, 203

Swanson, Katrina, 284

Tarrytown Automobile Plant, strike, 62

Taylor, Ferebee, 290

Tettegah, John K., 201

"third sex," 104

Thomas, Norman, 68

"Three Thousand Miles on a Dime in Ten Days" (short story), 50–51, 52, 154

Threshold (student magazine), 110

Thurman, Howard, 126

Title VII (Civil Rights Act), 212, 220, 222, 251; PM's memorandum on sex amendment to, 212–13

Transitional Year Program (TYP), at Brandeis University, 237–38

Trotskyist organizations, 95, 96, 98

Uncle Tom's Cabin (Stowe), 157

United Nations, 134, 172

United States, attitudes toward, 200–203

United States foreign policy on race relations, 202

University of California, Berkeley, 130, 133; law faculty doctorate admission decision, 136, 151

University of Ghana Law School, 195

University of North Carolina at Chapel Hill (UNC), 68, 147; PM application to, 68–69, 70–75; offer of honorary doctorate from, 290–91
uplift ideology, racial, 19, 22, 61, 128, 191, 200, 214, 229, 256

Vallejo, Calif., 49
Virginia Theological Seminary (VTS), 273–74, 276
Virginia Union University, 98

wage inequality at Brandeis University, 250–51
Walker, John T., 274, 282–83
Waller, Annie, 101, 103–4
Waller, Odell, 94–96, 99, 101–2, 104, 110–11
Waller trial and campaign, 96–105, 110–12, 168
Ware, Caroline, 115, 118, 120, 129–30, 159, 173–74, 186, 190, 203, 204, 208, 215, 219
Washington Evening Star (newspaper), 140
Watergate, 256
Watson, Emmett, 233
Wattley, James C., 280, 284–85
Well of Loneliness, The (Radclyffe Hall), 43
"What Is Africa to Me?" (unpublished article), 204
White, Walter, 73, 74, 88
White Citizens' Council, 193
White House, veto of PM's appointment to EEOC, 224
White v. Crook, 219–20
"Why Negro Girls Stay Single" (article), 148–49

Wilkins, Roy, 73, 74, 132, 194, 195
Williams, Robert F., 193–95
Women's Division of Christian Service, 159–60, 161, 164, 176, 223
Women's Studies Program, Brandeis University, 246
Workers Defense League (WDL), 80, 88, 89, 94, 106–8, 115, 119, 141, 151, 162, 169; involvement in Waller case, 96, 99, 101–5, 110–13
Workers' Education Project (WEP), 61–63, 230
workplace equality, 251
Works Progress Administration (WPA), 60–61, 63, 64, 68, 69, 76, 77, 146, 157, 230
World Council of Churches, Fourth Assembly, 235–36
World War II: impact on African Americans, 121, 132–33; reduction in student numbers, 123, 127, 130; comparisons between Nazism and racial supremacy in the United States, 122, 125, 132. *See also* returned servicemen
Wright, J. Robert, 273
Wynn, William "Billy" (husband), 46, 154

Yale Law School, 215, 217
Yale University, 130, 191, 203–4, 213–18, 223, 234, 243, 248, 262
Yaro (assistant in Ghana), 198
Young, Hugh Hampton, 67
Young Women's Christian Association (YWCA), 44–47

Ziman, Edmund, 171, 176, 186